Welcome!

For as long as I can remember, my love of food has been intrinsically linked to travel. I grew up in a family that took regular holidays to exotic places, so from a young age I discovered the joy of eating fresh pasta on a sun-drenched Tuscan patio, wild strawberries in the French countryside and spicy tagines in Moroccan souks.

These days, my journeys are usually planned around new food experiences, and when I get home, I like nothing better than experimenting with what I've learnt, often adding a twist or 'cheat' to make a dish my own. Along the way, I've broken bread with a host of dedicated farmers, producers and winemakers – and it's been the start of many of my most enduring friendships.

Each chapter in this book is inspired by my favourite cuisines, from spice-driven Indian and Mexican fare to the classic flavours of France and Italy. With my British upbringing, I couldn't resist including some new takes on childhood favourites, and of course I've included Australia, my adopted home, as I believe we have some of the most inspiring chefs and produce in the world.

So join me on a cook's tour of simple, beautiful recipes you'll love to make, eat and share. Enjoy!

Valli

LONDON
king's cros
Shannon Bennett's
P·A·R·I·S
THE FRENCH LAUNDRY
BRITISH PASSPORT
DESCRIPTION SIGNALEMENT
AUSTRALIA
PASSPORT

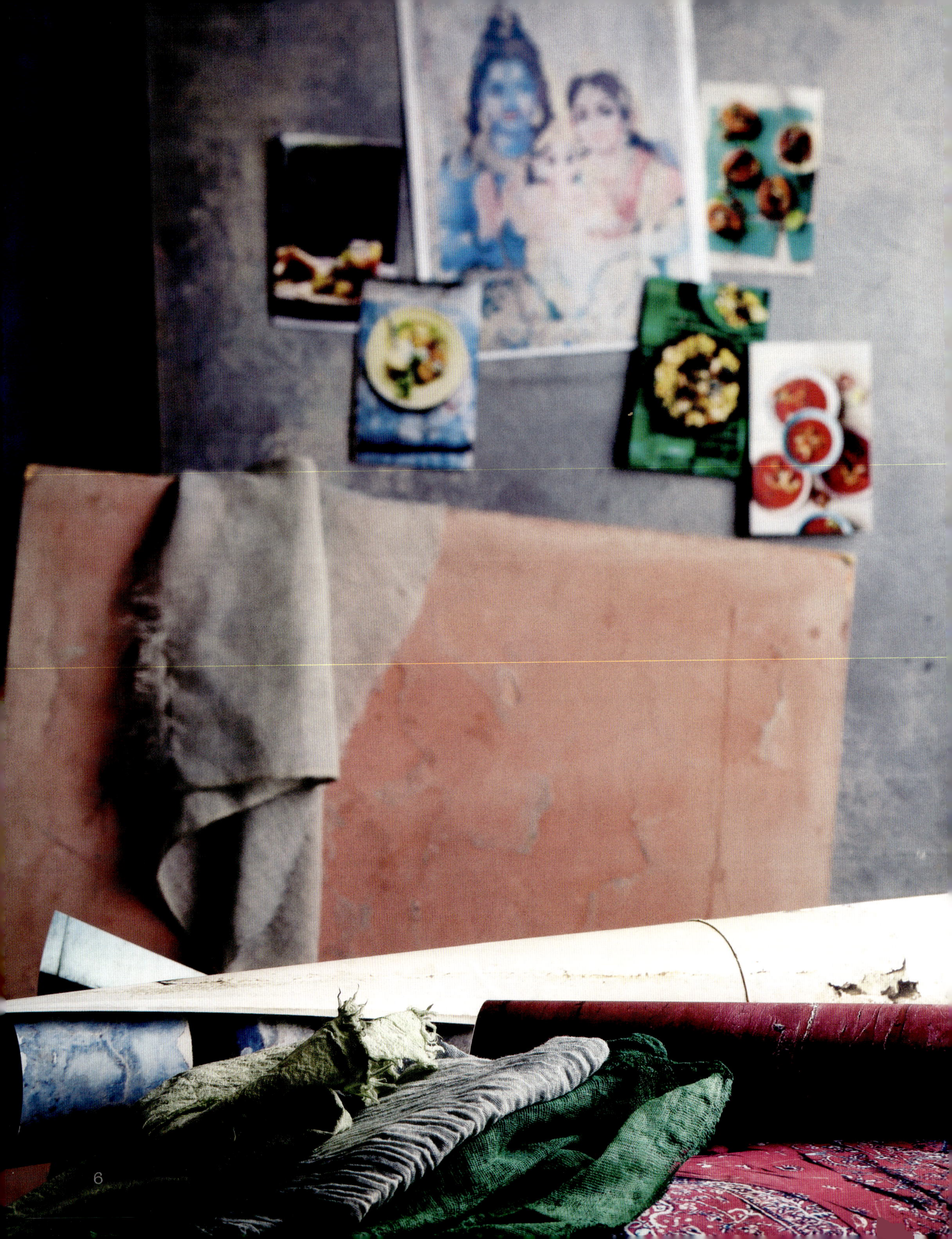

Contents

Italian	8
Spanish	36
Australian	64
Indian	92
American	120
Asian	148
Latin American	176
French	204
British	232
Middle Eastern	260
Menus	290
Basics	294
Index	298
Acknowledgements	302

ITALIAN

While Italian food is renowned for its regional specialties, there are ingredients that are used across the country. Take, for instance, olive oil, tomatoes, basil and cheeses, which add depth and richness. Then there's dried pasta in myriad shapes, polenta, risotto rice and crusty bread to eat fresh with meals, or to cook and toss through salads once stale. Desserts often rely on creamy mascarpone, matched with fortified wine.

PANTRY ESSENTIALS

Anchovies
Most commonly preserved in oil and/or salt, these tiny fish add a savoury richness when cooked with aromatics such as garlic and onion.

Balsamic vinegar
True balsamic, Aceto Balsamico di Modena, is made in the Emilia-Romagna region from grape juice that's cooked down to a thick, dark mosto (must). Aged in wooden barrels for at least 12 years, it has a more complex, rounded flavour than red wine vinegar.

Buffalo mozzarella
Buffalo mozzarella is a fresh stretched cheese made from buffalo milk; substitute 1 ball with 3 balls of bocconcini (made with cow's milk). Burrata is a 'pouch' of mozzarella filled with cream and offcuts or ritagli ('rags') of mozzarella. Both are available from selected delis and specialist food shops.

Campari & Marsala
Campari is an alcoholic aperitivo made with bitter herbs, often served mixed with soda. Marsala is a fortified wine from the region around the city of Marsala in Sicily. Both are available from bottle shops.

Cheese
Parmigiano-Reggiano, a hard cow's milk cheese from Emilia-Romagna, is the finest parmesan (substitute regular parmesan or Grana Padano). Taleggio is a soft, pungent washed-rind cow's milk cheese from Piedmont and Lombardy. Gorgonzola, a creamy blue-mould cow's milk cheese from Lombardy, is sold as dolce (sweet, or mild) or piccante (strong). All these cheeses are available from delis and selected supermarkets.

Mascarpone
A cow's milk cheese originating in Lombardy, made with cream and lemon juice or citric acid. It has a texture similar to thick, or clotted, cream.

Orecchiette
Small round dried pasta shapes, whose name translates aptly as 'little ears'.

Pancetta & prosciutto
Pancetta is a salt-cured meat made from pork belly, and is sold as 'flat' or 'round'. The round (rolled) type is usually served as part of an antipasti plate, while flat pancetta is more often used for cooking. Prosciutto is dry-cured ham, usually served crudo (raw). The finest examples come from Parma and San Daniele.

Passata
Also known as sugo, passata is blanched tomatoes, crushed and sieved to form a smooth, sauce-like consistency, then bottled.

Polenta
A coarse yellow cornmeal, available from supermarkets in regular and instant varieties.

Rice
While arborio is more commonly available from supermarkets, both carnaroli and vialone nano are considered superior for making risotto, as they keep their shape and 'bite' along with a beautiful creamy texture. They are both available from specialist food shops and Italian delis.

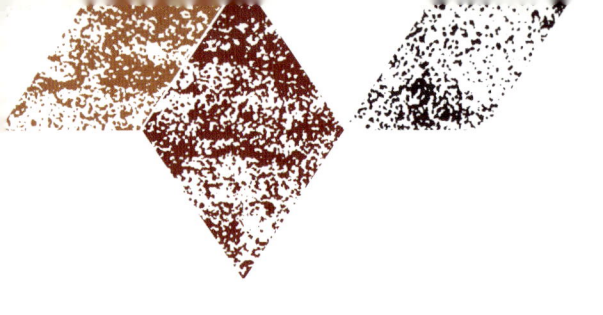

The new caprese

This is a take on the classic insalata caprese, whose colours represent the Italian flag. Grating tomatoes is an easy way to make a quick dressing.

4 vine-ripened tomatoes
1 garlic clove, crushed
4 anchovy fillets in oil, Ⓟ
　drained, finely chopped
Pinch of white sugar
⅓ cup (80ml) olive oil
2 tsp balsamic vinegar Ⓟ
4 small balls of burrata
　or buffalo mozzarella Ⓟ
Basil leaves and chargrilled
　sourdough or ciabatta,
　to serve

Grate the tomatoes on the large holes of a box grater, discarding skin. Transfer to a bowl and add the garlic, anchovy and sugar. Season, then stir in the olive oil and balsamic. Refrigerate for 20 minutes.

　Place a burrata on each serving plate. Spoon tomato dressing over. Serve with chargrilled bread, scattered with basil. **Serves 4**

Ⓟ See Pantry essentials, p 11.

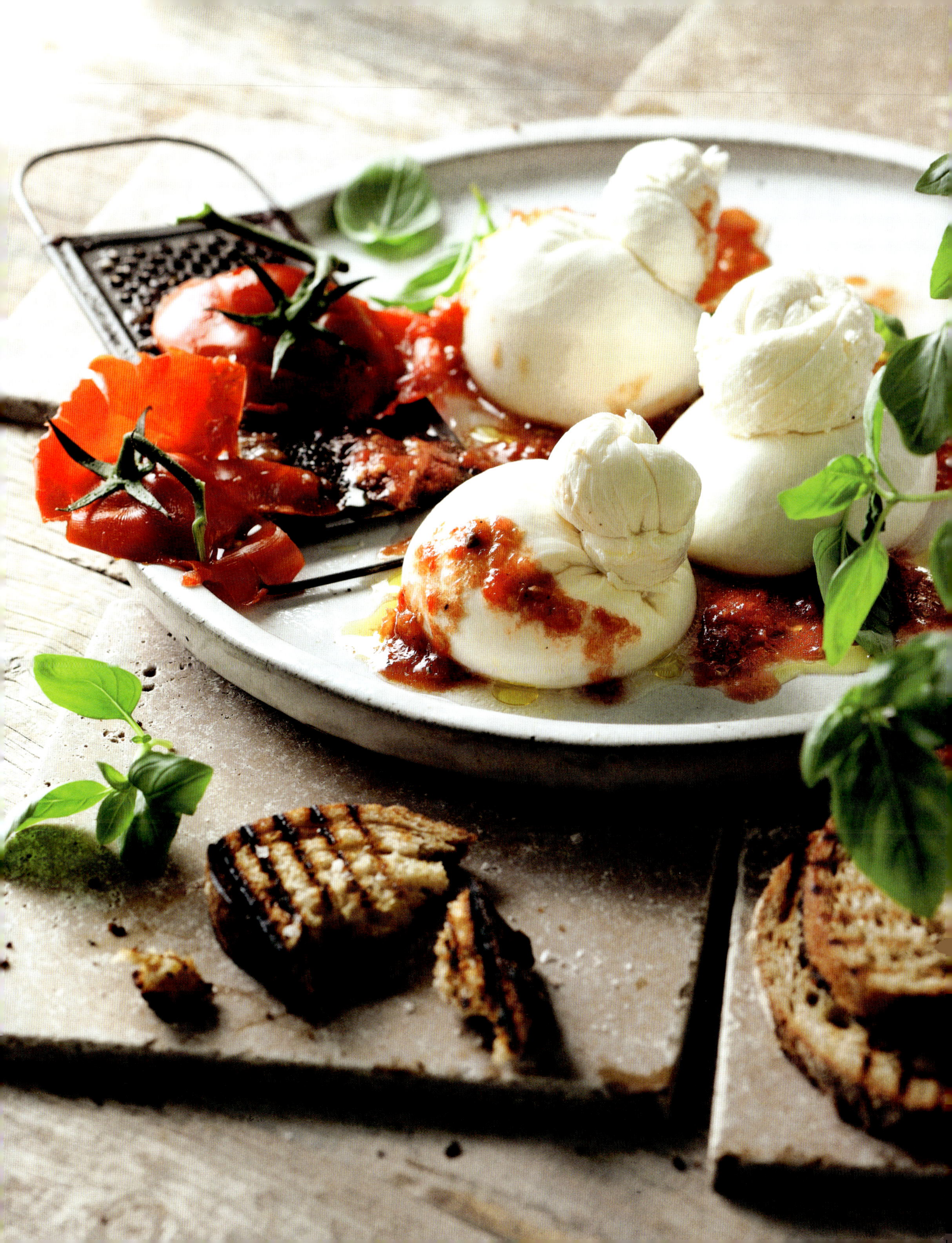

Carpaccio with strawberry panzanella

300g centre-cut beef eye fillet
½ cup (125ml) olive oil
1½ tsp whole black peppercorns, crushed
1½ tsp whole dried pink peppercorns, crushed
300g stale sourdough, crust removed, torn into chunks
500g strawberries
1 tbs balsamic vinegar ⓟ
½ telegraph cucumber, roughly chopped
1 small red onion, halved, thinly sliced
1 small bulb fennel, thinly sliced
½ bunch basil, leaves picked

Preheat the oven to 170°C.

Brush beef with 1 tbs oil and season with salt. Combine black and pink pepper on a plate, then roll beef in pepper mixture to coat completely.

Heat 1 tbs oil in a frypan over medium-high heat. Sear beef, turning, for 2 minutes or until browned all over. Remove from heat. Set aside to cool for 10 minutes. Wrap beef tightly in foil and freeze for 30 minutes (this will make it easier to slice thinly).

Meanwhile, toss the sourdough in 2 tbs olive oil, then spread over a baking tray and bake for 5-6 minutes until golden and crisp. Cool.

Crush half of the strawberries with a potato masher or fork. Combine with balsamic and remaining 1 tbs olive oil. Season.

Roughly chop the remaining 250g strawberries and place in a serving bowl with the cucumber, onion, fennel and croutons. Add the strawberry dressing and toss to combine.

Thinly slice beef, add to the salad and serve scattered with basil leaves. **Serves 4-6 as an antipasto or light lunch**
ⓟ See Pantry essentials, p 11.

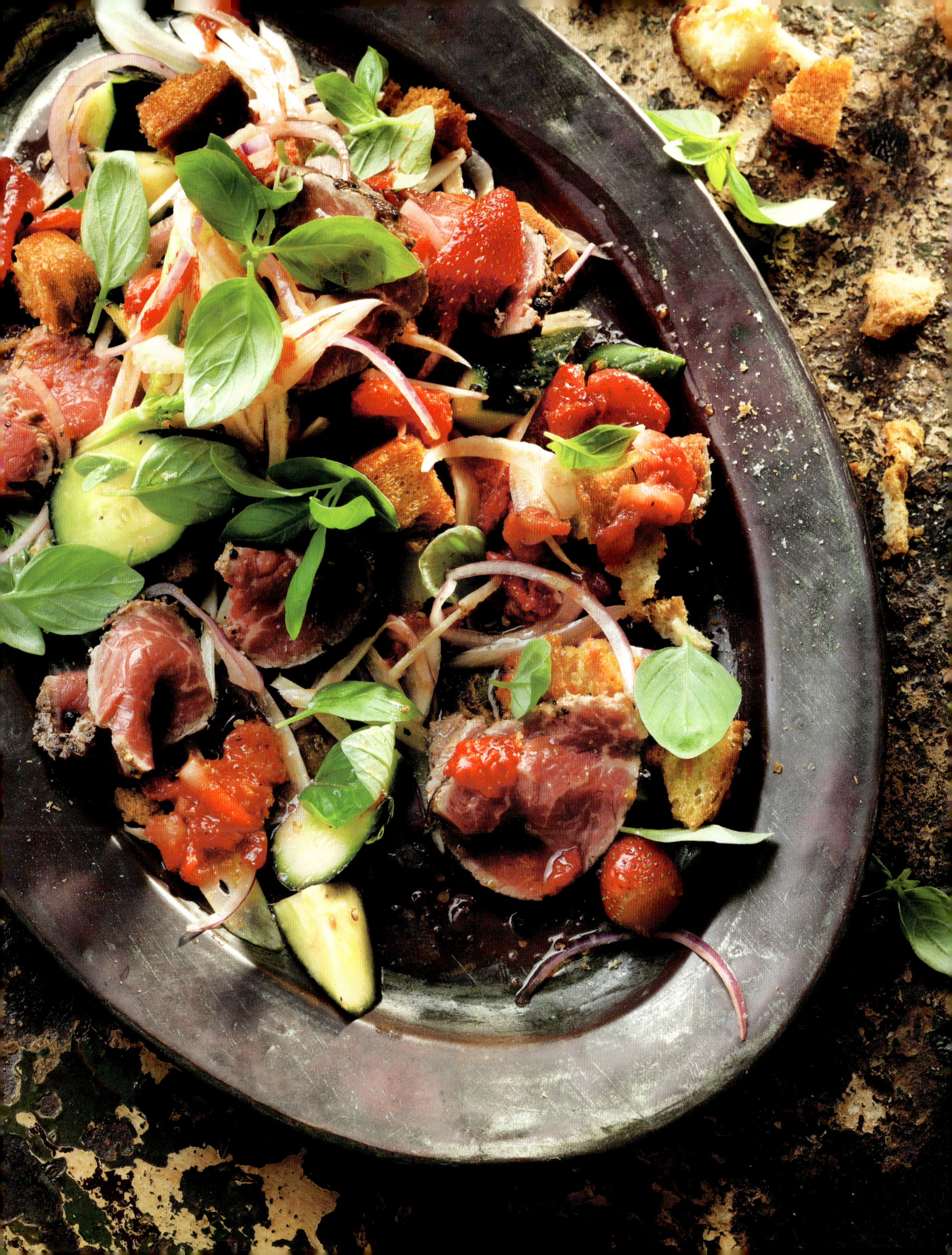

Scallops with peas and pancetta

- 6 slices flat pancetta ⓟ
- ¼ cup (60ml) olive oil
- ⅔ cup (50g) fresh breadcrumbs
- 1 garlic clove, finely chopped
- Finely grated zest and juice of ½ lemon
- 2 tbs chopped flat-leaf parsley
- 1 cup (250ml) chicken stock
- 2½ cups (300g) frozen or (400g) shelled fresh peas
- 1 tbs creme fraiche or sour cream
- 2 tbs chopped chervil or flat-leaf parsley
- 20g unsalted butter
- 12 scallops without roe

Preheat the oven to 180°C. Line a baking tray with baking paper.

Place pancetta on prepared tray and bake for 10-12 minutes until golden and crisp. Cool slightly, then break into shards.

Meanwhile, heat 2 tbs oil in a frypan over medium-high heat. Add breadcrumbs and garlic, and cook, stirring, for 3-4 minutes until golden. Add lemon zest, 1 tbs lemon juice and parsley, and stir to combine. Remove from the heat and set aside.

Bring the stock to the boil in a saucepan over medium heat. Add peas and simmer for 3 minutes (if cooking fresh shelled peas, simmer until tender). Drain, reserving stock.

Transfer peas to a food processor, season, then process, adding enough reserved stock to form a coarse paste. Add the creme fraiche and chervil. Cover and keep warm.

Heat butter and remaining 1 tbs oil in a frypan over medium-high heat. Cook scallops for 30 seconds each side or until golden but still rare in the centre.

To serve, divide pea puree among 4 plates, top each with 3 scallops and scatter with pancetta and crumb mixture.

Serves 4 as a starter

ⓟ See Pantry essentials, p 11.

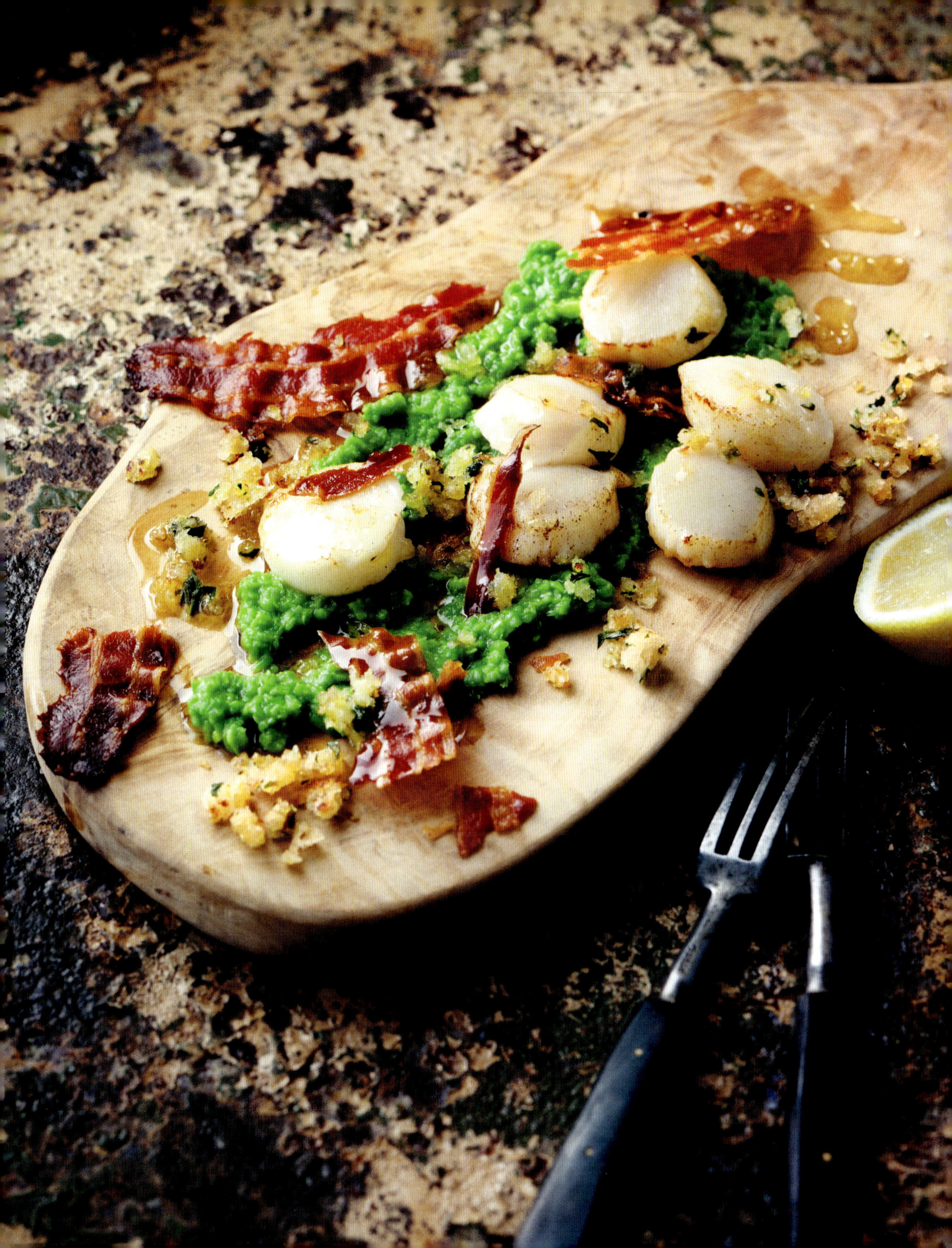

Taleggio & cauliflower risotto with hazelnut pangrattato

100g unsalted butter
¼ cup (60ml) olive oil
½ head cauliflower, cut into small florets
1.5L (6 cups) chicken or vegetable stock
1 leek, white part only, finely chopped
1 onion, finely chopped
2 garlic cloves, finely chopped
2 cups (400g) carnaroli rice Ⓟ
1 cup (250ml) white wine
200g Taleggio, Ⓟ rind removed, chopped
12 sage leaves

Hazelnut pangrattato
⅓ cup (80ml) olive oil
30g unsalted butter
2 tbs chopped sage
2 tbs chopped thyme leaves
1 cup (70g) fresh breadcrumbs
⅓ cup (50g) hazelnuts, roasted, skins removed, roughly chopped

Melt half the butter and 1 tbs oil in a frypan over medium-high heat. Add cauliflower and cook, turning, for 7-8 minutes until golden. Drain on paper towel. Keep warm.

Bring the stock to the boil in a large saucepan, reduce heat to low and keep at a gentle simmer.

Add leek, onion, garlic and remaining 50g butter to the frypan and cook for 3-4 minutes until softened but not browned.

Add rice and stir to coat the grains. Add the wine, then simmer for 1-2 minutes until the wine evaporates. Add hot stock, 1 cup at a time, stirring constantly, allowing each cup to be absorbed before adding the next, until all stock is used and the rice is creamy but still has bite (this will take about 20 minutes). Remove from heat, stir the Taleggio into the rice and cover with a lid.

Heat remaining 2 tbs oil in a frypan over medium-high heat. Cook sage leaves, turning, for 1 minute or until golden and crisp. Drain on paper towel.

For the pangrattato, heat the olive oil in a frypan over medium-high heat. Add butter to pan, then add chopped sage, thyme, breadcrumbs and hazelnuts. Cook, stirring, for 3-4 minutes until golden and crisp. Season.

Divide risotto among bowls and serve topped with cauliflower, hazelnut pangrattato and crisp sage leaves. **Serves 4-6**

Ⓟ See Pantry essentials, p 11.

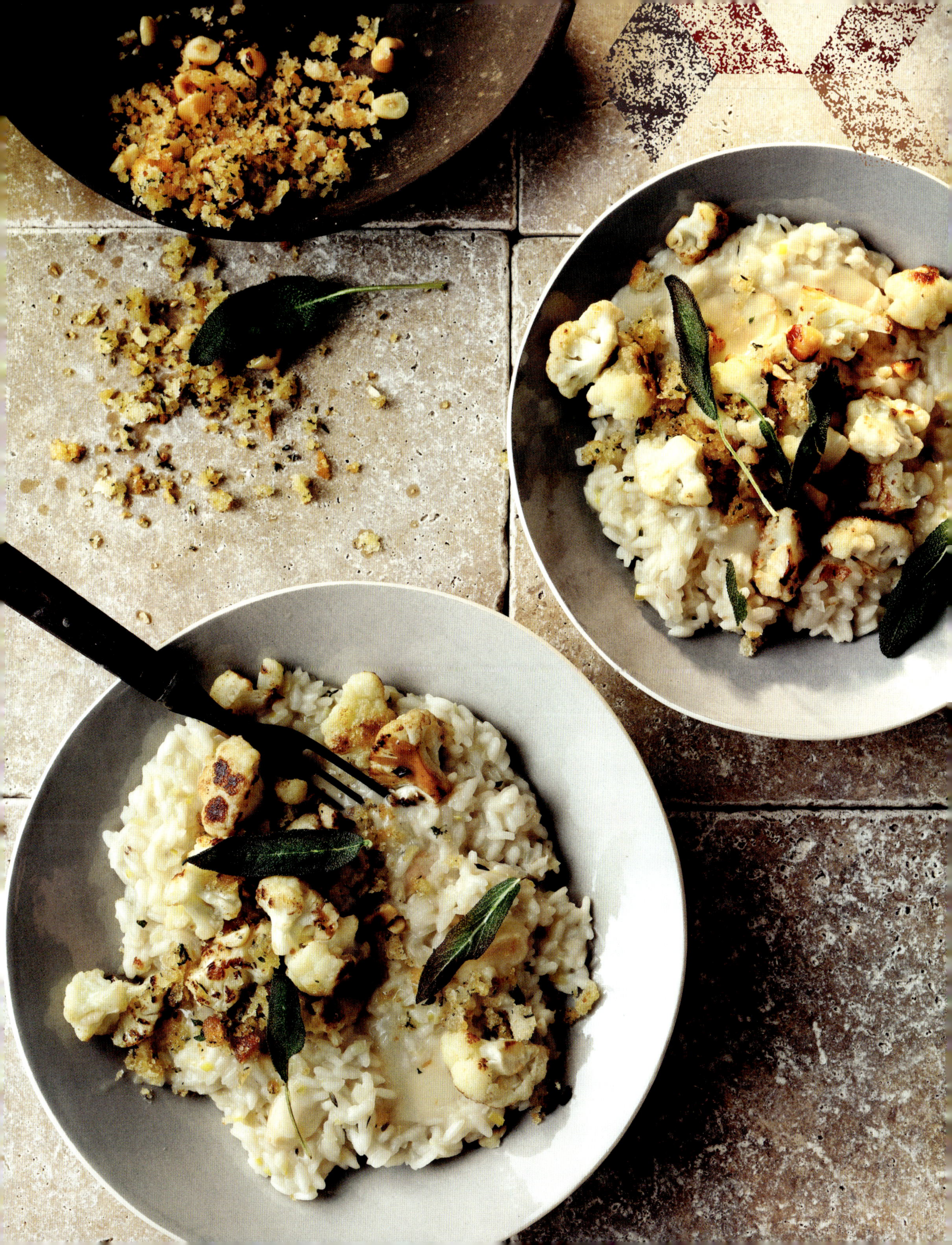

Piedmont peppers

I run a week of cooking classes in Piedmont each September and these delicious stuffed capsicums are a favourite starter for our long lunches.

4 red capsicums
4 tomatoes
8 anchovy fillets in oil, ⓟ drained, chopped
2 garlic cloves, thinly sliced
2/3 cup (165ml) olive oil
1 cup (150g) pitted kalamata olives

Preheat the oven to 180°C.
 Cut the capsicums in half lengthways, leaving stems intact, and remove the core and seeds. Place in a roasting pan.
 Cut a small cross in the stem end of each tomato and place in a heatproof bowl. Pour over enough boiling water to cover, then stand for 30 seconds. Drain, cool slightly, then peel, discarding skins. Cut the tomatoes into quarters lengthways. Place 2 quarters inside each capsicum half, then scatter with anchovy and garlic, and drizzle with oil.
 Cook for 45 minutes to 1 hour until the capsicums are soft. Add olives, then roast for a further 15 minutes. Cool to room temperature before serving. **Serves 6-8 as an antipasto**
ⓟ See Pantry essentials, p 11.

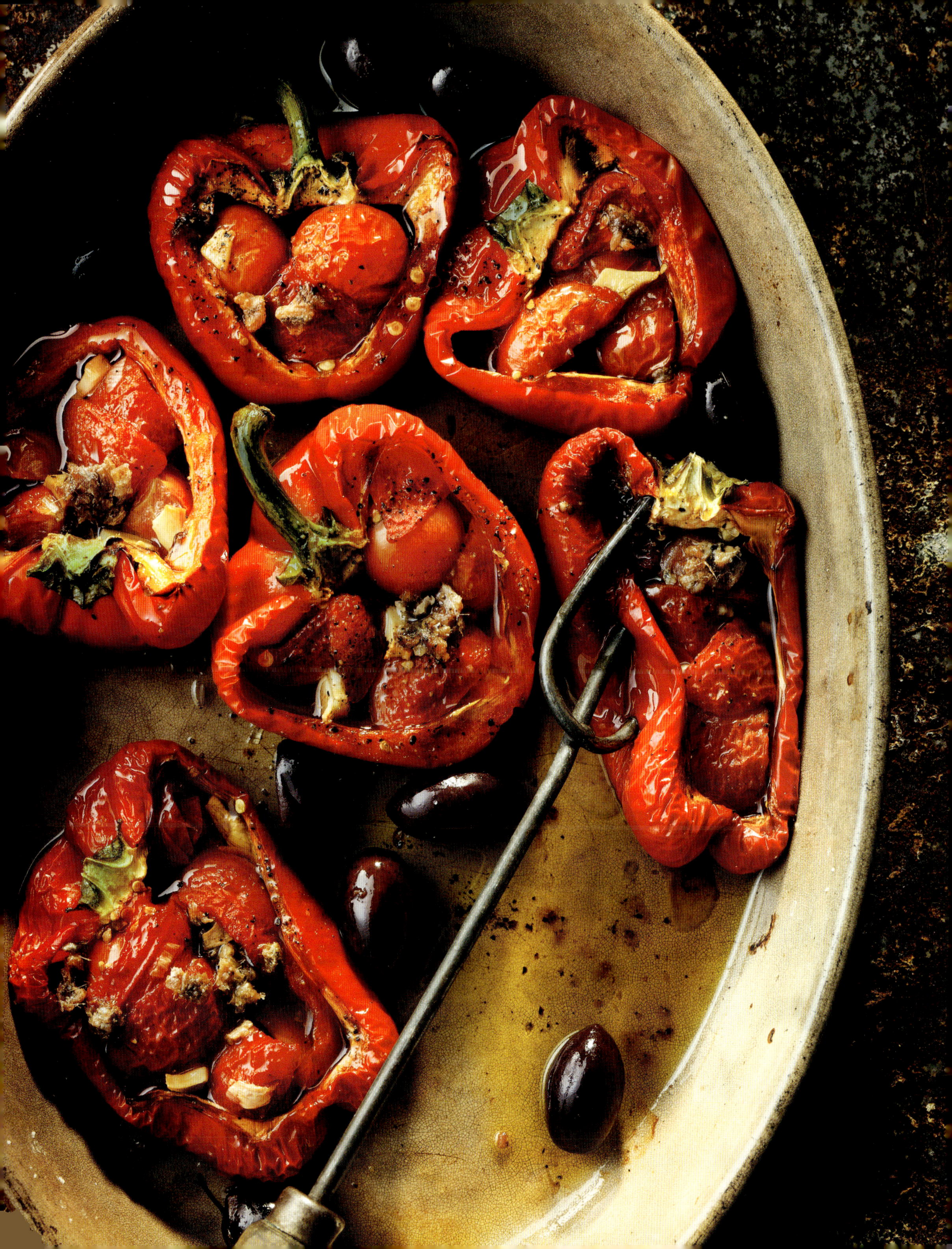

Spaghetti vongole

This simple classic is my husband's favourite, and is the first thing he orders whenever we go back to Italy.

400g spaghetti
⅓ cup (80ml) olive oil, plus extra to serve
3 garlic cloves, finely chopped
2 long red chillies, seeds removed, finely chopped
1kg clams (vongole), soaked in cold water for 15 minutes to remove any grit
½ cup (125ml) white wine
½ bunch flat-leaf parsley, finely chopped
Juice of ½ lemon

Cook the spaghetti in boiling salted water until al dente. Drain, reserving ¼ cup (60ml) cooking water.

Meanwhile, heat the olive oil in a large saucepan over low heat. Add garlic and chilli, and cook, stirring, for 1-2 minutes until fragrant but not browned. Add drained vongole and wine, increase heat to medium-high, cover with a lid and cook for 2-3 minutes until all the vongole have opened.

Add drained pasta to the vongole mixture with the reserved cooking water, parsley and lemon juice, and toss to combine. Season and serve drizzled with a little extra olive oil. **Serves 4**

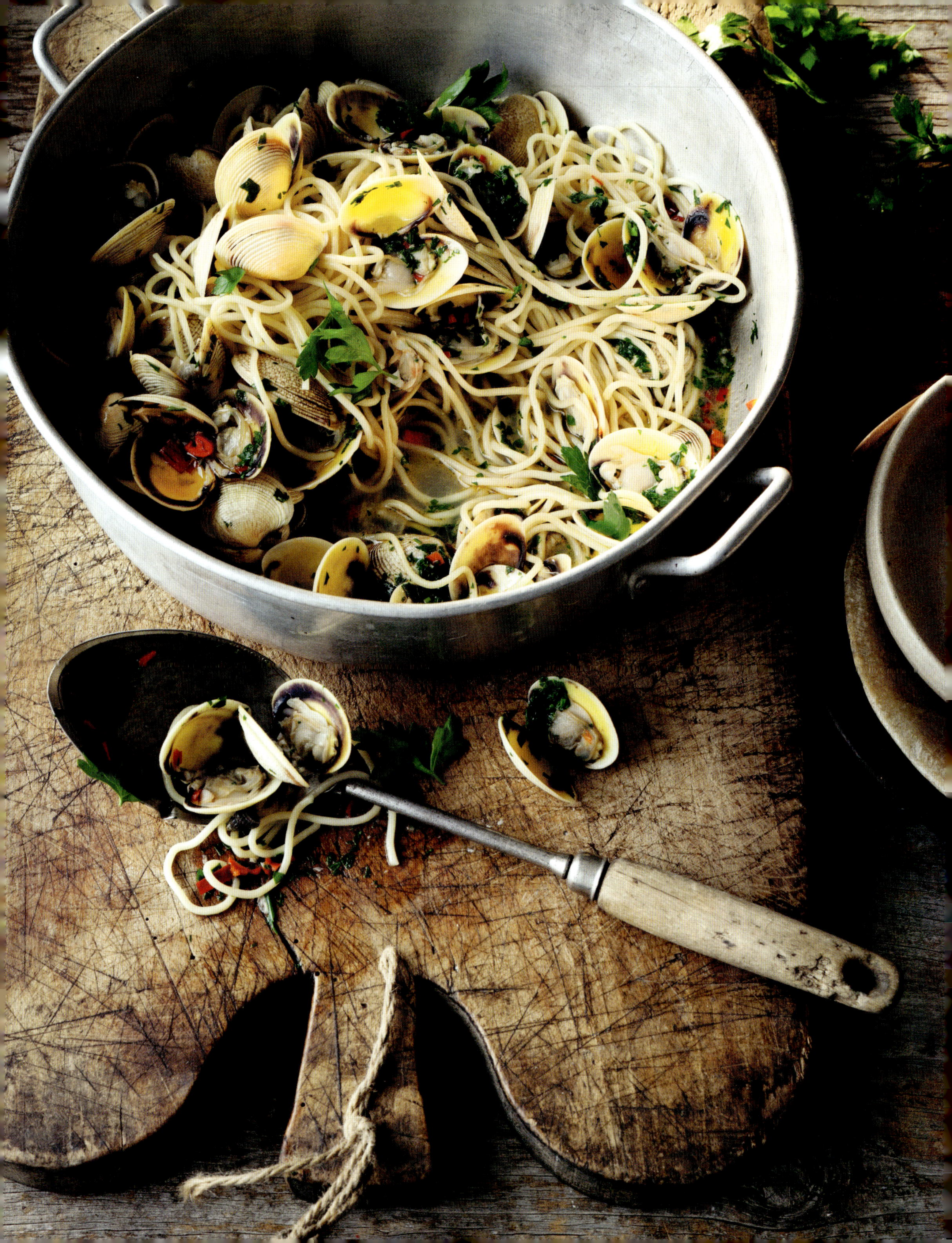

Roman chicken with creamy polenta

2 tbs extra virgin olive oil
8 chicken thigh cutlets
2 onions, finely chopped
2 garlic cloves, finely chopped
1 small red chilli, seeds removed, finely chopped
100g pancetta, Ⓟ chopped
600ml passata Ⓟ
1½ tbs chopped thyme, plus extra thyme sprigs to serve
Pinch of caster sugar
2 cups (500ml) chicken stock
1½ cups (250g) instant polenta Ⓟ
1 cup (250ml) milk
¼ cup (20g) grated parmesan Ⓟ
2 each roasted red and yellow capsicums, cut into strips
½ cup (90g) small black olives
Roughly chopped flat-leaf parsley leaves, to serve

Heat the oil in a large frypan over medium-high heat. Season the chicken thighs and cook, skin-side down, for 5-6 minutes or until golden. Remove from pan and set aside. Add onion, garlic, chilli and pancetta to the pan and cook, stirring, for 5-6 minutes until onion is soft. Add passata, thyme and sugar, then season. Return chicken to pan, skin-side up, cover with a lid and simmer over low heat for 25 minutes or until chicken is cooked through.

Meanwhile, bring the stock and 2 cups (500ml) water to the boil over medium-high heat. Gradually add polenta, whisking to combine, then reduce heat to low and simmer, stirring constantly, for 10 minutes or until thick. Add milk and parmesan, and stir to combine. Season, then cover with a lid.

Transfer chicken to a plate and cover loosely with foil. Add capsicum to the sauce, then cook, uncovered, for 3-4 minutes until sauce is reduced and thickened. Return chicken to the pan with the olives.

Serve chicken with polenta, scattered with parsley and extra thyme sprigs. **Serves 4-6**

Ⓟ See Pantry essentials, p 11.

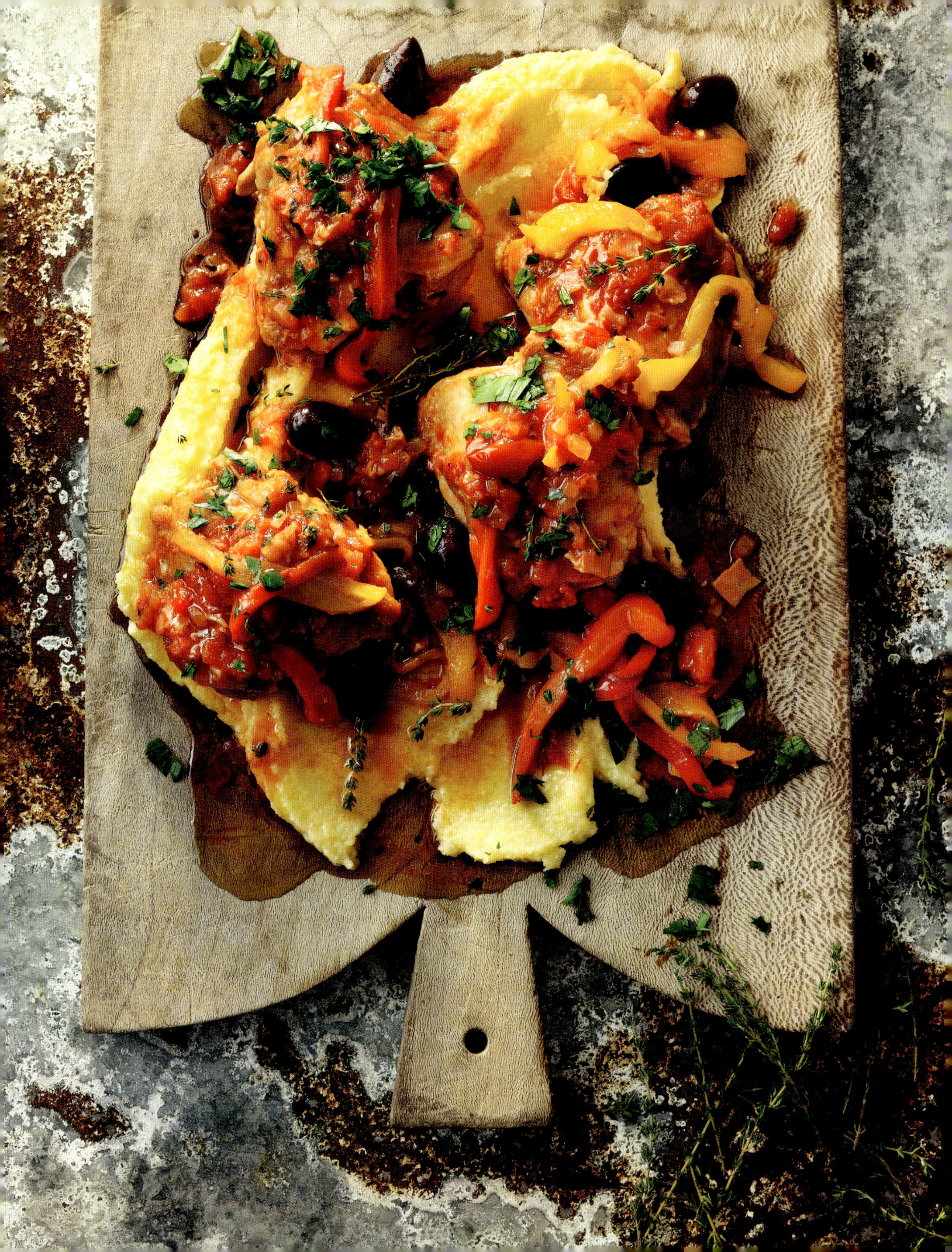

Baked gnocchi with spinach, figs and gorgonzola

Figs and gorgonzola are a match made in heaven, so combining them in this quick baked dish seemed like the natural thing to do.

500g good-quality potato gnocchi
150g baby spinach leaves
2 garlic cloves, crushed
300ml thickened cream
Pinch of freshly grated nutmeg
3 figs, quartered lengthways
200g gorgonzola dolce, ⓟ chopped
⅓ cup (25g) grated parmesan ⓟ

Preheat the oven to 200°C. Grease a 1L (4-cup) baking dish.

Cook the gnocchi in boiling salted water until they rise to the surface. Drain. Transfer to the prepared baking dish.

Meanwhile, blanch spinach in boiling water for 30 seconds. Drain, squeezing out any excess moisture.

Combine garlic, cream and nutmeg in a jug. Season.

Scatter spinach, figs and gorgonzola among the gnocchi in the baking dish, then pour over the cream mixture and sprinkle with parmesan.

Bake for 15-20 minutes until the gnocchi mixture is bubbling and golden on top. **Serves 4**

ⓟ See Pantry essentials, p 11.

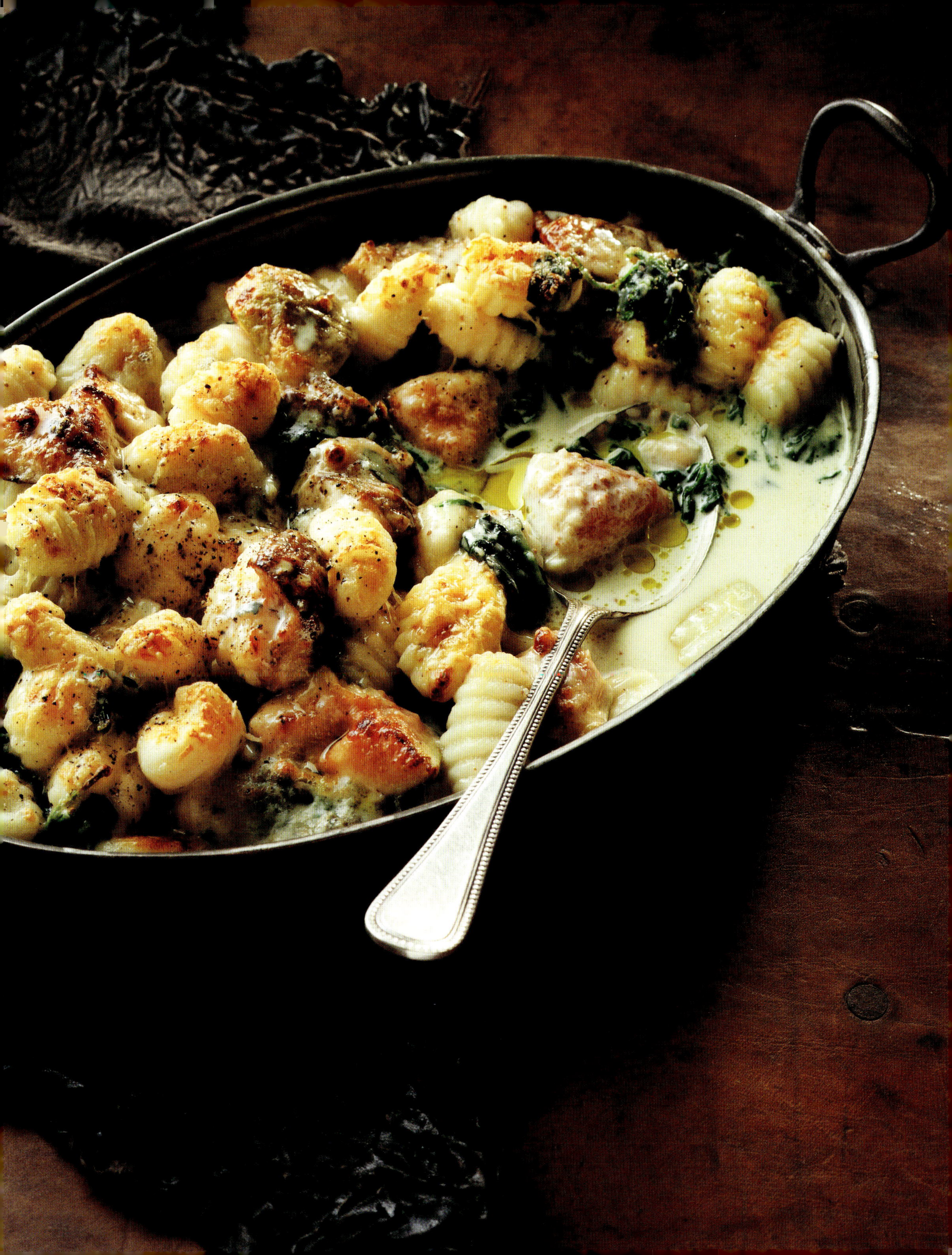

Tuscan pork with roast pumpkin and mustard fruits

Mostarda di frutta (mustard fruits) is a sweet, slightly spicy condiment served with meats and cheese. Start this recipe a day ahead.

2 tbs finely chopped rosemary
2 tbs fennel seeds
Finely grated zest of 1 lemon
⅓ cup (80ml) olive oil
1.5kg pork belly, skin on, scored
1kg jap pumpkin, cut into 3cm wedges
1 tsp chilli flakes

Mustard fruits
1L (4 cups) white wine vinegar
2½ cups (550g) caster sugar
1kg mixed whole dried fruit (we used apricots, pears, figs and glacé clementines)
⅓ cup (140g) wholegrain mustard
2 tsp mustard powder, dissolved in 2 tbs warm water
½ cup (125ml) lemon juice
4 garlic cloves, sliced
2 bay leaves

For the mustard fruits, combine the vinegar, sugar and 2 cups (500ml) water in a large saucepan over low heat, stirring until sugar dissolves. Add remaining ingredients and bring to the boil over medium heat, then reduce heat to low and simmer for 30 minutes. Using a slotted spoon, transfer fruits and remaining solids to a bowl. Increase heat to medium and simmer vinegar mixture, without stirring, for 20-25 minutes until reduced by half. Pack fruit mixture into a 2L (8-cup-capacity) sterilised jar, then pour over syrup to cover. Cool completely, then seal with a lid. Store in the fridge for up to 3 months.

Combine the rosemary, fennel seeds, lemon zest and 2 tbs olive oil in a bowl, then rub mixture all over the pork. Cover and refrigerate overnight.

Preheat the oven to 220°C.

Season pork with salt and place, skin-side up, on a roasting rack over a roasting pan. Fill pan with 2cm water. Roast pork for 30 minutes, then reduce heat to 180°C and cook for a further 2 hours, topping up water if necessary. Remove from the oven and set aside to rest, loosely covered with foil.

Meanwhile, 30 minutes before pork has finished cooking, place pumpkin in a roasting pan, drizzle with remaining 2 tbs oil and scatter with chilli flakes. Cover with foil, then roast, turning once, for 30 minutes or until tender.

Slice pork and serve with pumpkin and mustard fruits.

Serves 6

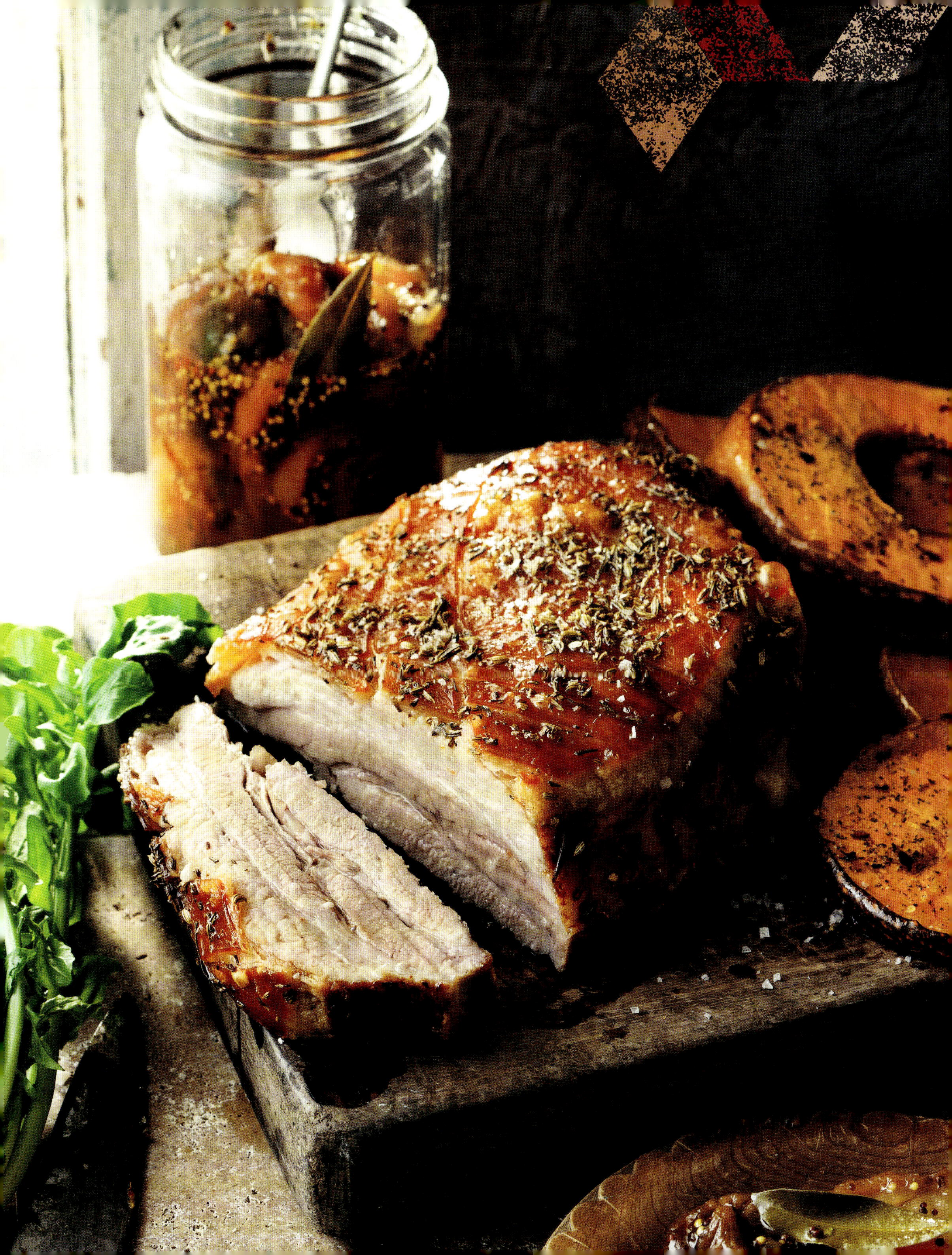

Orecchiette amatriciana

This pasta sauce is named after Amatrice, the town where it originated. Adding a little butter to give richness to the sauce is a tip I picked up from Italian food writer, the late Marcella Hazan.

8 slices pancetta ⓟ
2 tbs olive oil, plus extra to drizzle
1 onion, finely chopped
2 garlic cloves, crushed
800g can chopped tomatoes
30g unsalted butter
1 tsp caster sugar
2 tsp red wine vinegar
3 sprigs basil, plus extra basil leaves to serve
400g orecchiette ⓟ
Finely shredded parmesan, ⓟ to serve

Finely chop 4 slices pancetta. Heat oil in a saucepan over medium heat, then cook onion for 2-3 minutes until softened but not browned. Add chopped pancetta and garlic, then cook, stirring occasionally, for a further 3-4 minutes. Add tomatoes, butter, sugar, vinegar and basil. Season, then reduce heat to low and simmer for 30 minutes or until reduced and thickened.

Meanwhile, preheat the oven to 180°C. Line a baking tray with baking paper. Place the remaining pancetta on prepared tray and bake for 10-12 minutes until golden and crisp. Cool slightly, then break into large pieces.

Meanwhile, cook the pasta in boiling salted water until al dente. Drain, then add to the sauce with the pancetta and toss to combine.

To serve, remove and discard the basil stalks, then divide pasta among serving bowls. Drizzle with extra oil and scatter with parmesan and extra basil leaves. **Serves 4**

ⓟ See Pantry essentials, p 11.

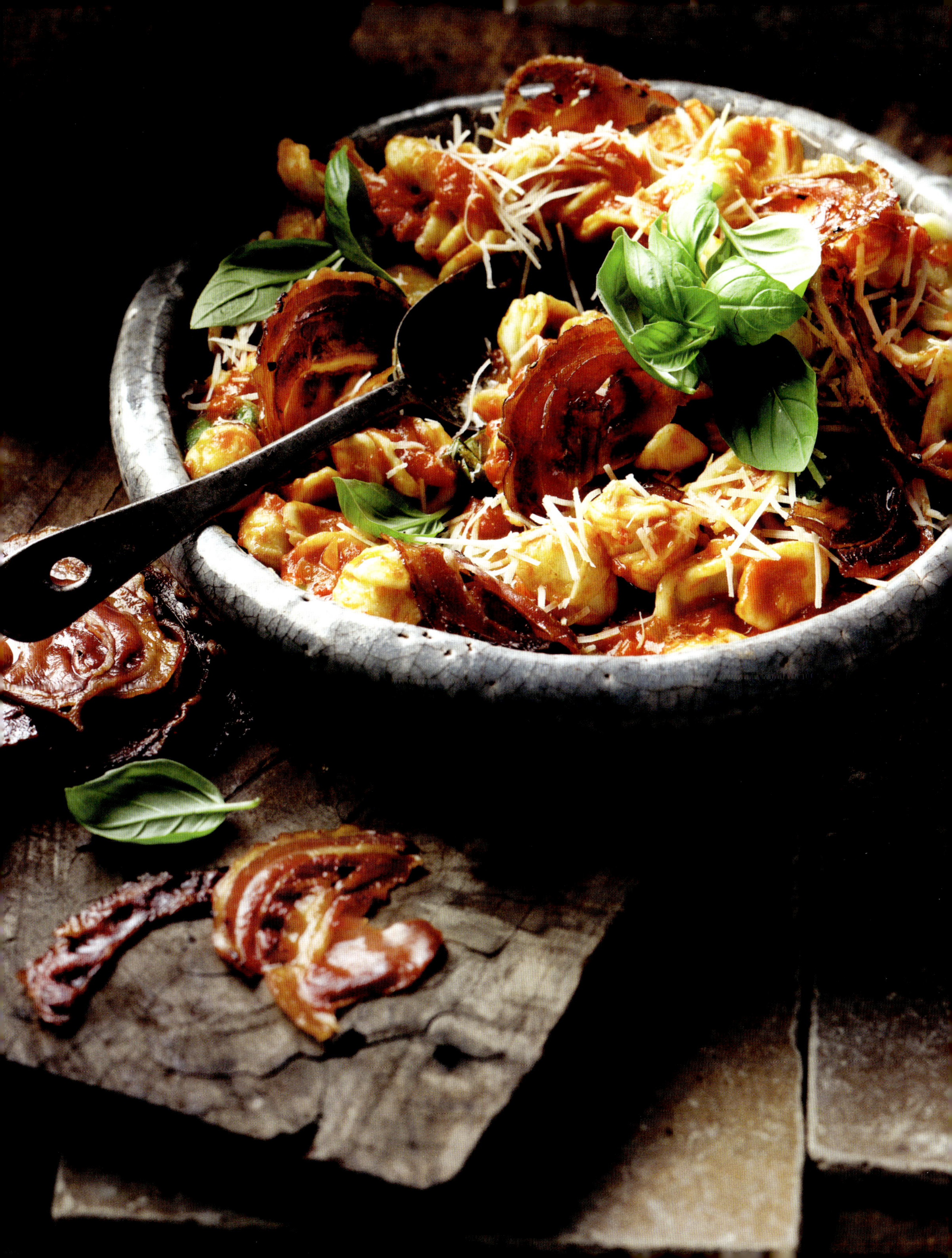

Negroni tart

The flavours of this dessert are inspired by that fabulous Italian cocktail comprising gin, red vermouth and Campari, served with an orange-zest garnish.

- 1 quantity sweet shortcrust pastry (see Basics, p 294) or 435g packet frozen vanilla bean sweet shortcrust pastry, thawed
- 1 cup (220g) caster sugar
- 1 vanilla bean, split, seeds scraped
- 6 oranges (seedless if possible, such as navels), 3 finely zested, then juiced, 3 peeled, pith removed, sliced
- 100ml Campari ⓟ
- 300ml thickened cream, whisked to stiff peaks
- 250g mascarpone ⓟ

Almond praline
- ¾ cup (105g) roasted slivered almonds
- 1 cup (220g) caster sugar

For the almond praline, line a baking tray with baking paper. Spread almonds over the baking paper. Combine sugar and 2 tbs cold water in a saucepan over low heat, stirring until sugar dissolves. Increase heat to medium-high and bring to the boil. Cook, without stirring, occasionally brushing down the sides of the pan with a damp pastry brush, until the mixture turns a golden caramel colour. Pour caramel over the almonds on the tray, then set aside until it hardens. Using a mortar and pestle or food processor, crush praline to coarse crumbs. Store in an airtight container.

Grease a 12cm x 36cm loose-bottomed tart pan. Line with pastry, then refrigerate for 15 minutes.

Preheat the oven to 180°C. Prick the pastry base with a fork, then line with baking paper and fill with pastry weights. Bake for 10-12 minutes until pale golden. Remove weights and paper, then bake for a further 5-6 minutes until pastry is dry and crisp. Cool in the pan.

Meanwhile, place the sugar and ⅓ cup (80ml) water in a saucepan over medium heat, stirring until sugar dissolves. Add vanilla pod and seeds, and bring to the boil, then reduce heat to medium-low and simmer for 2 minutes. Add orange juice, zest and Campari to the sugar syrup, then return to the boil and simmer for a further 2 minutes. Cool, then refrigerate.

Combine whipped cream, mascarpone and ½ cup praline. Spread over the tart shell and top with orange slices. Just before serving, drizzle over the orange syrup and sprinkle with extra praline crumbs. **Serves 6**

ⓟ See Pantry essentials, p 11.

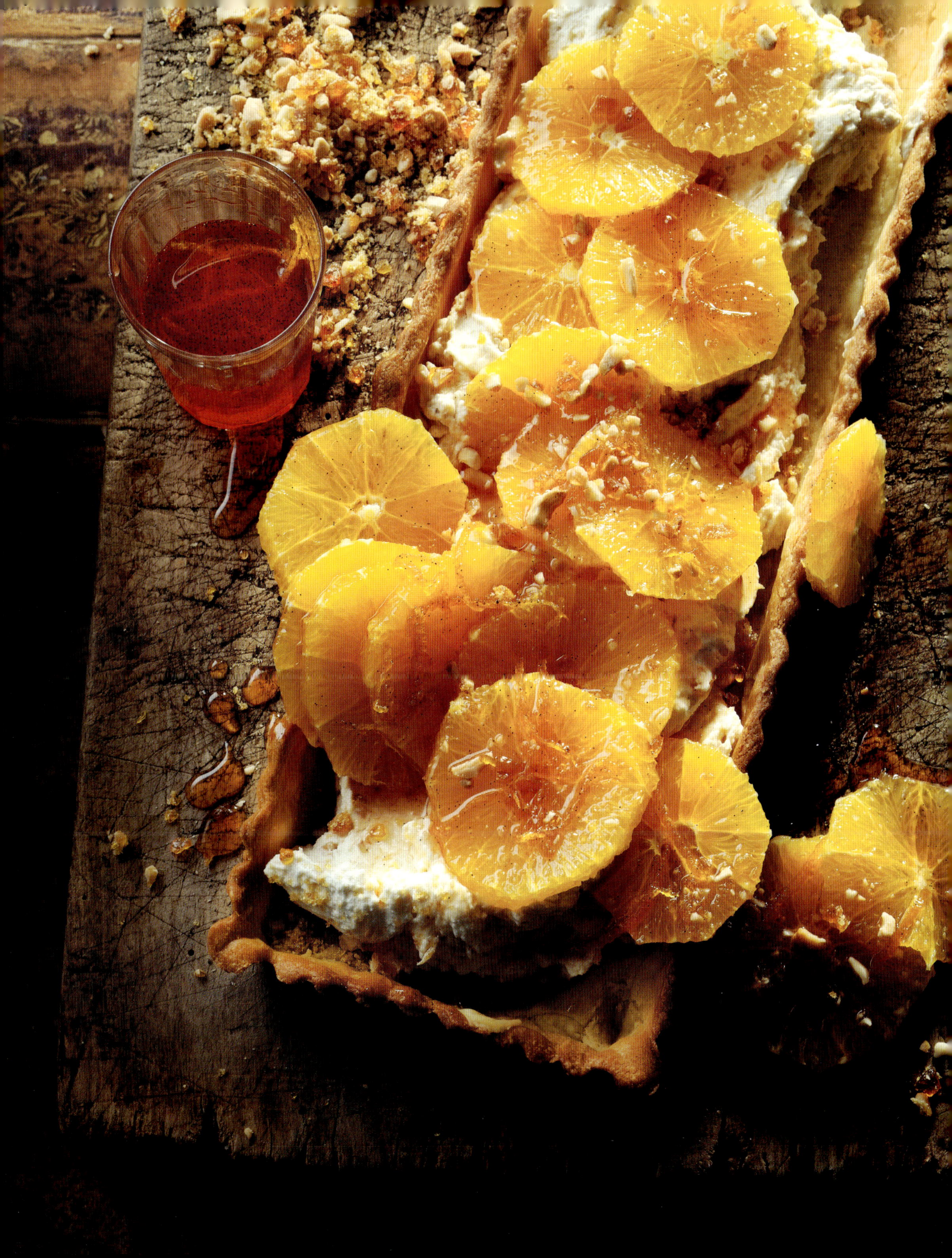

Minimisus

180g unsalted butter, softened
100g brown sugar
260g caster sugar
4 eggs
1 2/3 cups (250g) self-raising flour, sifted
12 amaretti biscuits, finely crushed
1/4 cup (60ml) coffee essence* or freshly brewed espresso, plus extra 2 tbs coffee essence for syrup
2 tbs Marsala ⓟ
100g ricotta
1 quantity Italian meringue (optional, see Basics, p 297) or 250ml whipped thickened cream, to serve
Chocolate-coated coffee beans, roughly chopped, to serve

Fillling
2 cups (500g) mascarpone ⓟ
Scraped seeds of 1 vanilla bean
1/3 cup (50g) icing sugar
1/4 cup (60ml) Marsala

Preheat the oven to 180°C. Line a 12-hole muffin pan with paper cases. Using an electric mixer, beat butter, brown sugar and 1/2 cup (110g) caster sugar for 3 minutes or until thick and pale. Add eggs, one at a time, beating well after each addition. Fold in flour, crushed amaretti, 1/4 cup (60ml) coffee essence and 1 tbs Marsala, then fold in ricotta until just combined. Divide batter among the muffin cases, then level tops. Bake for 25-30 minutes or until a skewer comes out clean. Cool for 10 minutes in pan, then transfer to a wire rack to cool completely.

For the filling, place all the ingredients in a bowl. Using a wooden spoon, stir until combined. Refrigerate until needed.

For the syrup, combine the remaining 2/3 cup (150g) caster sugar, remaining 1 tbs Marsala, extra 2 tbs coffee essence and 150ml water in a saucepan over low heat, stirring until the sugar dissolves. Increase heat to medium-high and cook for 5-7 minutes until reduced and syrupy. Cool.

Remove cakes from their cases and halve horizontally. Drizzle all the halves with a little cooled syrup, then spread 2 tbs filling over each base. Replace the tops. If using the Italian meringue topping, replace the cake tops, then dollop each with a spoonful of meringue. Using a kitchen blowtorch, lightly brulee the tops of the meringue. Alternatively, top with a dollop of whipped cream. Serve sprinkled with chocolate-coated coffee beans. **Makes 12**

* *Available in the coffee aisle of supermarkets.*
ⓟ *See Pantry essentials, p 11.*

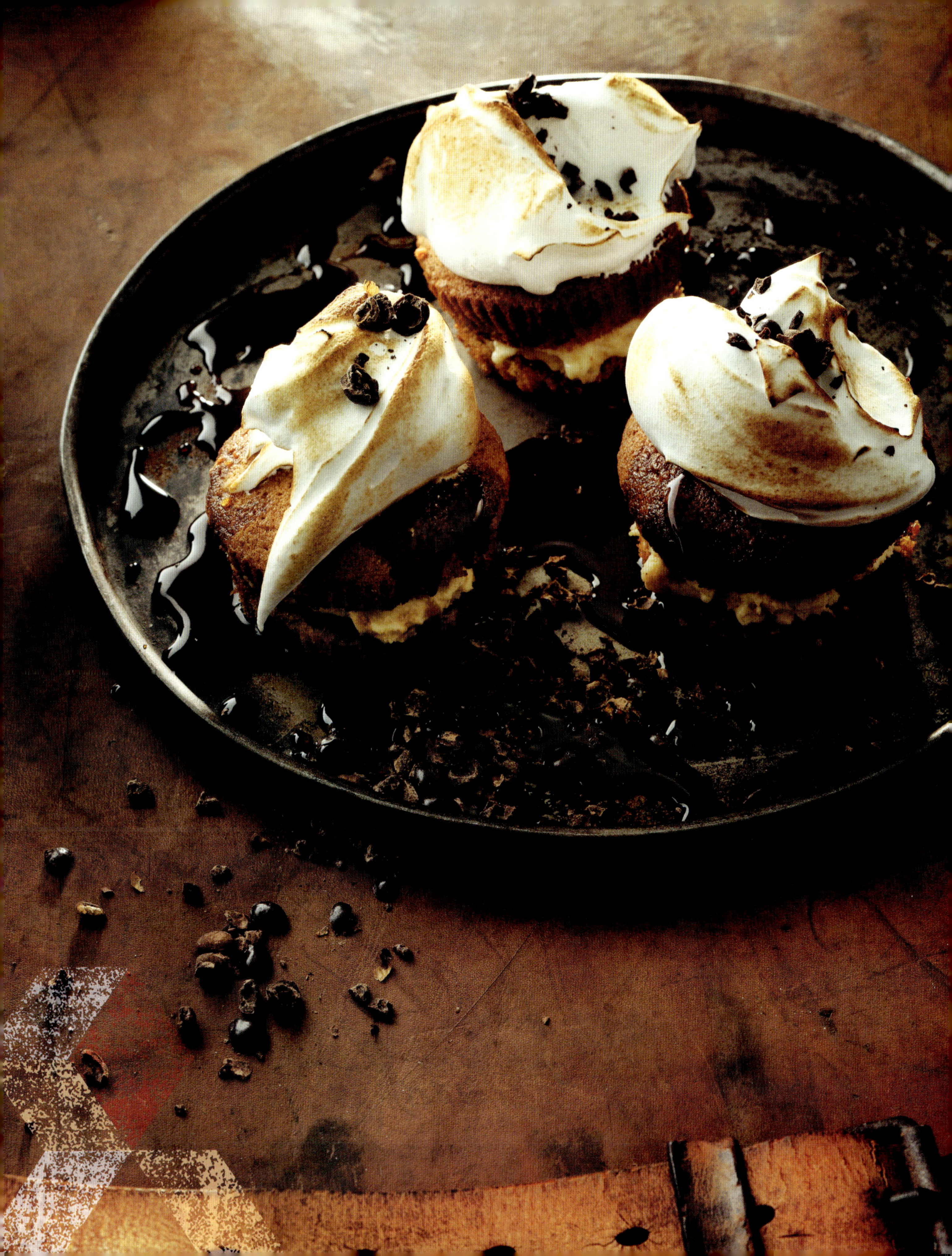

SPANISH

PANTRY ESSENTIALS

Almonds
Used as a tapas dish, in desserts and sweets, or to thicken sauces or soups.

Boquerones
Also known as white anchovies, these are preserved in vinegar and olive oil. From Spanish delis and specialist food shops.

Calasparra rice
A short-grain variety that holds its shape and texture even after absorbing large amounts of liquid. Available from Spanish delis and specialist food shops. Substitute arborio or other short-grain rice.

Chorizo
Fresh, dried or semi-dried, these pork sausages are flavoured with smoked paprika, garlic and chilli. Dried chorizo is from delis, supermarkets and butchers; fresh is from selected butchers and delis.

Jamon
Dried and salt-cured ham, the finest being jamon iberico, whose unique flavour is due to the acorns on which the pigs feed. Substitute jamon serrano or prosciutto.

Manchego cheese
A hard cheese, originally made with the milk of sheep from La Mancha. Available from Spanish and selected delis, and specialist cheese shops.

Pedro Ximénez
A rich, sweet, raisin-flavoured dark sherry made from a white grape variety of the same name, often abbreviated to 'PX'. Available from selected bottle shops.

Piquillo peppers
Usually sold roasted in jars or cans, these smoky, mild little red chillies are named for their beak-like shape. Available from delis and selected supermarkets.

Saffron threads
This highly prized spice is painstakingly harvested from the stigma (threads) of a variety of crocus. Use it sparingly, as not only is it expensive, but its sweet, musty flavour can be overpowering.

Sherry vinegar
True vinagre de Jerez is aged for at least six months. From delis and specialist food shops. Substitute red wine vinegar.

Smoked paprika (pimenton)
Spanish paprika comes in three varieties of heat – dulce (sweet or mild), agridulce (with a touch of heat) and picante (hot). The finest is pimenton de la Vera, which is smoked over oak, and adds a distinctive smoky flavour. We've used the sweet smoked version. Available from delis and specialist food shops.

Squid ink
Its delicate flavour and aroma are redolent of the sea. Available from gourmet food shops and selected fishmongers.

The Spanish kitchen reflects the country's imperial history and varied geography. Saffron, cinnamon and smoked paprika; olive oil and olives; legumes; and cured meats, such as morcilla (blood sausage), chorizo and jamon (ham) - all play their part in this vibrant cuisine.

Pear & manchego salad with jamon-wrapped breadsticks

2 firm beurre bosc pears
1 lemon, halved
1/3 cup (80ml) olive oil
2 tbs honey
2 tbs blood orange juice*
2 tbs sherry vinegar ⓟ
 or red wine vinegar
8 slices jamon ⓟ
8 breadsticks (grissini)
100g baby salad leaves (mesclun)
2 tbs roasted chopped walnuts
40g manchego cheese, ⓟ shaved

Cut the pears lengthways into 1cm-thick slices, leaving stalks intact. Rub pear with the cut side of half the lemon. Heat 1 tbs oil in a frypan over medium-high heat. Add pear and cook for 1-2 minutes each side or until light golden. Add honey and the juice of the remaining 1/2 lemon, swirling the pan to warm the honey mixture and coat the pear.

Whisk remaining 1/4 cup (60ml) olive oil, orange juice and vinegar in a small bowl. Season.

Wrap a slice of jamon around each breadstick. Using a slotted spoon, transfer pear slices to a bowl, reserving cooking juices. Add cooking juices to the dressing and whisk to combine, then toss with the pear and baby salad leaves. Scatter with walnuts and manchego, and serve with jamon-wrapped breadsticks. **Serves 4**

* If blood oranges aren't available, use regular oranges.
ⓟ See Pantry essentials, p 38.

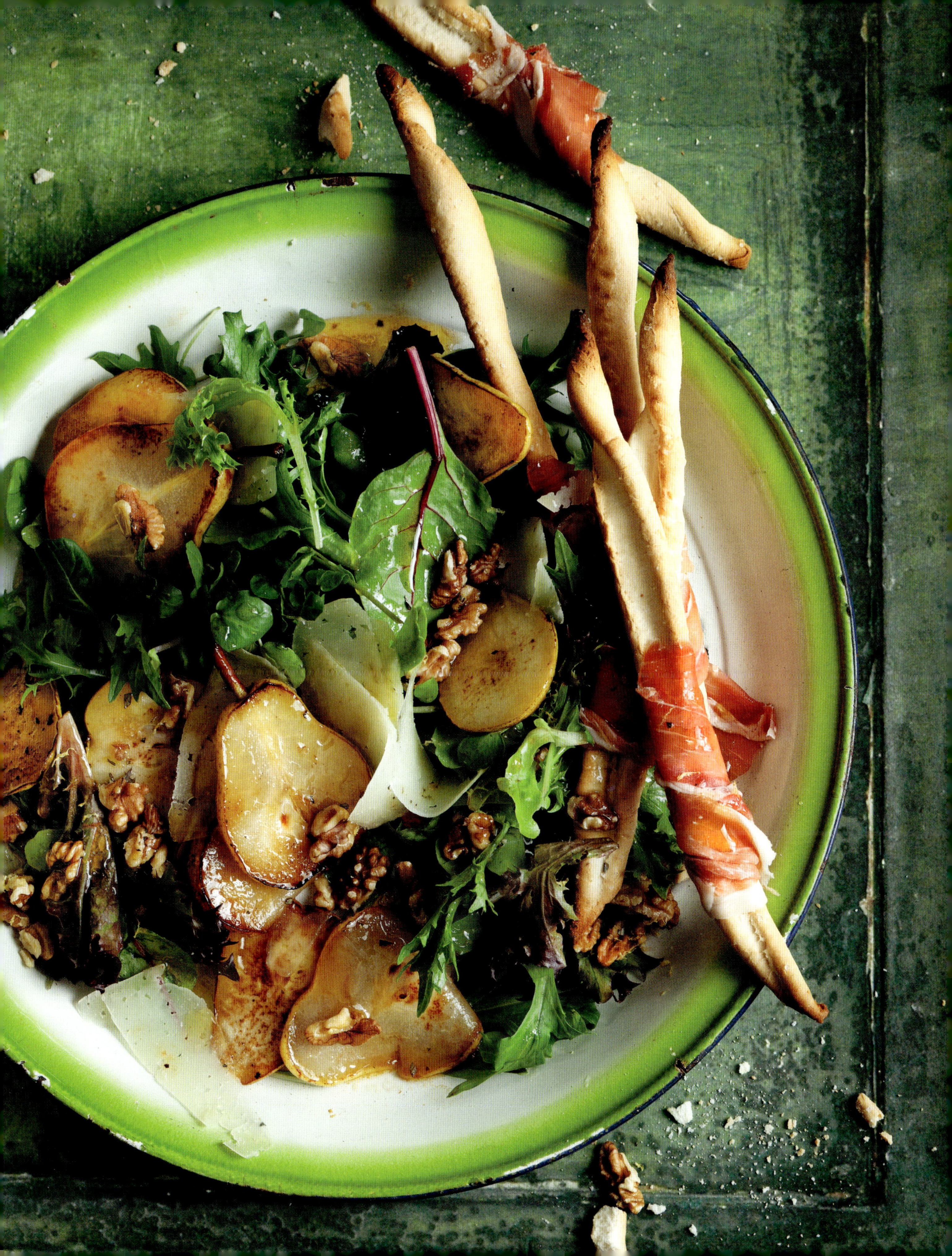

Jamon & manchego croquetas

2 large (600g) sebago potatoes, peeled, chopped
40g unsalted butter
1 small onion, finely chopped
¼ cup (60ml) thickened cream
120g jamon, Ⓟ finely chopped
120g manchego cheese, Ⓟ grated
¼ cup finely chopped chives
1 cup (150g) plain flour
2 eggs, lightly beaten
2 cups (100g) panko (Japanese) breadcrumbs
Sunflower oil, to deep-fry
½ cup flat-leaf parsley leaves
Aioli, to serve

Place potatoes in a saucepan and cover with cold salted water. Bring to the boil over medium-high heat, then reduce heat to medium and cook for 10-12 minutes until tender. Drain, then return potatoes to saucepan over low heat, shaking gently until excess liquid evaporates.

Meanwhile, melt half the butter in a saucepan over medium heat. Add onion and cook for 1-2 minutes until softened but not browned.

Using a potato ricer or masher, mash hot potatoes with remaining 20g butter until smooth. Transfer to a bowl and cool slightly. Add onion, cream, jamon, manchego and chives, then stir to combine. Refrigerate for 20 minutes to firm.

Place flour, egg and panko on separate plates. Roll chilled potato mixture into 12 oval shapes. Dust in flour, shaking off excess, dip in egg, then coat in breadcrumbs, pressing to secure. Place on a plate and refrigerate for 30 minutes to firm up.

Meanwhile, half-fill a deep-fryer or large saucepan with sunflower oil and heat to 190°C (a cube of bread will turn golden in 30 seconds when the oil is hot enough). Fry croquetas, in batches, for 2-3 minutes until golden. Drain on paper towel.

Dry flat-leaf parsley well with paper towel, then fry for 10 seconds or until crisp (be careful, as the oil may spit).

Scatter croquetas with fried parsley leaves and serve with aioli. **Makes 12**

Ⓟ See Pantry essentials, p 38.

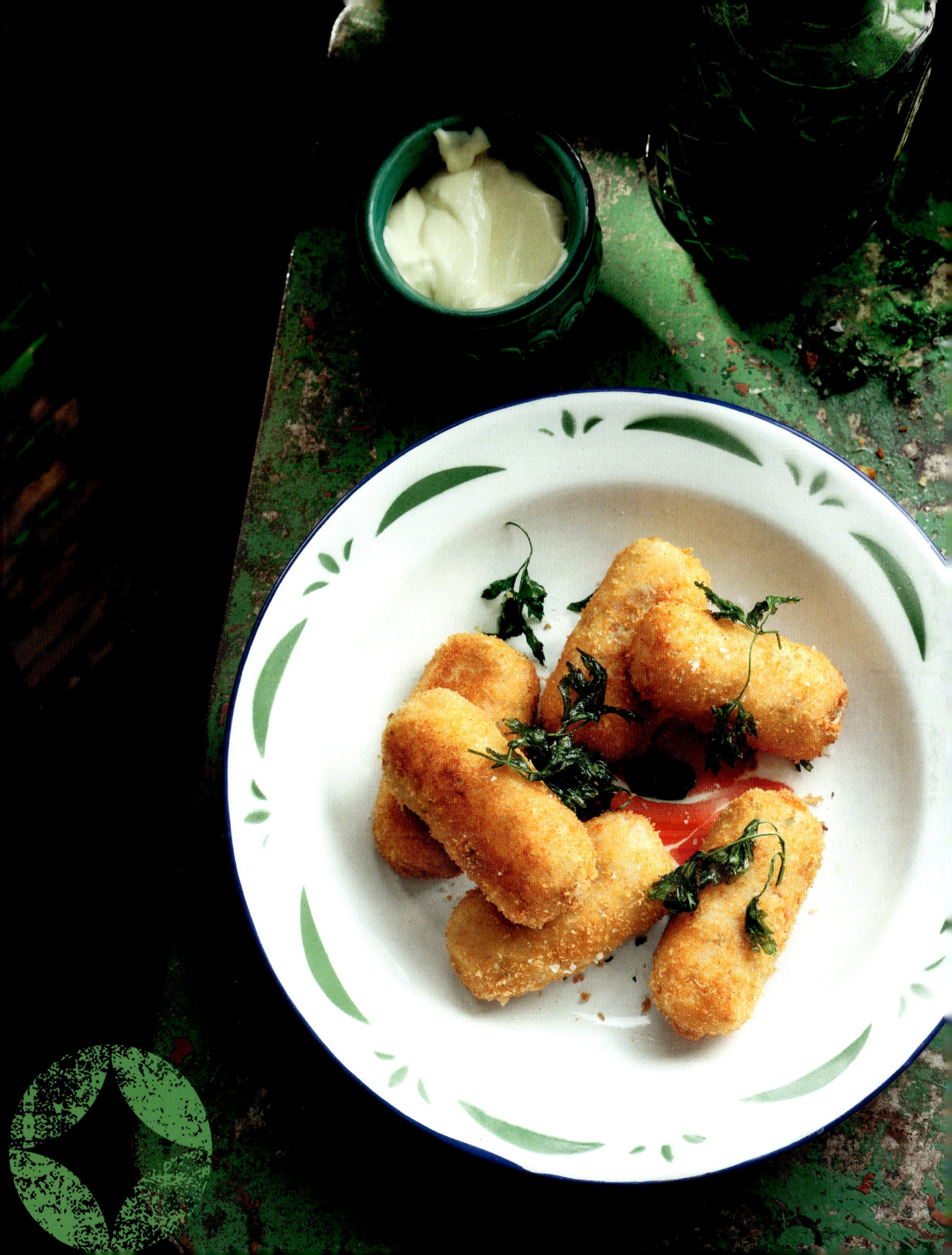

Chorizo burgers

150g fresh chorizo, ⓟ casing removed, crumbled
500g lean beef mince
2 tsp sweet smoked paprika (pimenton) ⓟ
2 tbs chopped parsley
2 tbs olive oil
1 onion, finely chopped
2 tomatoes, finely chopped
¼ cup (60ml) passata (sieved tomatoes)
4 slices jamon ⓟ or prosciutto
100g manchego cheese, ⓟ thinly sliced
4 brioche or burger buns, split, toasted
Rocket, to serve

Place chorizo, mince, 1 tsp paprika and 1 tbs parsley in a food processor and pulse to combine. Season, then form into 4 patties. Cover and refrigerate for 30 minutes to firm up.

Heat 1 tbs oil in a frypan over medium heat. Cook onion for 1-2 minutes until softened but not browned. Add chopped tomato, passata and remaining 1 tsp paprika, then cook for a further 3-4 minutes, stirring occasionally, until the mixture is the consistency of a relish. Stir through the remaining 1 tbs parsley and season.

Preheat a chargrill or frypan to medium-high. Cook jamon on both sides until crisp. Remove and keep warm. Brush patties with remaining 1 tbs olive oil and cook for 3 minutes each side or until cooked through. Place slices of manchego over each patty and cook for a further minute or until the cheese melts.

To serve, divide half the relish among the 4 bun bases, then top each with rocket, a patty, more relish, the crisp jamon and finally the bun lids. **Serves 4**

ⓟ See Pantry essentials, p 38.

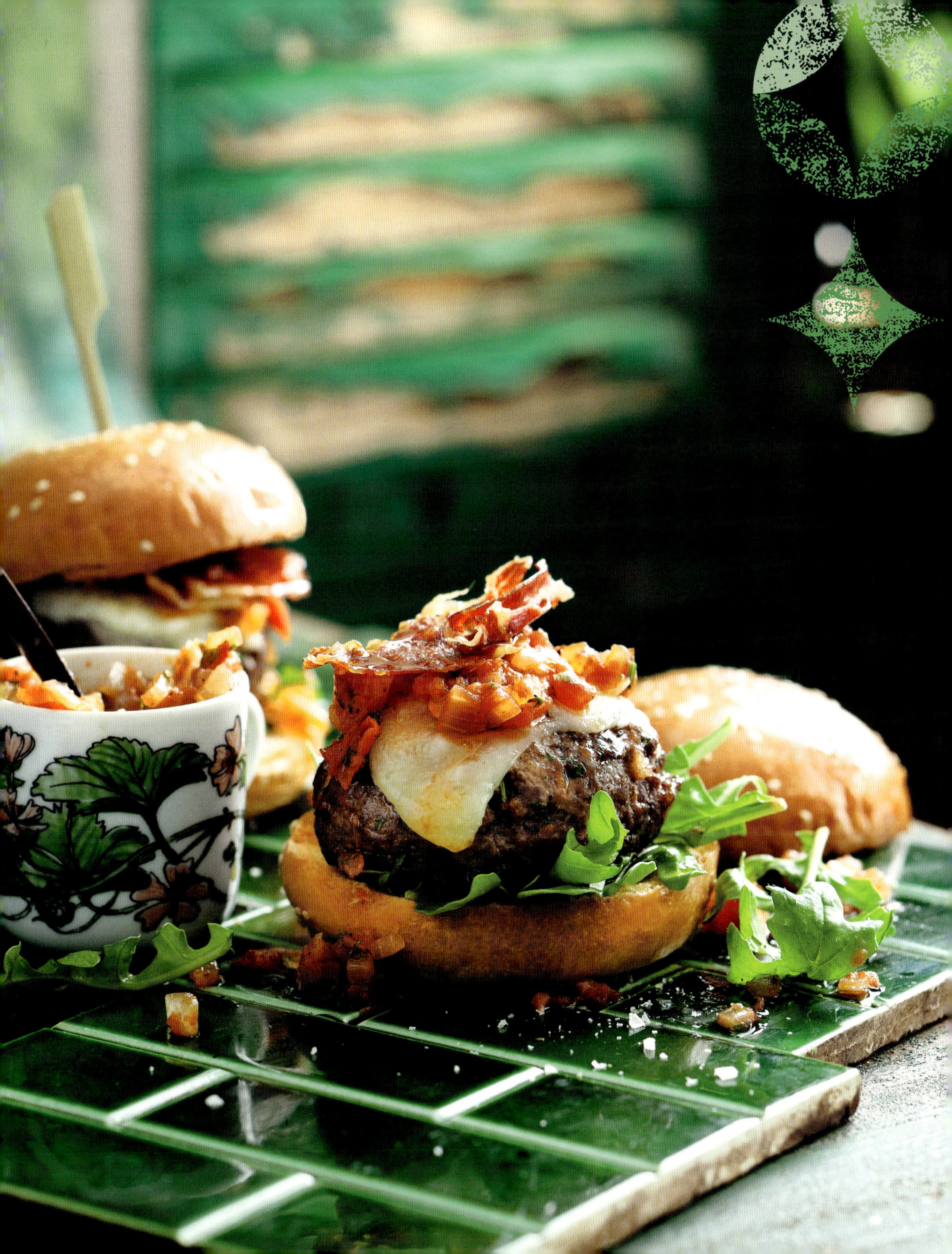

Chorizo-stuffed mushrooms

- 8 portobello mushrooms
- 150g fresh chorizo, ⓟ casing removed, crumbled
- 2 garlic cloves, chopped
- 1 tsp finely chopped thyme leaves
- 1 cup (70g) fresh breadcrumbs
- 2 tbs finely chopped flat-leaf parsley, plus extra to serve
- 1 tbs sundried tomato pesto
- 100g manchego cheese, ⓟ grated
- 2 tbs olive oil, plus extra to drizzle

Preheat the oven to 180°C. Line a baking tray with baking paper.

Trim stalks from the mushrooms and reserve. Place mushroom cups, concave-side up, on prepared tray. Place stalks in a food processor with the chorizo, garlic, thyme, breadcrumbs, parsley, pesto and 50g manchego. Add olive oil, then pulse until just combined. Season. Pile chorizo mixture into the mushroom cavities. Top with the remaining 50g manchego and drizzle with a little extra oil. Bake for 20-25 minutes until topping is crisp and mushrooms are tender.

Serve sprinkled with extra flat-leaf parsley.

Serves 8 as a tapa, or 4 as a main course

ⓟ See Pantry essentials, p 38.

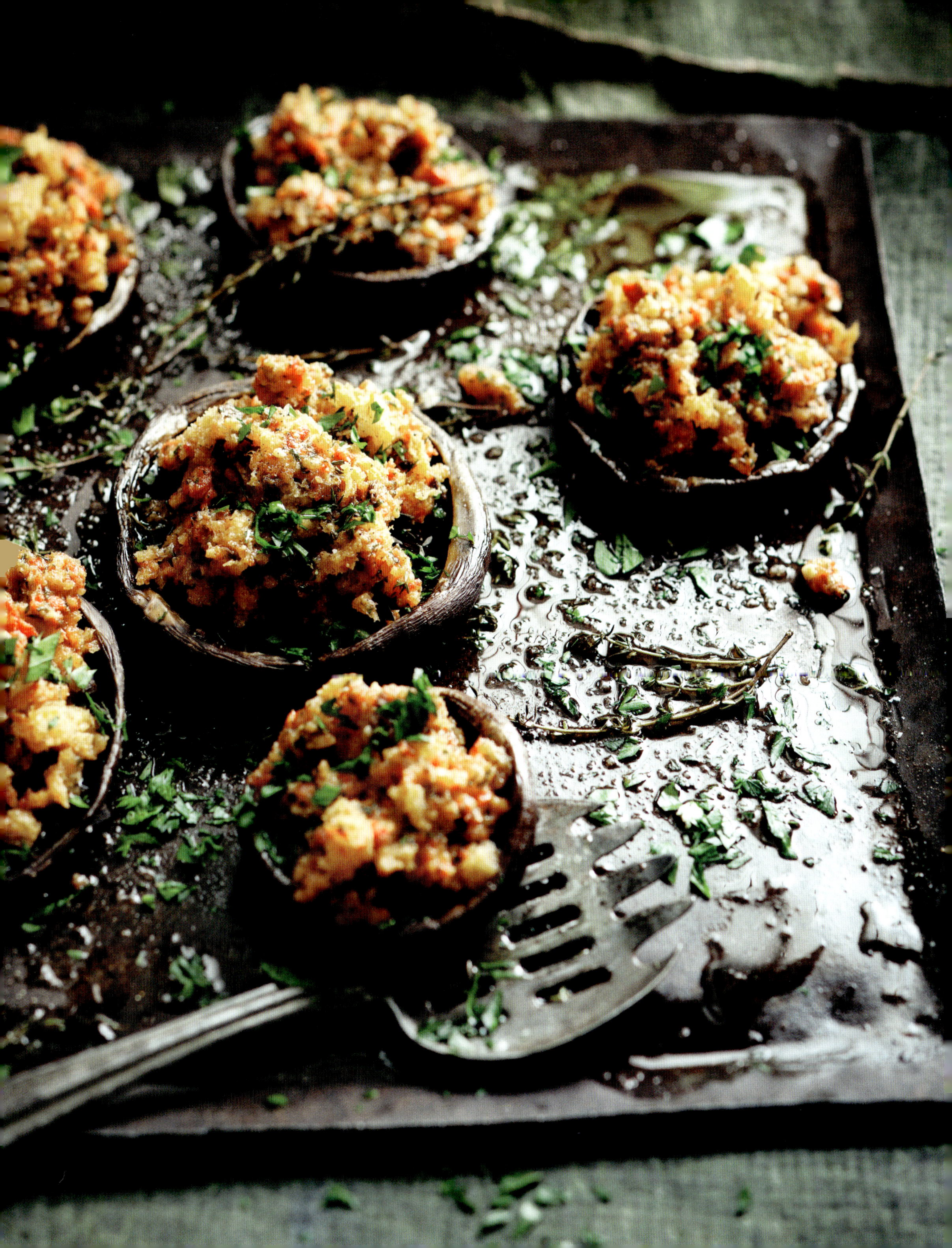

Prawns with arroz negro and chorizo crumbs

Arroz negro (black rice) is a Catalan and Valencian specialty cooked with squid ink. Here, I've served it with prawns rather than the more traditional squid or cuttlefish.

1 tbs olive oil
150g fresh chorizo, ⓟ casing removed, crumbled
2 cups (140g) roughly torn sourdough, crust removed
¼ cup flat-leaf parsley leaves
⅔ cup (100g) plain flour
½ cup (100g) rice flour
1 tbs sweet smoked paprika (pimenton) ⓟ
24 school prawns, unpeeled
Sunflower oil, to deep-fry

Arroz negro
2 tbs olive oil
1 small fennel bulb, finely chopped
1 leek (white part only), finely chopped
2 garlic cloves, finely chopped
350g Calasparra ⓟ or arborio rice
½ cup (125ml) white wine
3 cups (750ml) fish stock
30ml squid ink ⓟ

Heat olive oil in a frypan over medium-high heat. Add chorizo and cook for 2-3 minutes until starting to crisp. Add the torn sourdough and cook, stirring, until golden. Season. Stir through parsley, then set aside to cool slightly. Transfer chorizo mixture to a food processor and pulse to form coarse breadcrumbs.

For the arroz negro, heat the olive oil in a large pan over medium-low heat. Add the fennel, leek and garlic, and cook, stirring, for 2-3 minutes until softened but not browned. Add rice and stir to coat grains. Add wine, then increase heat to medium-high and cook for 2 minutes or until wine evaporates. Add stock and squid ink, reduce heat to low and simmer for 15-20 minutes until liquid is absorbed and rice is tender but still retains some bite.

Meanwhile, combine the flours, paprika and 1 tsp salt in a bowl. Toss prawns in flour mixture, shaking off excess.

Half-fill a large saucepan with sunflower oil and heat to 190°C (a cube of bread will turn golden in 30 seconds when the oil is hot enough). Fry prawns, in batches, for 1-2 minutes until crisp and golden. Drain on paper towel.

Serve prawns with arroz negro and chorizo crumbs.

Serves 4-6

ⓟ See Pantry essentials, p 38.

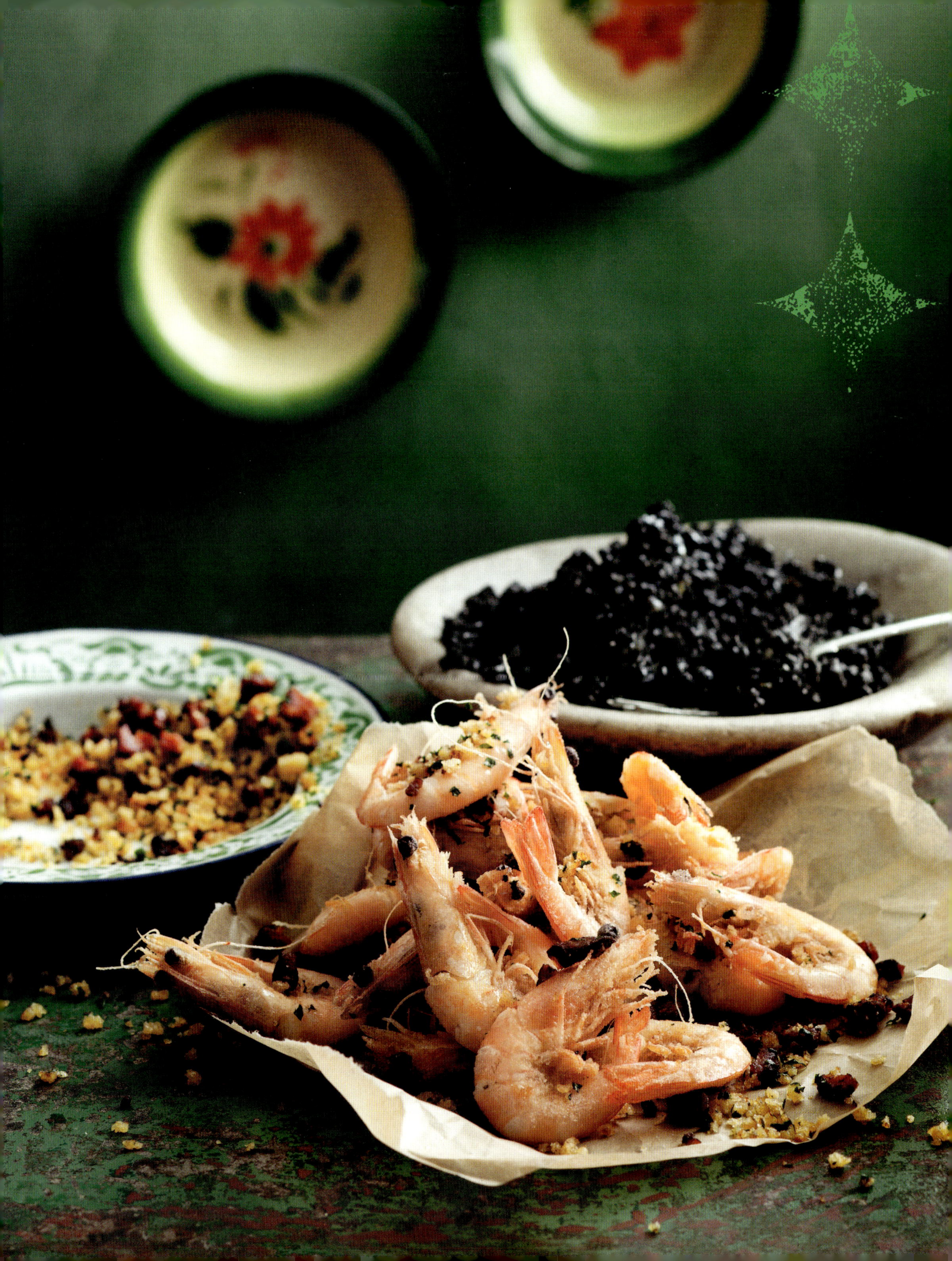

Braised pork with chorizo and olives

1/3 cup (80ml) olive oil
1kg boned pork shoulder, cut into 3cm pieces
2/3 cup (165ml) red wine
2 onions, chopped
6 garlic cloves, chopped
150g dried chorizo, ⓟ casing removed, thickly sliced
2 tsp sweet smoked paprika (pimenton) ⓟ
2 tbs tomato paste
400g can chopped tomatoes
2 cups (500ml) chicken stock
2 tbs finely chopped oregano
1 tbs finely chopped rosemary
1/4 cup (60ml) sherry vinegar ⓟ
2 tsp caster sugar
100g pitted black olives
Patatas bravas (see Basics, p 296) or rice, to serve

Heat half the oil in a large casserole or saucepan over medium-high heat. Cook pork, in batches, until browned, then transfer to a large bowl. Add the wine to the casserole, bring to a simmer and cook, scraping the base of the pan, for 3-4 minutes until slightly reduced. Pour over the pork in the bowl.

Heat remaining 2 tbs oil in the casserole over medium-high heat. Cook the onions, stirring occasionally, for 3-4 minutes until softened but not browned. Add garlic and chorizo, and cook, stirring, for a further 2 minutes. Add the paprika and tomato paste and cook for a further minute, then return the pork and cooking juices to the casserole with the tomatoes, stock and herbs. Season well, then bring to a simmer. Reduce heat to low, cover and cook for 1 hour.

Meanwhile, place vinegar and sugar in a small saucepan over low heat, stirring to dissolve the sugar. Increase heat to medium-high and simmer for 1 minute or until slightly reduced and syrupy. Add to the casserole with the olives and stir to combine. Cook, uncovered, for a further 30 minutes or until pork is meltingly tender. Serve with patatas bravas or rice.

Serves 4-6

ⓟ See Pantry essentials, p 38.

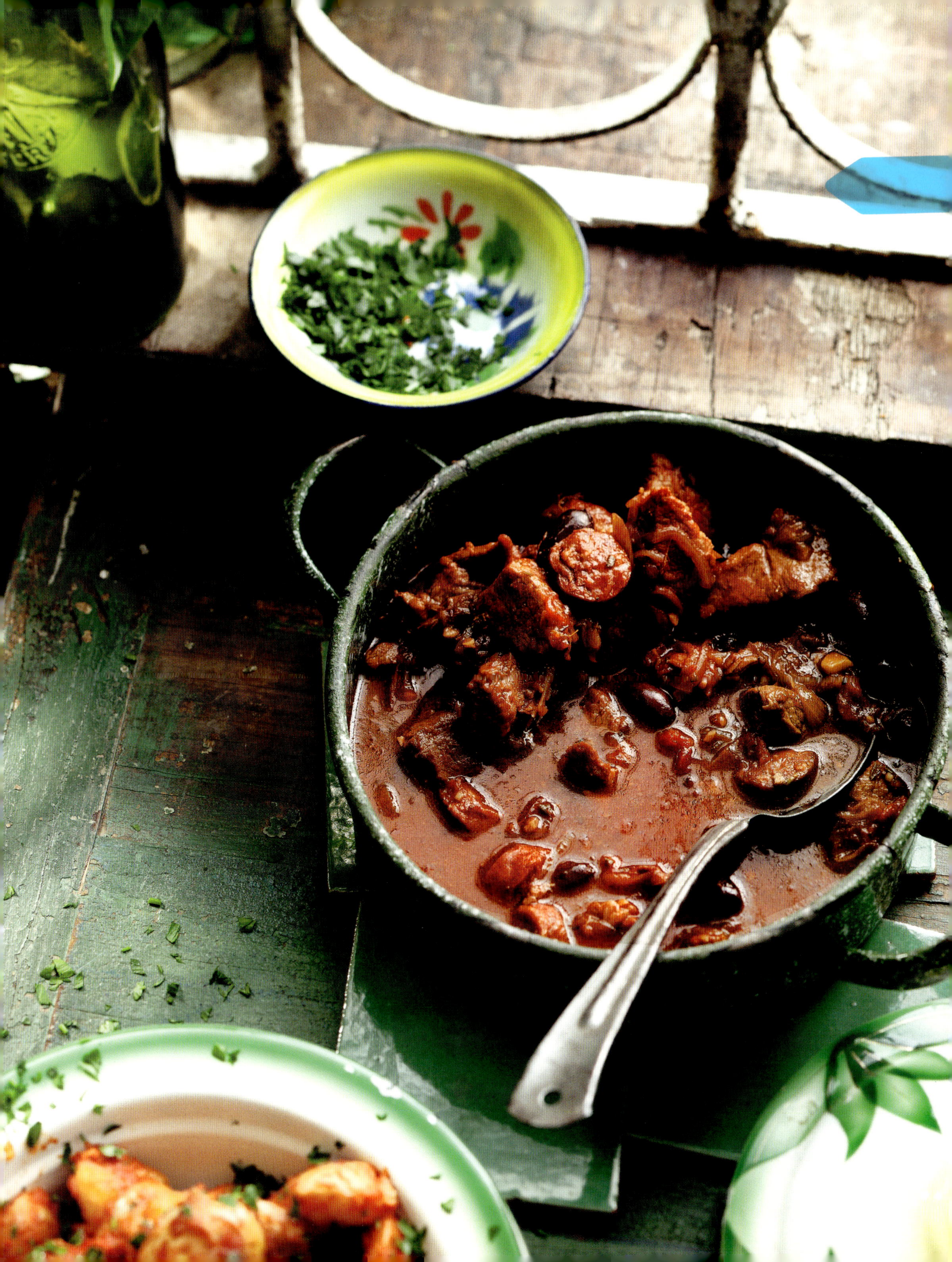

Rioja chicken

¼ cup (60ml) olive oil
1 onion, sliced
8 garlic cloves, sliced
150g fresh chorizo, Ⓟ
　casing removed, crumbled
2 cups (500ml) chicken stock
1 cup (250ml) Rioja or other
　red wine
400g can chopped tomatoes
1 tsp brown sugar
2 bay leaves
2 small dried red chillies
1.5kg whole chicken
400g can chickpeas,
　drained, rinsed
1 tbs finely chopped
　flat-leaf parsley
Saffron rice (optional, see
　Basics, p 295), to serve

Preheat the oven to 180°C.

Heat 2 tbs oil in a casserole over medium-high heat. Add onion and garlic, and cook for 1-2 minutes until softened but not browned. Add chorizo and cook, stirring occasionally, for 2-3 minutes until starting to crisp. Add stock, wine, tomato, brown sugar, bay leaves and chillies, and stir to combine. Place the chicken, breast-side up, on top of the sauce mixture. Cover with a lid and transfer to the oven. Cook for 1 hour, then remove lid and brush chicken with remaining 1 tbs oil. Season.

Return casserole to the oven and cook, uncovered, for a further 45 minutes. Remove chicken from casserole and transfer to a plate. Cover loosely with foil and set aside.

Place casserole on the stove over medium-high heat. Cook, stirring occasionally, for 3-4 minutes until sauce is reduced and thickened. Add chickpeas and stir to heat through.

Garnish chicken with parsley and serve with chickpea mixture and saffron rice, if using. **Serves 4**

Ⓟ See Pantry essentials, p 38.

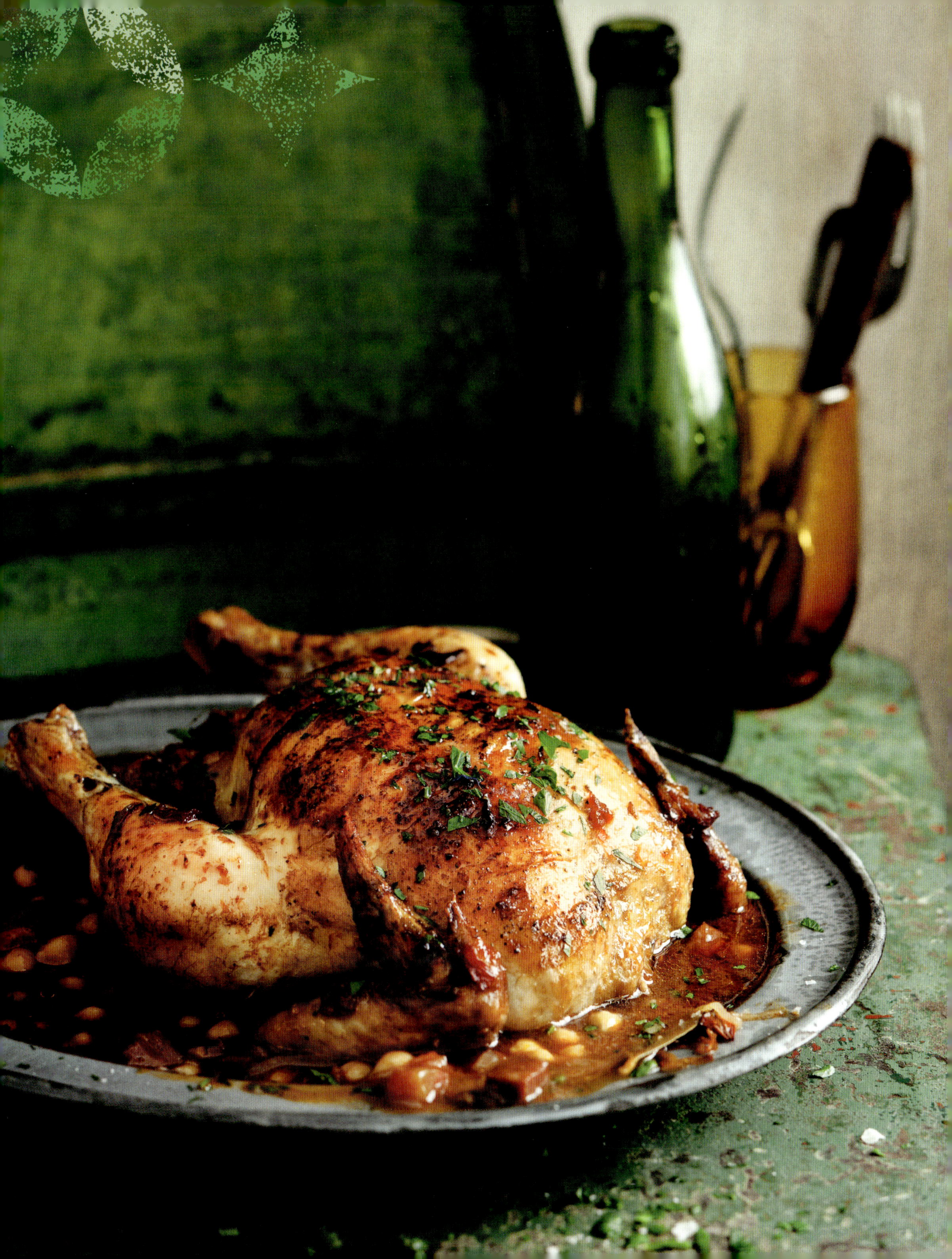

Paella

1-2 tbs olive oil
2 chicken thigh fillets, trimmed, cut into bite-size pieces
150g dried chorizo, ⓟ chopped
1 onion, finely chopped
1 red capsicum, chopped
2 garlic cloves, crushed
½ tsp saffron threads ⓟ soaked in 2 tbs boiling water
300g Calasparra ⓟ or arborio rice
½ cup (125ml) dry sherry
2 cups (500ml) chicken stock
12 pot-ready mussels
12 medium green prawns, peeled (tails intact), deveined
1 cup (120g) frozen peas
Finely chopped flat-leaf parsley and lemon wedges, to serve

Heat 1 tbs oil in a paella pan or large frypan over medium-high heat. Add the chicken and cook, stirring occasionally, for 3-4 minutes until golden and almost cooked through. Remove from pan and set aside.

Add the chorizo to the pan, adding a little more oil if necessary, and cook, stirring occasionally, for 2-3 minutes until starting to crisp. Add the onion, capsicum and garlic. Cook for 5 minutes or until the vegetables have softened.

Return the chicken to the pan, then add the saffron mixture and rice, and stir to coat grains. Add the sherry and stock, then cook over medium-low heat, stirring occasionally, for 12-15 minutes until the rice is almost cooked and most of the liquid has evaporated.

Place the mussels and prawns over the rice, then scatter over the peas. Cover with a lid or foil and cook for a further 5 minutes or until mussels have opened and prawns are cooked. Season.

Scatter with parsley and serve with lemon wedges. **Serves 4-6**
ⓟ See Pantry essentials, p 38.

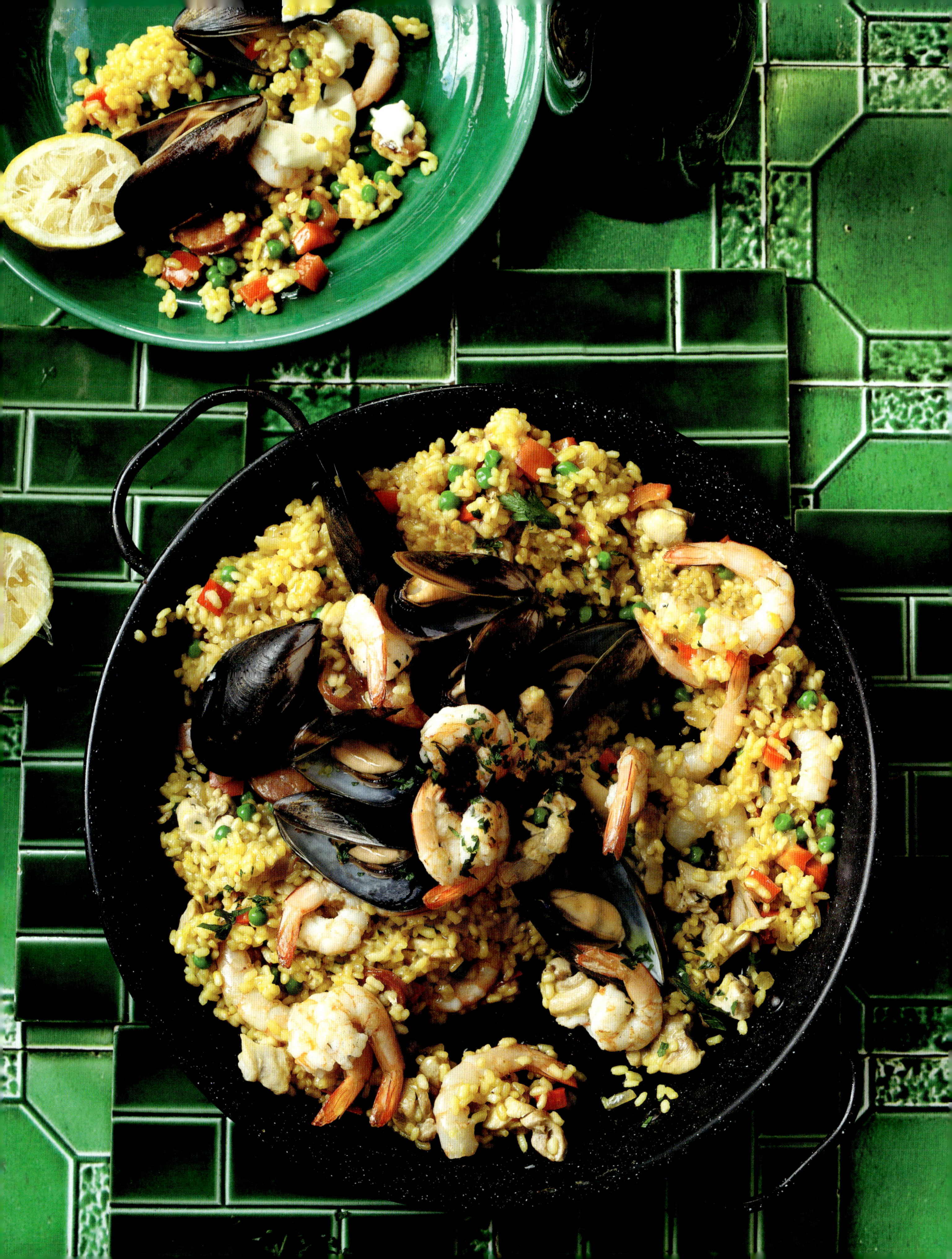

Steak with escalivada and manchego butter

Escalivada is a Catalan salad of smoky roasted vegetables. Its name is derived from the verb 'escalivar', which means 'to cook in hot ashes'.

¼ cup (60ml) olive oil, plus extra to brush
2 garlic cloves, crushed
2 tbs sherry vinegar ⓟ or red wine vinegar
2 tsp ground cumin
1 onion, cut into thin wedges
1 each roasted red and yellow capsicum, sliced
4 vine-ripened tomatoes, peeled, seeded, each cut into thin wedges
¼ cup finely chopped flat-leaf parsley
4 x 300g beef rib-eye steaks on the bone
Rocket, to serve

Manchego butter
60g manchego cheese, ⓟ grated
150g unsalted butter, softened
1 garlic clove, crushed
2 tbs finely chopped flat-leaf parsley
6 pitted green olives, finely chopped

For the manchego butter, place all the ingredients in a bowl and combine well. Form into a log on a piece of plastic wrap, then wrap tightly, twisting the ends to secure. Refrigerate for 30 minutes or until firm.

For the escalivada, whisk oil, garlic, vinegar and cumin in a bowl. Season. Preheat a chargrill or barbecue to medium-high. Toss onion in a little extra oil, then chargrill for 3-4 minutes, turning, until softened. Combine onion, capsicum, tomato and parsley in a large bowl and toss with dressing.

Brush the steaks with a little extra oil, then chargrill for 3-4 minutes each side for medium-rare or until cooked to your liking. Rest, loosely covered with foil, for 5 minutes.

Top each steak with a slice of manchego butter and serve with escalivada and rocket. **Serves 4**

ⓟ See Pantry essentials, p 38.

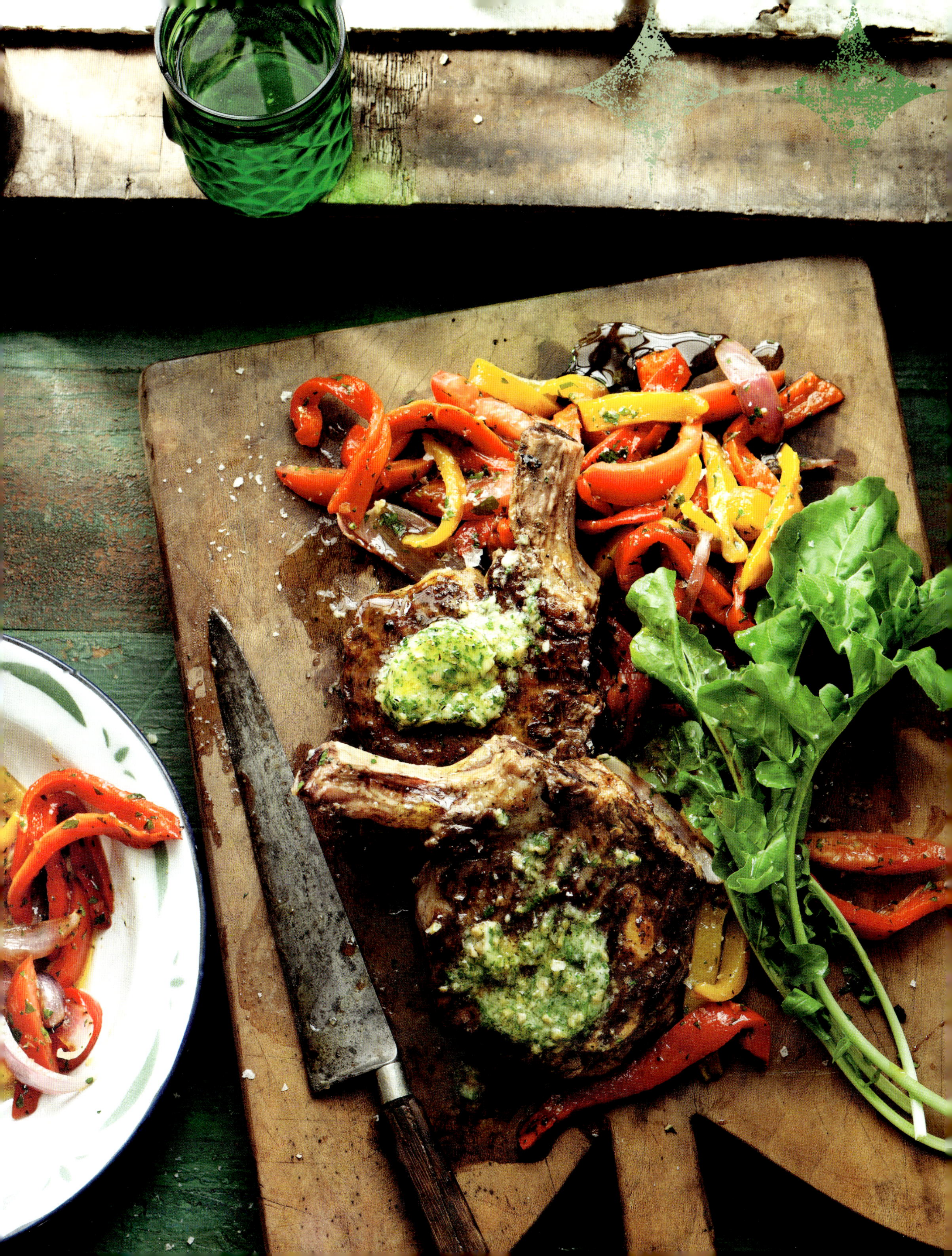

Crema Catalana

You will need a kitchen blowtorch for this recipe.

300ml milk
300ml pure (thin) cream
1 tbs finely grated orange zest
1 tbs finely grated lemon zest
2 cinnamon quills
4 egg yolks
160g caster sugar
2 tbs cornflour

Combine milk, cream, zests and cinnamon in a saucepan and bring to a simmer over low heat. Remove from heat and stand for 15 minutes for the flavours to infuse.

Using electric beaters, beat egg yolks, 80g caster sugar and cornflour until thick and pale. Reheat milk mixture over medium heat until almost boiling, then gradually strain through a sieve, whisking constantly, into the egg mixture. Discard solids. Return egg mixture to the pan over very low heat, stirring until thick enough to coat the back of a wooden spoon. Divide among 4 x ¾-cup (180ml) capacity ramekins. Cool, then refrigerate for 2-3 hours until chilled.

To serve, sprinkle 1 tbs remaining sugar over each custard, then use a kitchen blowtorch to caramelise. **Serves 6**

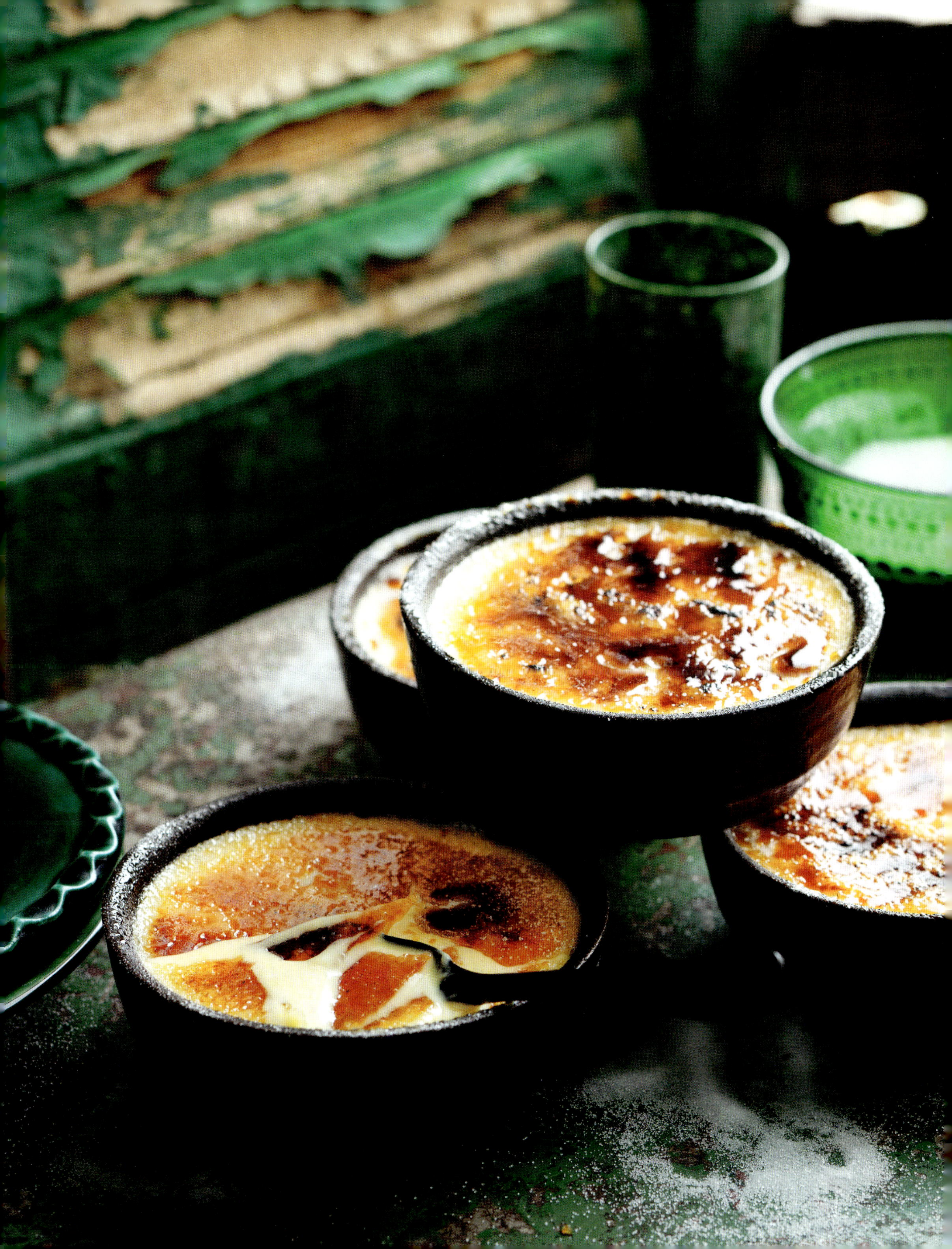

Chocolate-orange cake

This ultra-moist chocolate cake is based on Claudia Roden's classic boiled orange cake. It's a breeze to make and keeps well for up to 5 days.

2 oranges
6 eggs
250g caster sugar
2½ cups (250g) almond meal
1 tsp baking powder
½ tsp bicarbonate of soda
½ cup (50g) cocoa powder, plus extra to dust
Vanilla ice cream and extra orange wedges, to serve

Place the whole oranges in a saucepan and cover with cold water. Bring to the boil over medium-high heat, then reduce heat to low, cover with a plate or cartouche (a round of baking paper) to keep oranges submerged and simmer for 1-1½ hours, topping up water if necessary, until soft.

Preheat oven to 180°C. Grease and line a 22cm springform pan.

Remove oranges from saucepan and cool slightly. Quarter each orange and remove the seeds, then transfer to a food processor and whiz to a smooth puree. Add the remaining ingredients and pulse to combine. Pour batter into the prepared pan and bake for 45 minutes or until a skewer comes out clean. Cool for 10 minutes, then transfer to a rack to cool completely.

Dust with extra cocoa and serve with vanilla ice cream and orange wedges. **Serves 8**

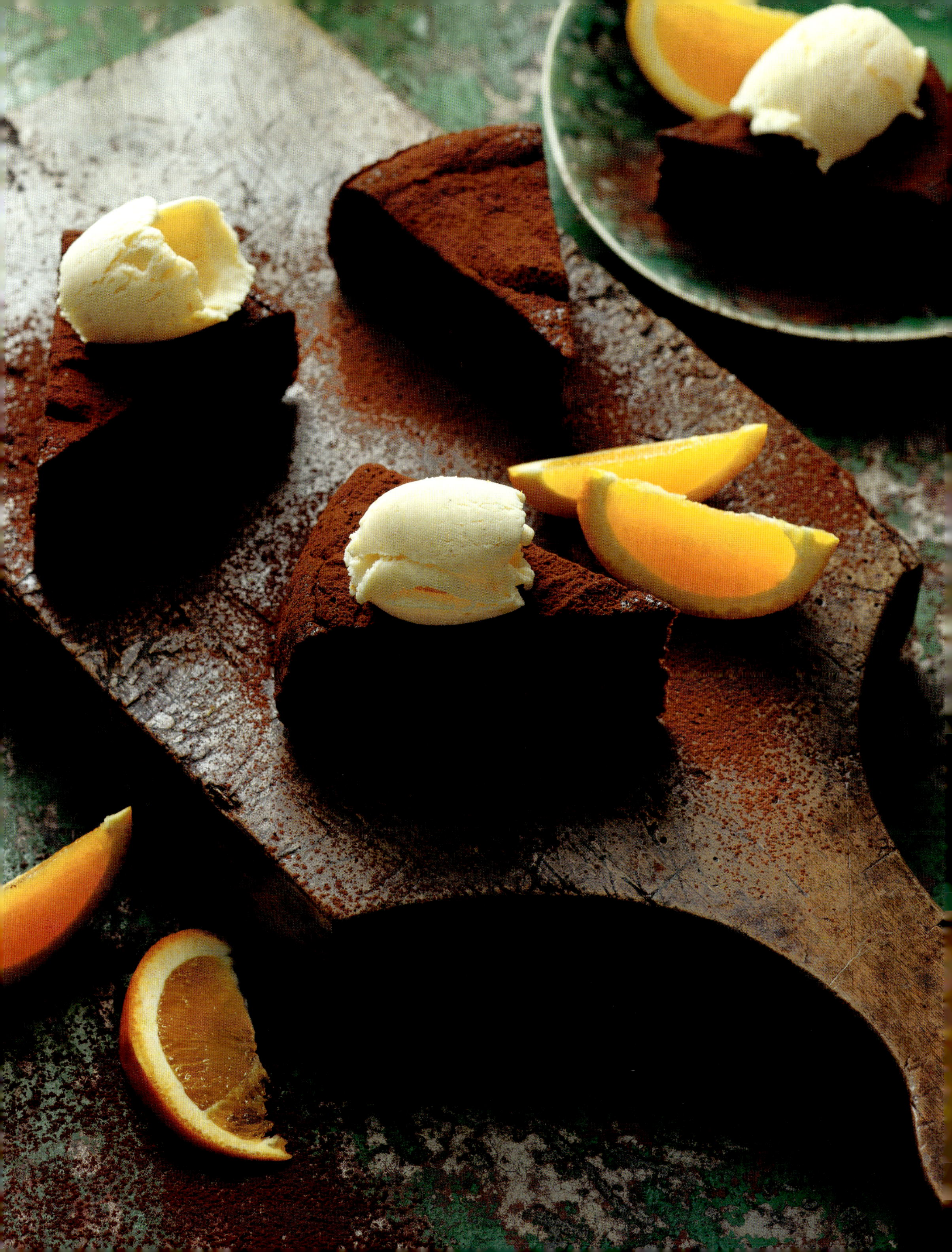

Hazelnut & Pedro Ximénez semifreddo with drunken raisins

You will need to start this recipe a day ahead.

1 cup (150g) roasted hazelnuts, skins removed
1 cup (220g) caster sugar
4 eggs, separated
2 tbs Pedro Ximénez ⓟ
400ml thickened cream, whisked to soft peaks

Drunken raisins
1½ cups (255g) raisins
⅓ cup (80ml) Pedro Ximénez
⅓ cup (75g) caster sugar

For the drunken raisins, soak the raisins in the Pedro Ximénez for 30 minutes. Combine sugar and ½ cup (125ml) water in a saucepan over low heat, stirring until sugar dissolves. Add raisin mixture and bring to a simmer for 3-4 minutes until slightly reduced and syrupy. Cool for 5 minutes, then refrigerate.

Line a baking tray with baking paper, then spread hazelnuts over the baking paper. Combine ¾ cup (165g) caster sugar and 150ml water in a saucepan over low heat, stirring until sugar dissolves. Increase heat to medium and simmer, without stirring, until mixture forms a golden caramel. Pour caramel over the hazelnuts, then set aside to cool. Break praline into shards, transfer to a food processor and process to coarse crumbs. Store in an airtight container.

Line a 1L (4-cup-capacity) terrine with plastic wrap, allowing enough overhang to completely cover the top. Using electric beaters, beat egg yolks with the remaining ¼ cup (55g) caster sugar until thick and pale. Fold in the Pedro Ximénez and cream. In a clean bowl, whisk eggwhites to stiff peaks, then fold into the egg yolk mixture with the hazelnut praline. Pour into the prepared mould, cover with the overhanging plastic wrap and freeze overnight.

Using the plastic wrap, remove semifreddo from the terrine and transfer to a platter. Serve sliced with drunken raisins and a glass of Pedro Ximénez. **Serves 8**

ⓟ See Pantry essentials, p 38.

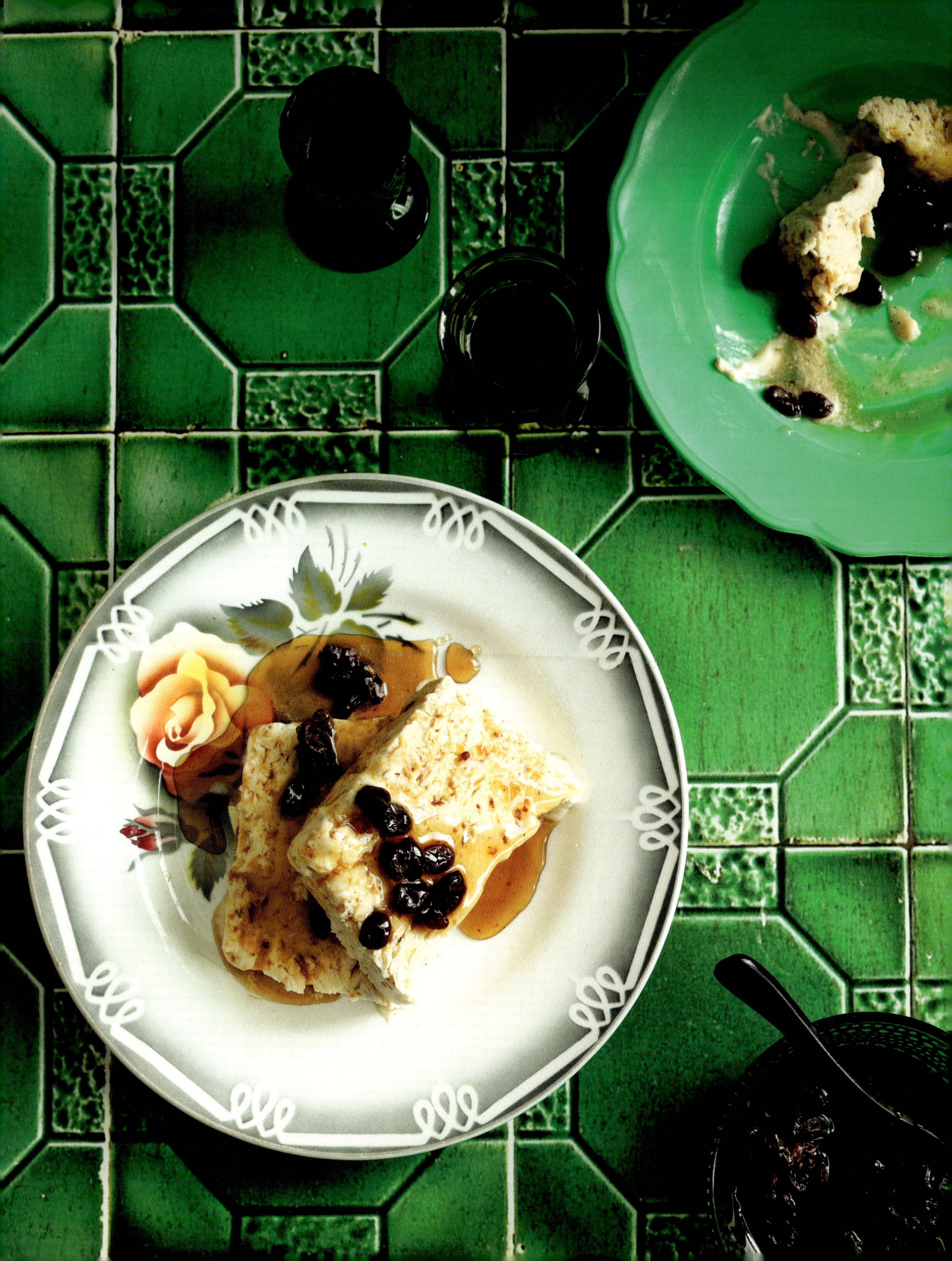

AUSTRALIAN

PANTRY ESSENTIALS

Australian mustard
A mild, slightly sweet style; substitute German or American mustard.

Honey
Most pure Australian honeys are sourced from native flowers, with flavours ranging from the mellowness of ironbark, yellow box and blue gum through to the stronger floral overtones of leatherwood, stringybark and red gum.

Kangaroo
A lean red meat with a slight gamy flavour, kangaroo suits fast cooking styles, as its low-fat content means it dries out and toughens easily if overcooked.

Lemon myrtle
The leaf has a soft citrus scent and flavour. Lemon myrtle-infused oil, ground lemon myrtle and lemon myrtle leaves are available from supermarkets and spice shops.

Macadamias & macadamia oil
Macadamias are indigenous to Australia, specifically north-east NSW and central and south-east Queensland. Macadamia oil is from specialist food shops and selected supermarkets.

Olives & olive oil
Australia produces a variety of world-class olives and olive oils, from boutique growers to supermarket brands. There is now a set of industry standards to ensure freshness and quality, so consumers can be assured they're buying oil that hasn't spent too long in the bottle, in transit or in poor storage conditions. Visit the Australian Olive Association website for details: australianolives.com.au.

Paperbark
Available in a roll, paperbark imparts a delicate, smoky flavour and aroma to food. You can also buy paperbark smoke oil to flavour ingredients. Visit dining-downunder.com.

Rabbit
Wild rabbit has dark, slightly gamy meat, which is best cooked slowly in a liquid or sauce. Farmed white rabbit has pale, tender meat and a little more fat, making it more suitable for faster cooking methods. However, there has been some controversy around farmed rabbit and production and subsequent availability have been affected. Wild rabbit is now available from selected butchers and supermarkets.

Australia's range of climate zones means we have access to an astonishing array of ingredients, from sea salt, seafood, beef and lamb, to wild game and indigenous ingredients such as native pepper berry, lemon myrtle and bush tomatoes. Then there are the fruit and vegetables, from mangoes and avocados to crunchy, salty samphire. Plus, no self-respecting Aussie would be without a jar of Vegemite, and not just for spreading on toast! Find many of the less commonly available ingredients at dining-downunder.com.

DEVONDALE
ORIGINAL
GIPPSLAND
1914
LIMITED EDITION
Fryar's
Penfolds

Barbecued sausage rolls with beer-braised onions

I've lost count how many (not always very good) sausages in rolls I ate at my two sons' rugby matches over the years. These little beauties take an Aussie favourite to a new level and wouldn't be out of place on a lunch or dinner menu.

¼ cup (60ml) olive oil
3 large onions, thinly sliced
150ml dark ale or stout
15g unsalted butter
¼ cup (55g) caster sugar
1 tbs red wine vinegar
4 good-quality pork sausages
4 crisp torpedo rolls
2 tbs Australian mustard ⓟ
Watercress or rocket, to serve

Heat the oil in a heavy-based frypan over medium-low heat. Add the onion and a good pinch of salt, and cook, stirring occasionally, for 30 minutes or until golden and soft. Add beer and cook until reduced. Add the butter, sugar and vinegar, and cook, stirring, for 5-6 minutes until dark and sticky. Set aside. (The onions can be made ahead and reheated, if preferred.)

Preheat the barbecue to medium-high and cook the sausages, turning frequently, for 10 minutes or until cooked through. Halve the rolls lengthways and lightly toast on the barbecue. Spread rolls on one side with mustard, then fill each with a sausage, watercress and onion. **Serves 4**

ⓟ See Pantry essentials, p 66.

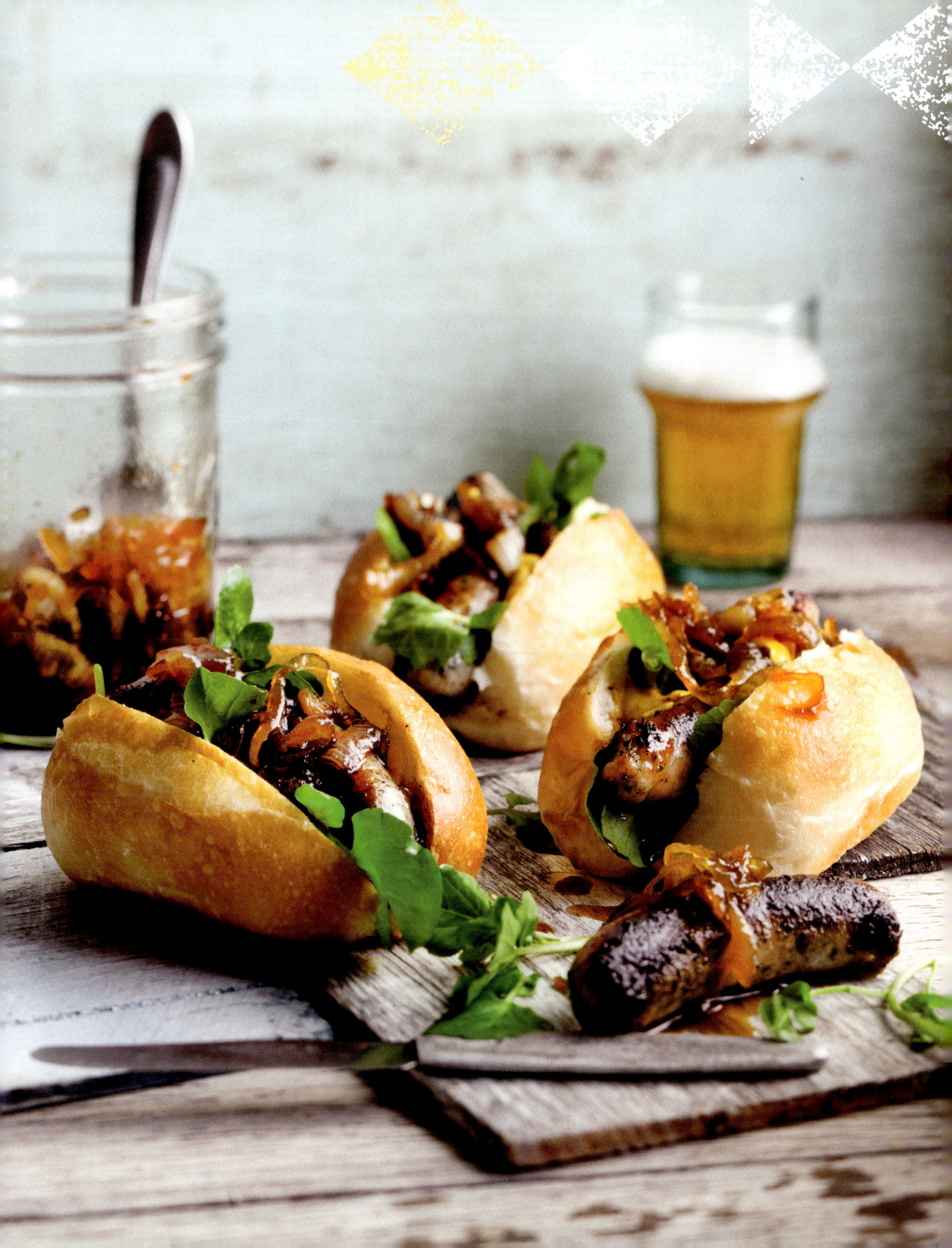

Barbecue chicken salad with passionfruit dressing

- 1 bunch coriander, leaves picked, roots reserved
- 3 garlic cloves, chopped
- 2 tbs olive oil
- 1 barbecue chicken, skin and bones removed, meat shredded
- 1 bunch snake beans, cut into 4cm lengths, blanched
- 1 avocado, chopped
- 1 Lebanese cucumber, very thinly sliced lengthways into ribbons
- 1 long red chilli, seeds removed, finely shredded
- ½ cup (75g) chopped toasted macadamias ⓟ or cashews
- 1 cup bean sprouts, trimmed
- ½ bunch Thai basil, leaves picked
- ½ cup fried Asian shallots

Passionfruit dressing
- ⅓ cup passionfruit pulp
- 2 kaffir lime leaves, finely shredded
- Juice of ½ lime
- 2 tsp fish sauce
- 1 tsp caster sugar
- 1 tsp grated ginger

For the passionfruit dressing, briefly whiz the passionfruit pulp in a small food processor to dislodge the seeds, then strain the juice, reserving 1 tsp seeds. Combine passionfruit juice with remaining ingredients and reserved seeds in a small bowl.

Using a mortar and pestle, pound the reserved coriander root with the garlic and 1 tsp salt to a paste. Alternatively, whiz in a small food processor. Stir in the olive oil, then toss with the chicken. Combine the snake beans, avocado, cucumber, chilli, nuts, bean sprouts, basil and shallots in a large bowl. Add the chicken mixture and coriander leaves and toss to combine. Drizzle with dressing and serve. **Serves 4-6**

ⓟ See Pantry essentials, p 66.

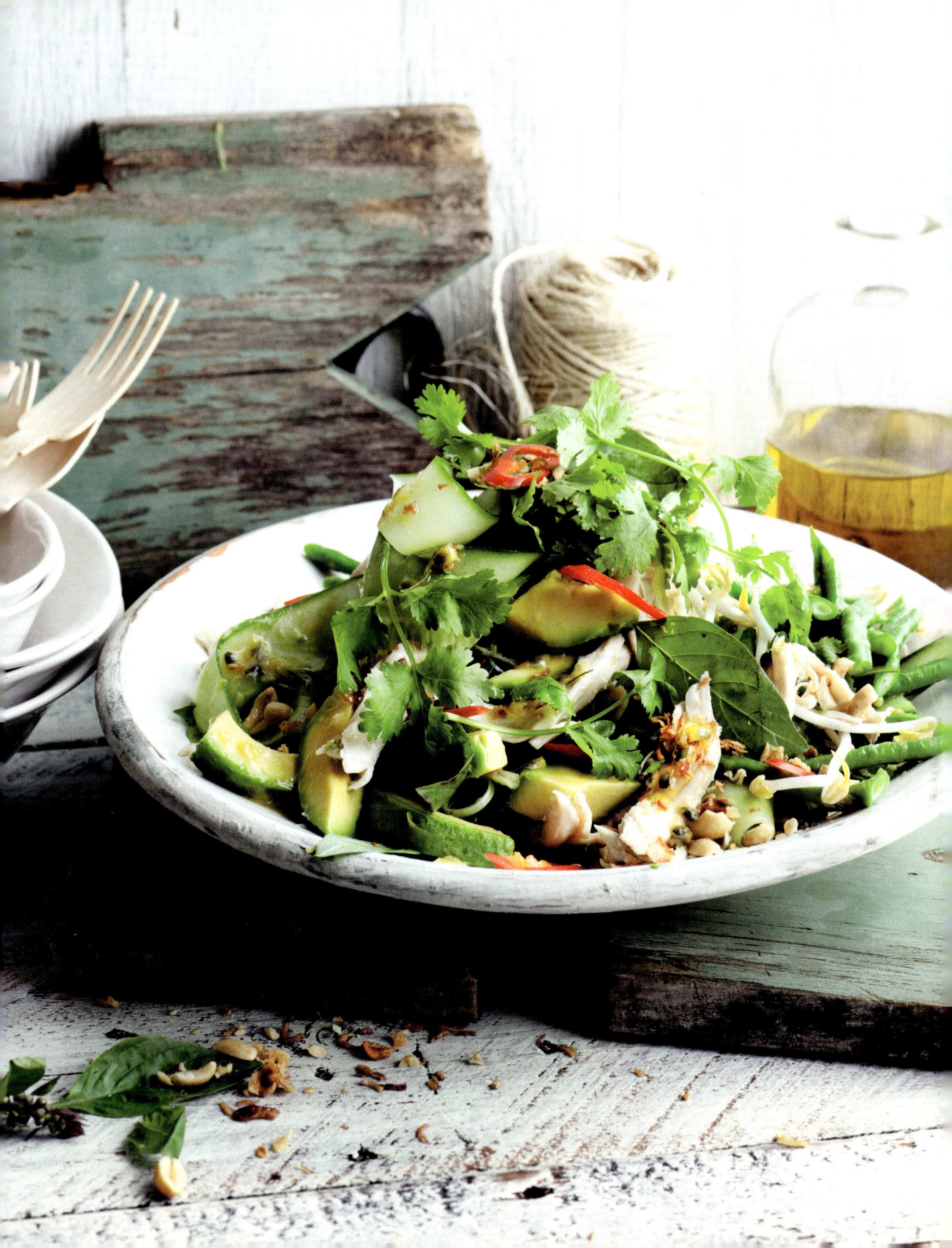

Rabbit pies

I like to make these hearty pies in cute individual springform pans that are available now in cookware shops, but deep individual pie dishes work well, too.

2 tbs olive oil
30g unsalted butter
1.6kg rabbit, ⓟ jointed (ask your butcher to do this for you)
2 rashers bacon, finely chopped
1 onion, finely chopped
1 carrot, finely chopped
2 garlic cloves, finely chopped
1 cup (250ml) dry cider
1½ cups (375ml) chicken stock
1 bay leaf
1 tbs chopped thyme
2 tbs chopped flat-leaf parsley
2 tbs cornflour
½ cup (125ml) thickened cream
1 tbs Dijon mustard
1 x quantity sour cream pastry (see Basics, p 294) or 2 x 375g packets frozen sour cream pastry*
1 egg, lightly beaten
Micro herbs (optional), to serve

Heat the oil and butter in a large frypan over medium-high heat. Brown the rabbit, in batches, for 2 minutes each side or until golden. Set aside. Add the bacon, onion, carrot and garlic to the pan and cook for 3-4 minutes until softened but not browned. Return rabbit to the pan, then add cider, stock and herbs, and bring to a boil. Season, then cover and reduce heat to medium-low and simmer for 1 hour or until the rabbit is just tender. Remove the rabbit from the pan and set aside to cool.

Combine cornflour with 2 tbs cold water and add to the pan, stirring until the sauce thickens. Add cream and mustard and stir to combine. Strain the sauce through a sieve into a jug, reserving solids. When the rabbit has cooled, shred the meat, discarding bones. Add reserved solids from the sauce and enough of the sauce (about half) to the rabbit mixture to moisten. Reserve the remaining sauce to serve.

Preheat the oven to 180°C. Grease 4 individual 10cm springform tart pans.

Roll out the pastry on a lightly floured surface to 5mm thick, then use to line the base and sides of the springform pans. Cut 4 rounds a little larger than the pans for the lids. Fill pastry cases with the cooled rabbit mixture, then top with lids, pressing gently to seal the edges. Brush tops with beaten egg, then bake for 35-40 minutes until filling is hot and tops are golden. Rest in pans for 10 minutes before turning out.

Scatter pies with micro herbs, if using, and serve with the reserved sauce. **Serves 6**

* We used Carême brand, available from specialist food shops. For stockists, visit: caremepastry.com.
ⓟ *See Pantry essentials, p 66.*

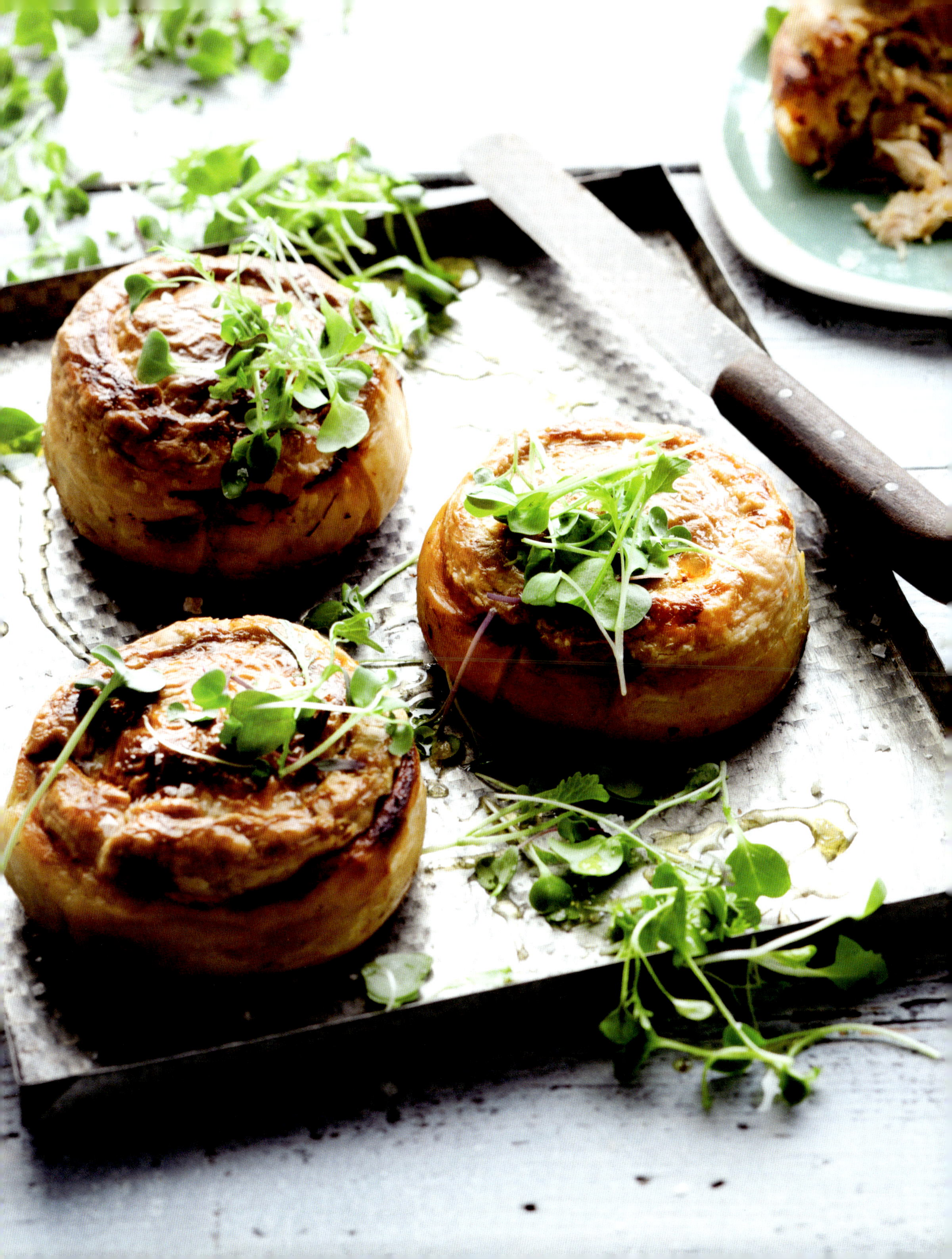

Pasta with prawns and macadamia pesto

This pesto will keep in an airtight container in the fridge for up to 2 weeks. The lemon juice prevents it from discolouring, but to be sure, pour over a thin layer of olive oil to seal it.

- 2 cups firmly packed basil leaves
- 2 tbs chopped chives
- 1/3 cup flat-leaf parsley leaves
- 1/2 cup (40g) grated parmesan
- 1/2 cup (125ml) extra virgin macadamia oil ⓟ or extra virgin olive oil, plus 1 tbs to fry
- 1 tsp lemon juice
- 2 cloves garlic, crushed
- 1/4 cup (35g) lightly toasted chopped macadamias ⓟ
- 400g spaghetti
- 250g cherry tomatoes, halved
- 400g cooked prawns, peeled (tails intact)
- 200g marinated feta, crumbled

Combine the basil, chives, parsley, parmesan, 1/2 cup (125ml) oil, lemon juice, garlic and macadamias in a food processor. Season, then whiz to a paste. Transfer to an airtight container and refrigerate until ready to use.

Cook the pasta according to packet instructions.

Meanwhile, heat the remaining 1 tbs oil in a large frypan over medium heat. Add the tomatoes, season and cook, stirring for 2-3 minutes until starting to soften. Add prawns and stir for 1 minute to warm through. Drain the pasta and add to the pan with all the pesto and gently toss to combine.

Serve pasta scattered with feta. **Serves 4**

ⓟ See Pantry essentials, p 66.

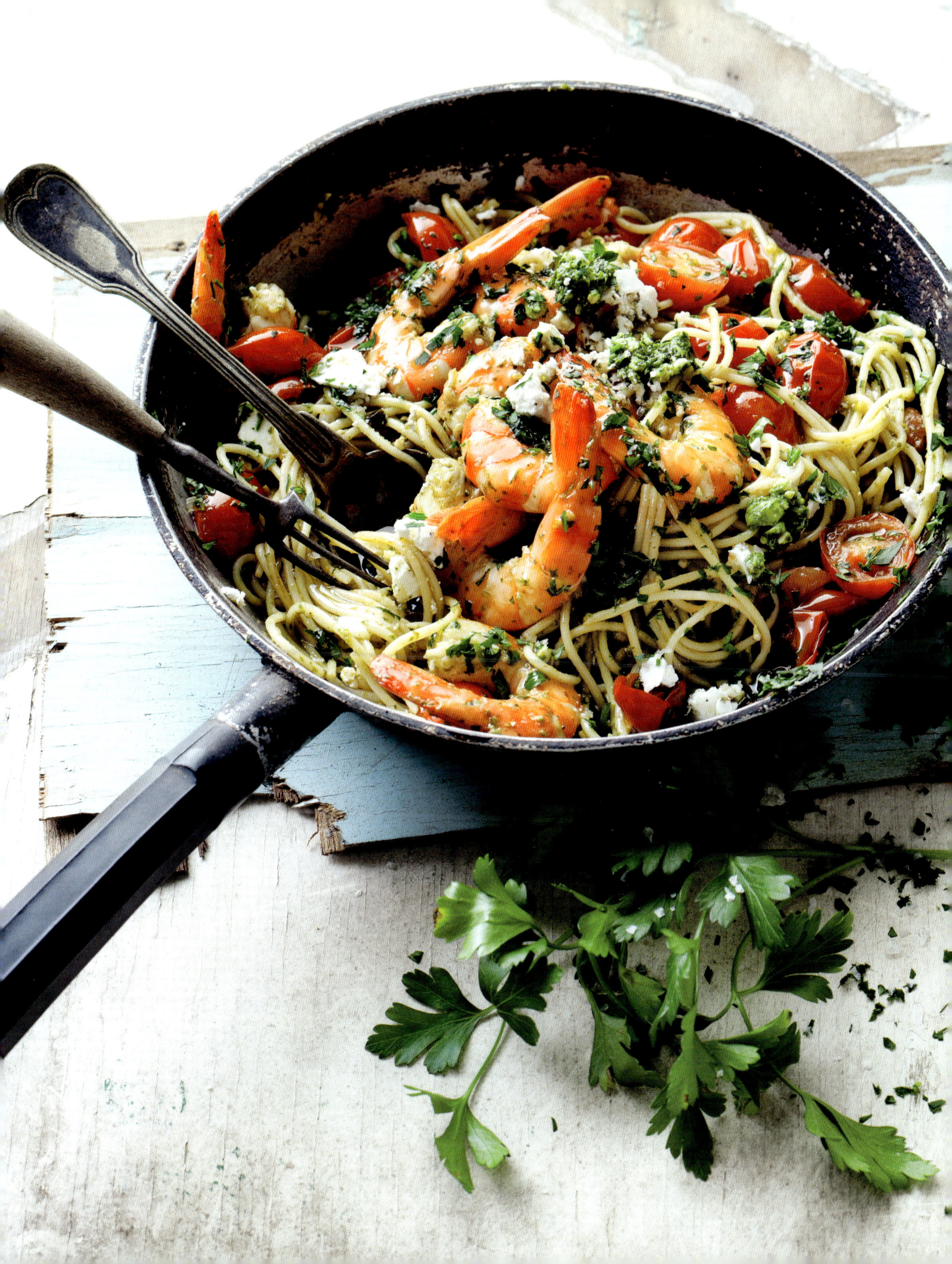

Barramundi baked in paperbark with chilli ginger dressing

Cooking fish in paperbark imparts a lovely smoky aroma and flavour. If you have difficulty sourcing it, just wrap the fish in baking paper, then foil, instead.

2 tbs sesame seeds
40cm x 40cm piece of paperbark ⓟ
1-1.5kg whole barramundi, cleaned, scaled
2 tbs olive oil, plus extra to brush
4 spring onions, finely shredded
4cm piece ginger, finely shredded
2 garlic cloves, thinly sliced
2 long red chillies, seeds removed, finely shredded
2/3 cup (165ml) soy sauce
1 tbs rice vinegar
1 tbs sesame oil
1 bunch coriander
Lime wedges and steamed rice, to serve

Preheat oven to 180°C or a lidded barbecue to medium-high.

Combine sesame seeds and 2 tsp sea salt in a small bowl. Place a wide sheet of foil, large enough to wrap the whole fish, on a work surface. Place the paperbark on top, then sit the fish on the paperbark. Brush the fish with a little extra olive oil, then sprinkle with sesame mixture. Enclose the fish in the paperbark, then tightly wrap in the foil.

Bake for 30-40 minutes until the fish is cooked through.

Meanwhile, place spring onion in a bowl of iced water to make them curl.

Heat olive oil in a small saucepan over medium heat. Add ginger, garlic and chilli, and cook, stirring, for 2 minutes or until softened slightly. Add soy, vinegar and sesame oil, stirring until warmed through. When the fish is cooked, open and discard the foil wrapping, then transfer the fish on the paperbark to a platter. Pour over the hot sauce and garnish with coriander and spring onion curls.

Serve with steamed rice and lime wedges. **Serves 4**

ⓟ See Pantry essentials, p 66.

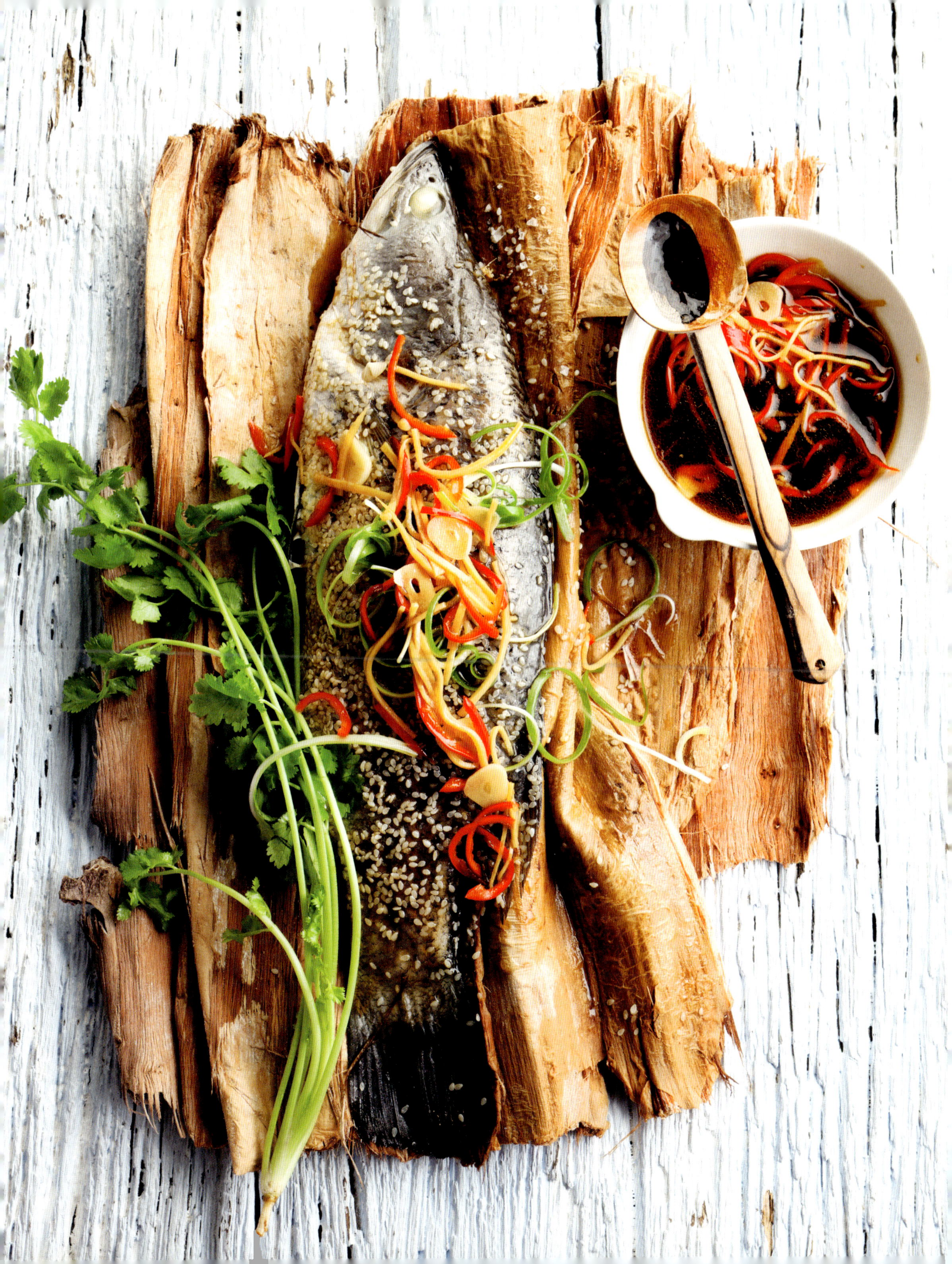

Kangaroo fillet with parsnip gratin and cherry chutney

6 (about 700g) parsnips, roughly chopped
½ cup (125ml) thickened cream
100ml milk
1 egg
90g unsalted butter, melted, cooled
Pinch of freshly grated nutmeg
½ cup (40g) finely grated parmesan
½ cup (35g) fresh breadcrumbs
2 tbs mixed peppercorns
1 tbs thyme leaves
2 x 300g kangaroo fillets Ⓟ
Olive oil, to brush
Flat-leaf parsley sprigs, to serve

Cherry chutney
600g pitted fresh or frozen cherries
½ cup (125g) brown sugar
2 cinnamon quills
2 tsp ground ginger
½ cup (125ml) red wine
2 tsp arrowroot

For the chutney, place all the ingredients except arrowroot in a saucepan over medium heat. Bring to a simmer, then reduce heat to low and cook for 6-8 minutes until the cherries release their juices. Combine arrowroot with 2 tbs cold water and stir until smooth. Add to the cherry mixture and cook for a further minute or until thickened. Remove from heat and set aside to cool. (Chutney can be made up to 2 days ahead.)

Preheat the oven to 180°C. Grease a 1L (4-cup-capacity) gratin dish. Place parsnip in a saucepan of cold salted water and bring to the boil over medium-high heat, then cook for 15 minutes or until tender. Drain. Transfer to a food processor and process until smooth. Add the cream, milk, egg, 60g melted butter, nutmeg and ¼ cup (20g) parmesan. Season, then spread into prepared dish. Top with breadcrumbs and remaining ¼ cup (20g) cheese, then drizzle with remaining 30g melted butter. Cook gratin for 25 minutes or until slightly puffed and golden.

Using a mortar and pestle or spice grinder, crush peppercorns and thyme, then stir in 1 tsp sea salt. Transfer to a plate. Brush the fillets with a little olive oil, then roll in peppercorn mixture. Cover with plastic wrap and refrigerate until 15 minutes before cooking (ensure fillets are well wrapped, as kangaroo meat oxidises quickly when exposed to the air).

Preheat a barbecue or chargrill to high. Bring the kangaroo to room temperature. Cook for 3 minutes on one side (do not turn before then, or the flesh will stick). Turn and cook for a further 3 minutes. Rest, loosely covered with foil, for 6-8 minutes. Slice and serve with the parsnip gratin, chutney and parsley sprigs. **Serves 4-6**

Ⓟ See Pantry essentials, p 66.

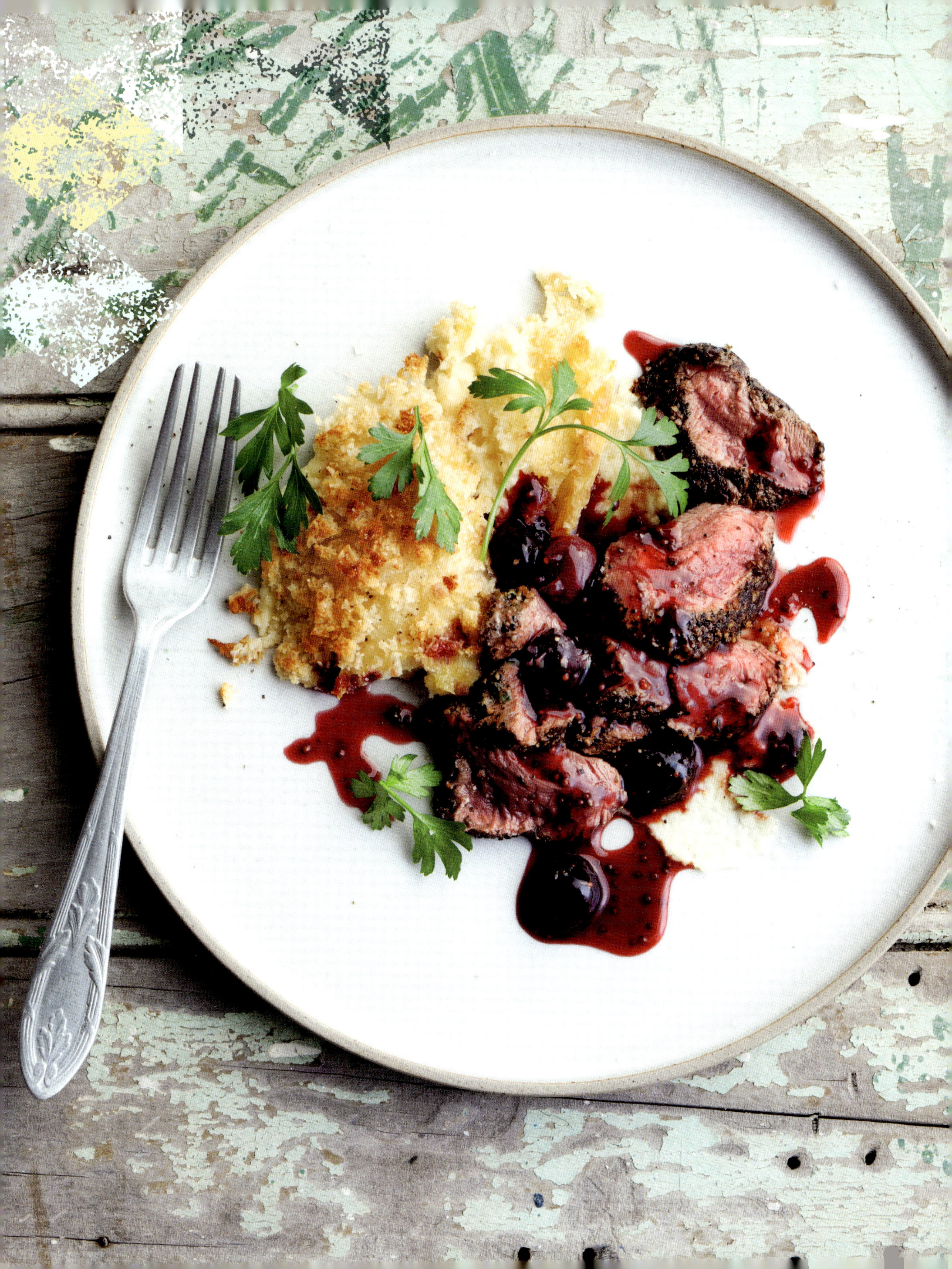

Vegemite roast chicken with macadamia couscous

Along with sweet, salty, sour and bitter, there is a fifth flavour, 'umami', the rich savouriness found in ingredients such as soy sauce, parmesan and, yes, Vegemite. I use it to enhance soups and stews, and here as a savoury butter.

1 tbs Vegemite
125g unsalted butter, softened
½ cup finely chopped flat-leaf parsley
1.8kg whole chicken
2 onions, thickly sliced
2 tbs extra virgin macadamia oil ⓟ or extra virgin olive oil
Finely grated zest of 1 small lemon, lemon reserved
1 cup (250ml) chicken stock
1 cup (200g) couscous
20 roasted macadamias, ⓟ roughly chopped
1 bunch broccolini, blanched

Preheat the oven to 180°C.

Using a wooden spoon, beat the Vegemite, butter and ¼ cup parsley in a bowl until combined. Alternatively, process in a small food processor.

Rinse the chicken inside and out and pat dry with paper towel. Gently loosen the skin from the breast meat with your hands, pushing as far as possible without tearing the skin. Spread the butter mixture all over the breast meat, then pat down the skin to cover. Spread the onion over the base of a roasting pan, then place the chicken, breast-side up, on top. Rub 1 tbs macadamia oil over the chicken and season. Place the reserved lemon inside the cavity, then truss the legs with kitchen string. Roast for 1 hour 10 minutes or until the juices run clear when the thickest part of the thigh is pierced. Set chicken aside to rest, loosely covered with foil, for 10 minutes.

Bring the stock to the boil in a saucepan over medium-high heat, then pour over the couscous in a bowl. Cover with a clean tea towel and set aside for 10 minutes. Add 1 tbs macadamia oil, season, then fluff with a fork. Add the macadamias, lemon zest, broccolini, roasted onion and remaining ¼ cup chopped parsley and stir to combine.

Using poultry scissors, cut chicken into quarters and serve with couscous, drizzled with pan juices. **Serves 4**

ⓟ See Pantry essentials, p 66.

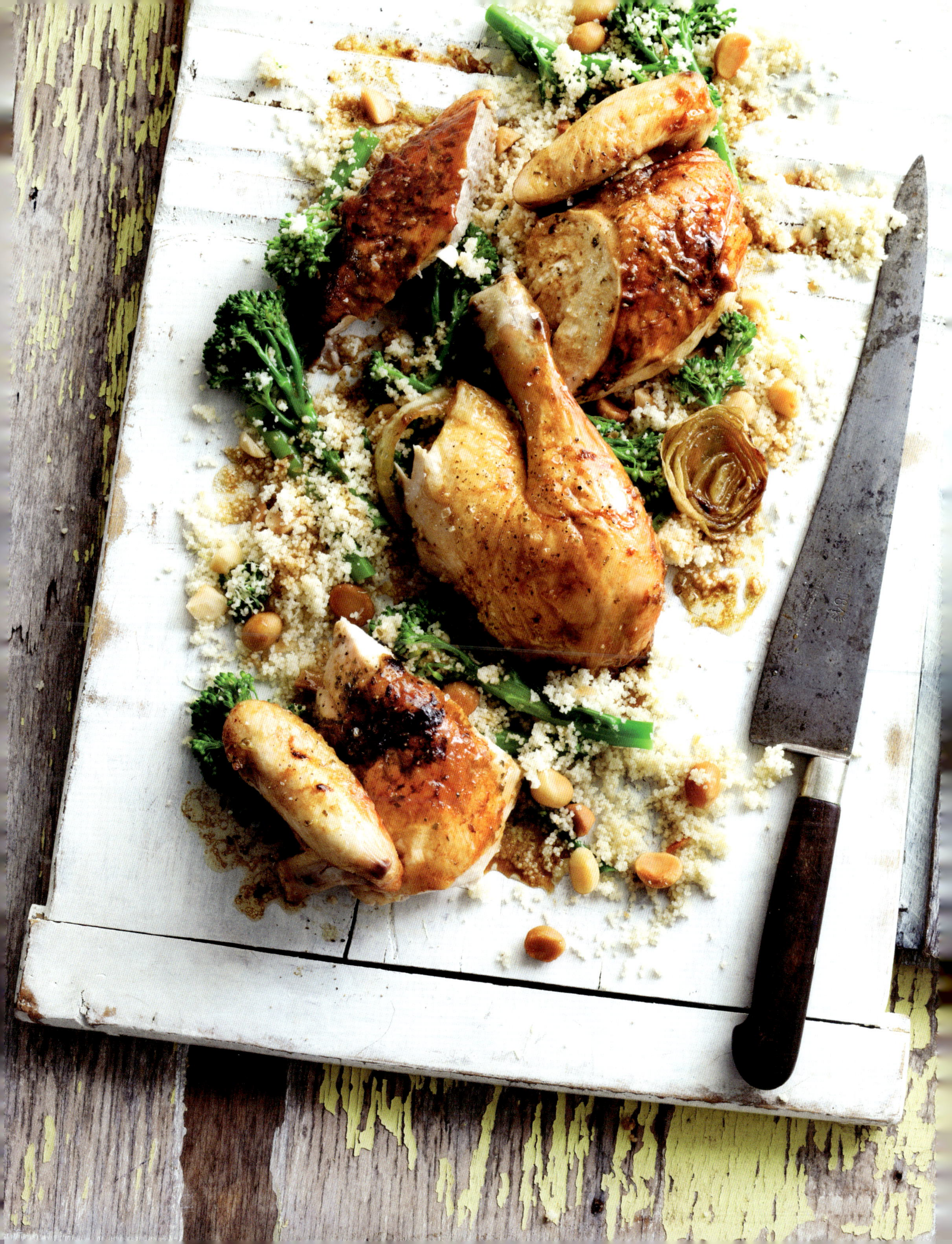

Roast leg of lamb with mint jelly and potato bake

2kg leg of lamb
3 garlic cloves, sliced
¼ cup (60ml) olive oil
1 quantity mint jelly (see Basics, p 296) or 1 cup (250g) good-quality store-bought mint jelly, plus extra to serve
1.5kg waxy potatoes (such as nicola or desiree), peeled
3 cups (750ml) chicken stock
100g unsalted butter, melted
½ bunch mint, leaves picked

Preheat the oven to 160°C. Make small slashes in lamb and insert garlic slices. Brush lamb with 1 tbs oil and 2 tbs mint jelly. Season and place in a roasting pan. Roast, uncovered, for 2½ hours, basting with remaining mint jelly every 20 minutes.

Meanwhile, grease a large shallow baking dish. Using a mandoline, cut potatoes into 5mm-thick slices. Layer in prepared dish (only up to 3 layers), seasoning each layer. Pour over stock, then brush top with one-third of the melted butter. Cover with foil and cook for 1 hour. Remove foil, brush with half the remaining butter. Cook for a further 1 hour.

Remove lamb from oven and set aside, loosely covered with foil, to rest. Increase oven to 190°C. Brush potato with remaining butter and cook for a further 15 minutes or until top is golden and crisp.

Heat remaining 2 tbs oil in a small frypan over medium-high heat. Fry mint leaves for 1 minute or until crisp.

Serve lamb with potato bake, garnished with fried mint leaves, with extra mint jelly. **Serves 6-8**

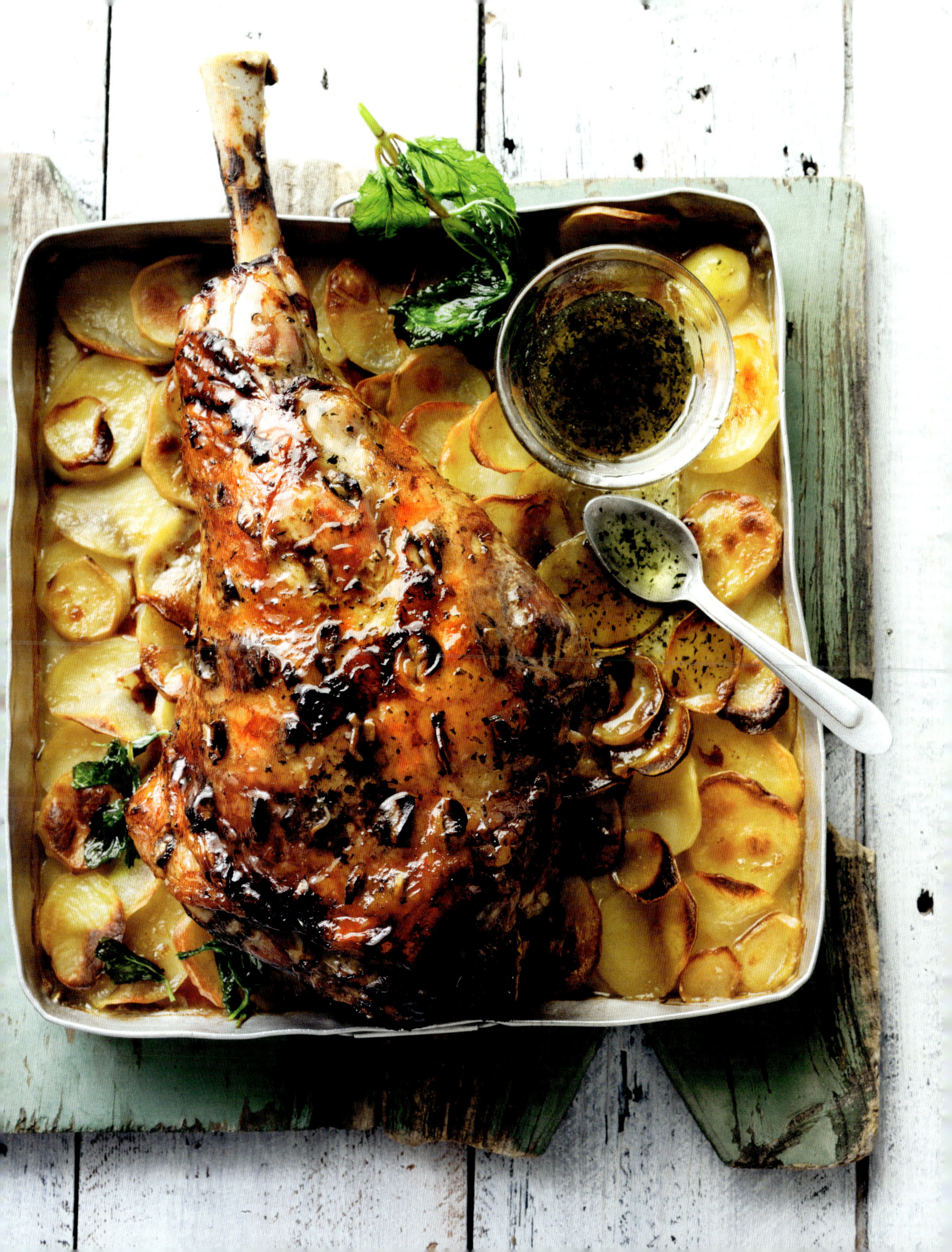

Chilli pineapple mini pavs

I couldn't write an Australian chapter without including a pavlova and, as for the debate as to whether it originated in Australia or New Zealand – who cares? It's still a favourite the world over.

4 eggwhites
250g caster sugar
2 tsp cornflour
1 tsp white wine vinegar
110g unsalted butter
30g demerara sugar
½ pineapple, peeled, cut into 3cm pieces
Pinch of dried chilli flakes
300ml thickened cream
2 tbs icing sugar
Finely grated zest and juice of ½ lime

Preheat the oven to 140°C. Line a baking tray with baking paper. Place the eggwhites and caster sugar in a bowl over gently simmering water. Using a large balloon whisk, whisk for 6-8 minutes until the sugar dissolves. Transfer the mixture to the bowl of an electric mixer and whisk until thick and glossy. Using a metal spoon, fold in the cornflour and vinegar. Place 6 dollops of meringue on prepared tray, making a shallow indent in the centre of each one. Bake for 1 hour, then turn off the oven and leave meringues in the oven with the door propped open until the oven is cold, or overnight.

Melt the butter in a frypan with the demerara sugar over medium heat, stirring until the sugar dissolves. Add pineapple and cook, turning, for 8-10 minutes until the pineapple softens and the sauce starts to thicken. Add chilli, then remove from heat and set aside to cool.

Whisk cream with the icing sugar to soft peaks, then whisk in lime zest and juice. Dollop cream mixture onto each meringue and top with chilli pineapple to serve. **Makes 6**

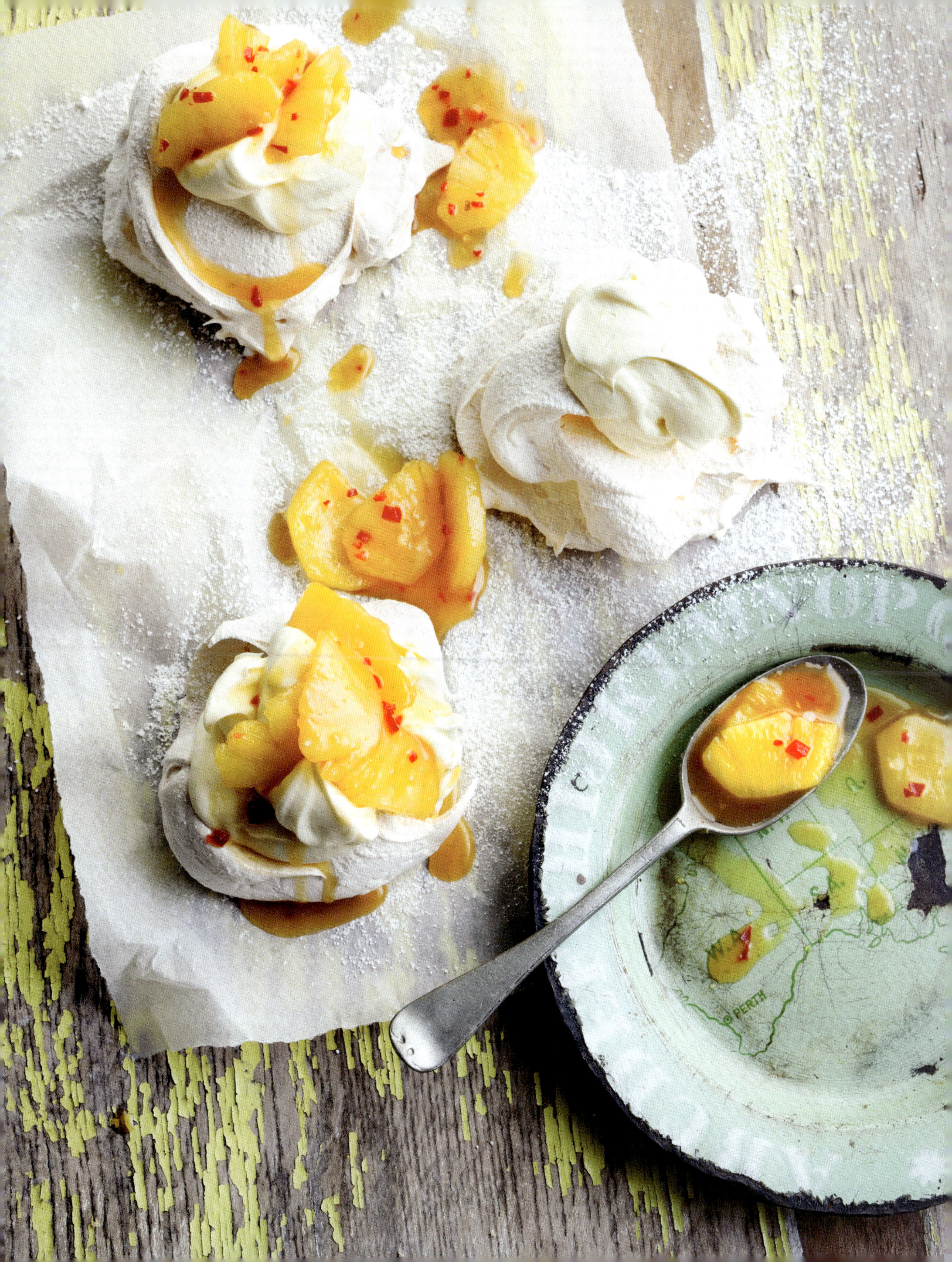
PERTH

Anzac ice cream sandwiches

The lovely no-churn vanilla ice cream in this recipe is from Gregory Llewellyn, chef/owner of Hartsyard in Sydney. The recipe makes more than you need to fill the biscuits, but hey, there's always room for ice cream in the freezer!

1 cup (90g) rolled oats
1 cup (150g) plain flour, sifted
1 cup (220g) caster sugar
¾ cup (65g) shredded or desiccated coconut
125g unsalted butter, chopped
2 tbs golden syrup
1 tsp bicarbonate of soda

No-churn vanilla ice cream
5 eggs, separated
¾ cup (165g) caster sugar
600ml thickened cream
⅓ cup (100gl) sweetened condensed milk
1 tsp vanilla extract

For the ice cream, line a shallow 40cm x 30cm metal tray with plastic wrap. Using a balloon whisk, whisk egg yolks and half the sugar in a heatproof bowl set over a saucepan of gently simmering water until thick and pale. Set aside to cool slightly. Using electric beaters, beat cream, condensed milk, vanilla and 1 tsp sea salt to soft peaks. In a separate bowl, whisk eggwhites and remaining sugar to soft peaks. Fold the egg yolk mixture into cream mixture until just combined, then gently fold in eggwhite mixture. Transfer mixture to tray so the mixture is about 3cm deep, then freeze for 4-6 hours or overnight until firm. (Makes 2.25L ice cream.)

Preheat the oven to 150°C. Grease and line a baking tray with baking paper.

Place oats, flour, sugar and coconut in a bowl. Place butter and golden syrup in a saucepan over low heat, stirring until butter melts. Combine bicarbonate of soda with 1 tbs boiling water in a small bowl, then add to the syrup mixture, stirring until it foams. Add the syrup mixture to the oat mixture and stir to combine. Roll heaped teaspoons of mixture into balls and place, 4cm apart, on prepared tray. Flatten slightly. Bake for 20 minutes or until golden. While the biscuit is still hot, cut into rounds using a 10cm round biscuit cutter. Cool, discarding (or eating!) the offcuts.

Using the same 10cm biscuit cutter, cut rounds from the ice cream, transfer to a lined baking tray and cover with plastic wrap. Keep frozen on the tray until ready to serve.

To serve, sandwich ice cream rounds between 2 Anzac biscuits. **Makes 10 sandwiches**

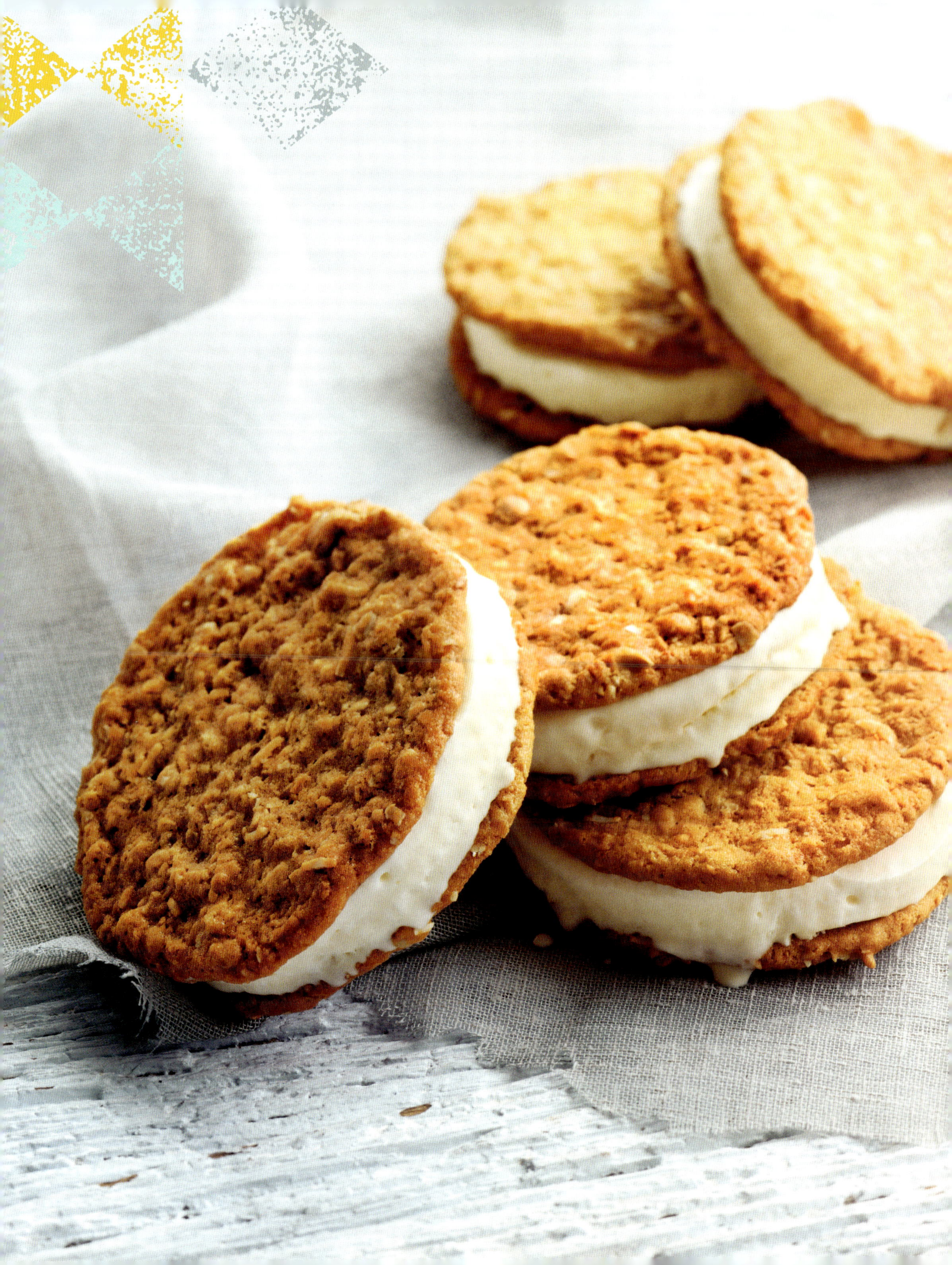

Tropical granola with lime yoghurt

To me, this epitomises Australian breakfast – fresh, healthy and best eaten looking out over a sun-drenched beach! It doesn't get much better than this.

20g unsalted butter
1 tbs olive oil
¼ cup (90g) golden syrup
⅓ cup (115g) Australian honey ⓟ
1 vanilla bean, split, seeds scraped
2 cups (180g) rolled oats
½ cup (75g) macadamias ⓟ
25g pistachio kernels
⅓ cup (70g) dried apricots, finely chopped
⅓ cup (55g) sultanas
⅓ cup (25g) shredded coconut
25g goji berries*
25g dried banana chips
1 cup (280g) thick Greek-style yoghurt
Finely grated zest of 1 lime
Sliced tropical fruit (such as mango or pineapple), to serve

Preheat the oven to 160°C. Line a large baking tray with baking paper.

Combine butter, oil, golden syrup, ¼ cup (90g) honey and vanilla seeds in a saucepan over low heat, stirring until butter melts and mixture is combined. Place oats, nuts, dried apricots, sultanas and coconut in a bowl. Pour over the butter mixture and toss to coat, then spread onto the prepared tray. Bake, turning every 10 minutes, for 30-40 minutes until golden and crisp. Set aside to cool completely, then stir in goji berries and banana chips. Store in an airtight container for up to 4 weeks.

Combine yoghurt with lime zest and remaining 1 tbs honey. Serve with granola and tropical fruit. **Makes 4 cups granola**

* *Goji berries are available from health food stores.*
ⓟ *See Pantry essentials, p 66.*

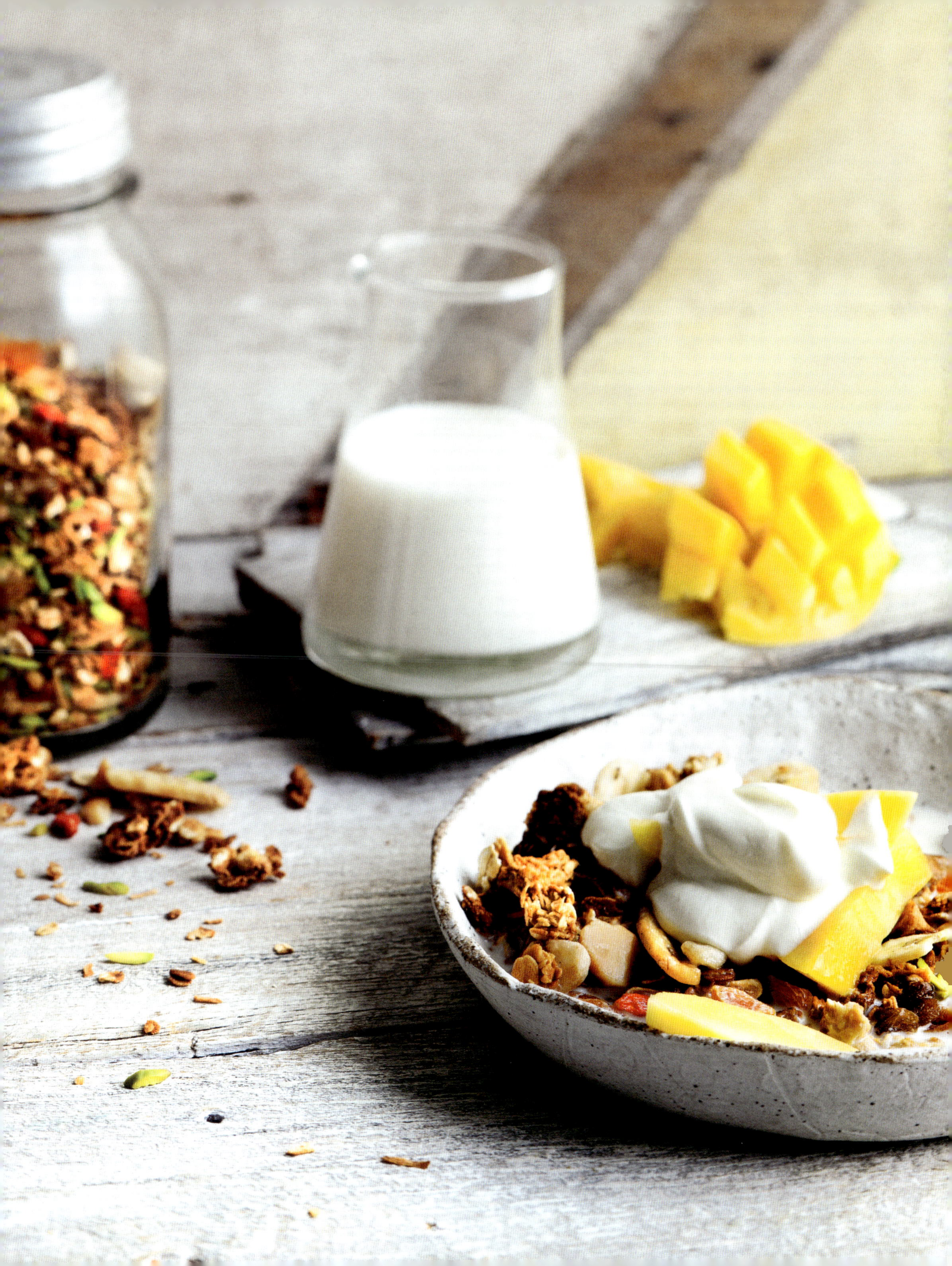

Lemon myrtle tapioca creams with passionfruit syrup

I've recently started playing with some of our native ingredients and have found that they add a unique depth to many dishes and marry particularly well with Southeast Asian flavours.

1/3 cup (65g) small tapioca pearls*
400ml coconut cream
1/3 cup (75g) caster sugar
10g dried lemon myrtle leaves ⓟ
1 cup (250ml) cold milk
1 cup (270g) chopped light palm sugar
6 passionfruit

Soak the tapioca in 1/2 cup (125ml) cold water for 45 minutes.

Meanwhile, place coconut cream, sugar and lemon myrtle in a pan over medium heat and bring to a simmer. Remove from heat. Drain the tapioca and add to the pan. Return pan to the stove and bring to the boil over medium-high heat, then reduce heat to low and simmer for 10 minutes, stirring, to prevent mixture from catching. Add the cold milk, stirring to combine. Remove the lemon myrtle and discard, then divide tapioca mixture among 6 x 1/2-cup-capacity (125ml) dishes or glasses. Cool for 10 minutes, then refrigerate for 2-3 hours.

Combine palm sugar and 1/3 cup (80ml) water in a pan over low heat, stirring until sugar dissolves. Simmer for 2-3 minutes, then set aside to cool. Scoop the pulp from the passionfruit, then briefly whiz the pulp in a small food processor to dislodge the seeds. Add pulp (and seeds, if desired) to the syrup and refrigerate until ready to serve.

Serve tapioca creams drizzled with passionfruit syrup.

Serves 6

* *Tapioca pearls are available from Asian food shops and selected supermarkets.*
ⓟ *See Pantry essentials, p 66.*

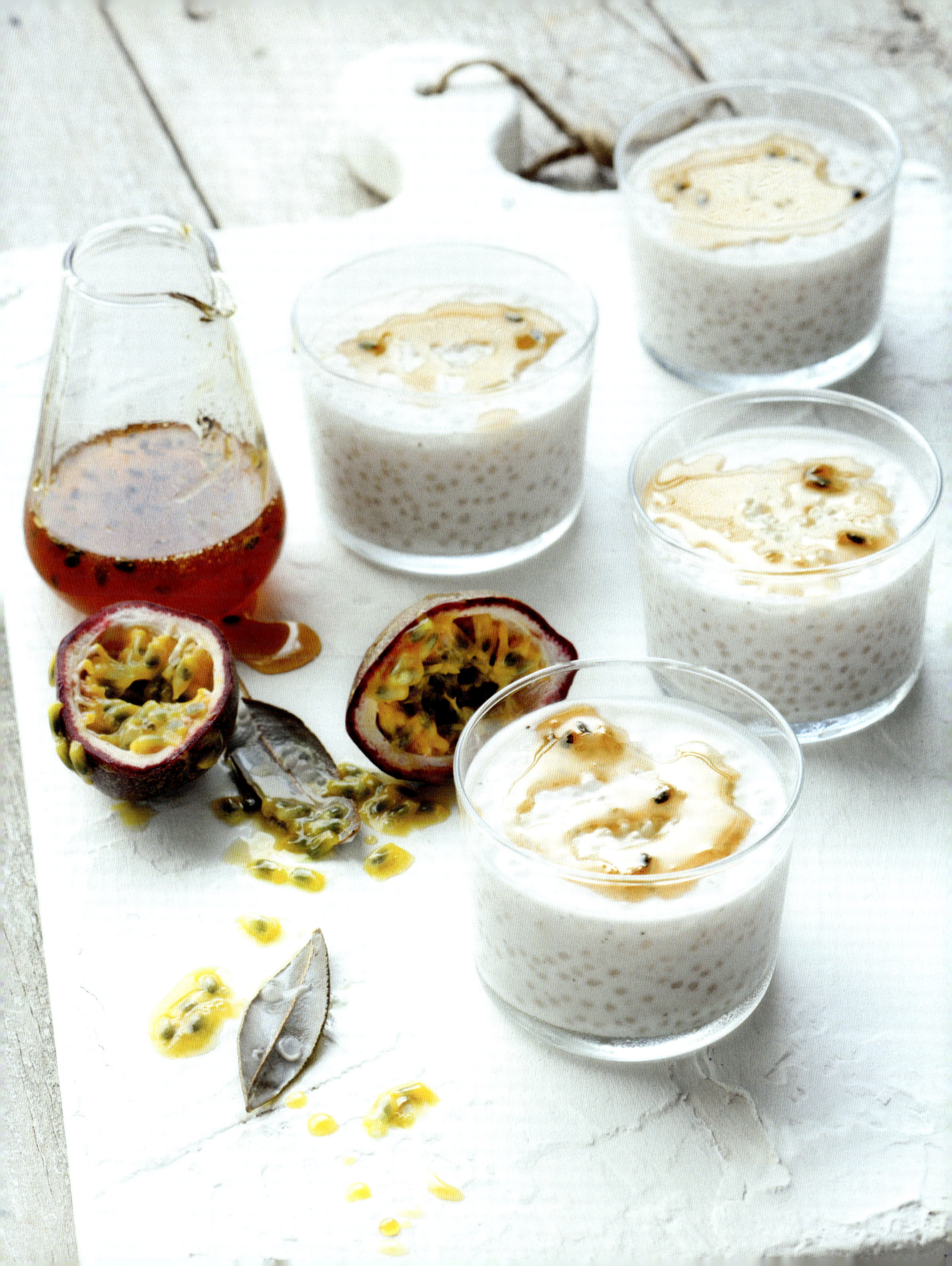

INDIAN

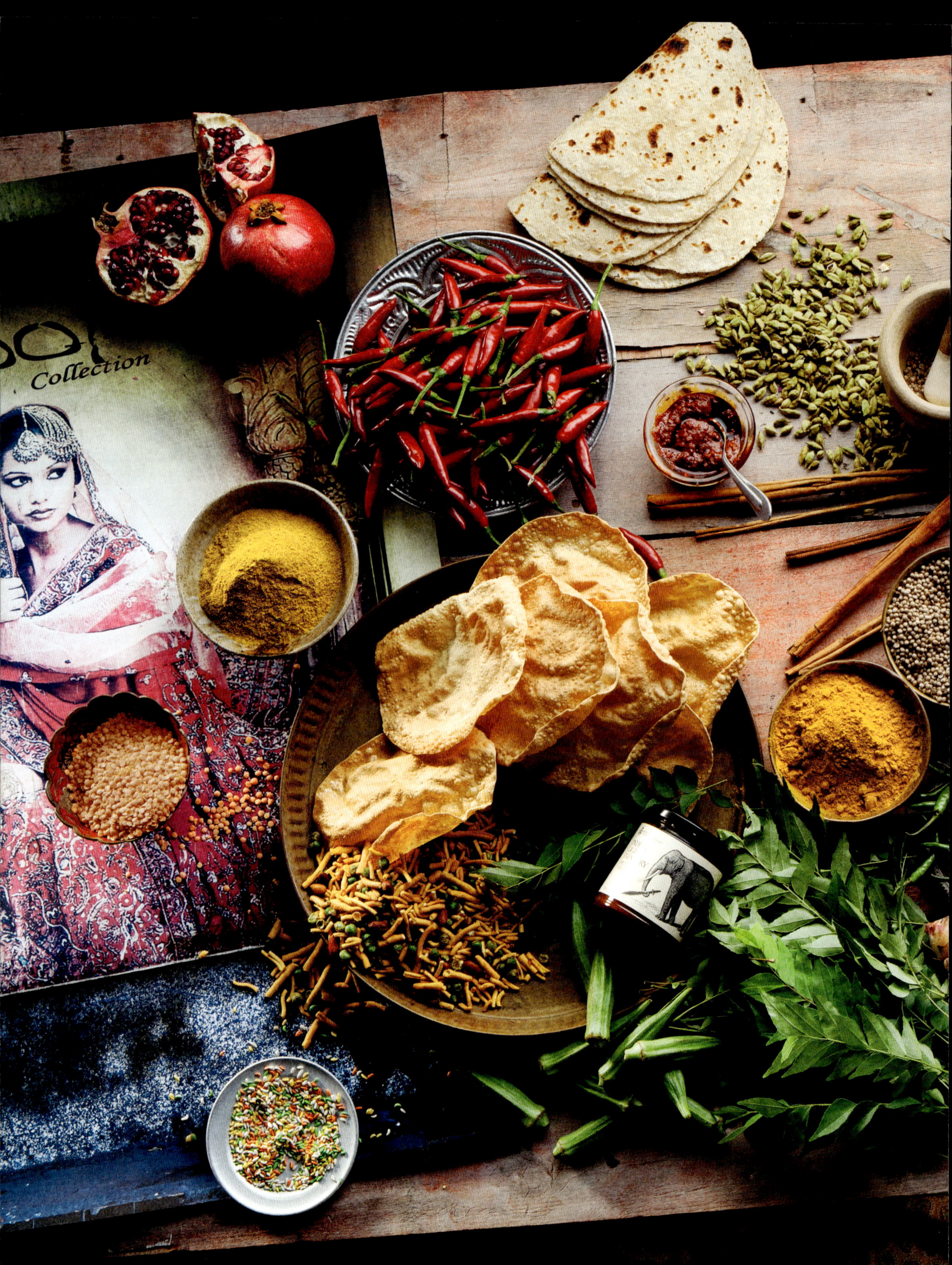
Collection

PANTRY ESSENTIALS

Basmati rice
A delicately flavoured long-grain rice, which is low to medium GI. Substitute other long-grain white rice.

Bread
Most breads are traditionally made with finely ground wholemeal flour called ata. Naan (or roti) is leavened bread baked in a clay oven (tandoor). Chapati and paratha are cooked on a flat or concave plate, called a tava; substitute a cast-iron frypan. Pappadams, made from lentil, chickpea (gram) or rice flour, are crisp-fried and often served as a snack.

Coconut
Particularly in the south, fresh grated coconut is used to thicken and flavour dishes, along with coconut milk. Desiccated coconut is an essential ingredient in burfi, a traditional sweet. Coconut oil is often used for cooking.

Curry leaves
Used fresh (available at greengrocers) or dried (from supermarkets), these have the distinctive spicy, citrus 'curry' fragrance. Dried curry leaves are less pungent, so you may want to increase the quantity.

Curry powders
Madras curry powder – mild or hot – is a good standby. The basis for classic rogan josh (lamb stew), bright red Kashmiri chilli powder varies in mildness depending on the amount of chillies it contains. Milder versions have more paprika. Vindaloo spice mix – originating from Portuguese-influenced Goa – is the hottest blend.

Garam masala
An aromatic spice blend generally comprising cloves, cardamom, cinnamon, cumin, black pepper and nutmeg. Best added towards the end of cooking or as a garnish.

Ghee
Clarified butter with a slightly nutty flavour. Used for cooking, finishing dishes and adding creaminess to dhals.

Gram flour
Also known as besan, it's made from ground chickpeas.

Jaggery
Made from sugar or palm cane, ranging in colour from golden (the purest) to dark brown. It's usually sold in solid blocks. Substitute dark brown sugar or palm sugar.

Panch phoron (panch phora)
Literally, 'five spices', this is a blend of five seeds – cumin, fenugreek, nigella, fennel and black mustard.

Paneer
A fresh white cheese made from drained milk curds to which lemon or citric acid has been added.

Tamarind puree
A thick, dark, sour-flavoured paste made from cooking down tamarind pods; substitute vinegar or lime juice.

Tandoori paste
A good marinade to mix with yoghurt for chicken, lamb and seafood. Traditionally used for 'dry' dishes roasted in a tandoor.

Spices, including cardamom, coriander, cumin, turmeric, fennel and chilli, are essential items, while a chopped onion, ginger and garlic mix often forms the base and thickening agent for curries. Keep lentils and other dried pulses on hand for dhals and other vegetarian dishes; and sweet mango chutney and sour lime pickle for condiments. Rice is the staple accompaniment in the south; bread in the north. Desserts are flavoured with cardamom, almond and rosewater, as is yoghurt, often drunk as a cooling lassi. Find many of these ingredients in supermarkets, or in spice shops and Indian food shops.

Potato wraps

Dipping store-bought chapatis into a chickpea flour batter makes them go wonderfully crisp, making them a perfect vessel for this traditional potato dish.

- 3-4 (about 600g) potatoes, peeled, cut into 2cm pieces
- 1/3 cup (80g) ghee ⓟ
- 1 onion, halved, thinly sliced
- 1 tsp grated ginger
- 1 tbs panch phoron ⓟ
- 1¼ tsp ground turmeric
- 1 tsp ground cumin
- 1 tsp mild curry powder ⓟ
- 12 curry leaves ⓟ
- 1/3 cup (50g) gram (besan) flour ⓟ
- 1/4 tsp chilli powder
- 6 chapatis ⓟ
- Mango chutney, to serve

Place potatoes in a saucepan of cold salted water and bring to the boil over medium-high heat. Reduce heat to medium and cook for 6-8 minutes until just tender. Drain.

Heat 1 tbs ghee in a frypan. Add the onion, ginger and panch phoron and cook for 2-3 minutes until the onion is softened but not browned. Add 1 tsp turmeric, cumin, curry powder and curry leaves, and cook, stirring, for 1-2 minutes until fragrant. Add the drained potatoes and cook, stirring occasionally, for 5-6 minutes until the potatoes start to crisp. Reduce heat to low, stirring occasionally to prevent the potato catching.

Place the gram flour, chilli powder and remaining 1/4 tsp turmeric in a bowl. Whisk in enough cold water (approximately 1/3 cup) a little at a time, to form a smooth, thick batter.

Heat remaining 1/4 cup (60g) ghee in a frypan over medium-high heat. Working in batches, dip 1 chapati in batter, shaking off excess, then cook for 1 minute each side until golden and crisp. Keep warm. Repeat with remaining chapatis and batter.

Serve chapatis with potato mixture and mango chutney.

Serves 4-6

ⓟ See Pantry essentials, p 95.

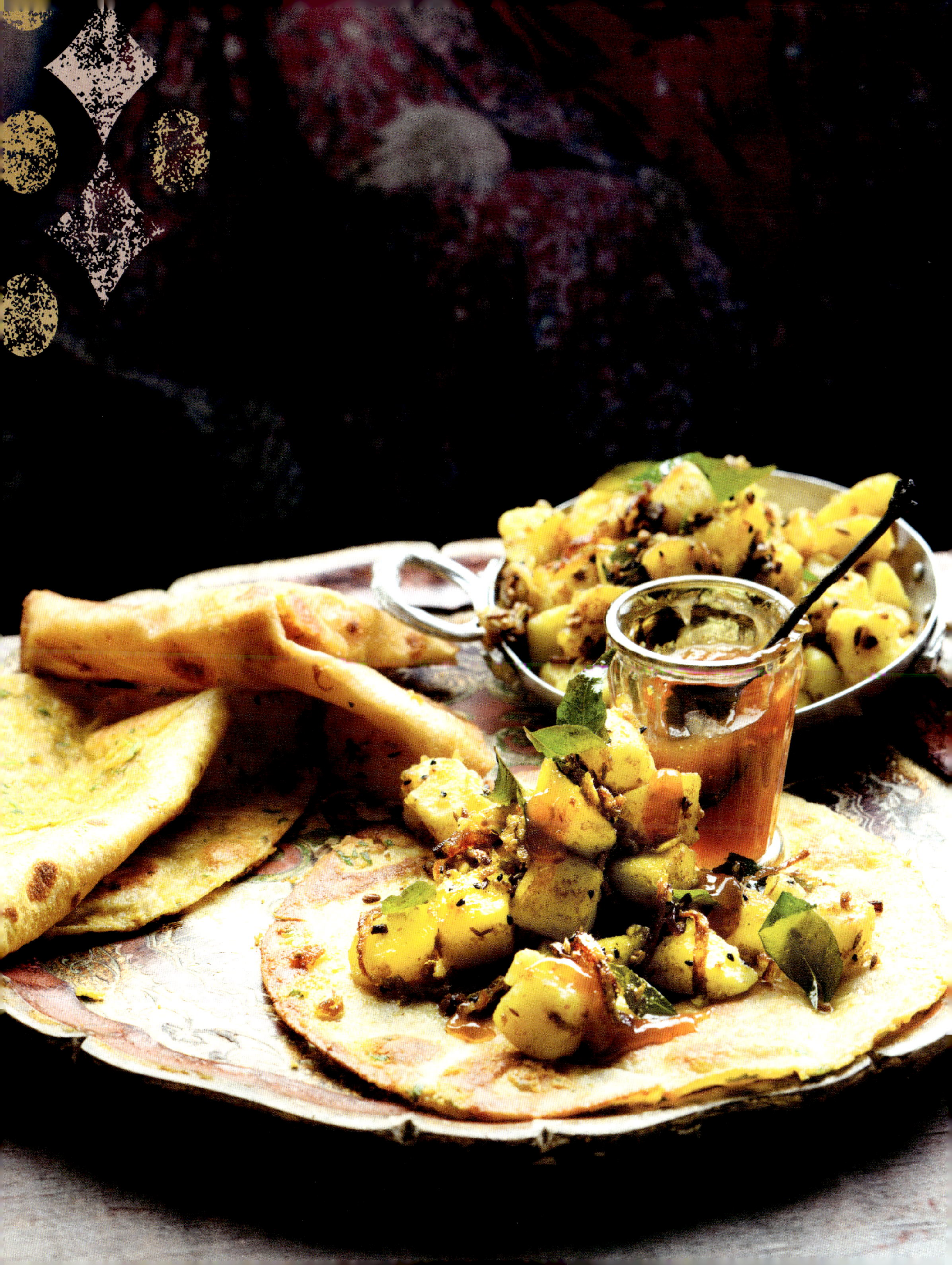

Indian salmon kebabs

⅓ cup (95g) natural yoghurt
1 tsp ground turmeric
1 tsp Kashmiri
 chilli powder ⓟ
¼ cup (70g) wholegrain
 mustard
3 garlic cloves, crushed
2cm piece ginger, grated
¼ cup (90g) honey
1 long green chilli, seeds
 removed, chopped
Finely grated zest and juice
 of ½ lemon
2 tbs finely chopped dill
2 tbs finely chopped
 coriander
600g piece skinless salmon,
 pin-boned, cut into
 3cm pieces
Warm chapatis or naan ⓟ
 and ½ iceberg lettuce,
 shredded, to serve

Spicy green sauce
½ cup (150g) whole-egg
 mayonnaise
1 cup coriander leaves
Juice of 2 limes
2 long green chillies, seeds
 removed, chopped
2 garlic cloves, chopped
1 tsp ground cumin

Combine yoghurt, turmeric, chilli powder, mustard, garlic, ginger, honey, green chilli, lemon zest and juice, dill and coriander in a bowl. Add salmon and turn to coat, then refrigerate for 30 minutes.

Meanwhile, soak 8 bamboo skewers in cold water for 30 minutes.

For the spicy green sauce, place all the ingredients in a small food processor and whiz to a smooth paste.

Preheat a chargrill or barbecue to medium-high. Drain salmon from excess marinade, thread the salmon onto the skewers, then cook for 3-4 minutes, turning, until golden but still a little rare in the middle. Serve with chapatis, lettuce and spicy green sauce. **Serves 4**

ⓟ See Pantry essentials, p 95.

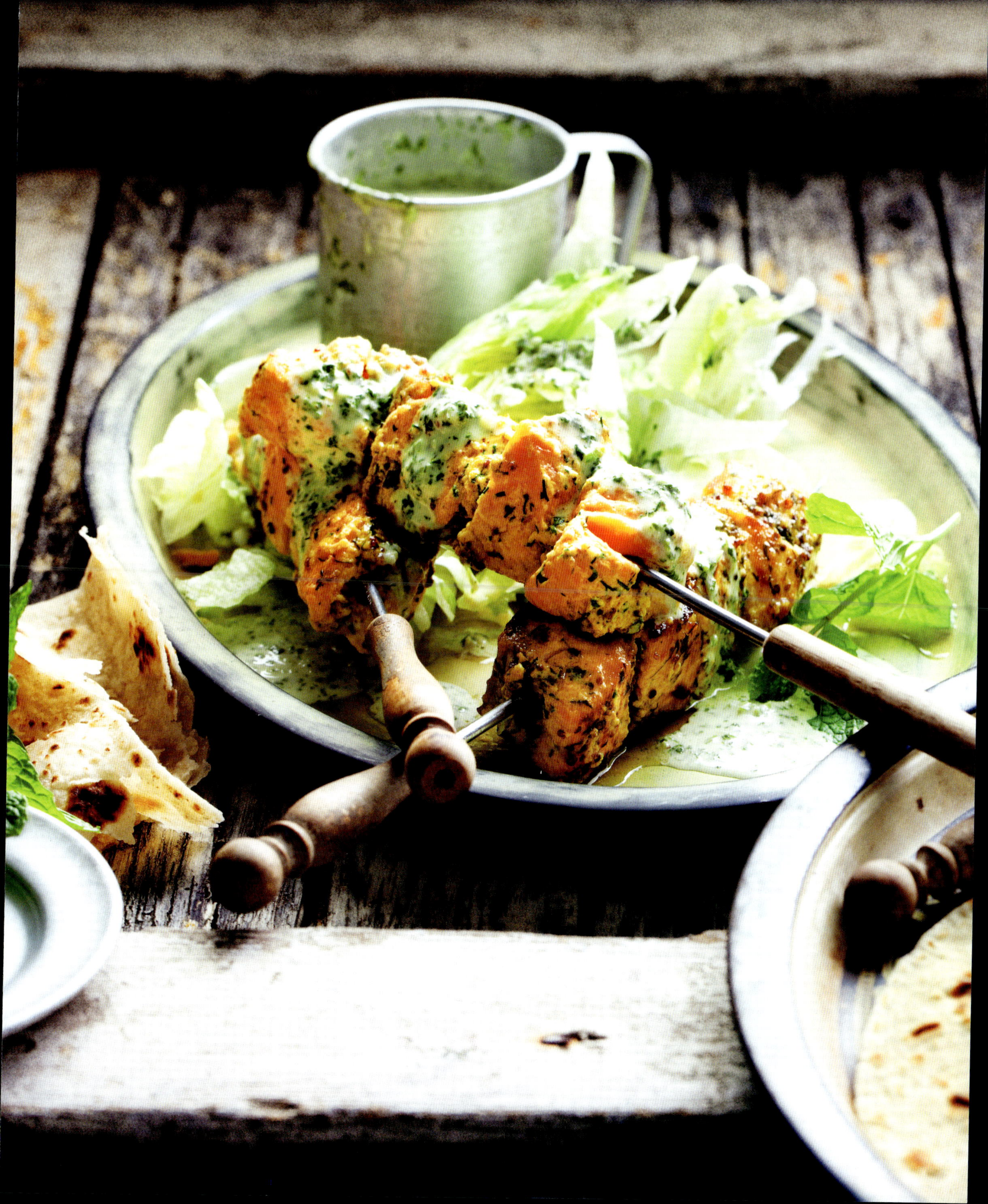

Prawn 'nizzas'

I've called these 'nizzas' because they are spicy Indian-style pizzas made with naan. You can vary the topping depending on what you have on hand.

4 naan breads ⓟ
½ cup (125ml) passata (sieved tomatoes), or pizza sauce
¼ cup (80g) mango chutney
20 medium cooked prawns, peeled (tails intact)
2 tsp mild curry powder ⓟ
1 cup (100g) grated mozzarella
½ cup (60g) grated paneer cheese ⓟ
2 tbs finely chopped coriander
2 tbs finely chopped mint, plus leaves to serve
Lime wedges, to serve

Preheat the oven to 220°C. Line 1 large or 2 small baking trays with baking paper. Place naan on tray.

Combine passata and mango chutney in a bowl. Toss prawns with the curry powder and season. Combine the cheeses with the chopped coriander and mint. Spread passata mixture over the naan, then top each with half of the cheese mixture. Top with prawns, then the remaining cheese mixture. Bake for 6-8 minutes until the cheese is melted and bubbling. Scatter with extra mint leaves and serve with lime wedges. **Serves 4**
ⓟ See Pantry essentials, p 95.

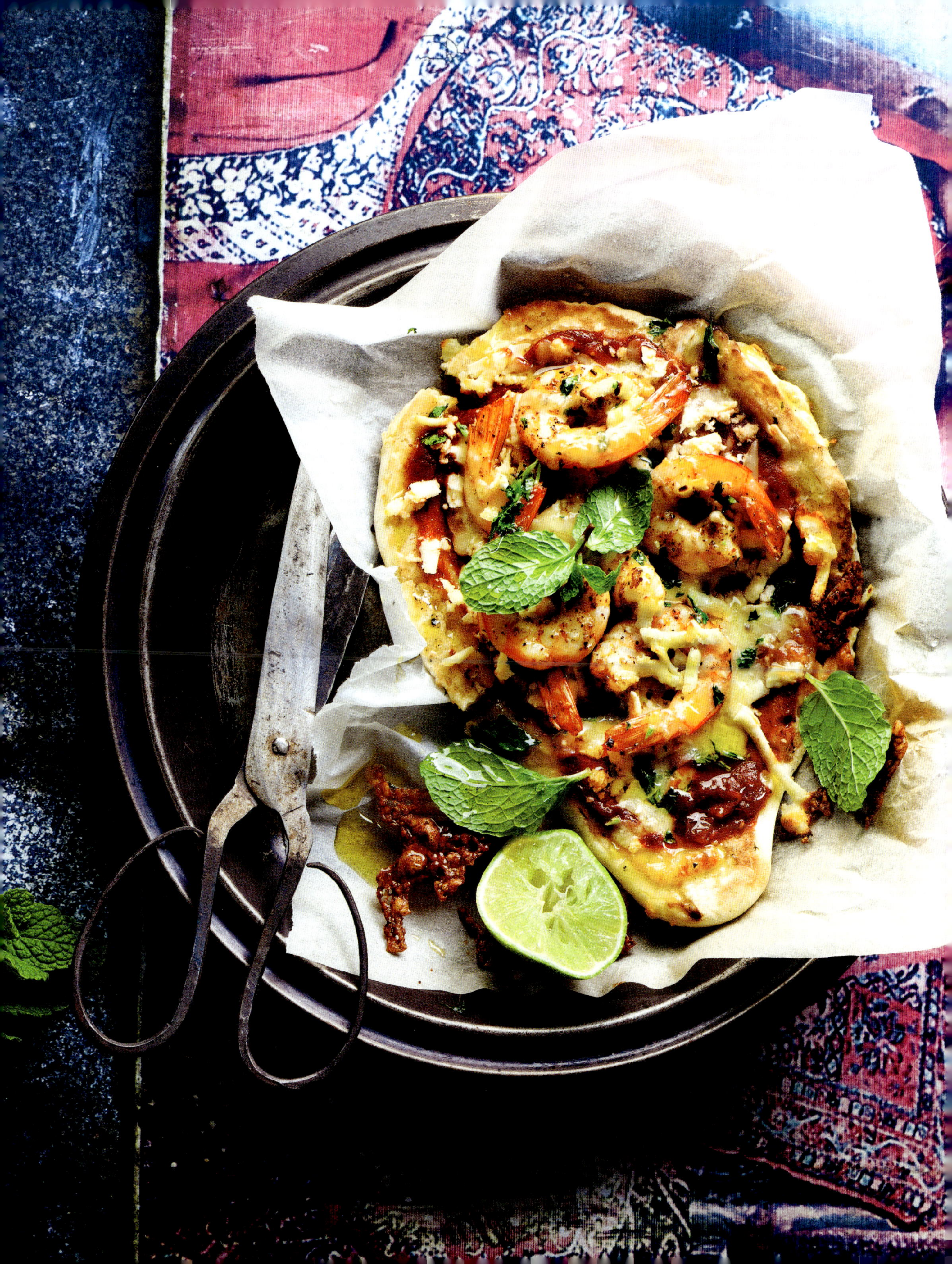

Tandoori swordfish with pilaf and coconut raita

½ cup (140g) plain yoghurt
2 tbs lemon juice
2 garlic cloves, chopped
2cm piece ginger, grated
1 long green chilli, seeds removed, chopped
1 tsp garam masala ⓟ
1 tsp ground turmeric
1 tsp ground coriander
1 tbs tandoori paste ⓟ
4 x 180g pieces swordfish
2 tbs ghee ⓟ
  or sunflower oil
Pilaf (see Basics, p 295), lime wedges and coriander and mint leaves, to serve

Coconut raita
200g thick Greek-style yoghurt
½ cup (50g) grated fresh or desiccated coconut
1 Lebanese cucumber, grated, squeezed dry
½ tsp caster sugar
¼ cup finely chopped coriander
¼ cup finely chopped mint
1 tbs lime juice

For the marinade, place yoghurt, lemon juice, garlic, ginger, green chilli, garam masala, turmeric, coriander, tandoori paste and ½ tsp salt in a food processor and pulse to combine. Place fish in a shallow bowl, add marinade and turn to coat the fish. Cover and refrigerate for 30 minutes.

Meanwhile, for the coconut raita, combine all the ingredients in a bowl, stirring until sugar dissolves. Refrigerate until ready to serve.

Heat a little ghee in a frypan over medium heat. Drain fish, discarding marinade, then cook for 2 minutes each side or until golden but still rare in the middle.

Serve swordfish with pilaf, coconut raita and lime wedges, topped with coriander and mint leaves. **Serves 4**

ⓟ See Pantry essentials, p 95.

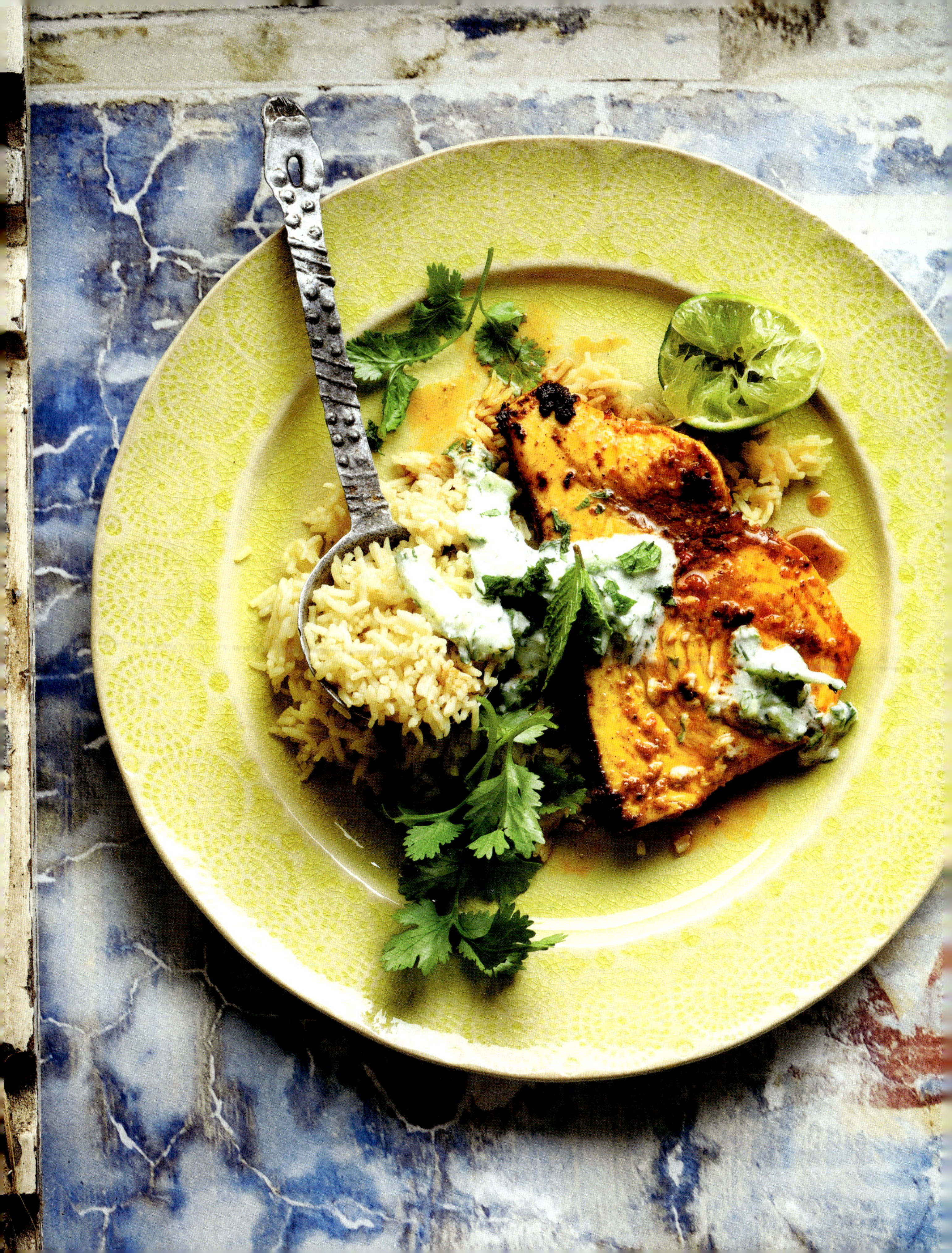

Tarka dhal with spinach and tomato

1½ cups (300g) red lentils
1 tsp grated ginger
½ bunch coriander, leaves picked, stalks finely chopped
300ml coconut milk
400g can chopped tomatoes
¼ cup (60ml) rice bran oil
1 tsp ground turmeric
½ tsp ground cumin
½ tsp ground coriander
1 tsp panch phoron ⓟ
1 long red chilli, seeds removed, finely chopped
8 curry leaves ⓟ
100g baby spinach leaves
Juice of 1 lemon
4 spring onions, thinly sliced
Pappadams, ⓟ to serve

Rinse the lentils in a sieve under cold running water, then place in a saucepan with the ginger, coriander stalks and 1 tsp salt. Add coconut milk and 600ml water, and bring to a simmer over medium-high heat. Reduce heat to low and cook, stirring occasionally, for a further 10 minutes. Add tomato and cook for a further 15 minutes or until the mixture is thick and lentils have started to break down.

Meanwhile, for the tarka spice mixture, heat the oil in a frypan over medium-high heat. Add spices, chilli and curry leaves, stirring until mixture is fragrant and seeds in the panch phoron start to pop. Remove from heat.

Using a wooden spoon, beat the lentil mixture until thick and creamy. Add three-quarters of the tarka mixture, then stir in the spinach, lemon juice and spring onion.

Serve tarka dhal sprinkled with coriander leaves, with pappadams and remaining tarka to sprinkle. **Serves 4-6**

ⓟ See Pantry essentials, p 95.

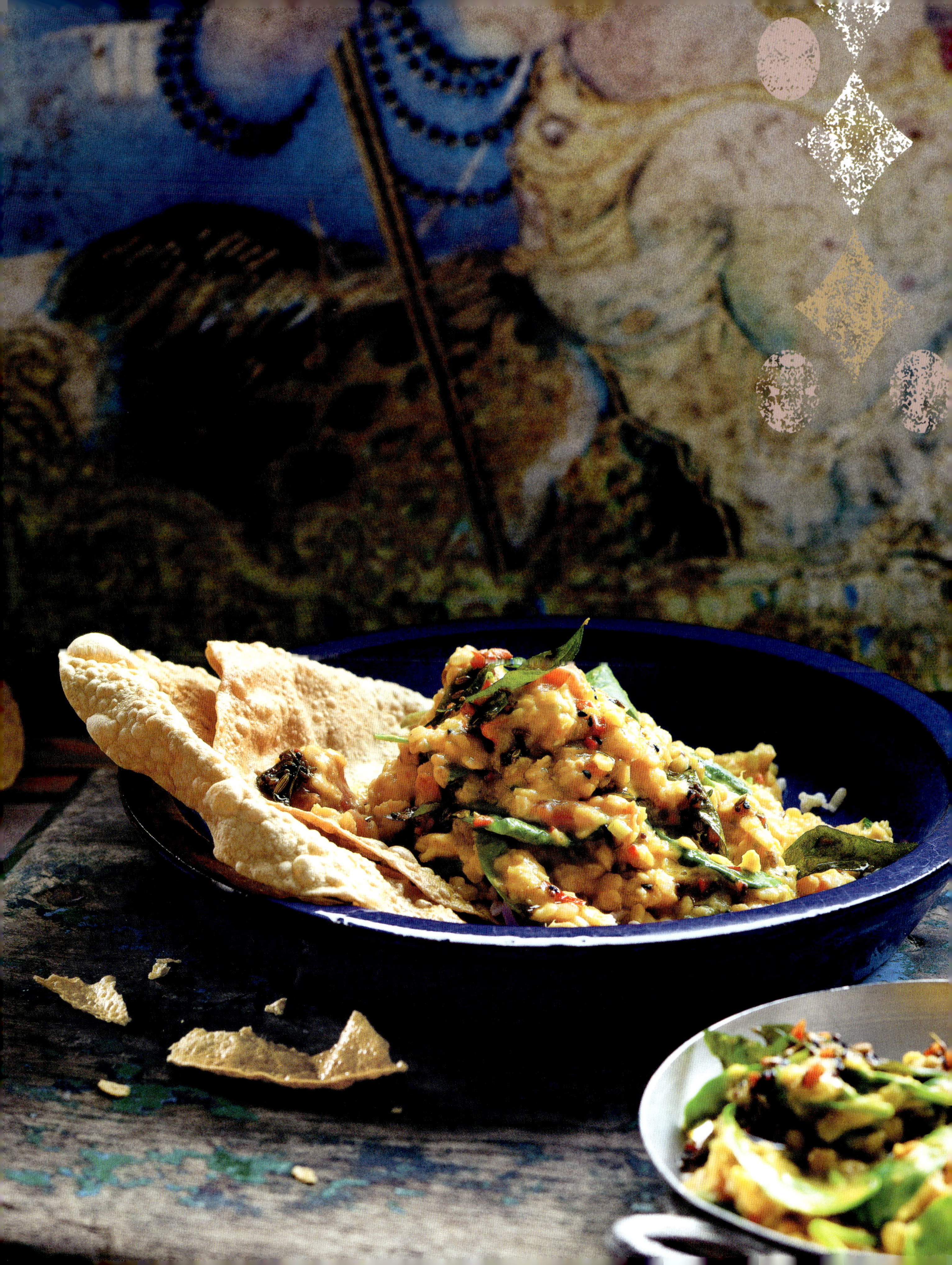

Kashmiri prawns

500g green prawns, peeled (tails intact)
1 tbs lemon or lime juice
2 tsp ground turmeric
½ bunch coriander, roughly chopped
300ml coconut cream
2 tbs ghee ⓟ or sunflower oil
1 onion, finely chopped
6 cardamom pods, lightly crushed
1 tsp Kashmiri chilli powder ⓟ
12 curry leaves ⓟ
1 cinnamon quill
3 garlic cloves, crushed
2cm piece ginger, grated
2 tbs fresh grated coconut or desiccated coconut

Place prawns in a bowl with the lemon juice, 1 tsp turmeric and 1 tsp salt, and toss to combine. Set aside for 5 minutes.

Place coriander, including stalks, in a blender or small food processor with the coconut cream and blend until smooth.

Heat the ghee in a large frypan over medium heat. Add onion and cook, stirring, for 2-3 minutes until softened but not browned. Add the cardamom, chilli powder, curry leaves and remaining 1 tsp turmeric, stirring until fragrant. Add cinnamon, garlic, ginger and prawns, and cook, stirring occasionally, for 2-3 minutes until prawns are just cooked.

Add coriander mixture to the pan with the grated coconut and simmer over medium heat for a further 1-2 minutes before serving. **Serves 3-4**

ⓟ See Pantry essentials, p 95.

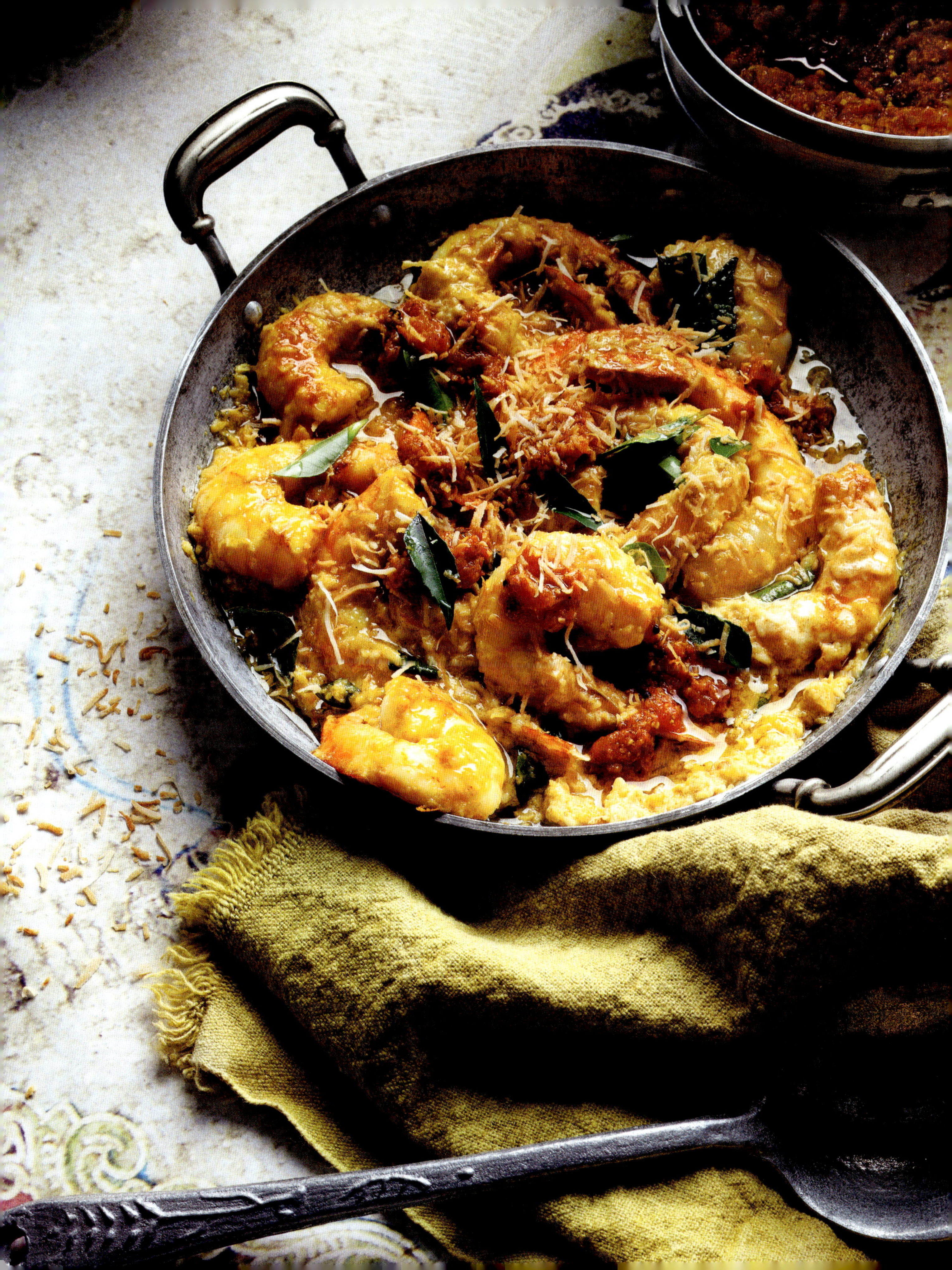

Oven-baked chicken curry

Warming the spices first gives such a great depth of flavour and makes your kitchen smell wonderful, like an Indian bazaar.

2 tsp each cumin, coriander and fenugreek seeds
1 tsp fennel seeds
2 tsp ground turmeric
1 onion, chopped
3 garlic cloves, chopped
2 long green chillies, seeds removed, chopped
1 bunch coriander, leaves picked, stalks chopped
3cm piece ginger, grated
2 tbs ghee Ⓟ
　or sunflower oil
1.8kg whole chicken, jointed into 8 pieces
1 tbs Madras curry powder Ⓟ
12 curry leaves Ⓟ
400g can chopped tomatoes
400ml coconut milk
1 cup (250ml) chicken stock
Thick Greek-style yoghurt and naan, Ⓟ to serve

Kachumber

2 large tomatoes, seeds removed, finely chopped
1 red onion, finely chopped
1 large Lebanese cucumber, finely chopped
2 tbs lemon juice

Preheat the oven to 180°C.

Combine the seeds and turmeric in a frypan over low heat and stir until fragrant. Transfer to a spice grinder or mortar and pestle, and grind to a powder.

Place onion, garlic, chilli, coriander stalks and ginger in a food processor and pulse to a paste.

Heat ghee in a frypan over medium heat. Season the chicken pieces, then cook, turning, in batches, for 3-4 minutes until golden. Transfer to a baking dish. Add the onion mixture to the frypan and cook, stirring, for 1-2 minutes until softened but not browned. Add spice mix, curry powder and curry leaves.

Place tomatoes and coconut milk in the food processor (there's no need to clean it after processing the onion mixture) and whiz to combine. Add to the frypan with stock and stir to combine. Bring to a simmer, then pour sauce over the chicken in the baking dish. Bake, basting chicken two or three times, for 1 hour or until chicken is tender.

Meanwhile, for the kachumber, finely chop three-quarters of the picked coriander leaves and combine with remaining ingredients in a bowl. Season.

Scatter remaining coriander leaves over curry and serve with kachumber, yoghurt and naan. **Serves 4-6**
Ⓟ See Pantry essentials, p 95.

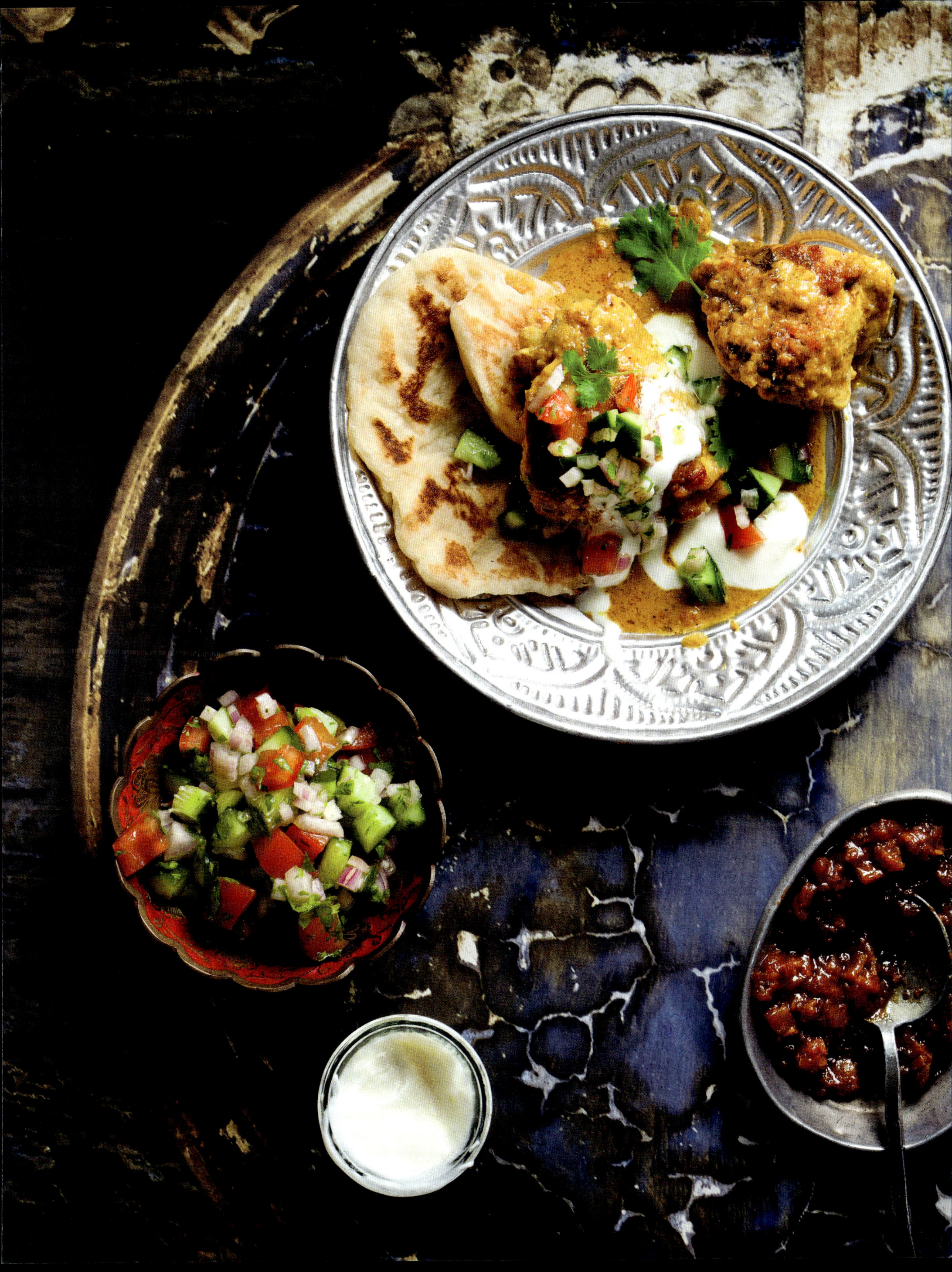

Coconut beef curry

2 onions, chopped
3 garlic cloves, chopped
2 tbs grated ginger
2 long red chillies, seeds removed, finely chopped, plus 1, thinly sliced lengthways, to serve
1 stalk lemongrass (inner core only), chopped
1/4 cup (60g) ghee ⓟ or sunflower oil
1.5kg beef chuck steak, trimmed, cut into 3cm pieces
12 curry leaves ⓟ
2 tbs ground cumin
2 tsp Kashmiri chilli powder ⓟ
2 tbs ground coriander
2 tsp ground turmeric
400ml coconut milk
1 1/2 cups (375ml) beef stock or consomme
2 cinnamon quills
1 tbs tamarind puree ⓟ
1 tbs brown sugar
Coconut rice (see Basics, p 295), thinly sliced red radishes and coriander leaves, to serve

Preheat the oven to 160°C.

Combine onions, garlic, ginger, chillies and lemongrass in a food processor and pulse to a coarse paste.

Heat 1 tbs ghee in a casserole or large ovenproof saucepan over medium-high heat. Cook beef, in batches, turning, until browned, then set aside. Add remaining 2 tbs ghee to the casserole and cook the onion mixture with the curry leaves, cumin, chilli powder, coriander and turmeric, stirring, for 1-2 minutes until fragrant. Return beef to the casserole, then add coconut milk, stock, cinnamon, tamarind and sugar, and stir to combine. Bring to the boil, then cover and transfer to the oven and cook for 2-2 1/2 hours until beef is meltingly tender.

Serve topped with sliced long red chilli, with coconut rice, radish and coriander leaves. **Serves 6**

ⓟ See Pantry essentials, p 95.

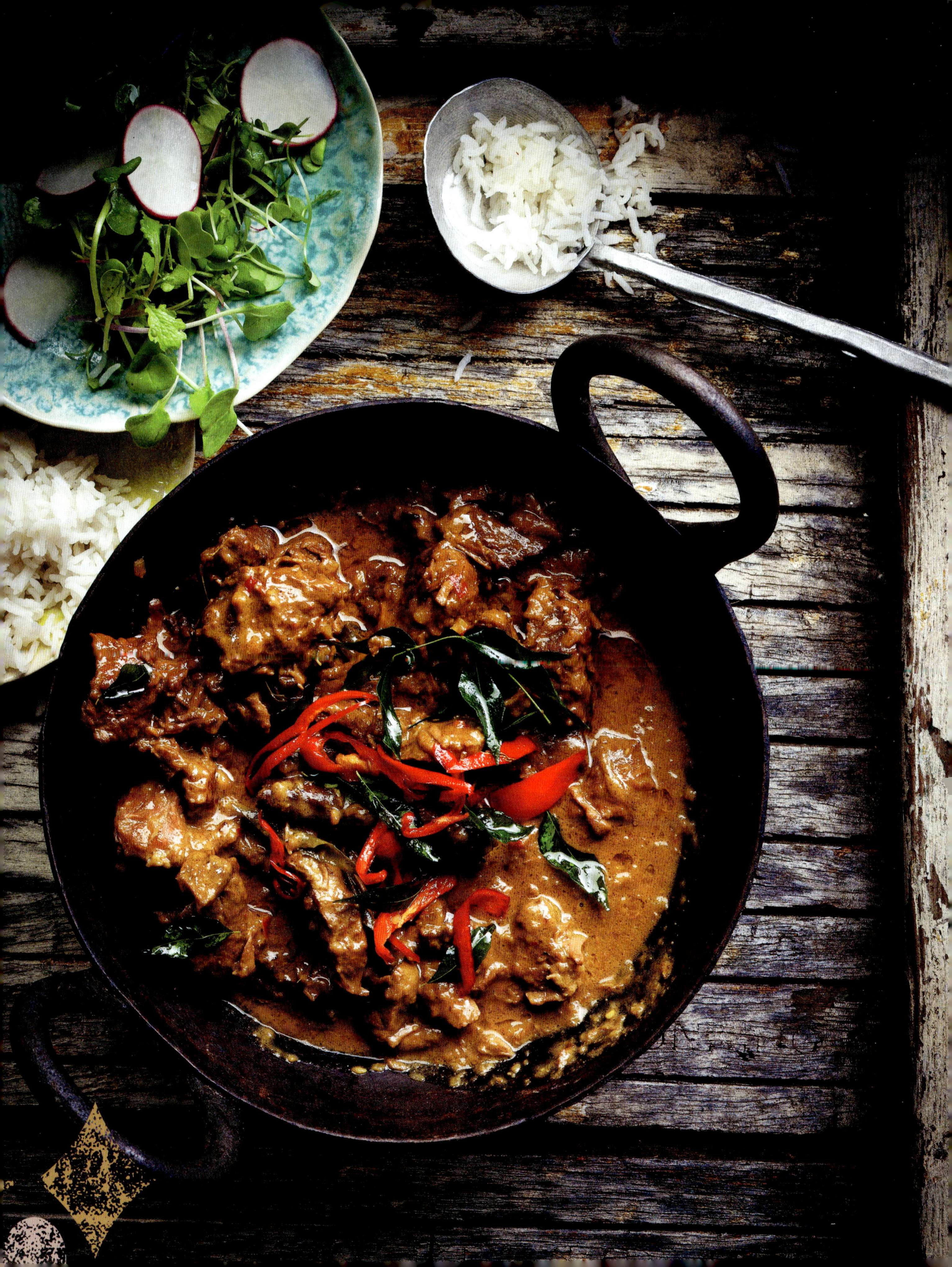

Tandoori lamb cutlets with sweet and sour tomatoes

½ cup (160g) tandoori paste ⓟ
2 tbs thick Greek-style yoghurt, plus extra to serve
2 tbs finely chopped coriander, plus extra leaves to serve
16 French-trimmed lamb cutlets
Sunflower oil, to brush

Sweet and sour tomatoes
8 tomatoes, quartered
2 long red chillies, halved lengthways
1 tbs black peppercorns, crushed
1 tbs panch phoron ⓟ
2 tsp ground turmeric
2 tbs ground cumin
2 tbs sweet paprika
⅓ cup (80ml) sunflower oil
⅓ cup (80ml) malt vinegar
½ cup grated fresh ginger
6 garlic cloves, crushed
⅓ cup (80g) brown sugar

Combine tandoori paste, yoghurt and coriander in a bowl, add cutlets and turn to coat. Refrigerate for 15 minutes to marinate.

Meanwhile, for sweet and sour tomatoes, place tomato and chilli in a bowl. Combine black peppercorns, panch phoron, turmeric, cumin, paprika and 1 tsp salt in a bowl. Heat the oil in a frypan over medium heat until almost smoking, then cook the spice mixture, stirring, for 1 minute or until fragrant. Add to the tomato mixture. In the same pan, combine the vinegar, ginger, garlic and brown sugar, stirring until sugar dissolves. Add to the tomato mixture and stir to combine. Set aside for at least 15 minutes for flavours to develop. The tomatoes can be served warm or at room temperature.

Brush a barbecue plate or frypan with oil, then preheat to medium-high. Drain the cutlets from marinade, then cook for 2 minutes each side or until lightly charred but still rare in the centre. Rest, loosely covered with foil, for 2 minutes.

Serve cutlets with sweet and sour tomatoes, and extra yoghurt and coriander. **Serves 4**

ⓟ See Pantry essentials, p 95.

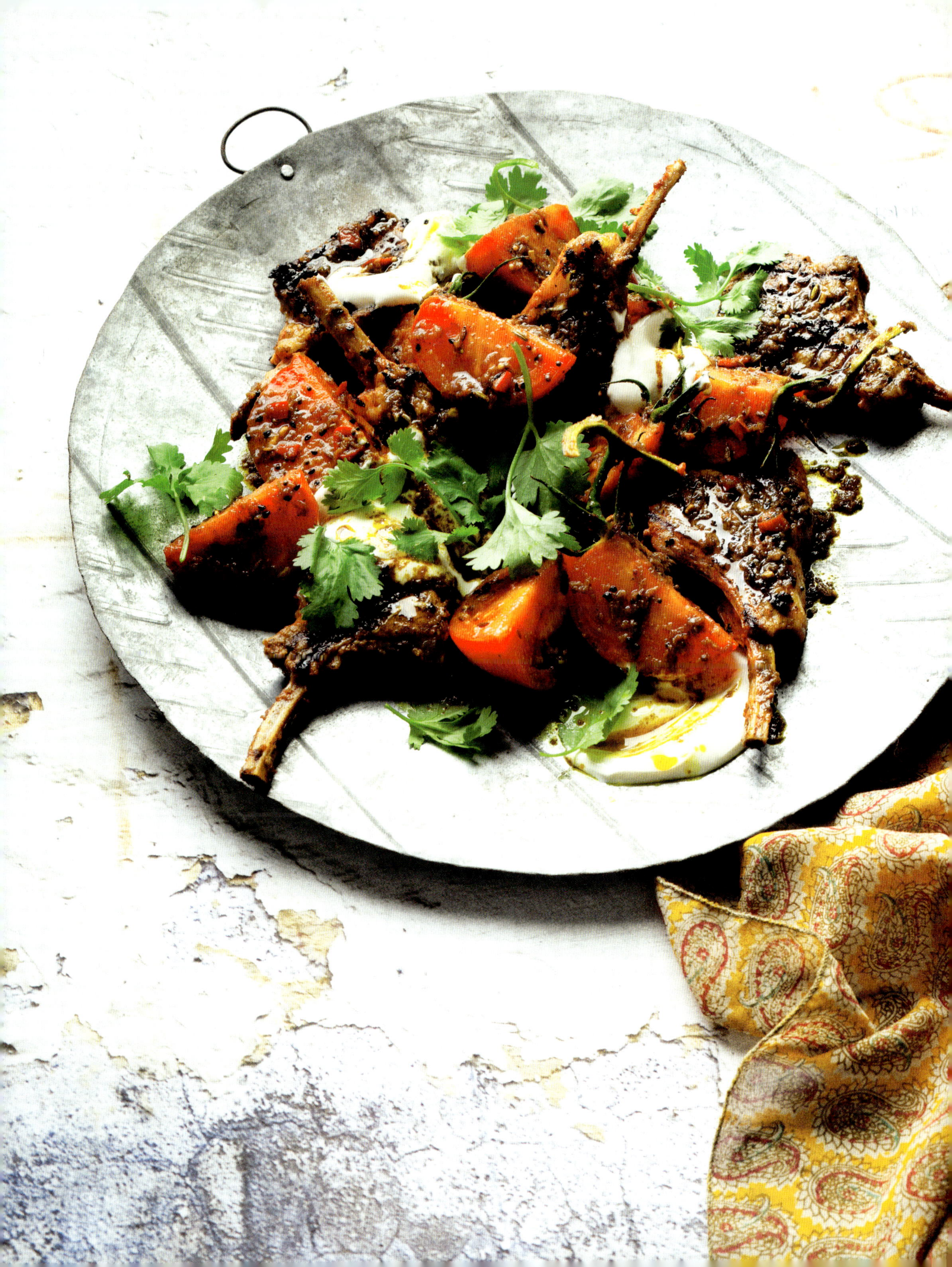

Coconut crepe layer cake

½ cup (125ml) milk
½ cup (125ml) thickened cream
1 cup (250ml) coconut cream, plus extra to serve
½ tsp ground cardamom
2 egg yolks
½ cup (110g) caster sugar
1 tbs finely grated lime zest
2½ tbs cornflour
300g desiccated coconut
375g jaggery ⓟ or dark palm sugar, chopped
16 crepes (see Basics, p 297), cooled
Icing sugar and sliced mango, to serve

Place milk, cream, coconut cream and cardamom in a saucepan and bring to a simmer over medium heat. Whisk egg yolks, sugar, zest and cornflour in a bowl. Whisking constantly, gradually pour the warm milk mixture into the egg mixture, then return mixture to the pan over a low heat, stirring until thickened. Remove from heat and stir in the desiccated coconut. Cool completely.

Meanwhile, place jaggery and 1½ cups (375ml) water in a saucepan over low heat, stirring until sugar dissolves. Increase heat to medium-high and cook, without stirring, until reduced and syrupy. Remove the jaggery syrup from the heat, pour into a jug and set aside.

Using a sharp knife, trim crepes to fit a 20cm springform cake pan. Place 1 crepe in the base of the pan, then spread with a thin layer of coconut filling. Repeat with remaining crepes and filling, finishing with a crepe. Cover with plastic wrap and refrigerate for at least 2 hours to firm up.

Transfer cake to a plate and dust with icing sugar. Slice and serve with mango, drizzled with jaggery syrup and extra coconut cream. **Serves 6-8**

ⓟ See Pantry essentials, p 95.

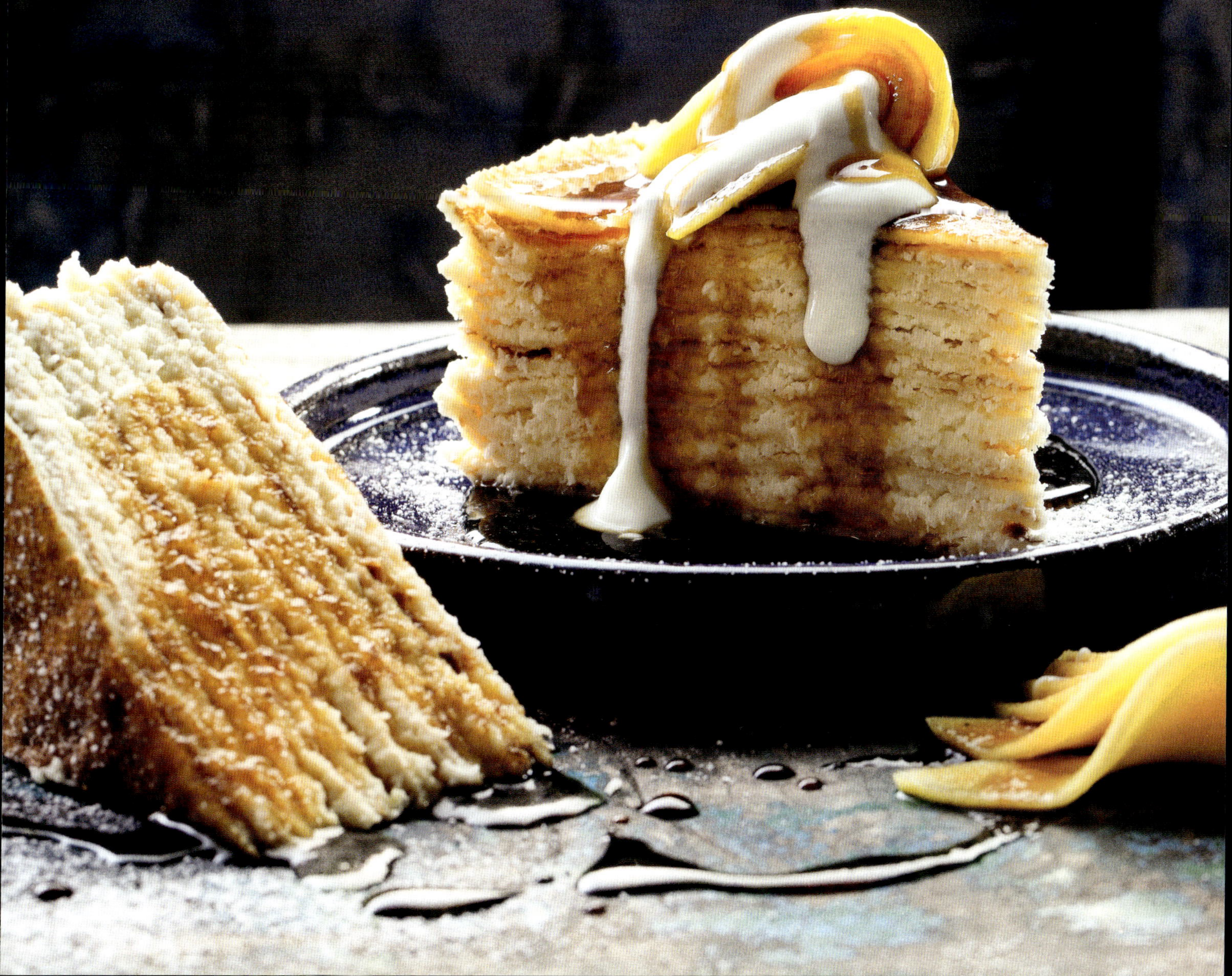

Almond milk cream with cardamom rhubarb

You will need to start this recipe a day ahead.

2 x gold-strength
  gelatine leaves*
400ml milk
¾ cup (75g) almond meal
½ cup (75g) icing sugar,
  sifted
1 tsp almond extract
300ml thickened cream
Edible silver leaf* (optional),
  to serve

Cardamom rhubarb
5 cardamom pods
⅓ cup (75g) caster sugar
300g rhubarb, trimmed,
  cut into 5cm lengths

Soak the gelatine in cold water for 5 minutes to soften.

Place milk in a saucepan with the almond meal. Bring to the boil over medium-high heat, then reduce heat to low and simmer, stirring, for 4-5 minutes. Remove from heat and transfer to a sieve placed over a bowl. Strain mixture, pressing with the back of a spoon, discarding solids. Squeeze out excess liquid from gelatine, then add gelatine to the milk mixture and stir until dissolved. Whisk in icing sugar and almond extract, then set aside to cool slightly.

Meanwhile, whisk cream to soft peaks, then fold through the milk mixture. Divide among 6 x 150ml-capacity dishes. Cover and refrigerate overnight.

For the cardamom rhubarb, preheat the oven to 160°C. Place cardamom pods in a small frypan over low heat and stir until fragrant, then crack pods and remove seeds. Using a mortar and pestle or a rolling pin, crush the seeds, then combine in a small bowl with the caster sugar. Place rhubarb in a glass or ceramic baking dish and sprinkle over the cardamom mixture. Cover with foil, then bake for 20-25 minutes until the rhubarb releases its juices and is just tender. Cool.

To serve, top almond milk creams with rhubarb and a little syrup. Decorate with silver leaf, if using. **Serves 6**

* *Gelatine leaves come in different setting strengths, and are available from specialist food shops. Edible silver leaf is of high purity and is sold as thin flakes or sheets at cake-decorating shops and stationery shops.*

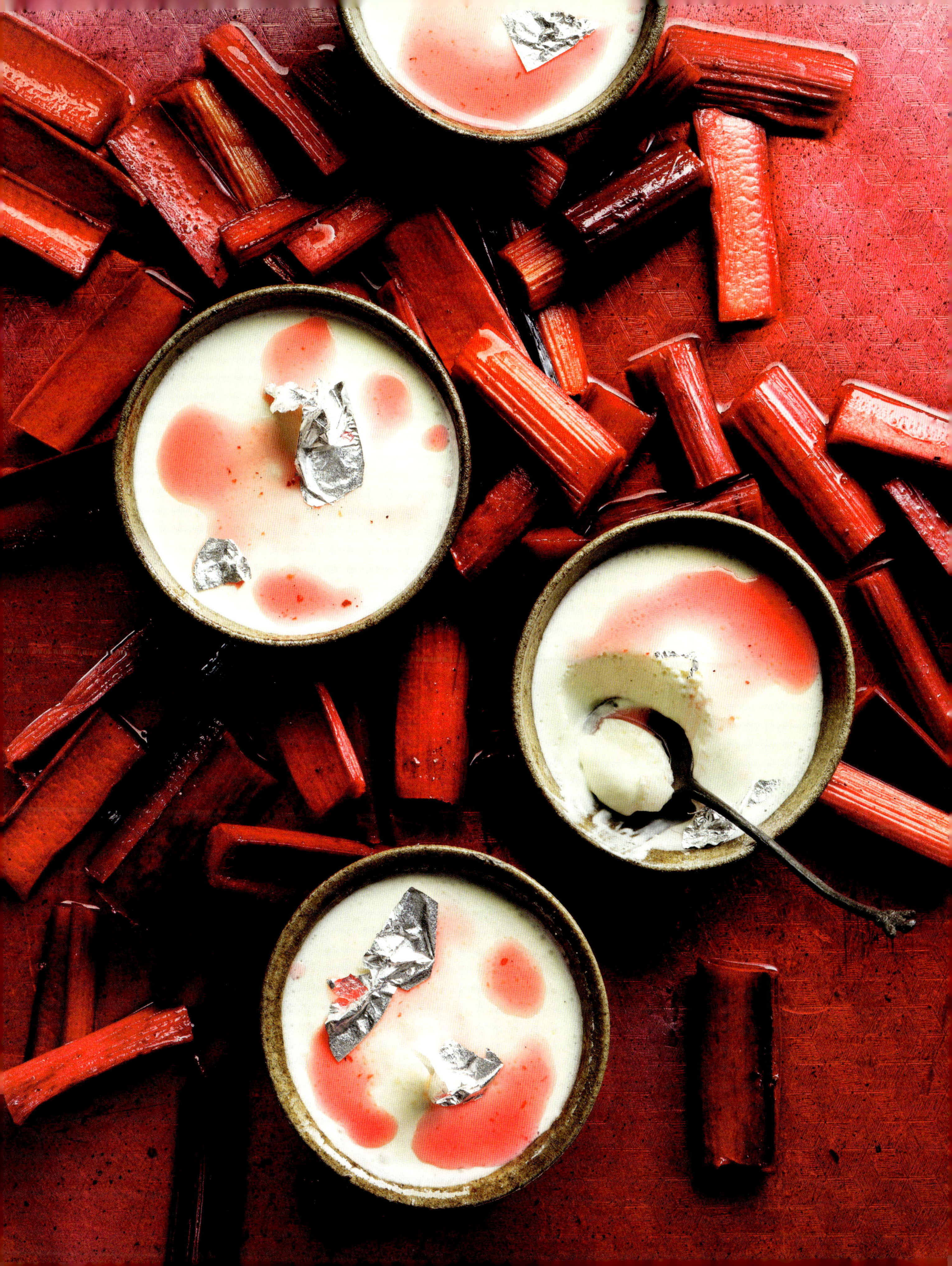

Shrikhand with sweet Indian biscuits

Shrikhand is a traditional dessert of strained sweetened yoghurt. You will need to start this recipe a day ahead.

2 cups (560g) thick Greek-style yoghurt
1/2 tsp saffron threads
1 tbs milk, warmed
1 tsp rosewater
1/2 cup (110g) caster sugar
Scraped seeds of 1/2 vanilla bean
1/2 tsp ground cardamom
2 tbs slivered or finely chopped pistachio kernels
Seeds from 1 pomegranate

Sweet Indian biscuits
100g ghee ⓟ or unsalted butter, at room temperature
2/3 cup (100g) icing sugar, sifted, plus extra to dust
125g plain flour
1/2 tsp ground cardamom
2 tbs finely chopped pistachio kernels

Line a sieve with a piece of muslin or clean Chux cloth and set over a bowl. Place yoghurt in lined sieve, fold over the muslin to cover, then refrigerate overnight to drain.

Add the saffron to the warmed milk in a small bowl, then set aside to infuse for 10 minutes. Place drained yoghurt in a bowl, discarding liquid. Add the saffron-infused milk, rosewater, sugar, vanilla and cardamom, and stir to combine. Cover and refrigerate until ready to serve.

For the biscuits, preheat the oven to 160°C. Line a baking tray with baking paper. Using electric beaters, beat ghee until thick and pale. Add the icing sugar, beating until combined. Add the flour, baking powder, cardamom and 1/2 tsp salt, then beat until just combined and the mixture comes together. Roll out on a lightly floured surface to 1cm thick. Using a 5cm round biscuit cutter, cut out rounds, re-rolling the dough offcuts. Place on the prepared baking tray and scatter with pistachios. Bake for 12-15 minutes until pale golden (do not overcook). Cool slightly on tray, then transfer to a wire rack to cool completely. Dust with extra icing sugar. Makes 12 biscuits.

Scatter the shrikhand with pistachios and pomegranate seeds, and serve with sweet Indian biscuits. **Serves 4**

ⓟ See Pantry essentials, p 95.

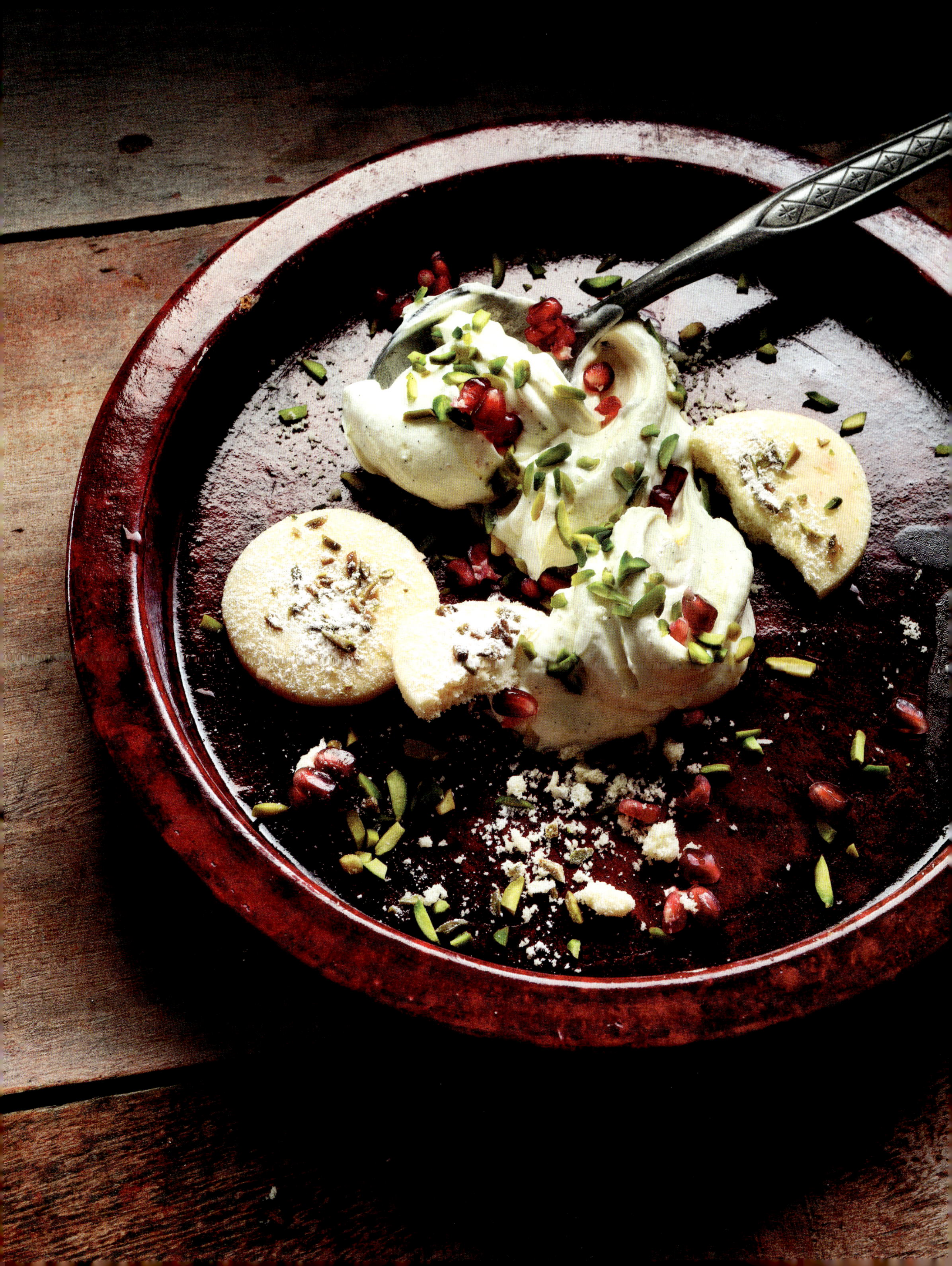

AMERICAN

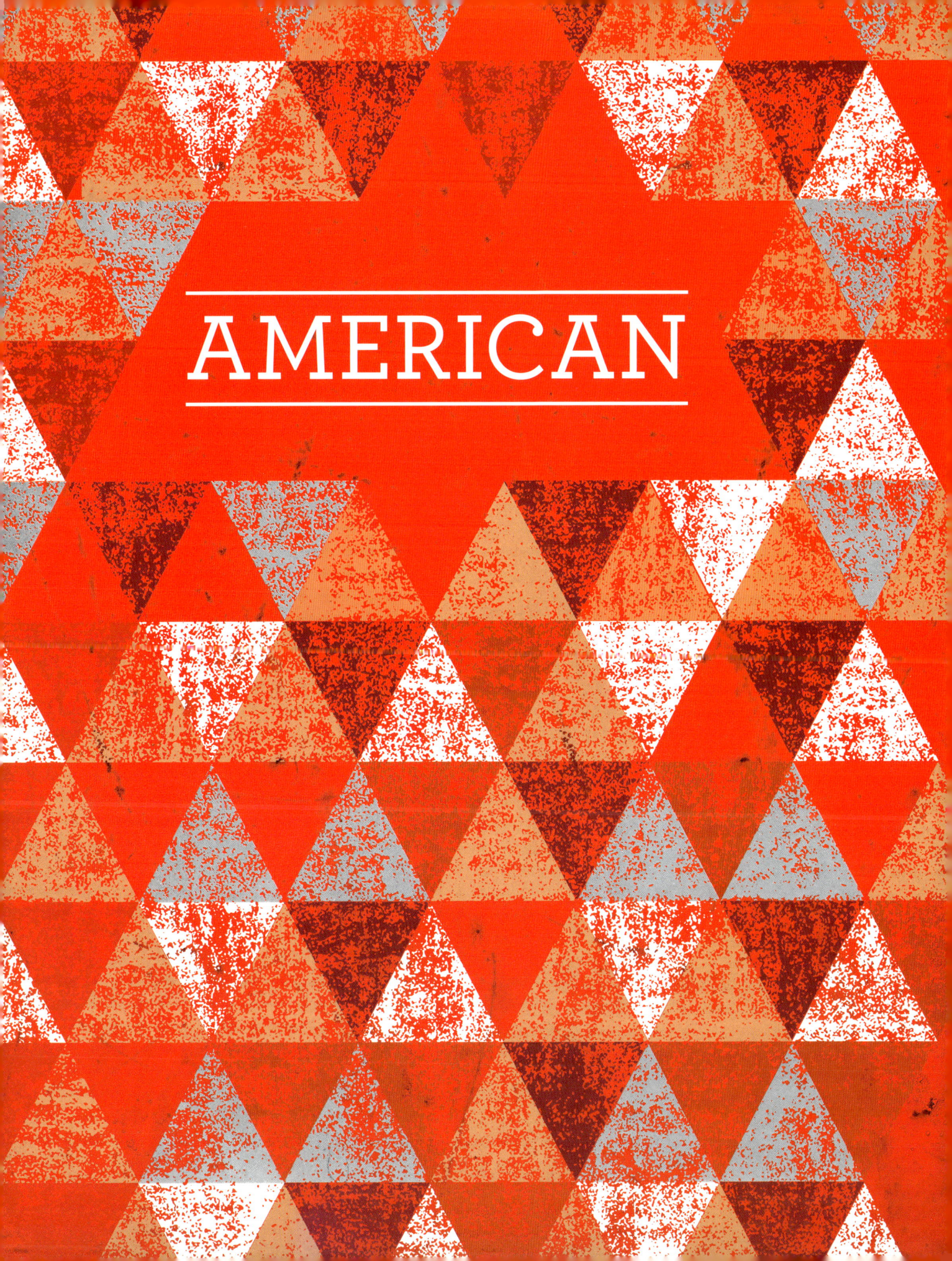

NOBLE
HANDCRAFTED
01
PIC'S REALLY GOOD
PEANUT BUTTER
ORIGINAL
BROOKLYN
McCLURE'S
POTATO CHIPS
CRINKLE CUT
SPICY PICKLE

PANTRY ESSENTIALS

American mustard
Also known as yellow or ballpark mustard, as it is commonly served in hot dogs at ball games, this bright yellow, mild-flavoured style is made with yellow and white mustard seeds, and turmeric.

Barbecue sauce
As many and varied as the styles of American barbecue cooking in the south-eastern states, the sauce base is usually made up of vinegar, sugar and tomato.

Buttermilk
Originally the by-product of the butter-making process, buttermilk is lower in fat than regular milk, but with a thicker consistency. Its slightly acidic profile means it works well with raising agents to create airiness in baking, as well as acting as a tenderiser for meat.

Corn syrup
A very sweet syrup used widely in processed foods. Substitute glucose syrup, but keep in mind that it is much thicker and may need thinning with a little water.

Crystal hot sauce
Produced by Baumer Foods in Louisiana since the early 1920s, it is made from aged cayenne peppers, distilled vinegar and salt, and is smokier and less vinegary than Tabasco. Available from selected delis.

Dill pickles
A New York Jewish deli staple, these cucumbers are brined with dill and garlic. They are often labelled as 'new' or 'half-sour', or 'old' or 'full-sour', depending on how long they've spent in the brining process.

Maple syrup
Sap sourced from a number of species of maple tree, principally in Canada, but also in the north-eastern states of America. The words caramel, smoky and woody are all used to describe its flavour. Buy pure maple syrup.

Tabasco
A peppery, vinegar-based hot sauce also produced in Louisiana since 1868, and now used around the world in everything from a Bloody Mary to Jamaican jerk chicken.

△

Italian, Chinese, Hispanic and Eastern European flavours have all enriched America's unique and varied food culture. While chefs Alice Waters and Thomas Keller blazed a trail with their use of native ingredients and artisan produce, good ol' hamburgers, mac 'n' cheese and southern fried chicken are still hard to resist. Stock up on peanut butter, mayonnaise, hot sauce, ketchup, macaroni and popcorn, plus marshmallows, maple syrup, corn syrup and ice cream for over-the-top desserts.

△

Maryland crab cakes with dill pickle mayo

While the original hails from the Chesapeake Bay area of Maryland, on America's east coast, crab cakes are a summer favourite around the country.

1¼ cups (85g) fresh breadcrumbs or torn white bread, crust removed
¼ cup (60ml) milk
250g picked crabmeat
2 spring onions, finely chopped
½ red capsicum, finely chopped
1 celery stalk, finely chopped
1 tbs finely chopped flat-leaf parsley
1 egg, lightly beaten
1 tsp American mustard ⓟ
¼ tsp cayenne pepper
¼ cup (60ml) olive oil
Seasoned flour, to dust
Mixed leaves and lemon wedges, to serve

Dill pickle mayo
1 cup (300g) whole-egg mayonnaise
1 tsp American mustard
2 tbs chopped dill pickles ⓟ
1 tbs lemon juice
1 tbs baby capers
1 tbs chopped dill

Soak the breadcrumbs in milk in a bowl for 5 minutes. Squeeze out excess liquid, discarding milk. Combine in a bowl with the remaining ingredients, except the oil, flour, mixed greens and lemon wedges. Form into 16 small patties, then cover and refrigerate for 30 minutes to firm up.

Meanwhile, for the dill pickle mayo, combine all the ingredients in a bowl, cover and refrigerate until ready to serve.

Heat oil in a frypan over medium heat. Lightly dust crab cakes with the seasoned flour, then fry, in batches, for 2-3 minutes each side until golden.

Serve with mixed leaves, dill pickle mayo and lemon wedges.

Serves 4 as a starter

ⓟ See Pantry essentials, p 123.

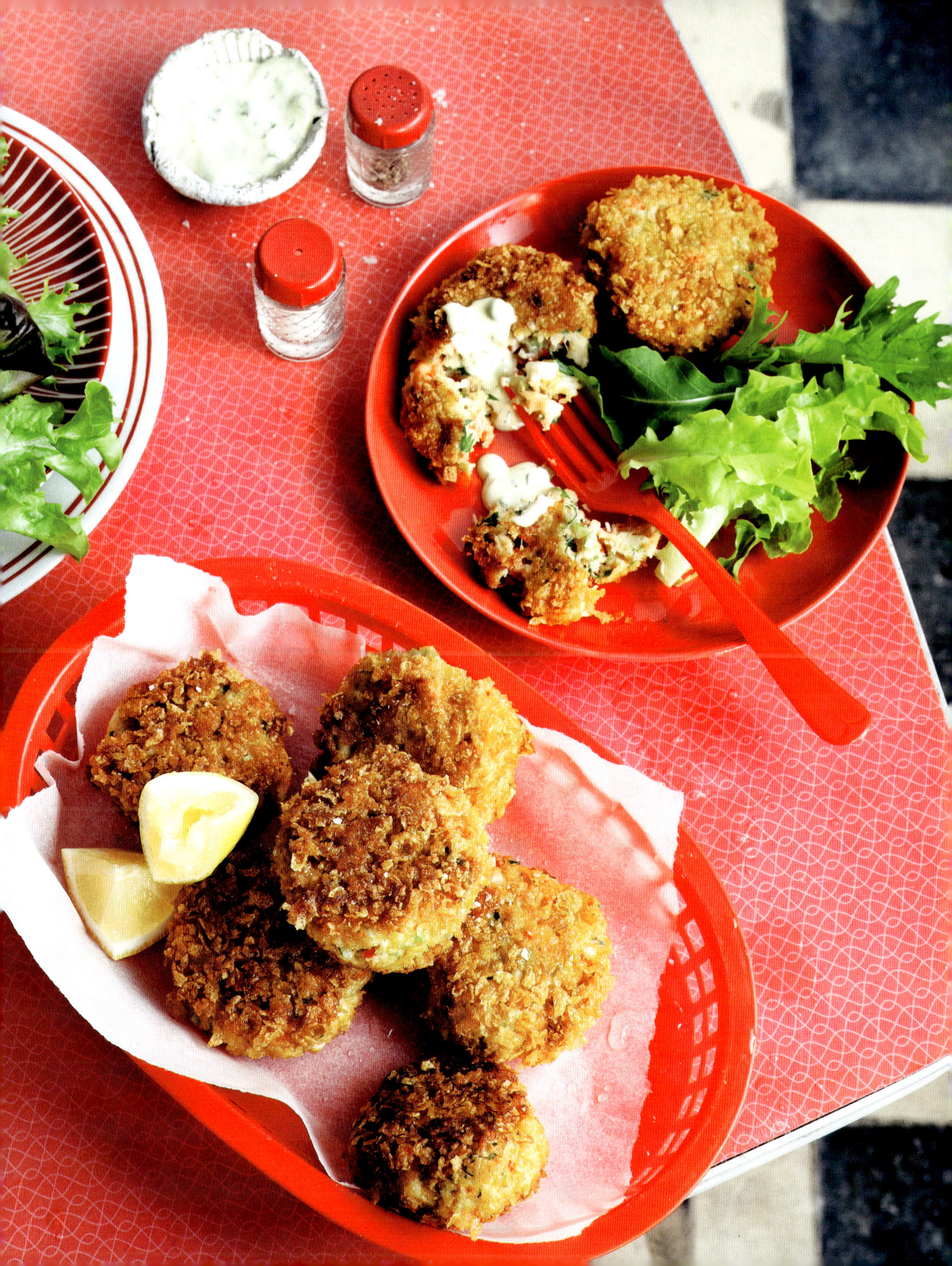

Popcorn prawns with ranch dipping sauce

50g cooked popcorn (¼ cup uncooked popcorn kernels)
1 cup (50g) panko (Japanese) breadcrumbs
⅓ cup (50g) plain flour
1 tsp chopped thyme leaves
2 eggs, lightly beaten
24 medium green prawns, peeled (tails intact)
Sunflower oil, to deep-fry

Ranch dipping sauce
¾ cup (180ml) buttermilk ⓟ
¼ cup (60g) sour cream
¼ cup (75g) whole-egg mayonnaise
2 tbs finely chopped flat-leaf parsley
2 tbs finely chopped chives
1 tbs white wine vinegar
1 garlic clove, crushed

For the ranch dipping sauce, place all the ingredients in a jar and season. Seal and shake well to combine. Refrigerate until ready to serve.

Whiz popcorn in a food processor to fine crumbs. Add breadcrumbs and pulse to combine. Transfer to a bowl. Combine flour and thyme in a separate bowl. Season. Place eggs in a third bowl. Dust prawns in seasoned flour, then dip in egg, shaking to remove excess, then the popcorn mixture. Repeat process to give prawns a double coating.

Half-fill a deep-fryer or large saucepan with oil and preheat to 190°C (a cube of bread will turn golden in 30 seconds when the oil is hot enough). Fry prawns, in batches, until golden and crisp. Drain on paper towel.

Serve prawns with ranch dipping sauce. **Serves 4**

ⓟ See Pantry essentials, p 123.

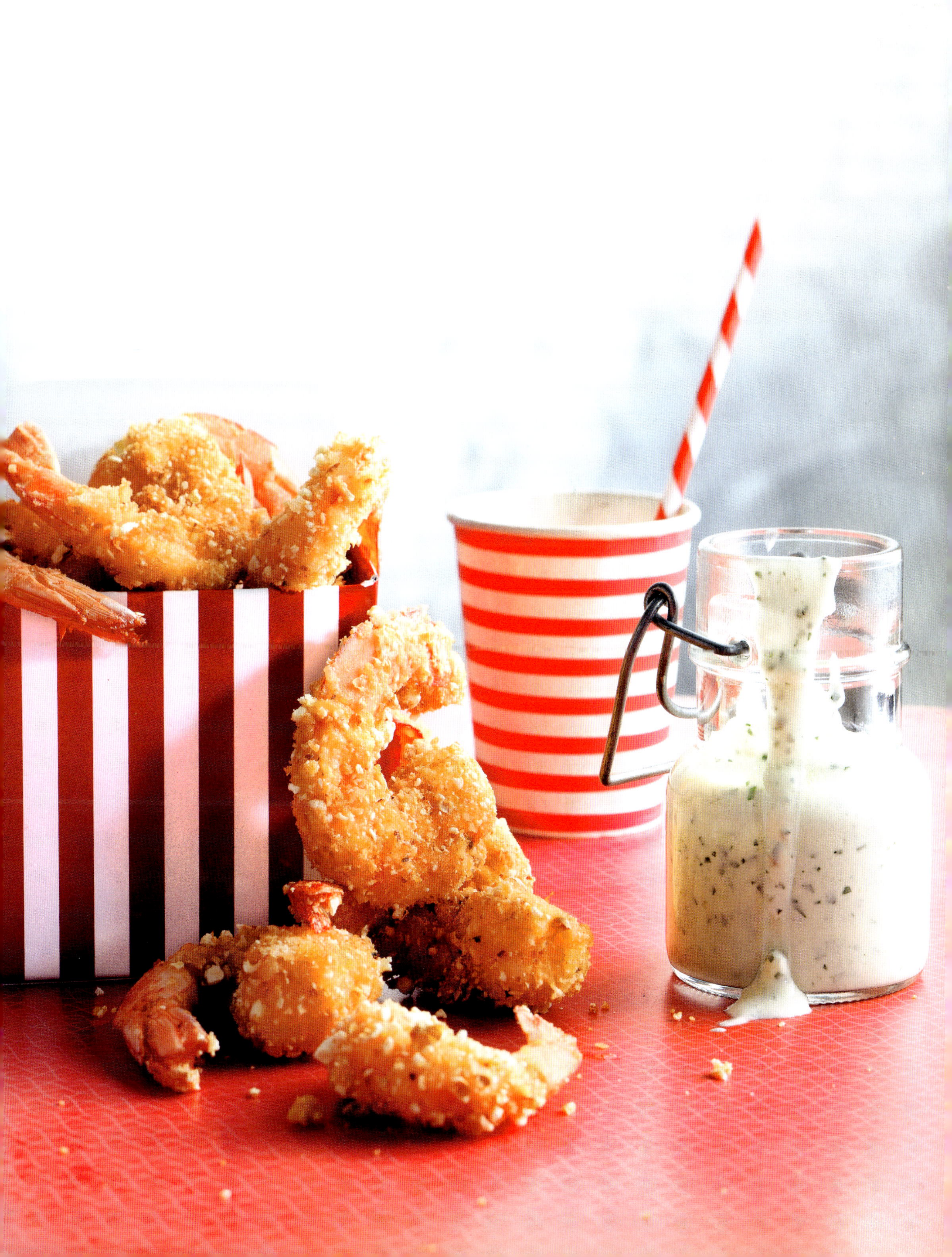

Meatball caesar

This new-look chicken caesar combines two iconic Italian-American inventions with delicious results.

500g chicken mince
1 small onion, finely chopped
2 tbs finely chopped chives
1 garlic clove, finely chopped
Few drops Tabasco ⓟ
1 tbs Worcestershire sauce
¼ cup (20g) grated parmesan, plus extra, shaved to serve
4 rashers bacon or flat pancetta
3 thick slices sourdough, crusts removed, torn into bite-size pieces
2 tbs olive oil
2 cos lettuce hearts, quartered lengthways
Finely chopped chives, to serve

Dressing
1 egg
1 garlic clove, chopped
Juice of 1 lime
1 tsp American mustard ⓟ
½ tsp Worcestershire sauce
150ml extra virgin olive oil
½ cup (40g) grated parmesan

Preheat oven to 200°C. Line 2 baking trays with baking paper.

Place chicken in a bowl with the onion, chives, garlic, Tabasco, Worcestershire sauce and 2 tbs parmesan. Using clean, damp hands, mix well, then form into 20 balls. Place on a prepared baking tray, cover and refrigerate for 15 minutes to firm up.

Place bacon on the second prepared tray and bake for 10 minutes or until crisp. Remove from tray, reserving tray, and set aside to cool. Spread bread over the reserved tray. Drizzle over 1 tbs olive oil and toss to coat. Set aside.

Drizzle meatballs with the remaining 1 tbs oil, then bake for 10 minutes. Place the croutons on the oven shelf underneath the meatballs, then bake meatballs and croutons for a further 10 minutes until meatballs are cooked through and croutons are golden and crisp.

Meanwhile, for the dressing, whiz the egg, garlic, lime juice, mustard and Worcestershire sauce in a small food processor. With the motor running, slowly add the oil in a steady stream until emulsified. Transfer to a bowl, season and stir in parmesan.

To serve, tear lettuce onto a platter. Top with meatballs, bacon and croutons, drizzle with dressing and scatter with shaved parmesan and chives. **Serves 4**

ⓟ See Pantry essentials, p 123.

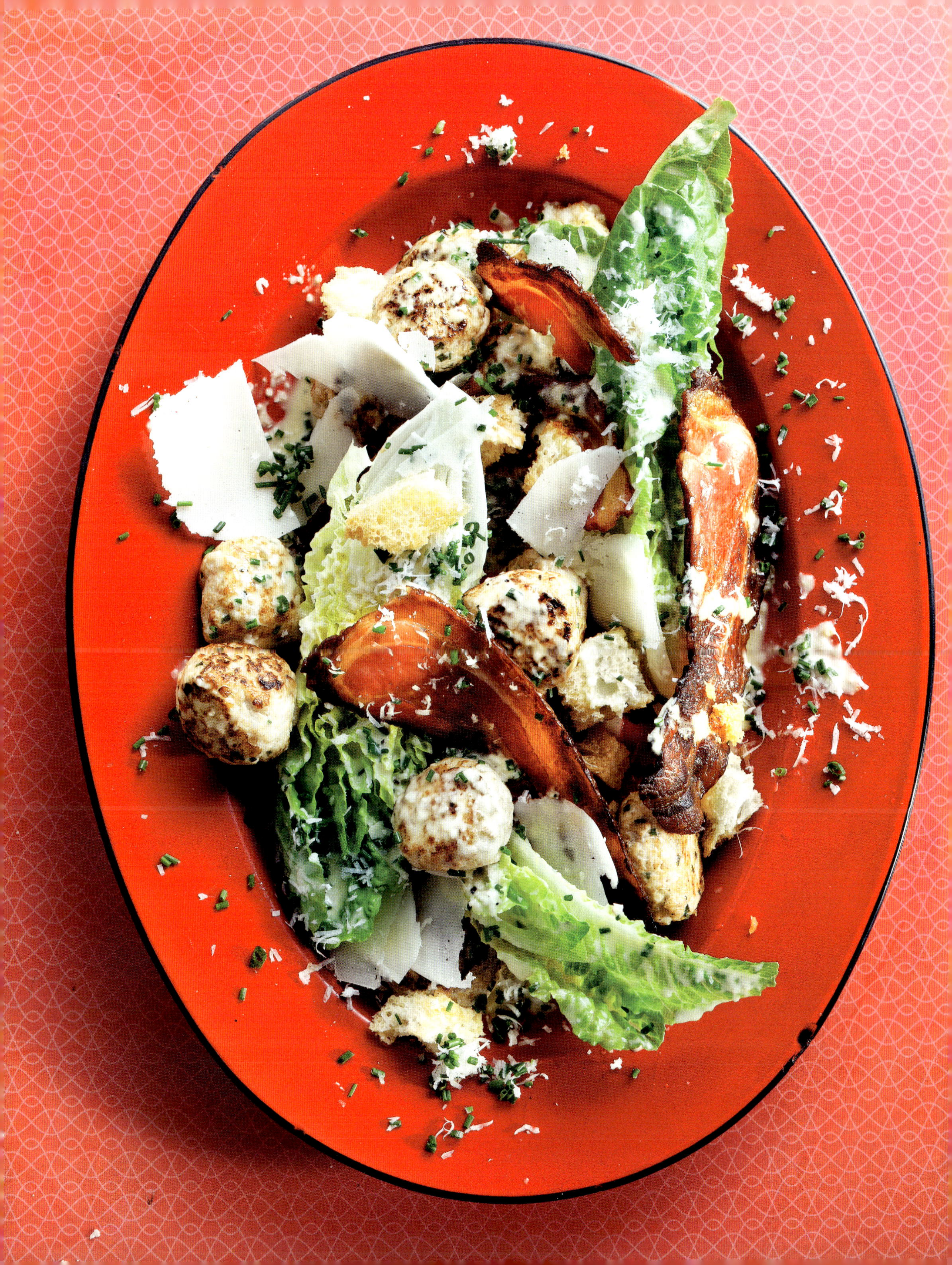

Not so sloppy Joes

Sloppy Joes are basically unconstructed hamburgers – the filling being more like a sauce than a patty. My version transforms the mixture into little meatballs – far less messy to eat with your hands!

1/4 cup (60ml) olive oil
1 onion, finely chopped
5 garlic cloves, finely chopped
200g pork mince
5 Italian-style sausages, casings removed, meat crumbled
2 eggs
Finely grated zest of 1 lemon
1 tbs dried oregano
1 cup (70g) fresh breadcrumbs
1 cup (80g) parmesan
3 cups (750ml) passata (sieved tomatoes)
1/2 tbs caster sugar
6 long ciabatta-style rolls
1 cup (100g) grated mozzarella
1/2 red onion, halved, thinly sliced
Flat-leaf parsley leaves and aioli (optional), to serve

Heat 1 1/2 tbs oil in a deep frypan over medium heat. Add the onion and 3 garlic cloves and cook for 2-3 minutes until softened but not browned. Transfer to a bowl, reserving frypan, and set aside to cool completely.

Place pork mince, sausage meat, eggs, lemon zest, 2 tsp oregano and cooled onion mixture in a food processor and pulse to combine. Season, then add breadcrumbs and parmesan and pulse to combine. Divide mixture into 18 portions and roll into walnut-sized balls. Heat remaining 1 1/2 tbs oil in the reserved frypan over medium-high heat. Cook meatballs, turning, until golden. Add passata, sugar and remaining 2 garlic cloves and 2 tsp oregano, and stir gently to combine. Season, then simmer, uncovered, over low heat for 30 minutes or until sauce is reduced and meatballs are cooked through.

Preheat the grill to high. Split the rolls lengthways and place on a baking tray. Sprinkle over the mozzarella, then grill until the cheese is melted and bubbling.

To serve, fill rolls with meatballs and sauce, a little red onion and parsley, and a drizzle of aioli, if using. **Serves 6**

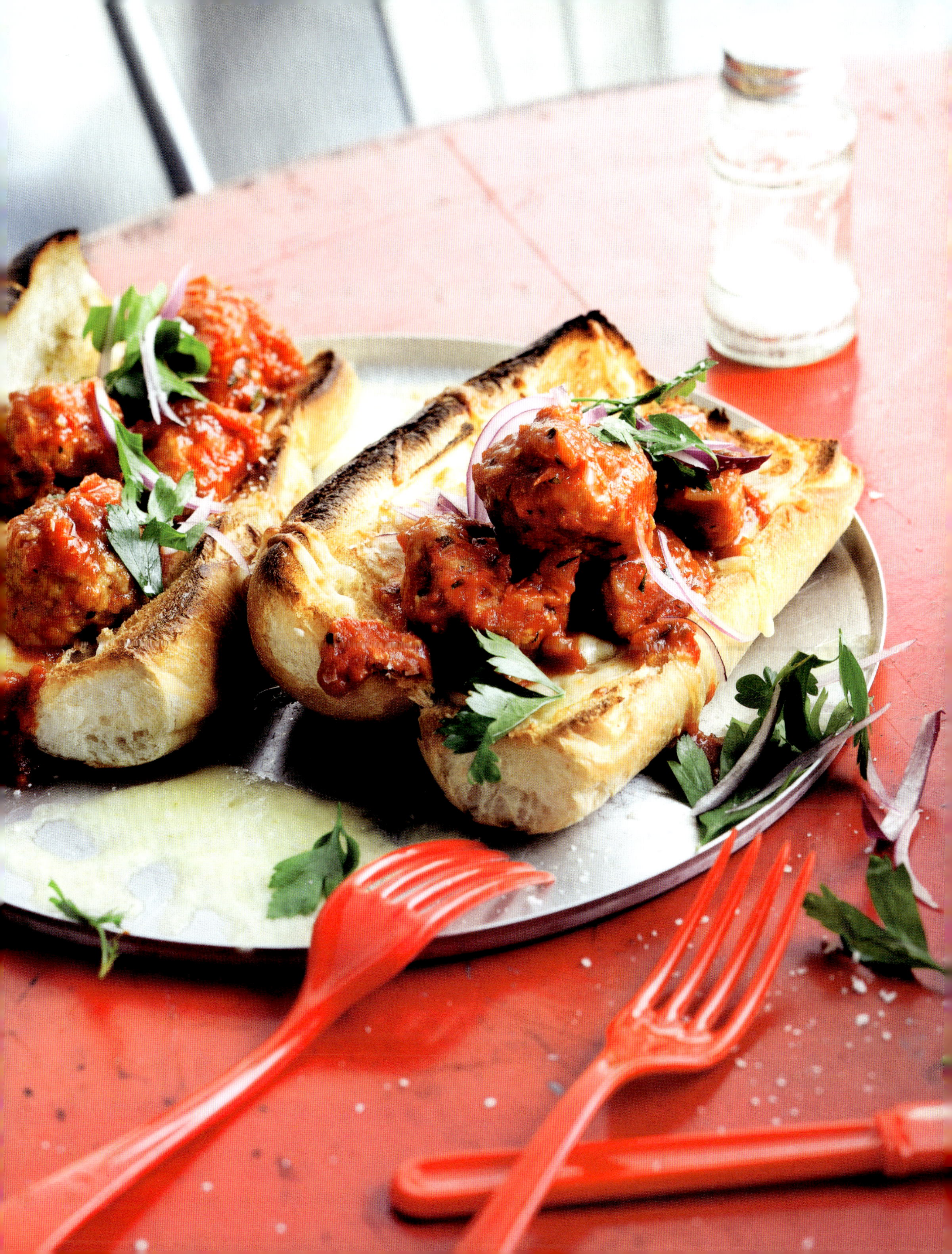

Boston baked beans

You will need to start this recipe at least a day ahead.

3¾ cups (750g) dried cannellini beans (sometimes sold as American beans)
1 smoked ham hock
2 onions, finely chopped
2 cups (500g) tomato ketchup
½ cup (125g) brown sugar
⅓ cup (80ml) maple syrup ⓟ
⅓ cup (120g) treacle
1 tbs Worcestershire sauce
1 tsp sweet smoked paprika (pimenton)
1 tbs English mustard powder
2 bay leaves

Place beans in a large bowl, cover with cold water, then set aside to soak overnight.

Preheat the oven to 120°C.

Drain the beans, rinse under cold water and drain again. Transfer to a large saucepan and cover with cold water. Bring to a simmer over medium-high heat, skimming any scum from the surface, then simmer for 15 minutes. Drain, reserving the cooking liquid. Transfer beans to a casserole or ovenproof saucepan with the remaining ingredients and enough of the cooking water to cover by 3cm. Cover with a lid, then cook for 8 hours or overnight.

Remove the ham hock and allow to cool slightly, then shred the meat, discarding skin and bone. Stir meat through the bean mixture and warm through before serving. **Serves 4-6**

ⓟ See Pantry essentials, p 123.

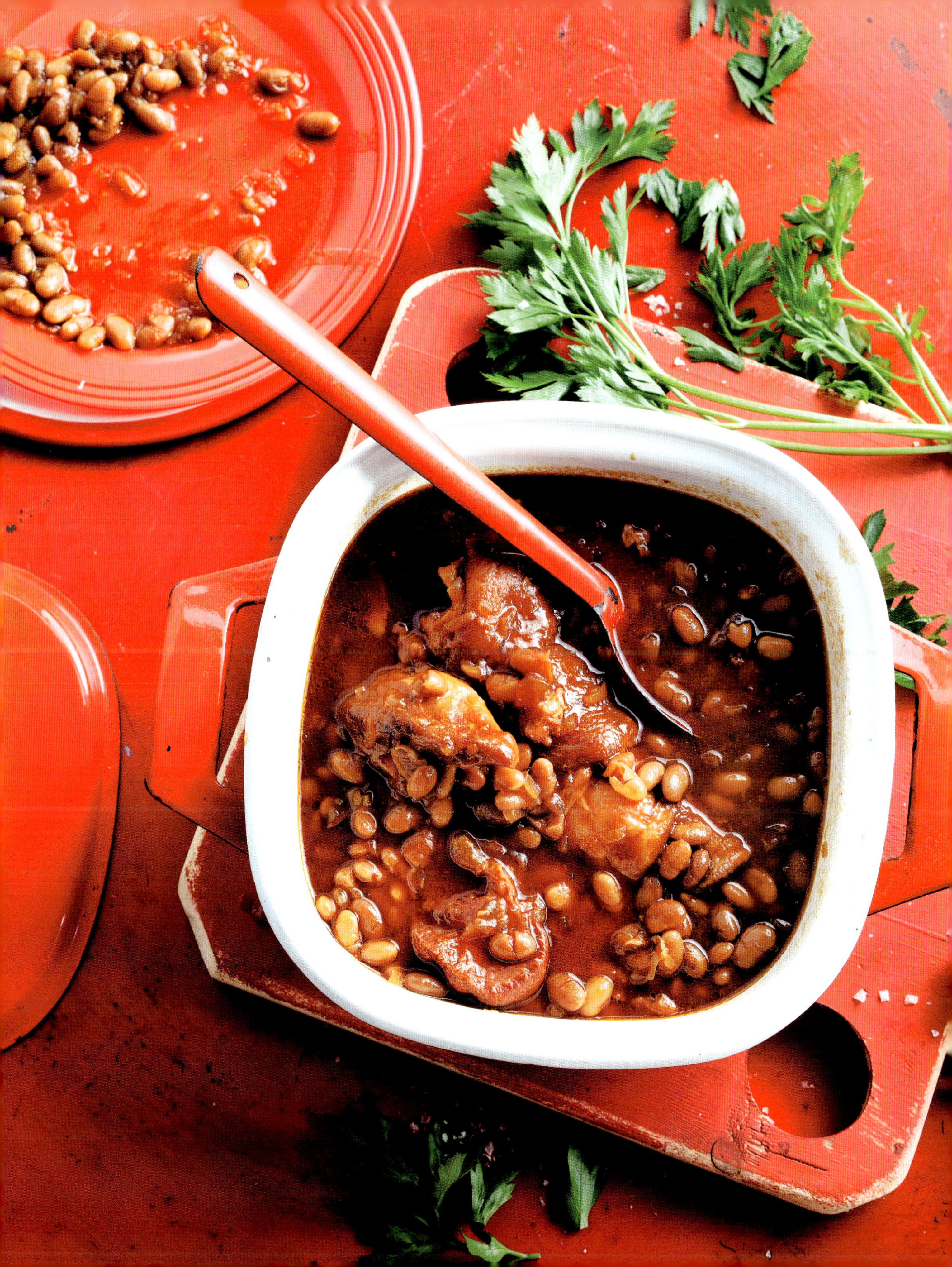

Southern fried chicken

Proper fried chicken is delicious. The secret is not to have the oil too hot, as you want to make sure the chicken cooks all the way through to the bone. I like to give it a few minutes in the oven after frying just to make sure.

1 cup (250ml) buttermilk
½ cup (125ml) Crystal hot sauce ⓟ or 2 tbs Tabasco ⓟ
4 chicken thigh cutlets (on the bone) and 4 drumsticks
2 cups (300g) plain flour
2 tbs onion powder
1 tsp cayenne pepper
2 tsp mustard powder
1 tsp paprika
1 tbs celery salt
1 tsp ground black pepper
Sunflower oil, to deep-fry
Creamy mashed potato, to serve

Coleslaw
¼ white cabbage
¼ red cabbage
2 carrots
1 tsp caster sugar
1 tbs white wine vinegar
2 tbs sour cream
125g whole-egg mayonnaise
1 tbs horseradish cream
2 spring onions, finely chopped
2 tbs finely chopped flat-leaf parsley

Combine buttermilk, hot sauce and 2 tbs salt in a bowl. Add the chicken and turn to coat well. Cover and refrigerate for 4 hours.

Meanwhile, for the coleslaw, using a mandoline, finely shred the cabbages and place in a large bowl. Grate the carrots on the large hole of a box grater and add to the cabbage. Whisk the sugar, vinegar, sour cream, mayonnaise and horseradish with 2 tbs warm water to make a loose dressing. Season, then add the dressing with the spring onion and parsley to the cabbage mixture and toss to combine. Cover and refrigerate until ready to serve.

Preheat oven to 170°C. Line a baking tray with baking paper.

Combine flour, onion powder, cayenne, mustard powder, paprika, celery salt and black pepper in a bowl. Drain the chicken, shaking off excess buttermilk, then coat well in the flour mixture. (If you have enough flour mixture, do a double coat.) Half-fill a deep-fryer or large saucepan with oil and heat to 160°C (a cube of bread will turn golden in 90 seconds when the oil is hot enough), then fry the chicken, in batches, until deep golden. Transfer to the prepared baking tray and transfer to the oven for 5-6 minutes until cooked through.

Serve the chicken with coleslaw and creamy mashed potato. **Serves 4**

ⓟ See Pantry essentials, p 123.

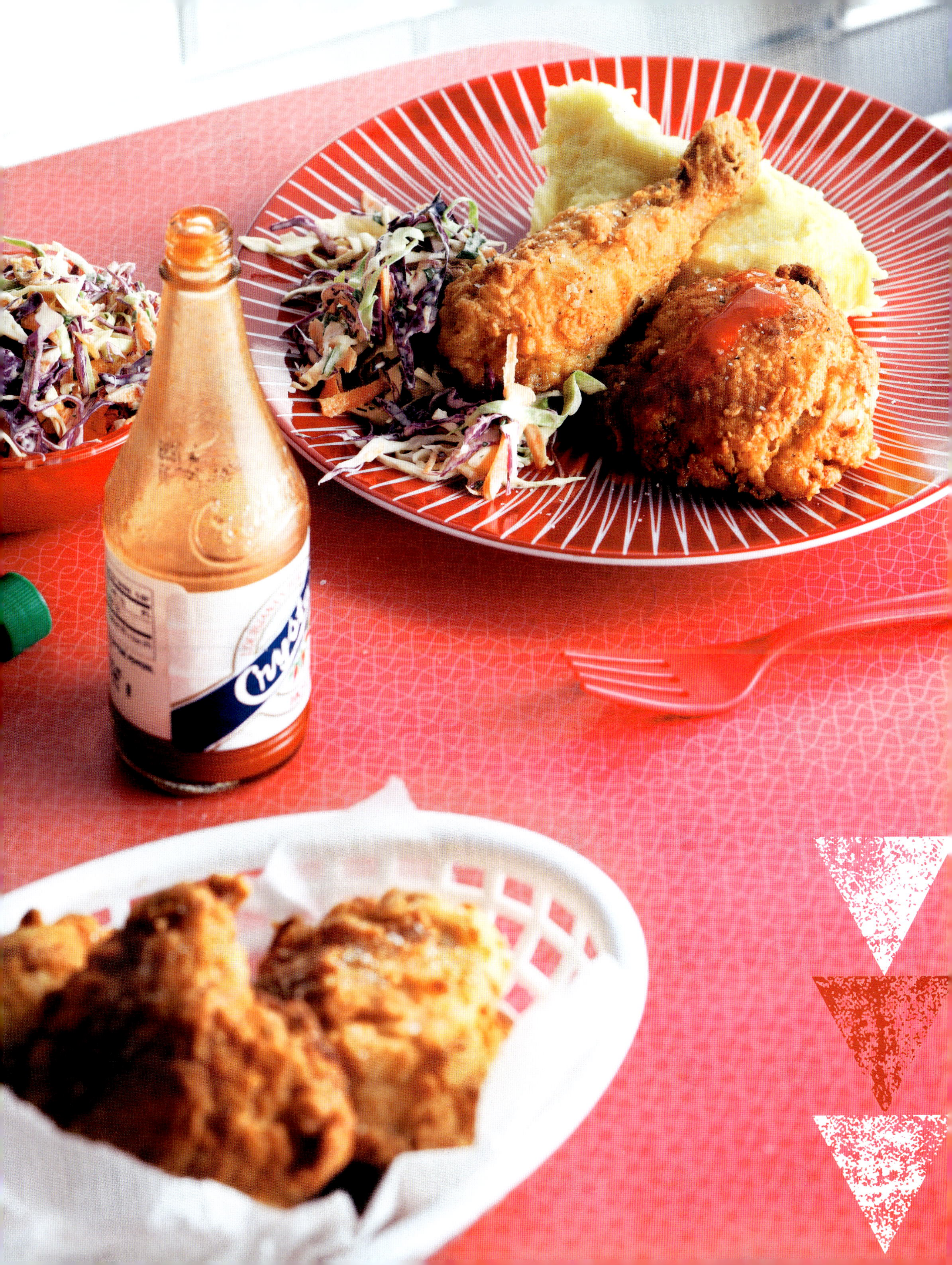

Deep-pan pizza

This style of pizza takes longer to bake than a traditional thin-crust pizza, but it's definitely well worth the wait.

1 tsp dried yeast
¼ tsp cream of tartar
1 tsp caster sugar
250g strong (baker's) flour
¼ cup (60ml) olive oil, plus extra to drizzle
1 small eggplant, cut into 2cm pieces
1 red capsicum, cut into 2cm pieces
1 zucchini, cut into 2cm pieces
1¼ cups (125g) grated mozzarella
⅓ cup (25g) grated pecorino
1 garlic clove, halved
400ml good-quality pizza sauce
Basil leaves, to serve

Combine yeast, cream of tartar, sugar and 150ml warm water in a bowl. Set aside for 10 minutes or until the mixture starts to froth. Place flour in a bowl with 1 tsp salt. Add yeast mixture and oil, then bring the dough together with your hands. Transfer to a floured surface and knead for 5-6 minutes until smooth and elastic. Transfer to an oiled bowl, cover with plastic wrap and set aside in a warm spot for 1 hour or until doubled in size.

Meanwhile, preheat the oven to 180°C. Line a baking tray with baking paper. Place eggplant, capsicum and zucchini on tray, drizzle with extra oil and season. Roast for 15 minutes or until tender. Set aside. Increase oven temperature to 200°C.

Combine the mozzarella and pecorino in a bowl.

Brush a 22cm or 24cm cast-iron pan with a little extra oil, then rub all over with the cut side of the garlic. Knock down dough, then, using your hands, stretch dough until it is large enough to line the pan halfway up the side (or roll out with a rolling pin). Scatter over half the cheese mixture, then the roasted vegetables, then the pizza sauce. Top with the remaining cheese mixture. Bake for 25 minutes or until the dough is puffed and golden around the edges, and the cheese is bubbling. Stand in the pan for 5 minutes before serving topped with basil. **Serves 2**

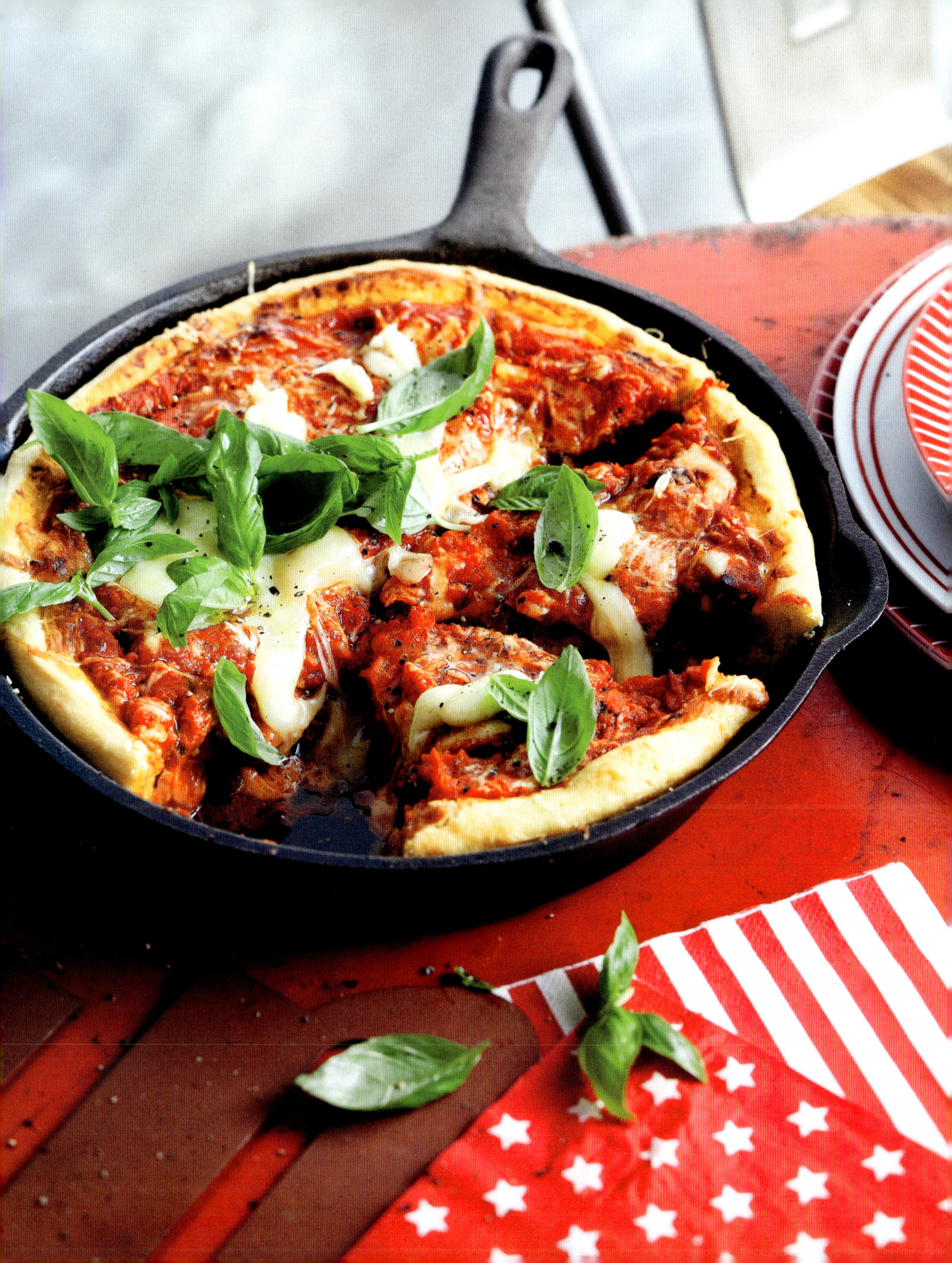

Mac 'n' cheese slice

This makes a large quantity, but once baked, it will keep in the fridge for 3-4 days, so you can fry up a slice whenever you feel like a snack. Alternatively, halve the quantities and bake in a 1-litre terrine. Start this recipe a day ahead.

400g macaroni
Olive oil, to drizzle
2 cups (500ml) milk
1 onion, halved
2 bay leaves
2 sprigs thyme
¼ tsp grated fresh nutmeg
80g unsalted butter
¼ cup (35g) plain flour
1¼ cups (150g) strong cheddar, grated
1¼ cups (155g) gruyere, grated
1¼ cups (100g) grated parmesan
1 egg, lightly beaten
Plain flour, to dust
Tomato wedges and rocket, to serve

Cook the macaroni in boiling salted water according to packet instructions. Drain and refresh in cold water. Transfer to a bowl, drizzle over a little olive oil and toss to combine.

Combine milk, onion, bay leaves, thyme and nutmeg in a saucepan over medium heat and bring to a simmer. Set aside for 30 minutes for the flavours to infuse.

Preheat the oven to 180°C. Grease and line a 12cm-deep, 12cm x 28cm terrine or loaf pan with baking paper.

Melt 40g butter in a saucepan over low heat. Add the flour and cook, stirring, for 1-2 minutes. Strain the milk into the pan, discarding solids, and whisk until smooth and thickened. Add the cheeses and stir to combine. Add the egg and stir to combine. Season. Add the sauce to the macaroni and toss to coat. Transfer macaroni mixture to the prepared terrine and bake for 30 minutes or until golden. Cool in the pan for 30 minutes, then refrigerate overnight.

Cut mac 'n' cheese into 2cm-thick slices and dust with flour. Heat the remaining 40g butter in a heavy-based frypan over medium-high heat and cook mac 'n' cheese for 2-3 minutes each side until golden and crisp.

Serve with tomato and rocket. **Serves 10-12**

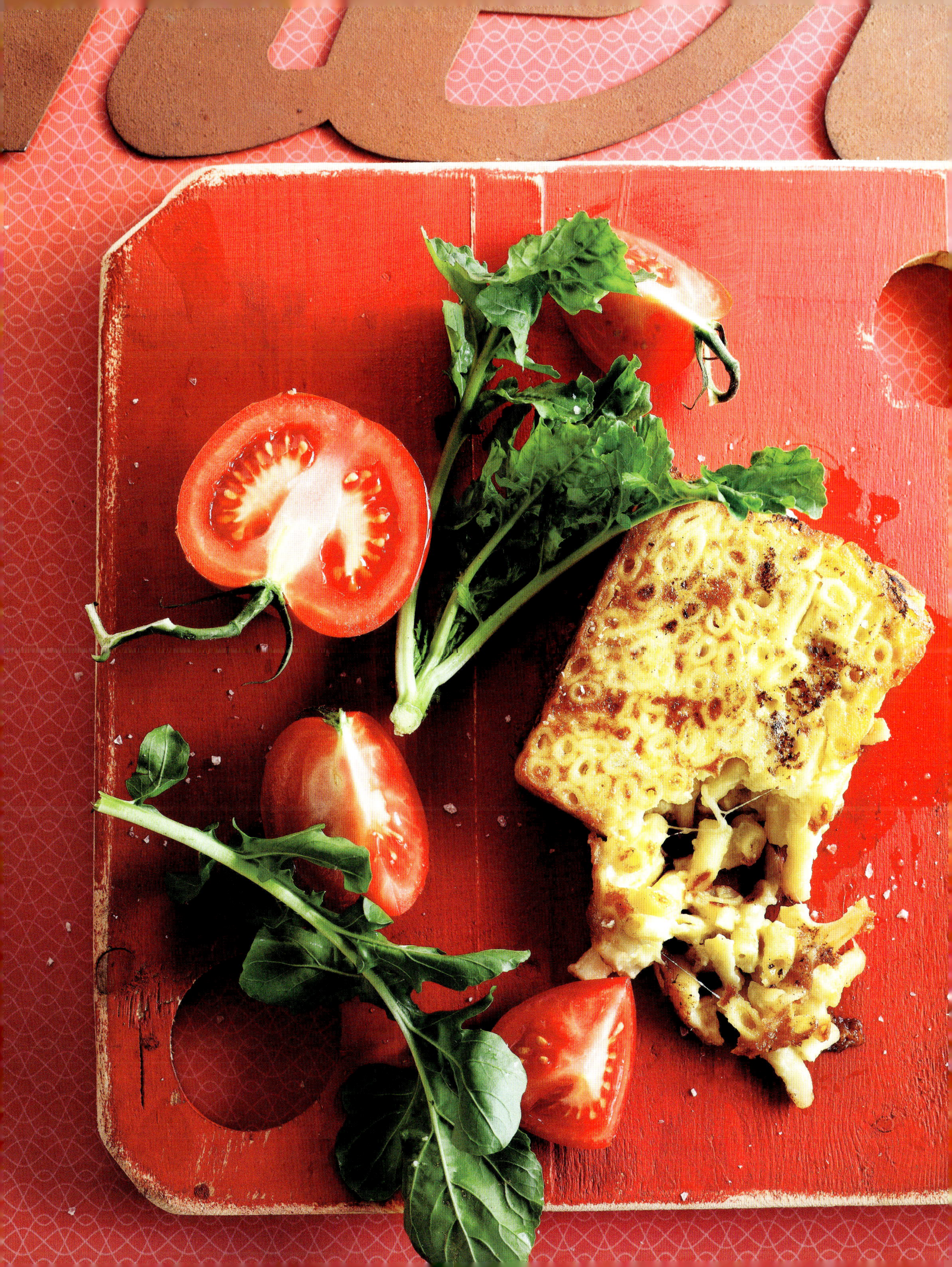

Cioppino

This hearty seafood stew originated in San Francisco and is considered a true Italian-American hybrid. Grilled sourdough, another San Fran invention, makes the perfect accompaniment to soak up the delicious sauce.

500g clams (vongole)
¼ cup (60ml) olive oil
1 thick Italian-style pork sausage, casing removed, crumbled
1 fennel bulb, finely chopped
1 onion, finely chopped
4 garlic cloves, finely chopped
2 tbs tomato paste
1 cup (250ml) dry white wine
3 cups (750ml) fish or chicken stock
400g can chopped tomatoes
2 tsp fish sauce
200g firm white boneless fish fillets (such as ling), cut into bite-size pieces
12 medium green prawns, peeled, deveined
500g pot-ready mussels
Juice of ½ lemon
2 tbs finely chopped flat-leaf parsley
Grilled sourdough, to serve

Soak clams in cold water for 15 minutes to remove any grit.

Heat 1 tbs oil in a large saucepan over medium heat. Add the sausage meat and cook, stirring, until browned and cooked through. Remove from pan and set aside. Wipe the pan clean with paper towel, then add remaining 2 tbs oil. Add the fennel, onion and garlic, and cook for 2-3 minutes until softened but not browned. Add the tomato paste and cook, stirring, for 1-2 minutes (this will add depth of flavour to the sauce). Add the white wine and cook for 3-4 minutes until reduced by half.

Add the stock, tomatoes and fish sauce, then simmer for 2-3 minutes. Add the fish and cook for 1 minute. Add the drained clams, prawns and mussels, cover with a lid and cook for 2-3 minutes until the clams and mussels have opened and prawns are cooked through. Season, then stir through the lemon juice and parsley. Serve the cioppino with grilled sourdough. **Serves 4-6**

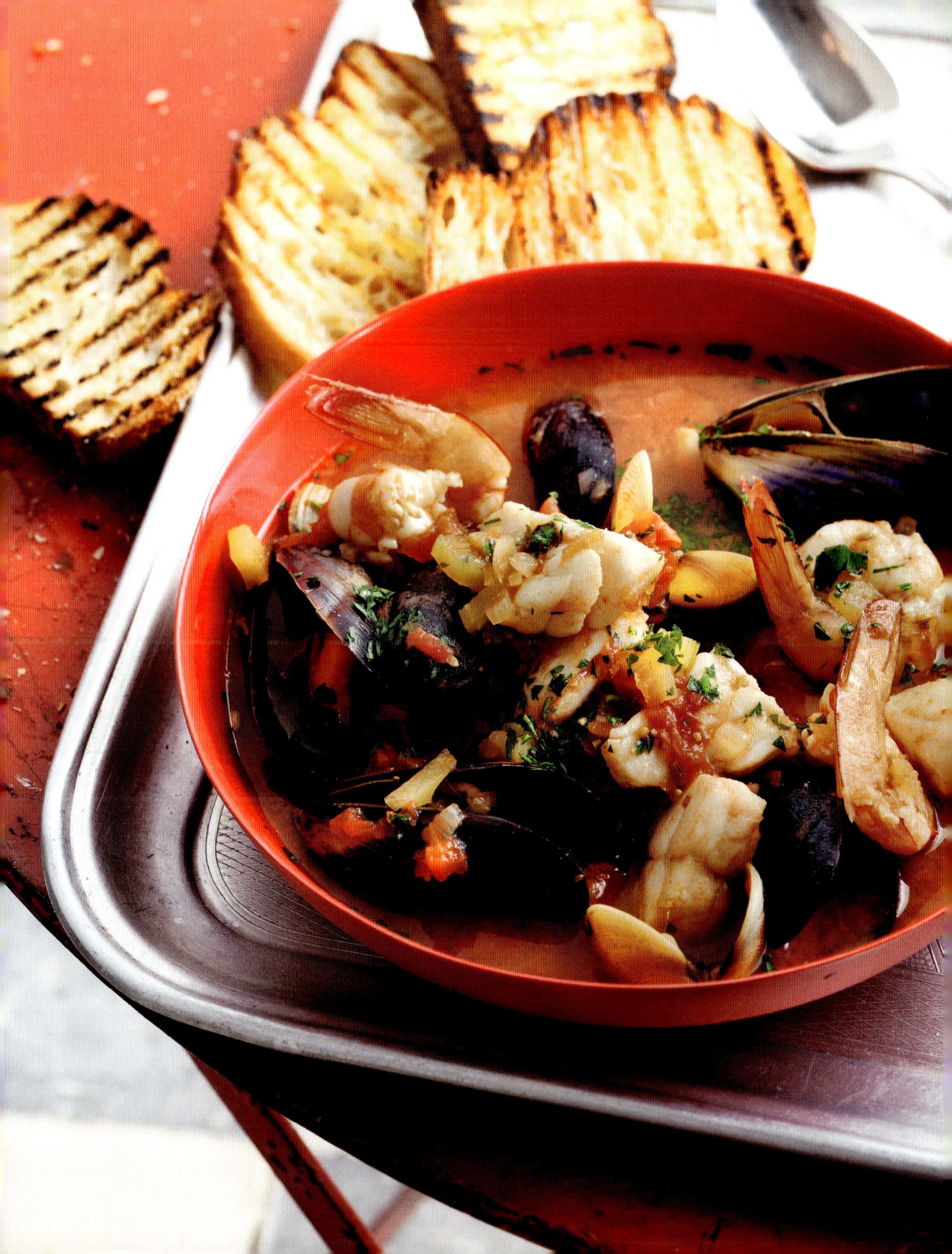

Plum cobbler

I love some of the crazy names of American desserts – cobblers, grunts and buckles to name but a few. This one may have got its name because the scone topping resembles cobblestones. You can make it with any seasonal fruit.

800g red plums, halved, stones removed
130g caster sugar
2 tsp cornflour
1 tbs lemon juice
½ tsp ground cinnamon
130g unsalted butter
1½ cups (225g) self-raising flour
1 egg
⅓ cup (80ml) buttermilk ⓟ
Icing sugar, to dust
Pure (thin) cream or vanilla ice cream, to serve

Preheat the oven to 180°C.

Place plums in a bowl and toss with ¼ cup (55g) sugar. Set aside for 30 minutes, stirring occasionally to release the juices. Drain plums, reserving juice, then transfer to a 1.5L (6-cup-capacity) baking dish.

Combine the cornflour with the reserved plum juice. Add lemon juice and cinnamon, and stir to combine. Pour over the plums, then dot with 30g butter. Bake for 15 minutes or until plums have softened. Remove from the oven and set aside to cool slightly.

Sift the flour and a pinch of salt into a bowl, then, using your fingers, rub in the remaining 100g butter until the mixture resembles coarse breadcrumbs. Stir in the remaining ⅓ cup (75g) sugar. Whisk the egg and buttermilk in a jug, then add to the flour mixture, stirring until a sticky dough forms. Transfer to a floured surface and roll out dough to 1cm thick. Using a 6cm plain cutter, cut out 12-14 rounds (the dough will be quite wet, so dip the cutter in flour each time to prevent it from sticking). Place dough rounds, very slightly overlapping, over the plum mixture, then bake for 20-25 minutes until golden.

Dust with icing sugar and serve with cream or vanilla ice cream. **Serves 6**

ⓟ See Pantry essentials, p 123.

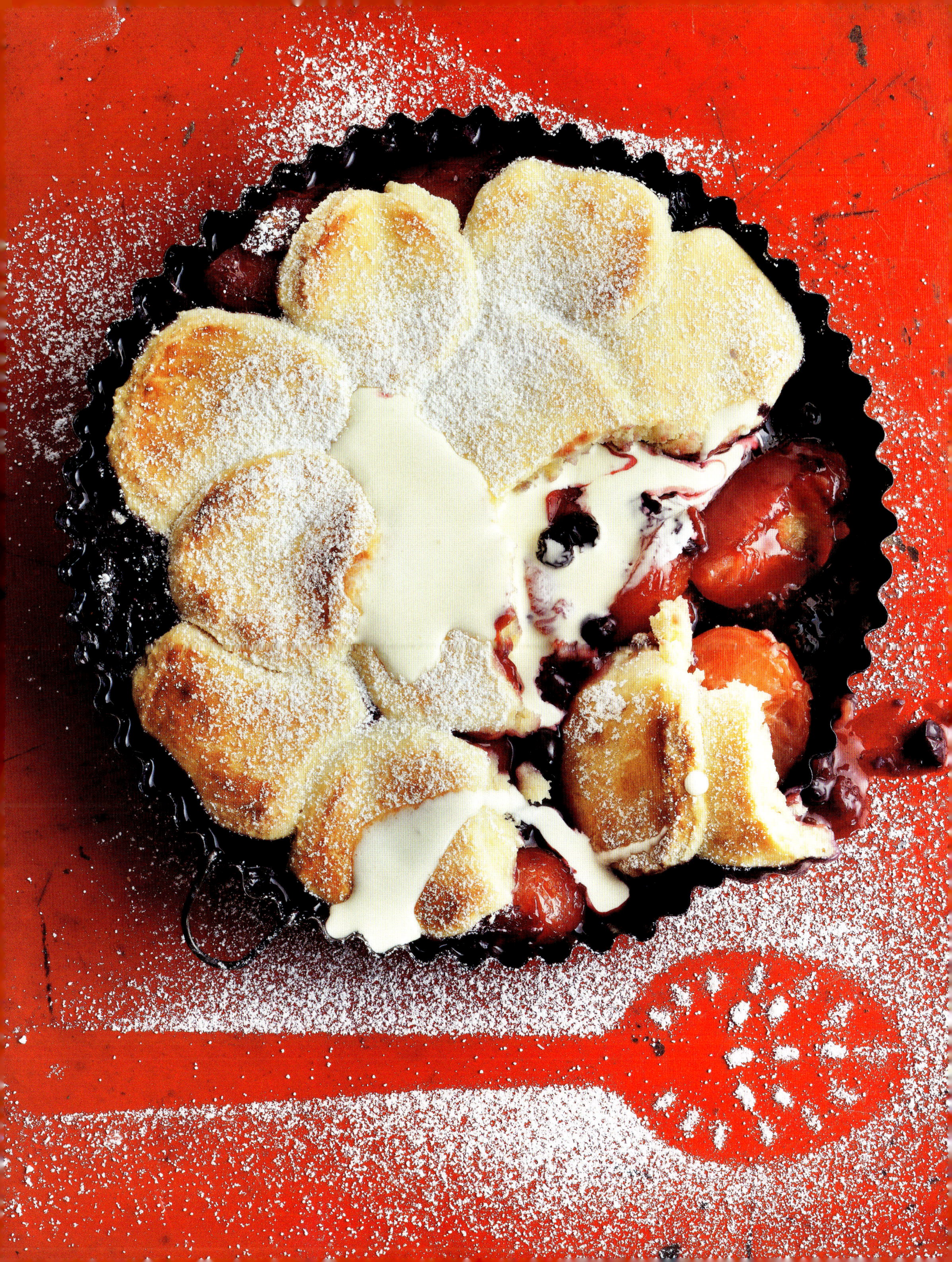

Cola cakes

We baked these cute little cola cakes in small glass jars, but you can make the recipe as a whole cake, if you prefer.

1½ cups (225g) plain flour
1 tsp bicarbonate of soda
1 cup (220g) caster sugar
65g unsalted butter
⅓ cup (80ml) sunflower oil
100g mini marshmallows
¼ cup (25g) cocoa powder
200ml cola
100ml buttermilk ⓟ
2 eggs, lightly beaten
Vanilla ice cream, to serve

Preheat the oven to 180°C. Grease 6 x 1-cup-capacity (250ml) jars or grease and line a 25cm cake pan.

Sift flour and bicarbonate of soda into a bowl. Add the sugar and stir to combine. Combine the butter, oil, marshmallows, cocoa and cola in a saucepan over medium heat and bring to the boil, whisking gently to melt the marshmallows and dissolve the cocoa. Add to the flour mixture and stir to combine. Add the buttermilk and eggs, and stir to combine. Divide mixture among jars or pour into the prepared cake pan. Bake cakes in jars for 25 minutes, or cake in pan for 45 minutes or until a skewer comes out clean. Cool slightly.

Serve cakes warm, topped with vanilla ice cream.

Serves 6 (in jars) or 8 as a whole cake

ⓟ See Pantry essentials, p 123.

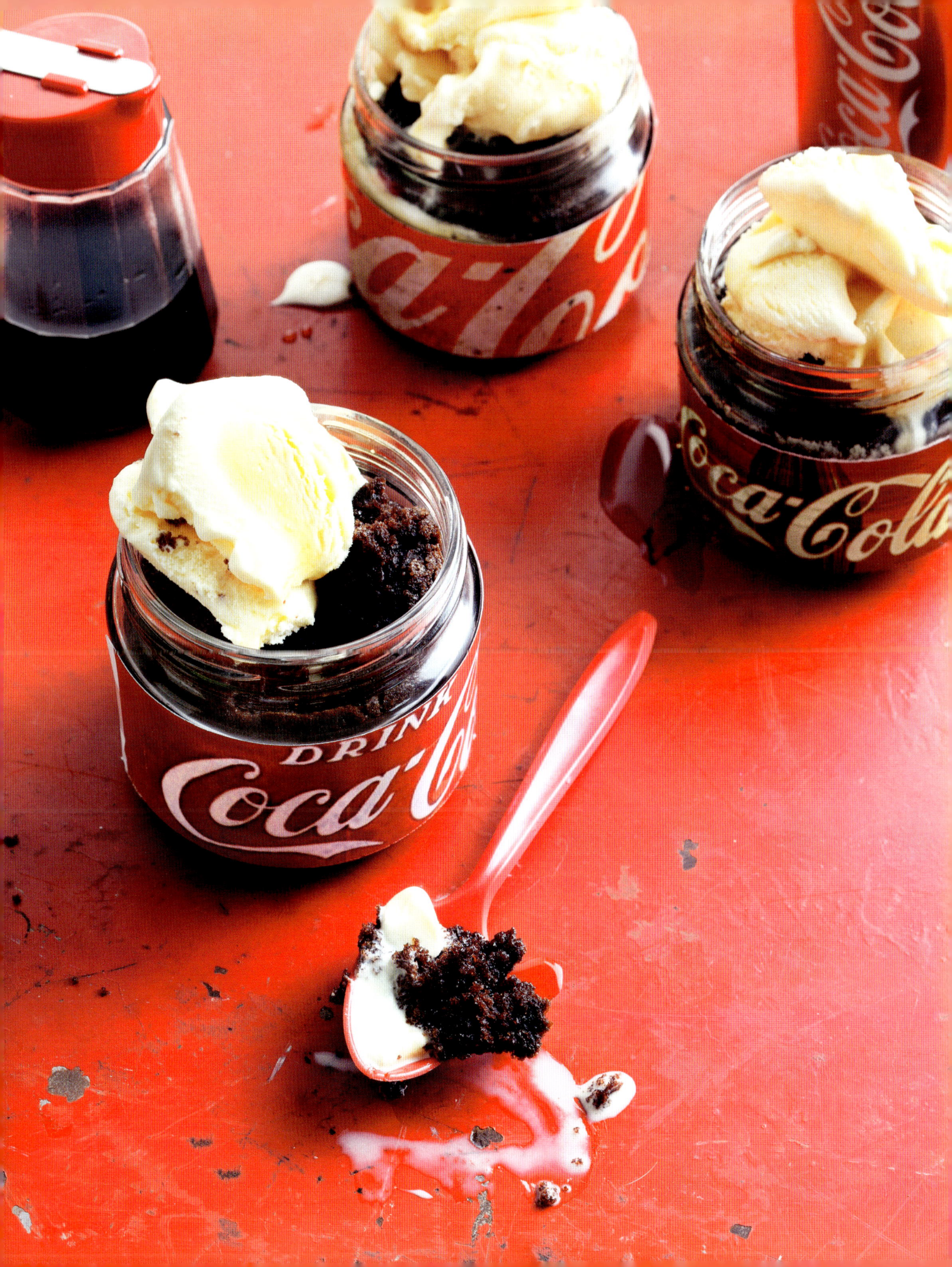
DRINK

Mississippi mud pie

300g frozen dark chocolate shortcrust pastry*, thawed or 1 quantity chocolate shortcrust pastry (see Basics, p 294)
400g dark chocolate, chopped
175g unsalted butter, softened
350g dark muscovado or dark brown sugar
4 eggs
1/3 cup (35g) cocoa powder
300ml thickened cream, whisked to soft peaks
2 tbs creme de cacao (chocolate liqueur, optional)
50g white chocolate, chopped

Preheat the oven to 160°C. Grease a 26cm, 3cm-deep loose-bottomed tart pan. Roll out pastry and use to line the pan. Refrigerate for 15 minutes. Prick the pastry base with a fork, then line with baking paper and fill with pastry weights. Bake for 10 minutes. Remove paper and weights, and return to the oven for a further 3 minutes or until the pastry is dry and crisp. Cool slightly in pan.

Melt 200g dark chocolate in a heatproof bowl set over a small saucepan of simmering water (don't let the bowl touch the water) and stir until smooth. Set aside to cool.

Using an electric mixer, beat the butter and sugar until thick and creamy. Add the eggs, 1 at a time, beating well after each addition. Add the cooled chocolate and beat until combined. Sift over the cocoa and fold into the mixture, then fold in the whipped cream and creme de cacao, if using. Pour mixture into the pastry case, then bake for 45-50 minutes until just set (the centre should still be quite wobbly). Turn off the oven and leave the pie in the oven for a further 30 minutes or until set. Remove from the oven and set aside in the pan to cool completely.

To make the topping, melt the white chocolate and remaining 200g dark chocolate separately in heatproof bowls set over a small saucepan of simmering water (don't let the bowls touch the water) and stir until smooth. Set aside to cool slightly. Pour the melted dark chocolate over the tart and spread by tipping the tart gently until the chocolate covers the tart to the edge. Place the melted white chocolate in a small piping bag and drizzle in thin lines across the top of the dark chocolate glaze.

Serve pie immediately or set aside for 30 minutes for chocolate to set before serving. **Serves 8-10**

* *We used Carême brand, available from specialist food shops. For stockists, visit: caremepastry.com.*

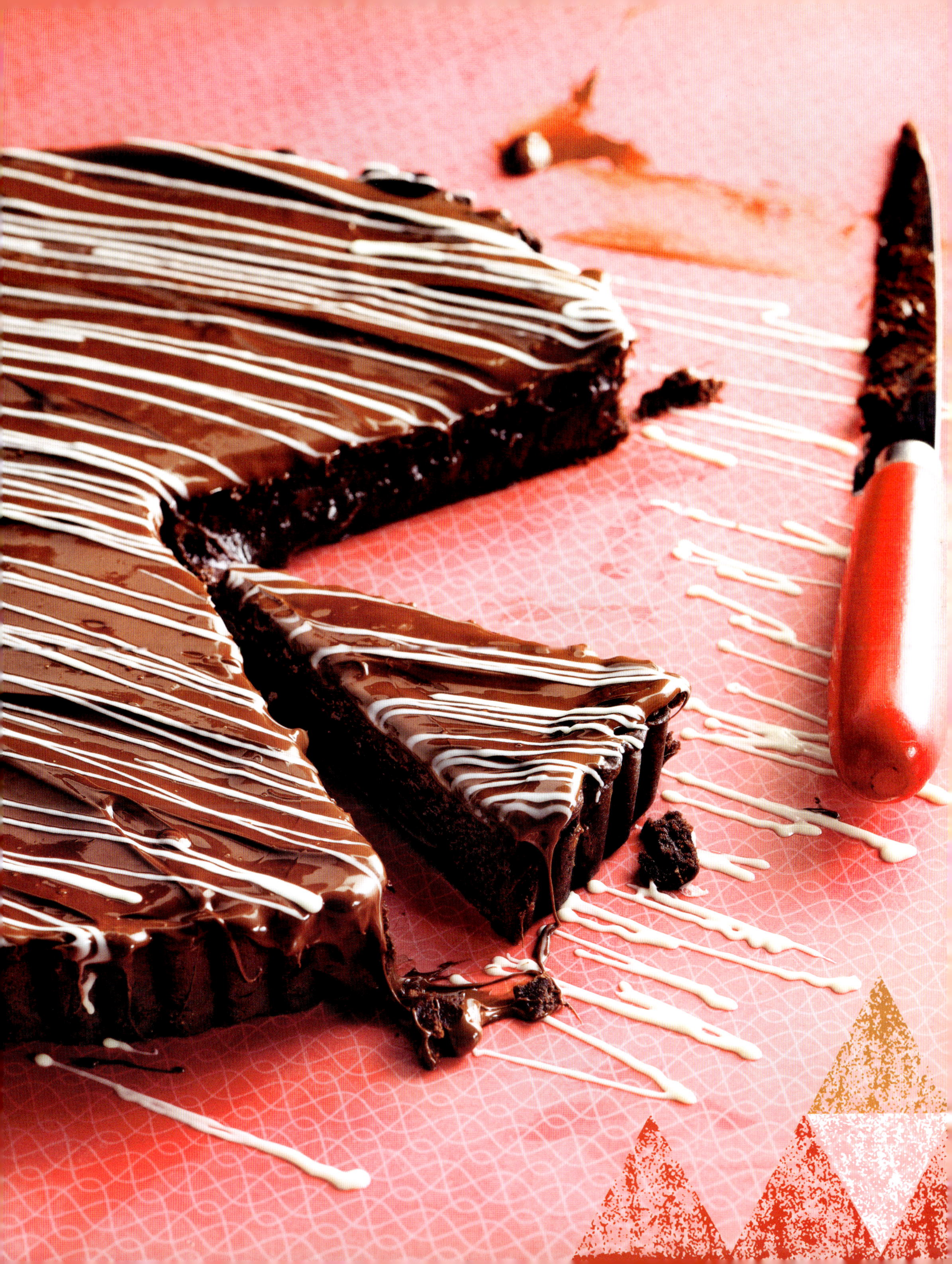

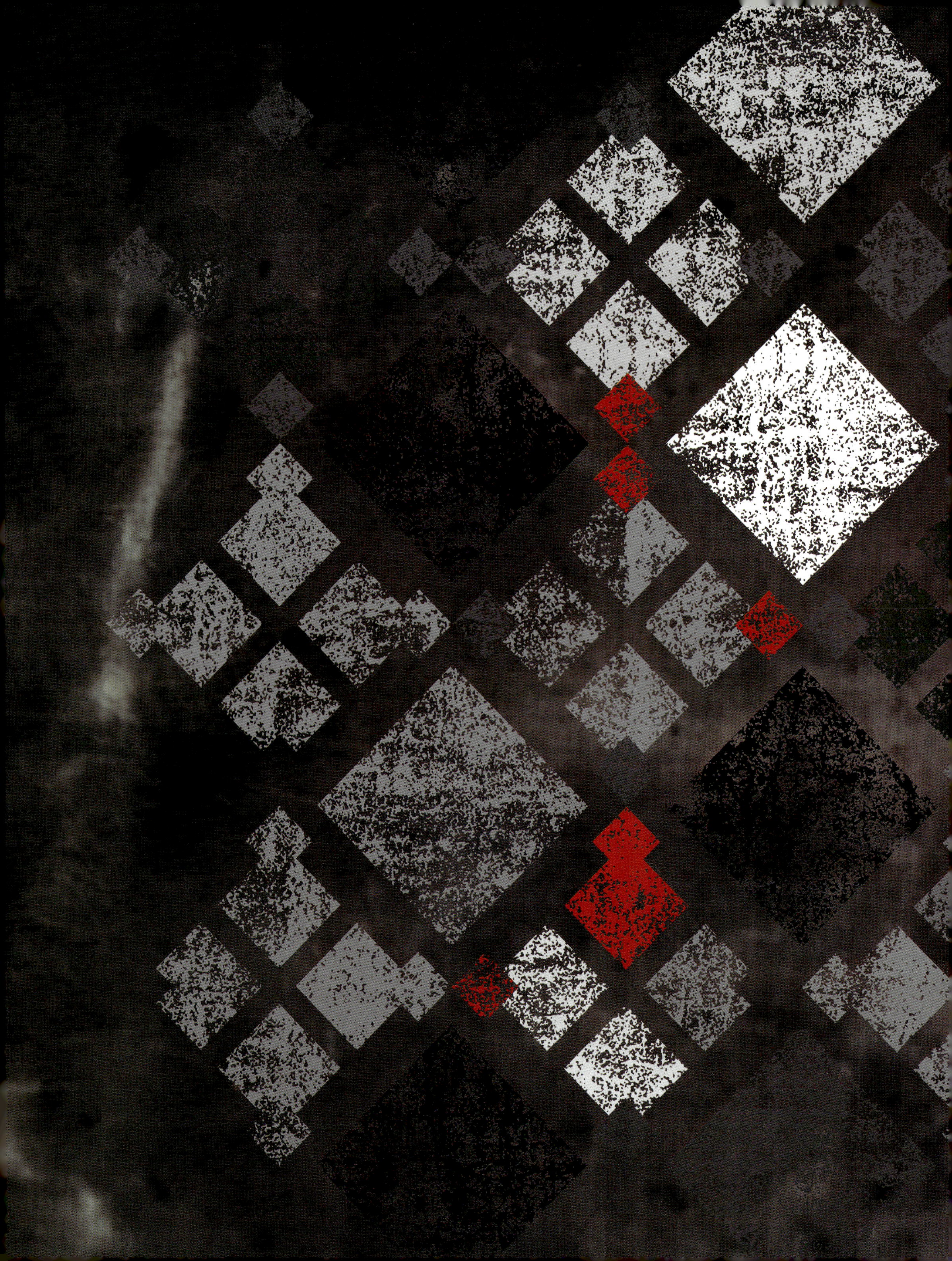

ASIAN

While such a broad canvas requires a book of its own, Asian staples include peanut or sunflower oil and toasted sesame oil; rice vinegar and wine; rice and noodles; coconut milk and cream; and sauces including light and dark soy, tamari, hoi sin, oyster and sriracha. Garlic, ginger, onion, fresh chillies, herbs and lime add to this powerhouse of flavours. Available from Asian food shops and increasingly in supermarkets and greengrocers.

PANTRY ESSENTIALS

Asian (red) eschalots
This red-skinned variety is more pungent than regular golden eschalots, which can be substituted.

Chillies
From searingly hot tiny red 'scuds' and birdseye chillies to milder long red and green varieties.

Chinese black (chinkiang) vinegar
Traditionally used as a dipping sauce for dumplings, it also adds complexity to braises and stir-fries.

Chinese rice wine (shaohsing)
Made from fermented glutinous rice with a mild, sake-like flavour; substitute dry sherry.

Coconut milk & cream
Used to enrich and thicken Southeast Asian curries. Coconut cream is used in desserts and to finish salads and savoury dishes.

Curry pastes
Massaman for rich, meat-based curries, green curry for poultry and fish; tom yum for spicy soups and stir-fries.

Fish sauce
Made from fish fermented with sea salt, and integral to that holy quartet of flavour balance in Thai cooking – salty, sour, sweet and bitter.

Fried Asian shallots
Thinly sliced and deep-fried, they're used to add crunch and texture, and as a garnish.

Herbs
Thai basil (substitute sweet basil), Vietnamese mint, kaffir lime leaves, lemongrass and coriander.

Mirin
A low-alcohol Japanese rice wine used to flavour rice and sauces; substitute dry sherry with a pinch of sugar.

Oyster sauce
Produced by slowly cooking down oysters to form an intense, dark syrup. Adds savour and richness.

Palm sugar
Varies in colour and consistency, and is often sold in blocks that need to be grated or shaved to use. Substitute brown or dark brown sugar.

Panko breadcrumbs
Coarse Japanese breadcrumbs that give a very crisp finish; substitute dried breadcrumbs.

Pickled ginger (gari)
Thinly sliced fresh ginger, pickled in vinegar and sugar.

Rice vinegar
A pale, mild style; substitute white vinegar with a pinch of sugar. Seasoned rice vinegar has added sugar and salt and is used to flavour sushi rice.

Sesame oil
Used to add flavour to finished dishes or in dressings.

Sriracha
A Thai bottled condiment containing chillies, vinegar, sugar, garlic and salt.

Tamarind puree
A thick, dark, sour paste made by cooking down tamarind pods; substitute vinegar or lime juice.

Wasabi peas
Dried green peas coated with wasabi (the hot, mustard-like brassica used to make green wasabi paste), sugar and salt.

Wonton wrappers
Thin wheat-flour and egg pastry sheets, about 8cm square, sold in packets. Spring-roll (lumpia) wrappers are slightly thinner and made with rice flour.

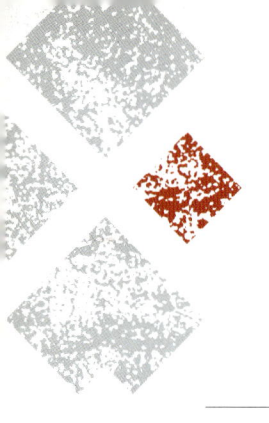

Korean beef with quick kimchi

Kimchi is considered the national dish of Korea, with as many variations as there are family kitchens. At its most basic, this piquantly sour dish is simply fermented cabbage, but here I've added aromatics for flavour and heat.

500g beef fillet, cut into strips across the grain
2 tbs soy sauce
2 tbs mirin ⓟ
½ tsp mustard powder
2 garlic cloves, crushed
2 tsp sesame oil ⓟ
⅓ cup (50g) sesame seeds
Steamed rice (optional), to serve

Quick kimchi
½ Chinese cabbage (wombok), torn into 3cm pieces
1 small red onion, halved, thinly sliced
2 garlic cloves, finely chopped
2 tbs drained finely shredded pickled ginger ⓟ
1 long red chilli, seeds removed, finely chopped
¾ cup (180ml) rice vinegar ⓟ
2 tbs Sriracha sauce ⓟ
¼ cup (55g) caster sugar

For the quick kimchi, combine cabbage in a 1L (4-cup-capacity) jar with the onion, garlic, ginger and chilli. Combine vinegar, Sriracha, sugar and ½ cup (125ml) water in a saucepan over low heat, stirring until the sugar dissolves. Pour vinegar mixture over the cabbage, then seal the lid and shake well to combine. Refrigerate for at least 2 hours before using. Store in the refrigerator for up to 1 week.

Soak 12 bamboo skewers in cold water for 30 minutes. Place beef in a bowl. Combine soy, mirin, mustard powder, garlic, sesame oil and 2 tbs sesame seeds in a bowl, and stir to combine. Add marinade to the beef and toss to coat. Set aside for 1 hour.

Heat a chargrill or barbecue to medium-high. Thread beef onto skewers, then cook for 2-3 minutes, turning, until lightly charred. Sprinkle with remaining 2 tbs sesame seeds and serve with quick kimchi and steamed rice, if using. **Serves 4-6**
ⓟ See Pantry essentials, p 151.

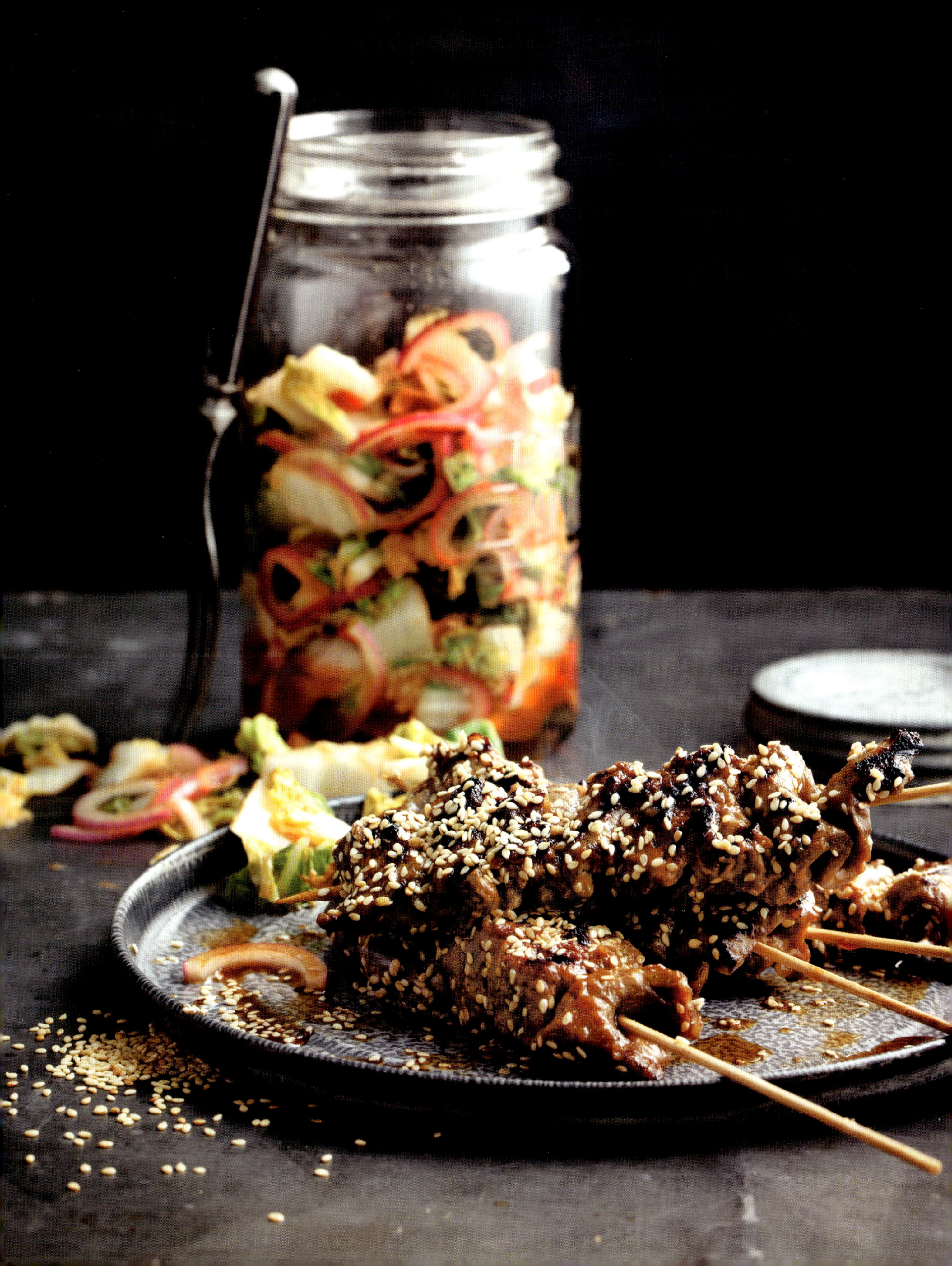

Chicken & banana blossom salad

¼ cup (60ml) peanut oil
3 Asian (red) eschalots, ⓟ finely chopped
3 garlic cloves, finely chopped
2 long red chillies, seeds removed, finely chopped
⅓ cup (80ml) fish sauce ⓟ
½ cup (135g) grated palm sugar ⓟ or brown sugar
⅓ cup (80ml) lime juice
1 banana blossom*
2 tbs lemon juice
500g shredded cooked chicken
2 cups each Thai basil, ⓟ mint and coriander leaves
4 spring onions, finely shredded
¼ cup (10g) toasted coconut flakes
¼ cup fried Asian shallots ⓟ

Heat peanut oil in a saucepan over medium heat, add the eschalot and cook, stirring, for 1-2 minutes until softened. Add garlic and chilli, and cook, stirring, for a further 30 seconds or until fragrant. Add the fish sauce, palm sugar and lime juice. Simmer for 1 minute, then remove from heat and cool.

Remove and discard the dark outer leaves from the banana blossom, reserving 4 medium-sized leaves to serve. Peel away the inner leaves, discarding the stamens, and finely shred. Immediately transfer to a bowl of cold water with the lemon juice (this will prevent the leaves from going brown). When ready to serve, drain the banana blossom and pat dry with paper towel. Place in a bowl with the chicken, herbs, spring onion, coconut and fried shallots. Toss with enough dressing to coat. Pile chicken mixture into the reserved leaves and serve with remaining dressing on the side. **Serves 4**

* *Banana blossoms are the buds of the banana plant, available from Asian grocers and selected greengrocers and supermarkets.*
ⓟ *See Pantry essentials, p 151.*

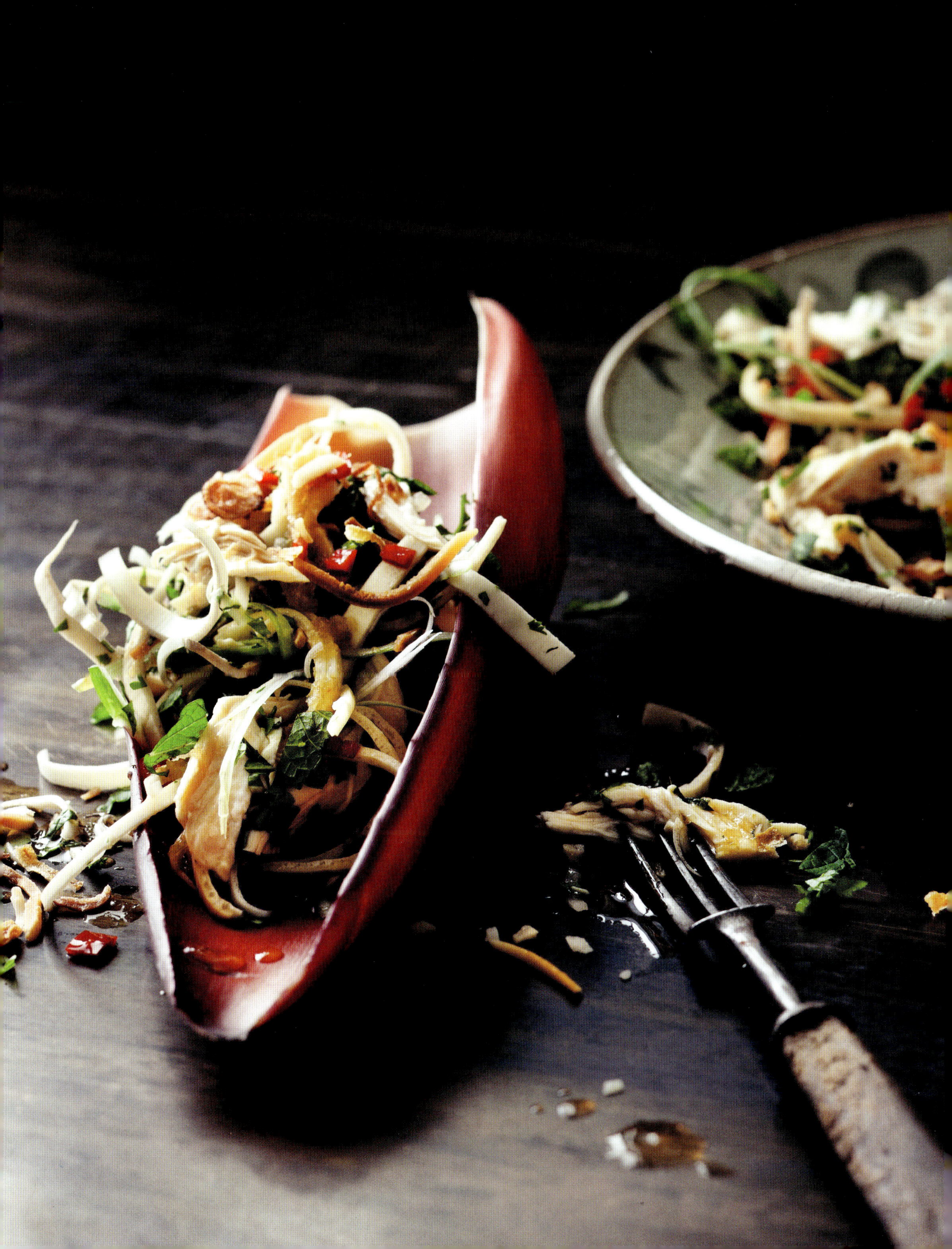

Wasabi-crumbed squid with chilli dipping sauce

¼ cup (60ml) soy sauce
1 tbs mirin ⓟ
1 tbs rice vinegar ⓟ
2 tsp caster sugar
1 long red chilli, seeds removed, finely chopped
100g wasabi peas ⓟ
2 cups (100g) panko (Japanese) breadcrumbs ⓟ
⅔ cup (100g) plain flour
3 eggwhites, lightly whisked
1kg small squid, cleaned, tentacles reserved, tubes cut into 1cm rings
Peanut or vegetable oil, to deep-fry

For the chilli dipping sauce, combine soy, mirin, rice vinegar, caster sugar and chilli in a small bowl, stirring until the sugar dissolves. Set aside until ready to serve.

Using a food processor, whiz the wasabi peas until finely crushed. Add breadcrumbs and pulse to combine, then transfer to a bowl. Place flour and eggwhite in separate bowls. Dust squid in flour, shaking off excess, then dip in eggwhite, then wasabi crumbs, shaking off excess.

Half-fill a deep-fryer or large saucepan with oil and heat to 190°C (a cube of bread will turn golden in 30 seconds when the oil is hot enough). Fry the squid, in batches, for 2-3 minutes until golden and crisp. Drain on paper towel.

Serve with chilli dipping sauce. **Serves 4-6 as a starter**
ⓟ See Pantry essentials, p 151.

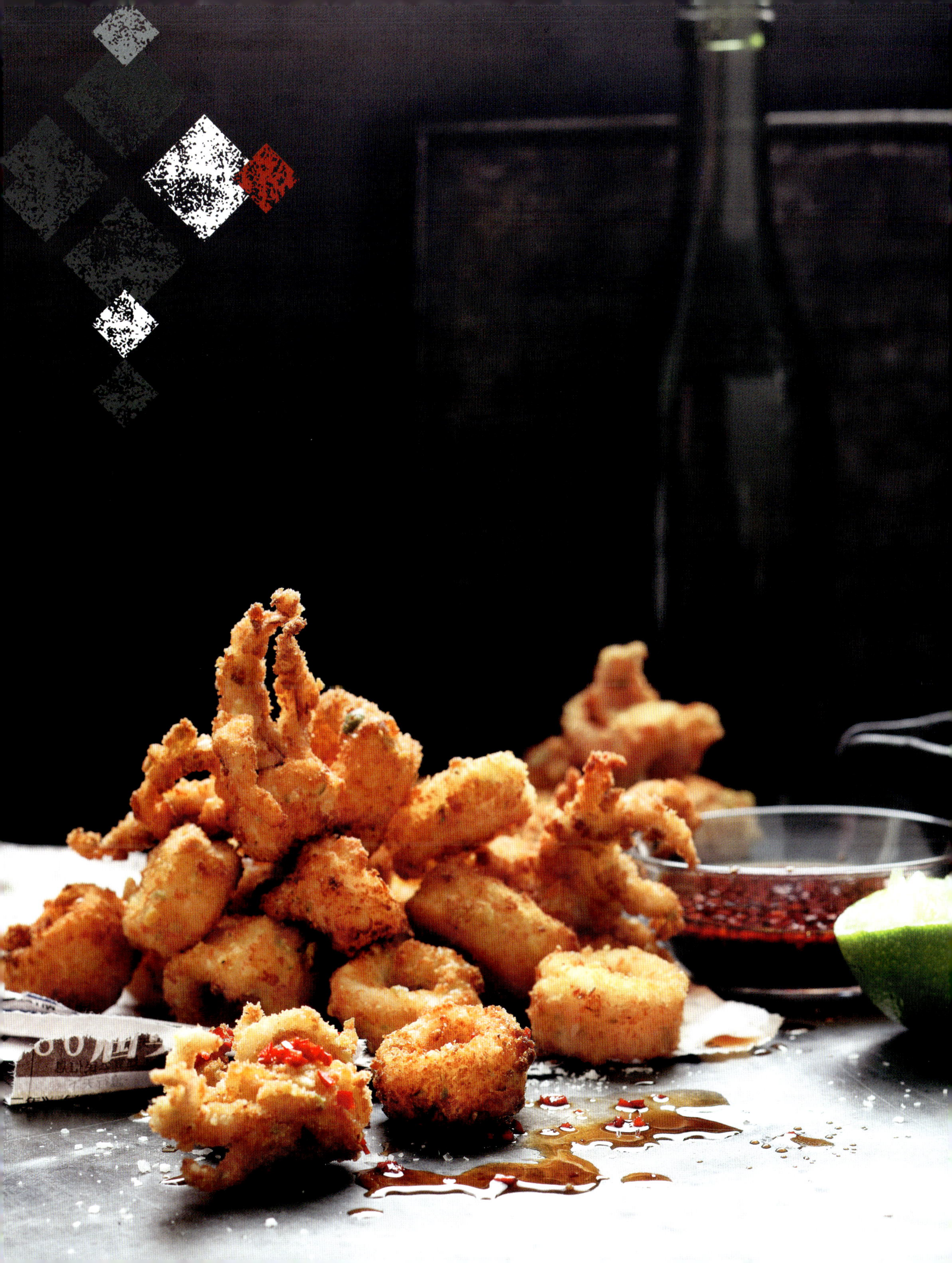

Crying tiger beef with dipping sauce

Its Thai name, 'suea rong hai', translates to 'crying tiger', as its fiery dipping sauce is said to bring tears to the eyes. I've tamed this one a little, in the hope that it will bring tears of joy!

2 tbs fish sauce ⓟ
1 tbs oyster sauce ⓟ
1 tbs soy sauce
2 tbs brandy
2 garlic cloves, crushed
¼ cup (60ml) peanut oil
1 tsp caster sugar
500g beef eye fillet, trimmed
Snow pea shoots or watercress, to serve

Dipping sauce
1 long red chilli, seeds removed, chopped
1 long green chilli, seeds removed, finely chopped
Pinch of chilli flakes (optional)
1 tbs caster sugar
¼ cup (60ml) lime juice
¼ cup (60ml) fish sauce
2 Asian (red) eschalots, ⓟ thinly sliced

Combine sauces, brandy, garlic, oil and caster sugar in a large ziplock bag. Add the beef and massage to coat well. (Alternatively, place mixture in a bowl, add beef and turn to coat well.) Refrigerate for 4 hours or overnight.

For the dipping sauce, combine all the ingredients in a small bowl, stirring until the sugar dissolves.

Preheat a chargrill or barbecue to medium-high. Remove beef from marinade, discarding marinade, and cook, turning, for 8-10 minutes until charred but still quite rare or until cooked to your liking. Rest the beef, loosely covered, for 10 minutes. Thinly slice and serve with the dipping sauce and snow pea shoots. **Serves 4-6**

ⓟ See Pantry essentials, p 151.

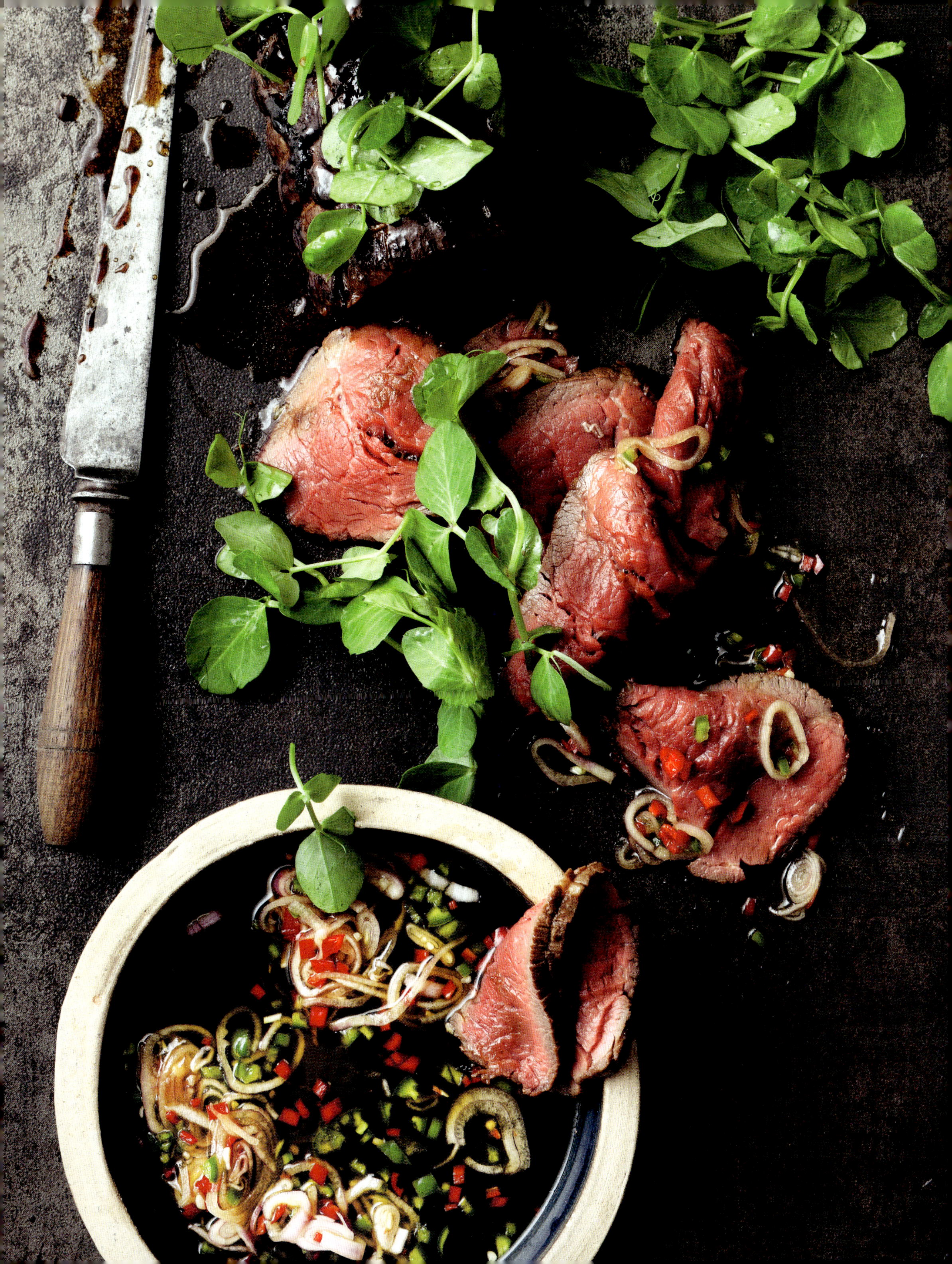

Asian tartare with crisp wontons

This simple and refreshing tartare is perfect to serve as a canape before an Asian meal, and can be put together in minutes.

Peanut oil, to shallow-fry
12 wonton wrappers ⓟ
250g piece skinless salmon, pin-boned, finely chopped
2 tbs fish sauce ⓟ
Juice of 1 lime
1 tbs light soy sauce
1 tsp caster sugar
1 long red chilli, seeds removed, finely chopped
2 Asian (red) eschalots, ⓟ finely chopped
½ garlic clove, crushed
2 tbs finely chopped coriander
1 tbs finely chopped Vietnamese mint ⓟ
1 tbs finely chopped mint, plus extra leaves to serve
Salmon roe (optional), to serve

Heat 2cm oil in a frypan over medium-high heat. Fry the wonton wrappers for 1 minute or until golden and crisp. Transfer to a plate lined with paper towel and sprinkle with sea salt.

To make the tartare, place all the remaining ingredients, except roe, in a bowl and stir to combine. Top with salmon roe, if using, and extra mint leaves and serve with crisp wontons.

Serves 3-4 as a starter

ⓟ See Pantry essentials, p 151.

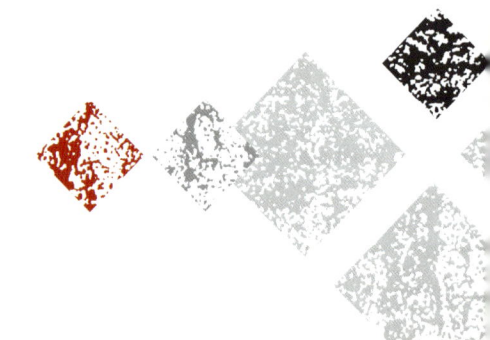

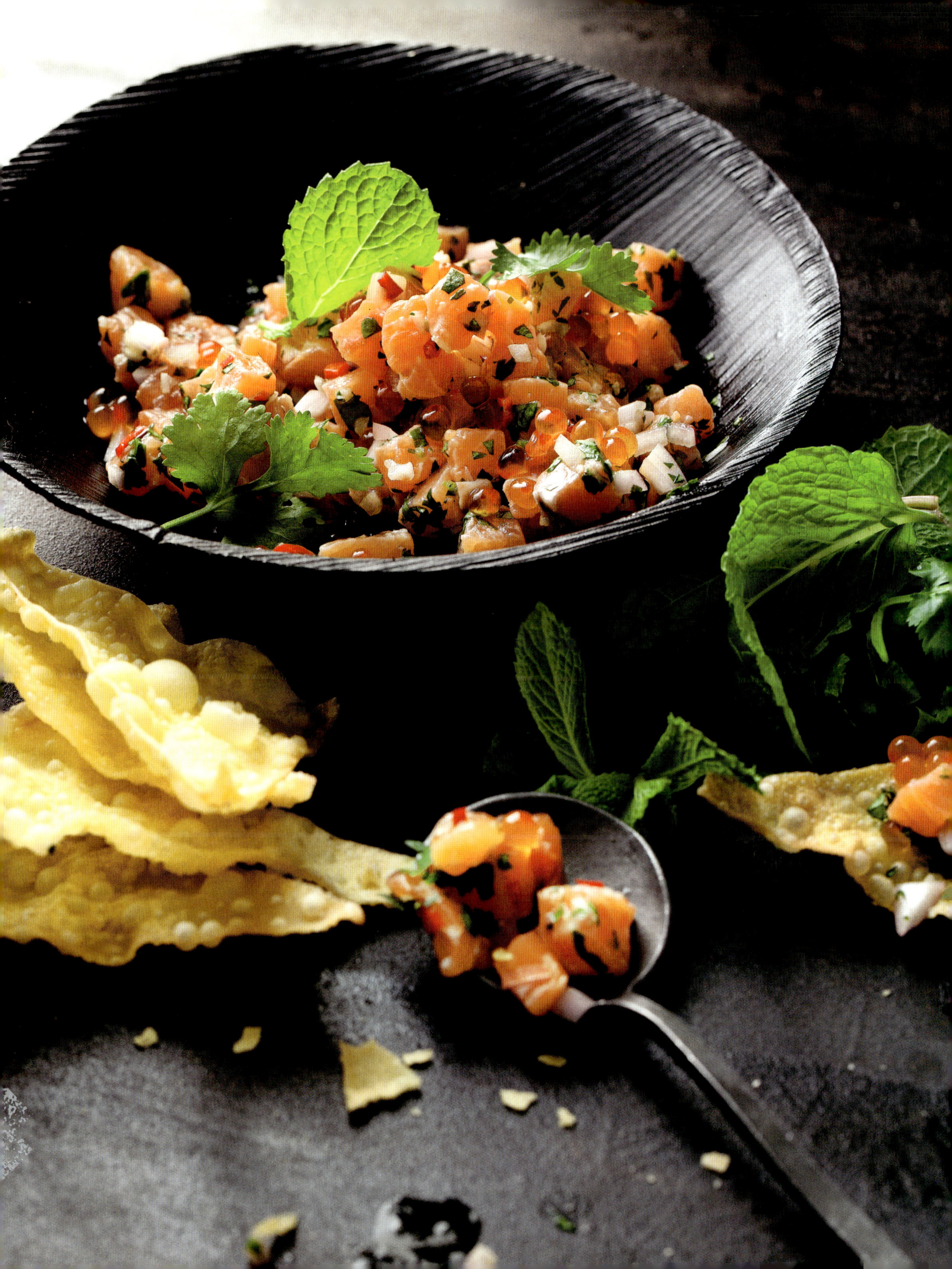

Baked ocean trout with smashed cucumber salad

I know it sounds crazy smashing cucumbers, but this method tenderises them, as well as allowing them to absorb more of the dressing. This is a great salsa to serve with any simple Asian-style baked fish.

2/3 cup (160ml) soy sauce
150ml maple syrup
3cm piece ginger, grated
3 garlic cloves, crushed
1 side (1kg) boneless, skinless ocean trout

Smashed cucumber salad
2 telegraph cucumbers
2 garlic cloves, finely chopped
1 red onion, halved, very thinly sliced
1/4 cup (70g) drained, finely shredded pickled ginger Ⓟ
Micro herbs (optional), to serve

Line a large baking tray with baking paper.

Place soy, maple syrup, ginger and garlic in a small bowl and stir to combine. Place trout on prepared baking tray and pour over marinade. Cover and refrigerate for 1 hour.

Meanwhile, for the smashed cucumber salad, peel and halve cucumbers lengthways, scoop out seeds and discard. Transfer cucumber to a large ziplock bag, seal, then bash with a rolling pin. Using your hands, break into chunks. Add garlic and 2 tsp salt to the bag and rub into cucumber. Add onion, shake to combine, then seal, removing as much air as possible. Refrigerate for 15 minutes.

Preheat the oven to 140°C. Cook the trout, uncovered, for 15 minutes or until just cooked through.

Meanwhile, drain cucumber mixture, discarding liquid, then toss with ginger in a bowl. Serve the trout with smashed cucumber salad, topped with micro herbs, if using. **Serves 6-8**
Ⓟ See Pantry essentials, p 151.

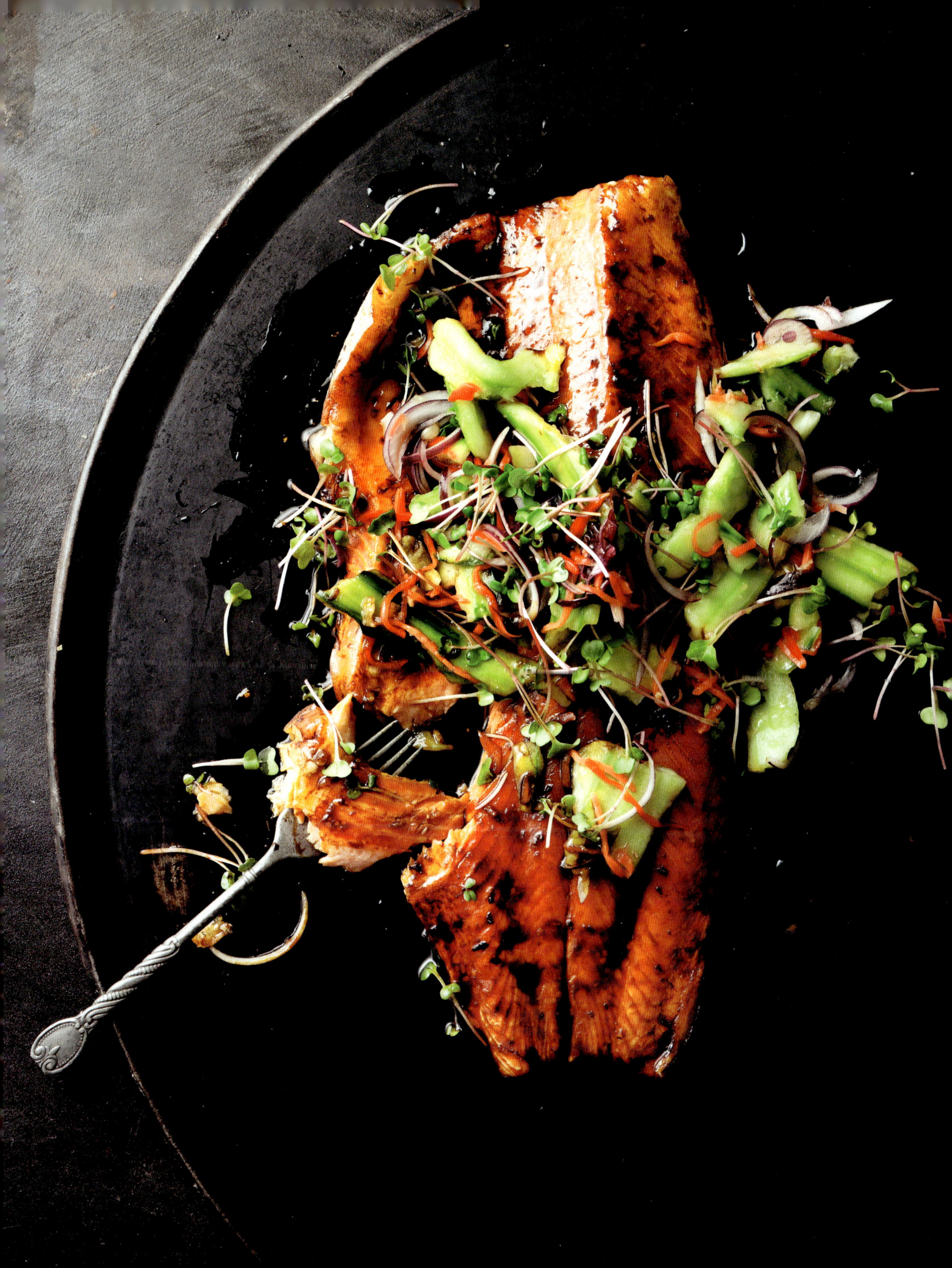

Massaman duck curry with pineapple

1 tbs sunflower or peanut oil
4 duck marylands
2 tbs grated light palm sugar or brown sugar
¼ cup (75g) massaman curry paste ⓟ
400ml coconut milk ⓟ
2 tbs fish sauce ⓟ
Juice of 1 lime
1 tbs tamarind puree ⓟ
4 kaffir lime leaves, ⓟ 2 whole, 2 very finely shredded
4 chat potatoes, halved
½ small pineapple, peeled, cut into wedges
2 tbs roughly chopped unsalted peanuts
1 long red chilli, seeds removed, thinly sliced on the diagonal
1 cup Thai basil leaves ⓟ
½ cup Vietnamese mint ⓟ
1 cup coriander leaves
Steamed rice, to serve

Preheat the oven to 160°C.

Heat the oil in a casserole or large ovenproof saucepan over medium-high heat. Cook the duck, skin-side down, for 2-3 minutes until golden. Remove duck and set aside. Drain all but 2 tbs fat from the casserole. Add palm sugar and cook, stirring, for 1-2 minutes until caramelised. Add the curry paste and cook, stirring, for 1-2 minutes until fragrant. Add the coconut milk, fish sauce, lime juice, tamarind, the whole kaffir lime leaves and ½ cup (125ml) water. Return duck to the casserole, cover and transfer to the oven for 1 hour.

Meanwhile, place potatoes in a saucepan of cold salted water, bring to the boil over medium heat and simmer for 5-6 minutes. Drain, then add potatoes and pineapple to the casserole. Cover and return to the oven for a further 30 minutes or until the duck is tender.

Scatter curry with chopped peanuts, chilli, Thai basil, mint, coriander and shredded kaffir lime leaves, and serve with steamed rice. **Serves 4**

ⓟ See Pantry essentials, p 151.

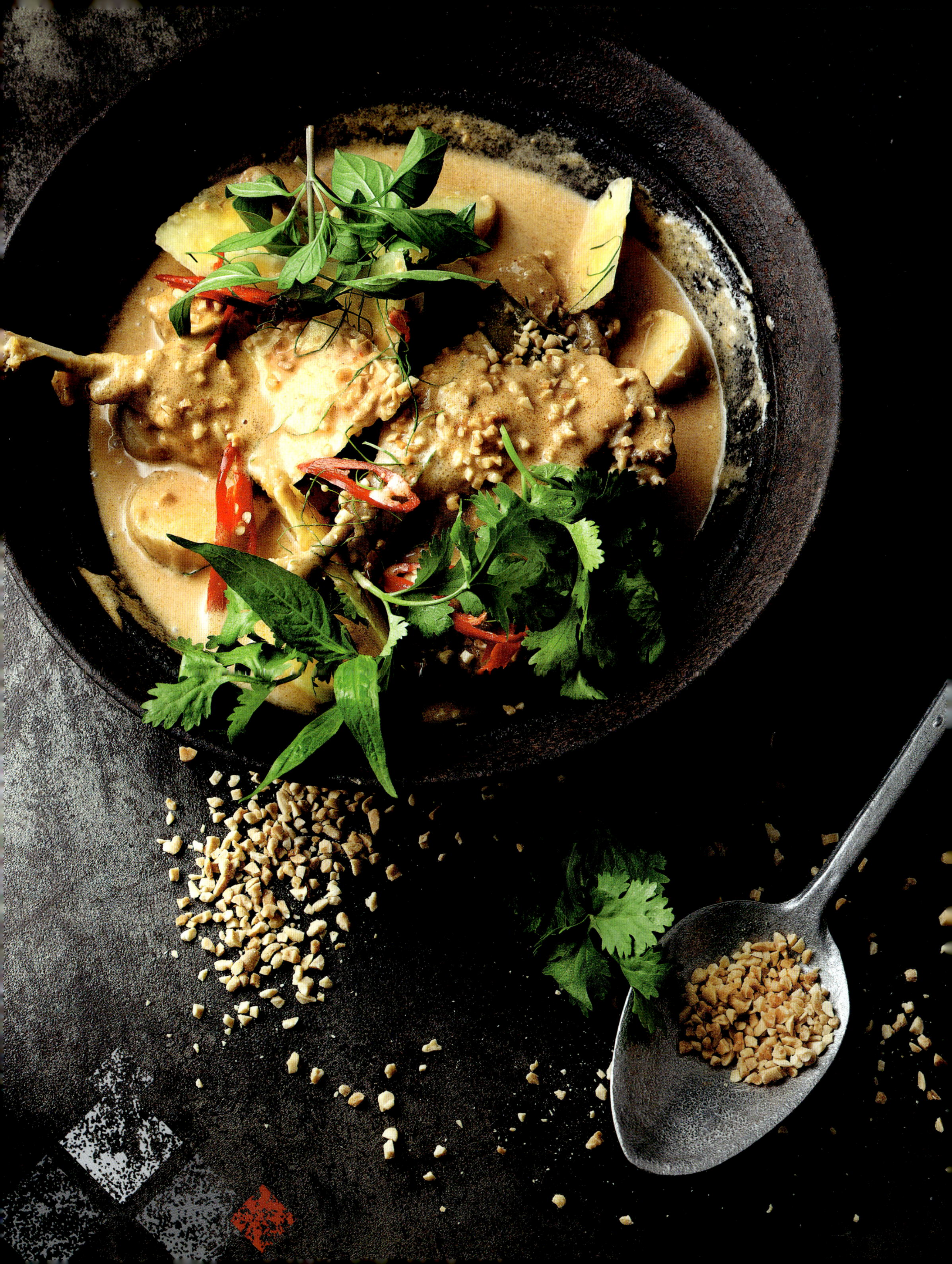

Braised pork belly with black vinegar and pickled chillies

2 tbs dark soy sauce
1 cup (250ml) Chinese rice wine (shaohsing) ⓟ
2kg piece pork belly, skin removed, cut into 5cm pieces
¼ cup (60ml) peanut oil
2 garlic cloves, thinly sliced
3cm piece ginger, grated
¼ tsp chilli flakes
100ml Chinese black (chinkiang) vinegar ⓟ
1 tsp five spice
2 star anise
⅔ cup (160g) brown sugar
3 cups (750ml) beef stock or consomme
2 long red chillies, thinly sliced
¼ cup (60ml) seasoned rice vinegar ⓟ
Asian greens and steamed rice, to serve

Combine soy sauce and 50ml wine in a large bowl. Add pork and turn to coat in marinade. Set aside for 1 hour.

Heat 2 tbs oil in a casserole or large saucepan over medium-high heat. Cook pork, in batches, turning and adding extra oil if necessary, until browned. Remove from casserole and set aside. Add remaining 1 tbs oil to the casserole, then add garlic, ginger and chilli flakes, and cook, stirring, for 1-2 minutes until fragrant. Add black vinegar, five spice, star anise, sugar, stock and remaining 200ml rice wine, and stir to combine. Return pork to the casserole and bring to the boil. Reduce heat to low, cover and cook for 1½ hours.

Meanwhile, for the pickled chillies, combine sliced red chillies and seasoned rice vinegar in a bowl and set aside for 1 hour.

Remove the casserole lid and increase heat to medium-high. Cook pork for a further 30 minutes or until the sauce is reduced and syrupy, and the pork is very tender.*

Serve the pork with the pickled chillies, Asian greens and steamed rice. **Serves 4-6**

* *Depending on how fatty the pork belly is, you may want to skim off excess fat from the dish before serving.*

ⓟ *See Pantry essentials, p 151.*

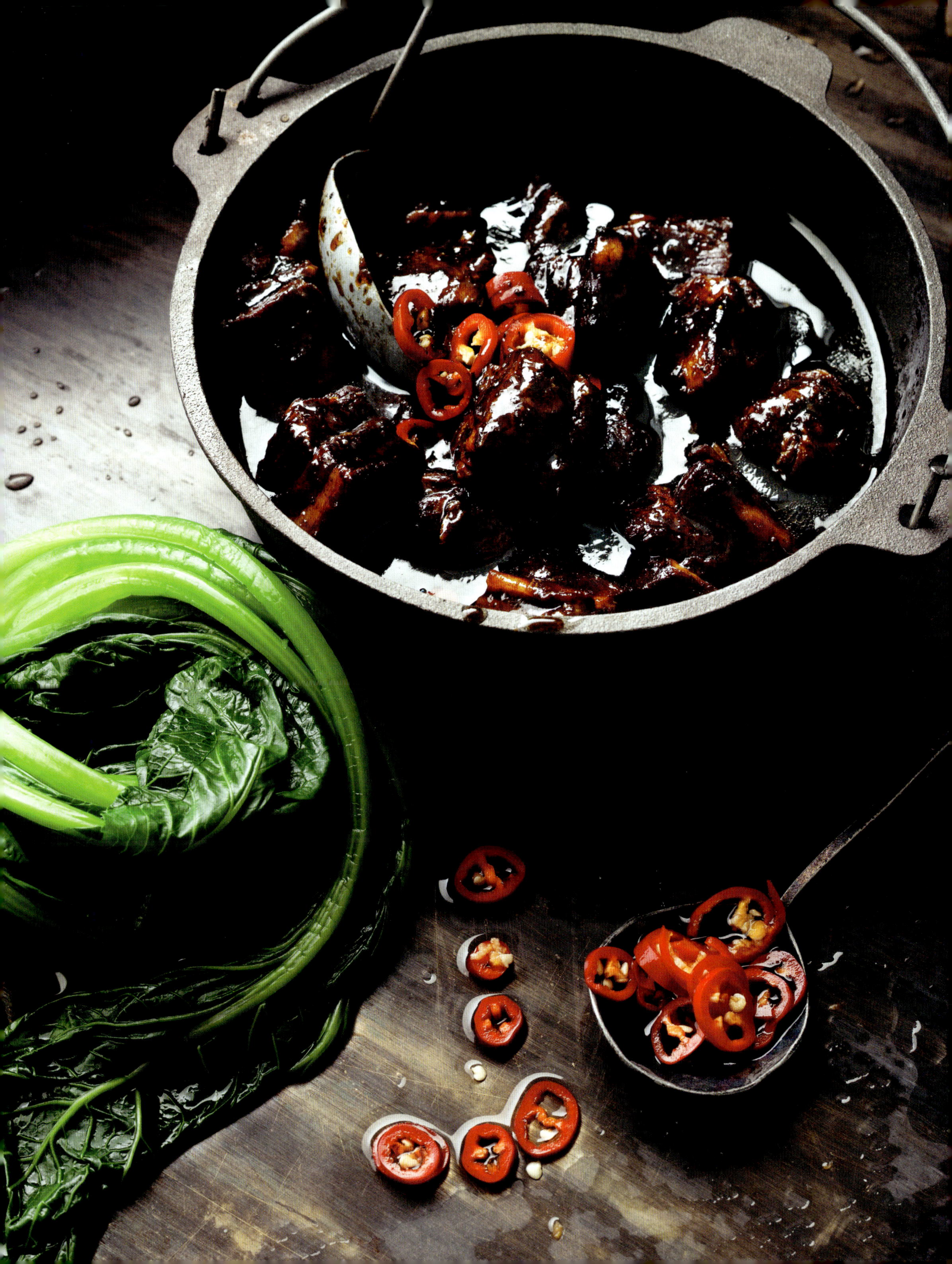

Tom yum fried rice

I like to serve this version of fried rice with chopped fresh tomato and lime, just as you would with tom yum soup.

3 cups (750ml) vegetable stock
1 tbs sunflower oil
3 Asian (red) eschalots, ⓟ finely chopped
3 garlic cloves, finely chopped
¼ cup (75g) tom yum paste*
1¼ cups (250g) jasmine rice
300g peeled green prawns
100g small snow peas, trimmed, blanched
1 bunch broccolini, trimmed, blanched
1 cup Thai basil leaves, ⓟ plus extra to serve
Lime and tomato wedges, to serve

Heat stock in a large saucepan over medium heat.

Meanwhile, heat the oil in a frypan over medium-low heat. Add eschalots and cook, stirring, for 1-2 minutes until just softened. Add garlic and tom yum paste, and cook, stirring, for 2 minutes or until fragrant. Add the rice to the frypan and cook, stirring, until grains are coated. Add hot stock to the rice mixture, partially cover with a lid, then reduce heat to low and cook, stirring occasionally to prevent the rice catching, for 8-10 minutes until the rice is tender. Add the prawns, cover with a lid and cook for a further 3 minutes or until the prawns are cooked through. Add vegetables and cook for 1 minute or until just warmed through.

Serve rice topped with basil, with lime and tomato wedges.

Serves 4

* Different brands of tom yum paste will vary in heat, so use an amount according to your taste.
ⓟ *See Pantry essentials, p 151.*

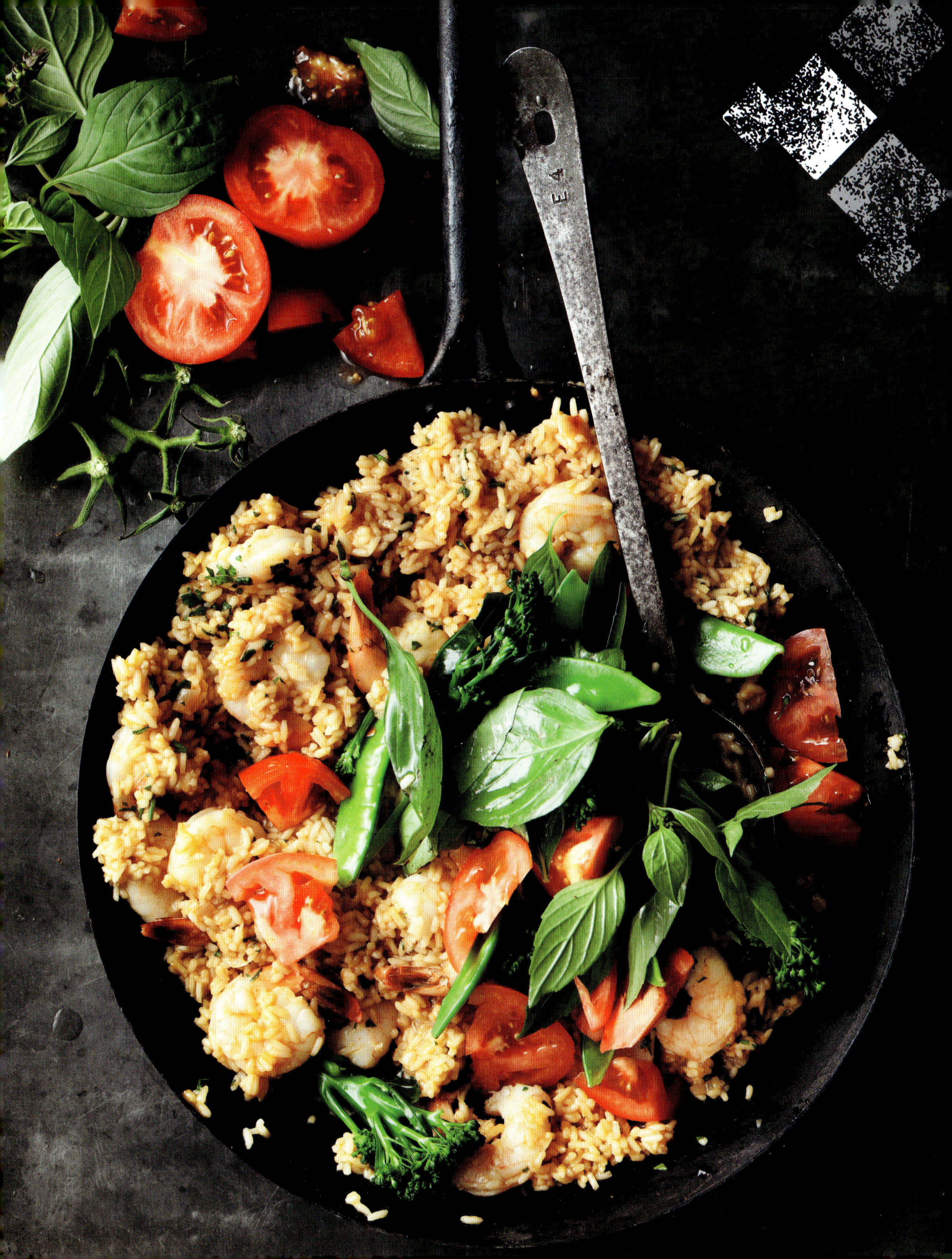

Japanese cheesecake with raspberries

500g cream cheese, softened
¾ cup (165g) caster sugar
60g unsalted butter, softened
6 eggs, separated
300ml thickened cream
2 tsp lemon juice
1 tsp vanilla extract
½ cup (75g) plain flour, sifted
Icing sugar, to dust

Raspberry sauce
250g raspberries, plus extra to serve
2 tbs caster sugar

Preheat the oven to 160°C. Grease and line a 22cm square cake pan, allowing some overhang to help remove the cake.

Using electric beaters, beat cream cheese and ¼ cup (55g) caster sugar for 2-3 minutes until well combined. Add the butter and beat until combined. Add the egg yolks, 1 at a time, beating after each addition, then add the cream, lemon juice and vanilla. Fold through the sifted flour, then transfer mixture to another bowl. In a clean bowl, whisk the eggwhites to stiff peaks. Add the remaining ½ cup (110g) caster sugar, in 3 batches, whisking well after each addition, until thick and glossy. Gently fold the eggwhite mixture into the cream cheese mixture, then transfer to the prepared pan, gently tapping the pan on the bench to remove any air bubbles. Place pan in a deep baking dish and pour in enough boiling water to come halfway up the sides of the cake pan. Bake for 1 hour (if the top is browning too quickly, loosely cover with foil), then reduce heat to 140°C and bake for a further 30 minutes. Turn off the oven and leave the cake in the oven for 15 minutes with the door ajar. Remove the cake from the oven and cool completely, then refrigerate for 1-2 hours until firm.

Meanwhile, for the sauce, place the raspberries, sugar and 2 tbs water in a small saucepan over medium heat. Cook, stirring, for 2-3 minutes until the berries have released their juices and broken down. Strain through a fine sieve over a bowl or jug, discarding solids, then refrigerate.

Using the baking paper, remove cheesecake from pan, dust with icing sugar and serve with raspberry sauce and extra whole raspberries. **Serves 6**

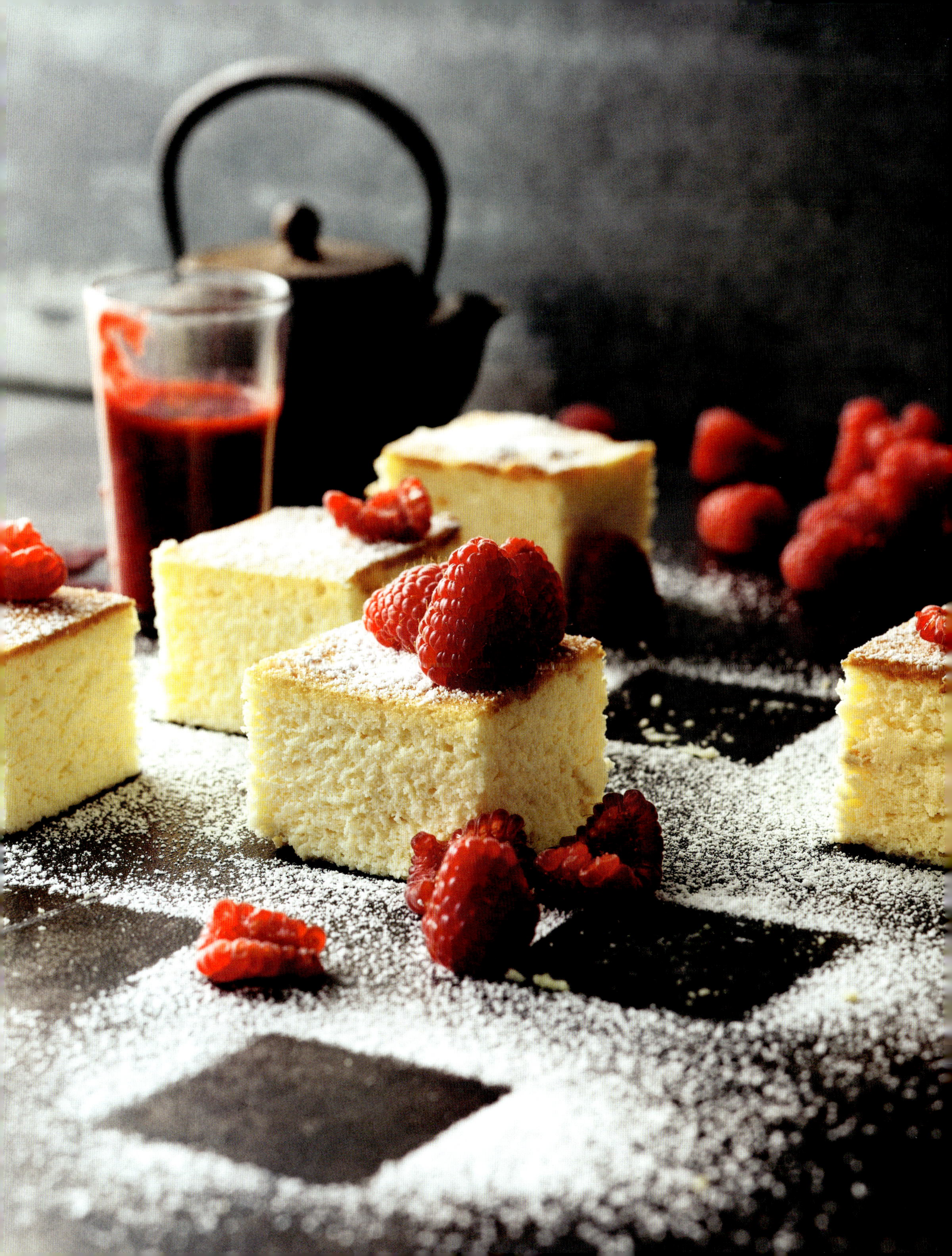

Chilli pears with sweet wontons and ginger cream

8 pears (such as corella or beurre bosc)
1 lemon, halved
125g caster sugar
1 long red chilli, seeds removed, halved lengthways
2 star anise
2cm piece ginger, thinly sliced into rounds
300ml thickened cream
2 tbs icing sugar
1 tsp ground ginger

Sweet wontons
12 wonton wrappers ⓟ
1 eggwhite
2 tbs honey
1 cup (80g) flaked almonds, lightly crushed
¼ cup (55g) caster sugar
1 tsp ground ginger

Peel the pears, leaving stems intact. Rub the pear flesh with the cut side of a lemon to prevent them from browning. Place sugar, chilli, star anise and ginger in a saucepan with 2 cups (500ml) water over low heat, stirring until sugar dissolves. Add pears and poach for 8-10 minutes until tender (timing will depend on the ripeness of the pears). Using a slotted spoon, remove the pears and set aside. Increase heat to medium-high and simmer poaching liquid for 5-6 minutes until reduced and syrupy. Return pears to pan, then cool.

For the sweet wontons, preheat the oven to 200°C. Line 2 large baking trays with baking paper. Place wonton wrappers on tray. Using a fork, lightly whisk the eggwhite and honey in a bowl. In a separate bowl, combine almonds, caster sugar and ground ginger. Brush wonton wrappers on one side with the eggwhite mixture, then sprinkle with the almond mixture. Bake for 7-8 minutes until golden. Cool.

Combine the cream, icing sugar and ground ginger in a bowl and whisk to soft peaks.

Serve the pears drizzled with syrup, with sweet wontons and ginger cream. **Serves 4**

ⓟ See Pantry essentials, p 151.

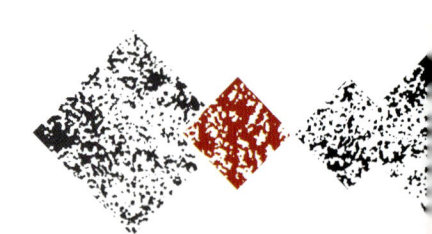

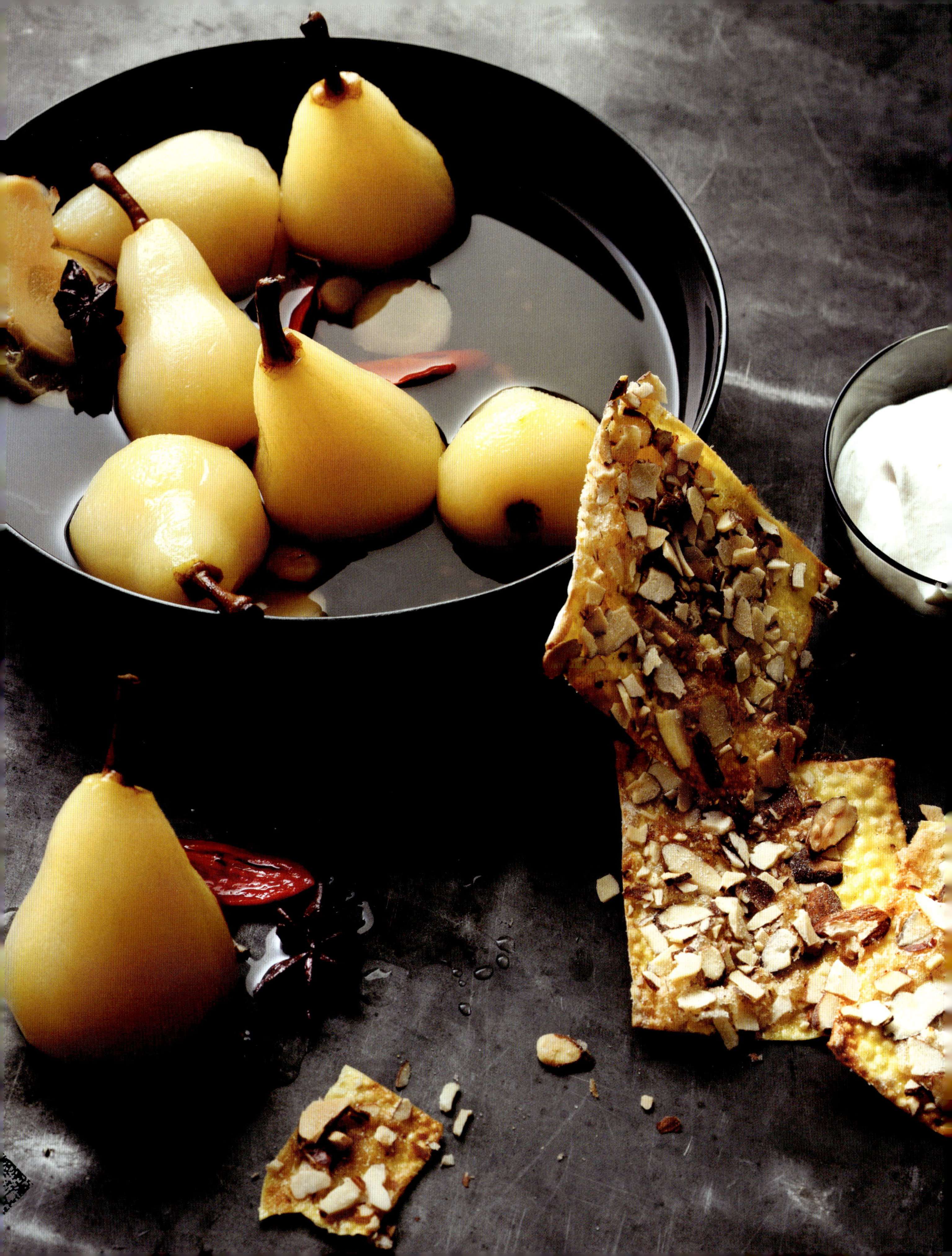

Coconut sorbet with fruits in lemongrass syrup

In summer, I like to serve this sorbet with mango and papaya, but it goes just as well with winter fruits such as poached quince or rhubarb. The liqueur gives the syrup a little kick, but only use it if you have some lying around.

400ml coconut cream Ⓟ
300ml thickened cream
1²/₃ cups (370g) caster sugar
Finely grated zest and juice of 1 lime
1 lemongrass stalk (inner core only), bruised
2 kaffir lime leaves Ⓟ
1 tbs Malibu or Cointreau (optional)
2 mangoes, sliced
2 oranges, peeled, pith removed, cut into rounds
1 red dragonfruit, sliced
2 nectarines, stones removed, sliced
Pulp of 5 passionfruit
Micro coriander (optional), to serve

Place the coconut cream, thickened cream and ½ cup (110g) caster sugar in a saucepan over medium heat, stirring until sugar dissolves. Increase heat to medium-high and simmer for 5 minutes. Remove from heat, then transfer to a bowl set over a bowl of iced water to chill. Pour mixture into a 1L plastic container and freeze for at least 3 hours or until firm enough to scoop. Alternatively, churn in an ice cream machine according to manufacturer's instructions.

Combine lime zest, lemongrass, kaffir lime leaves, remaining 260g caster sugar and 1 cup (250ml) water in a saucepan over medium heat, stirring until sugar dissolves. Increase heat to medium-high and simmer for 3 minutes. Add the lime juice and liqueur, if using, then remove from the heat and set aside for 30 minutes for the flavours to infuse. Strain, discarding solids. Refrigerate until chilled.

Serve scoops of sorbet with mango, orange, dragonfruit, nectarine and passionfruit, drizzled with syrup and garnished with micro coriander, if using. **Serves 4**

Ⓟ See Pantry essentials, p 151.

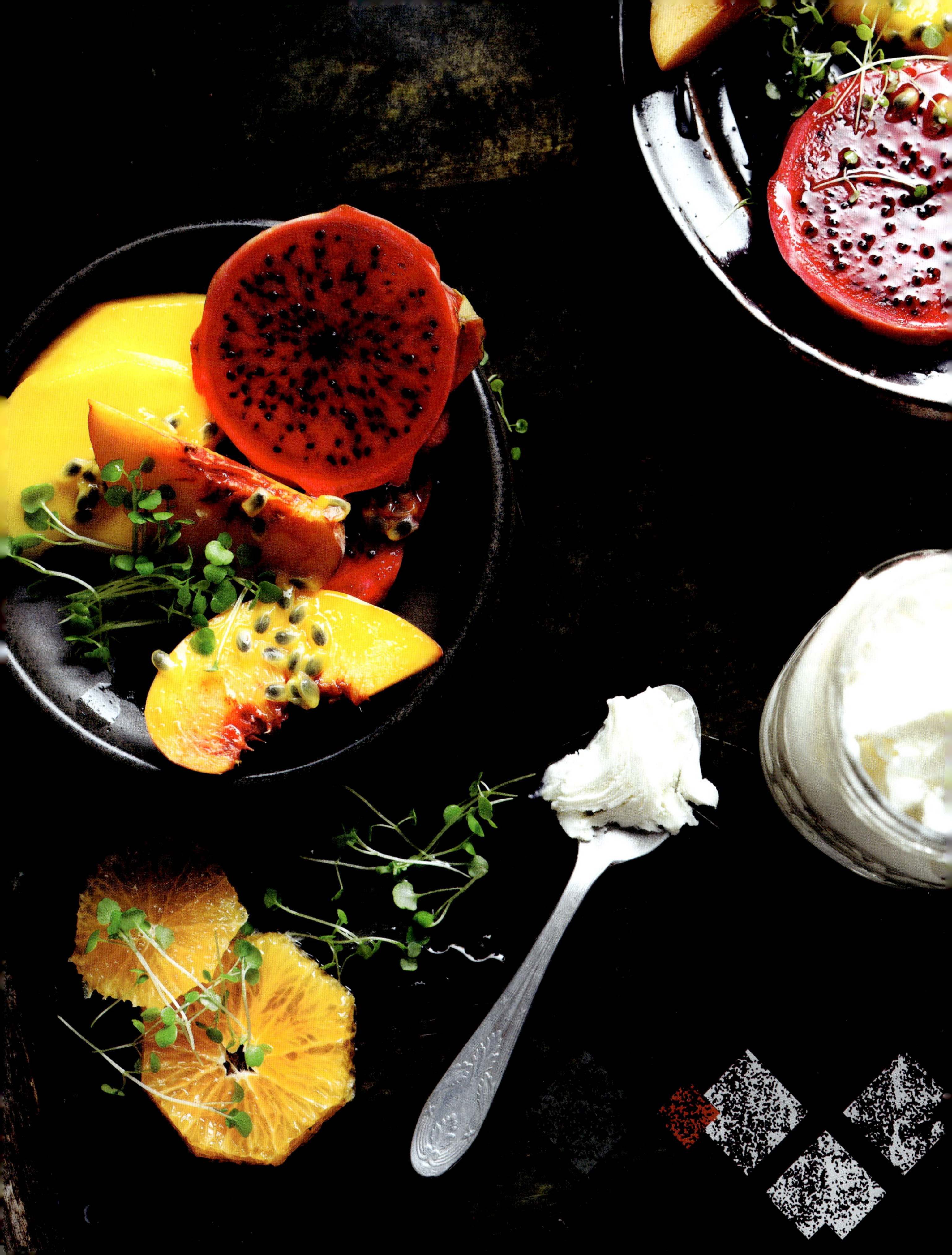

LATIN AMERICAN

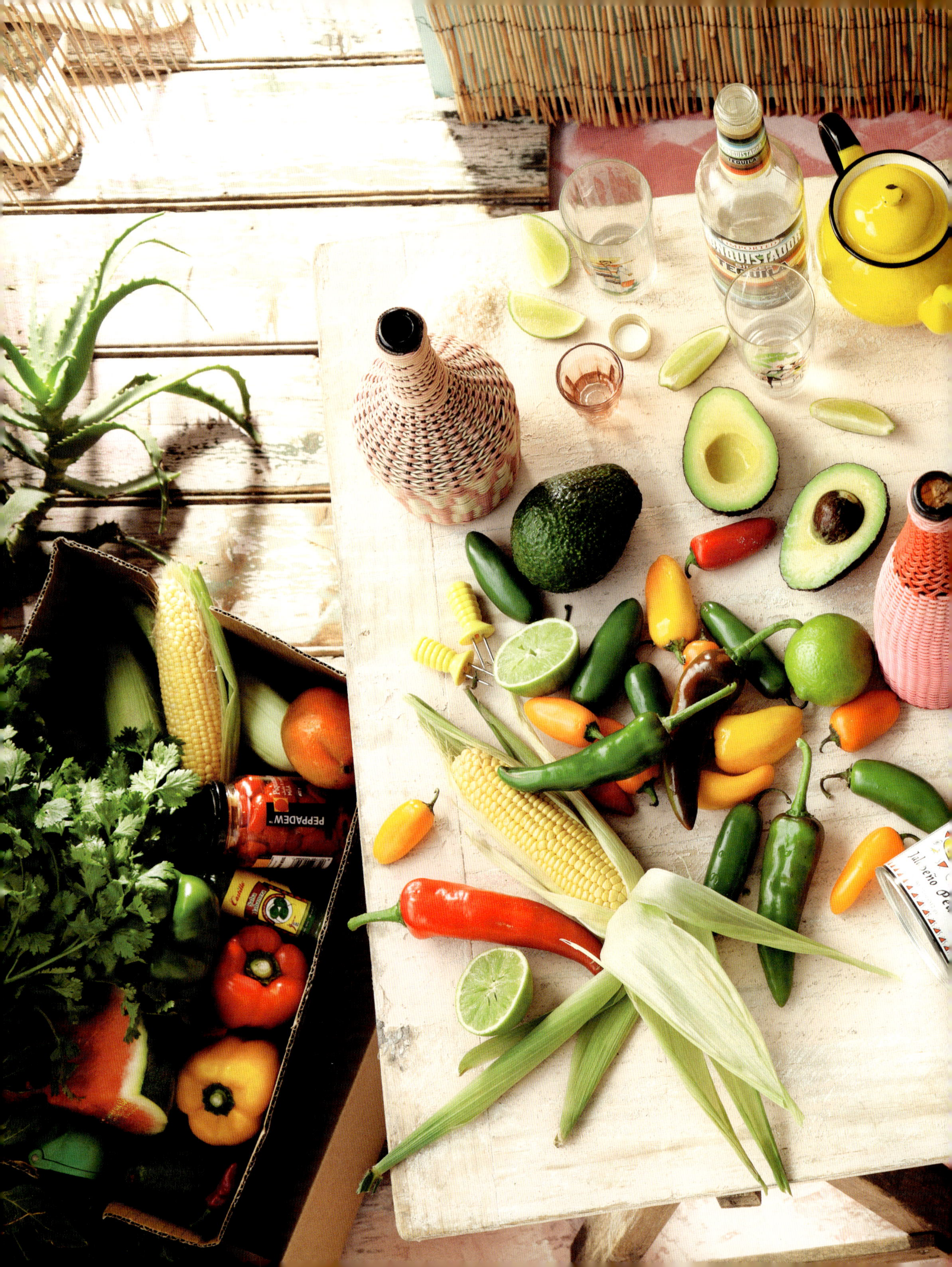
PEPPADEW

PANTRY ESSENTIALS

Ancho chilli powder
Made with ground poblano chillies, with a mild flavour and rich, dark red colour, this is used widely in Mexican cooking. You can also buy whole, dried ancho chillies, but they need to be soaked in hot water before using.

Black (turtle) beans
A small black legume. Available dried (they need to be soaked overnight) or canned from selected supermarkets, delis and specialist food shops.

Dulce de leche
Literally 'milk sweet', this is sweetened milk cooked down to a thick, smooth, caramel-coloured paste. The consistency can range from almost solid to a smooth drizzling sauce.

Habanero chillies
Small, squat and very hot chillies, ranging in colour from orange to red, with a slightly citrus flavour. Habanero hot sauce is a staple Mexican condiment.

Jalapenos
Jalapenos range from moderate to extremely hot. Once dried and smoked, they take on a rich, sweet, smoky flavour and are known as chipotle. They're also pickled and sold in cans as chipotle chillies (or peppers) in adobo sauce.

Masa harina
A corn-based flour used to make tortillas and other Mexican dishes. Regular maize or corn flour will not give the same results, so if you can't find masa harina, stick with regular wheat-flour tortillas.

Tequila
A liquor made by distilling the blue agave plant. There is now an increasing selection of quality boutique brands available from selected bottle shops.

Tortillas
Originally made with masa harina, these Mexican staples are a thin flatbread used in a number of dishes, including tacos, enchiladas and burritos.

Latin American food – from Argentinian barbecue to Mexican mole – is having its day in the sun. Chillies, dried or fresh, hot or mild, are used in abundance, as are a variety of hot sauces. Dried beans and corn form the base of many dishes, while lime, avocado, tomato, coriander, oregano and garlic rev things up in sauces and salsas. Many ingredients are now available from supermarkets, delis and specialist food shops, or visit fireworksfoods.com.au or herbies.com.au.

Empanadas

1 egg
2 tbs olive oil, plus extra to shallow-fry
1 onion, finely chopped
2 garlic cloves, crushed
1 long red chilli, seeds removed, finely chopped
350g minced beef
1 tsp ground cumin
40g sultanas soaked in 2 tbs dry sherry or water for 10 minutes
1/3 cup (50g) pimiento-stuffed green olives, chopped
2 tbs sundried tomato pesto
2 tbs finely chopped flat-leaf parsley
6 sheets frozen puff pastry, thawed
1-2 tsp habanero hot sauce ⓟ
1 cup (240g) sour cream

Bring the egg to the boil in a saucepan over medium-high heat, then simmer for 8 minutes or until hard-boiled. Refresh under cold running water until cool enough to handle. Peel and set aside to cool completely.

Heat oil in a saucepan over medium heat, then add the onion, garlic and chilli, and cook, stirring, for 2-3 minutes until softened but not browned. Add the mince and cook, breaking up with a wooden spoon, until browned. Add cumin, sultanas and their soaking liquid, olives and tomato pesto, and stir to combine. Season, then set aside to cool completely. Chop hard-boiled egg and add to the cooled mince mixture with the parsley.

Line a baking tray with baking paper. Working in batches, use a 10cm round biscuit cutter to cut out 4 rounds from each pastry sheet. Place 1 tbs filling on one half of each round, brush the edge of the pastry with a little cold water, then fold over pastry to form a half-moon shape. Crimp the edges with a fork to seal. Place on the prepared baking tray and refrigerate until ready to cook.

Heat 4cm oil in a deep frypan over medium-high heat and cook empanadas, in batches, turning halfway with tongs, for 2-3 minutes until golden. Drain on paper towel. Alternatively, preheat the oven to 180°C, brush empanadas with a little beaten egg or milk and bake for 15-20 minutes until golden.

Stir habanero hot sauce through the sour cream and serve with the empanadas. **Makes 24**

ⓟ See Pantry essentials, p 179.

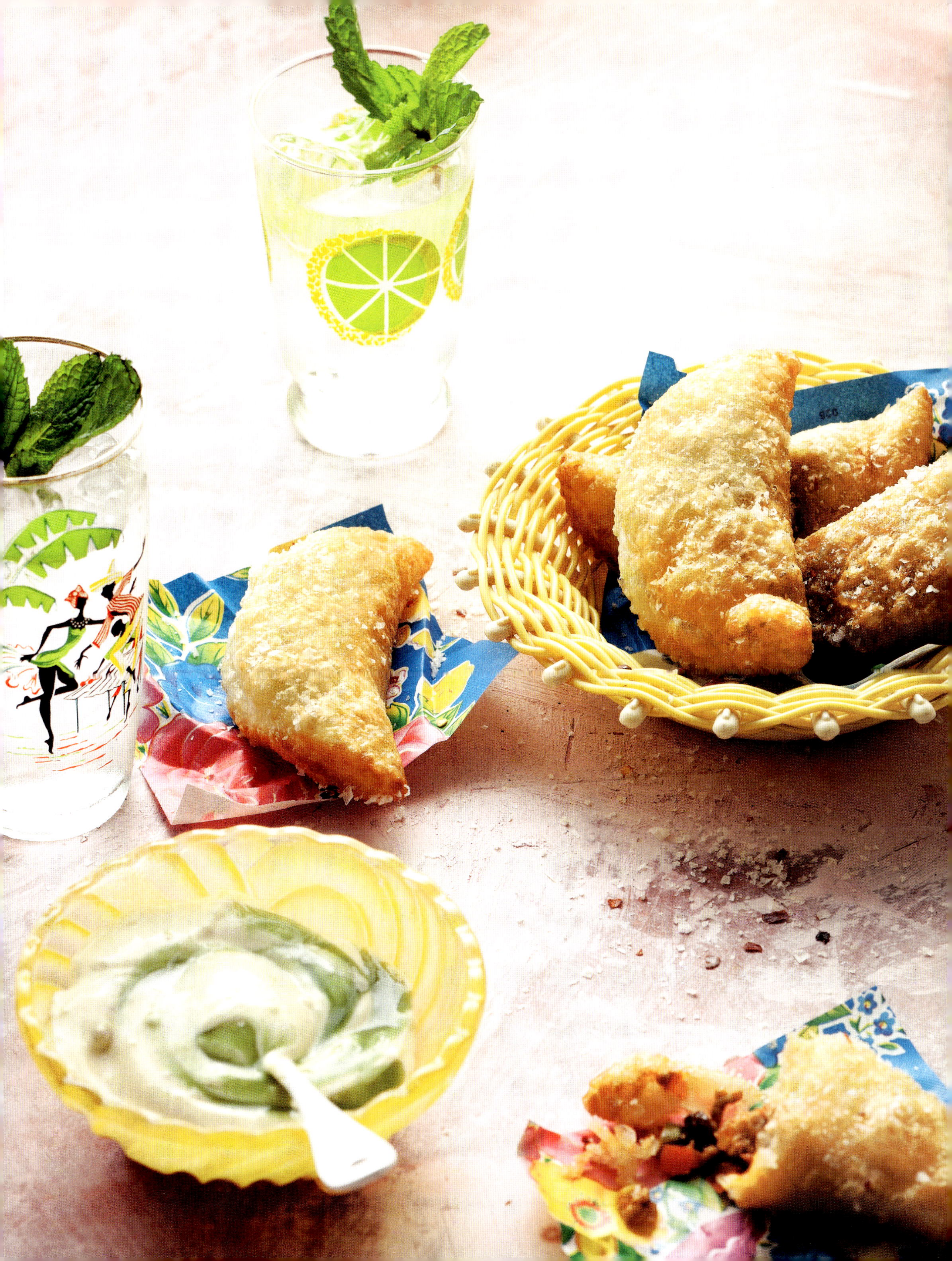

Smoky pepper soup with drunken prawns

This soup is just as delicious served chilled as it is hot.

1 tbs olive oil, plus extra to drizzle
1 red onion, chopped
1 small bulb fennel, chopped
1 carrot, chopped
3 garlic cloves, chopped
1 tbs thyme leaves
2 tsp cumin seeds, toasted
½ tsp dried chilli flakes
1 tbs tomato paste
400g can chopped tomatoes
3 cups (750ml) vegetable stock
1 tsp caster sugar
1 roasted red capsicum, chopped
1 tsp sweet smoked paprika (pimenton)
12 cooked prawns, peeled, (tails intact), deveined
⅓ cup (80ml) tequila Ⓟ
1 quantity small fried croutons (see Basics, p 296), to serve
2 tbs finely chopped coriander, to serve

Heat oil in a saucepan over medium heat. Add the onion, fennel and carrot, and cook, stirring for 3-4 minutes until softened but not browned. Add garlic, thyme, cumin and chilli, and cook for a further minute. Add tomato paste and cook, stirring, for a further minute. Add chopped tomatoes, stock, sugar, capsicum and paprika, and bring to the boil. Reduce heat to medium-low and simmer for 15-20 minutes until vegetables are tender. Cool slightly.

Meanwhile, combine prawns in a bowl with the tequila, cover and refrigerate for 15 minutes.

Using a blender or food processor, whiz cooled tomato mixture to a puree. Strain puree through a sieve into a clean saucepan and reheat. Alternatively, if serving the soup chilled, strain into a bowl and refrigerate until ready to serve.

To serve, divide soup among bowls and top with prawns, croutons and coriander, then drizzle with a little extra olive oil.

Serves 4-6

Ⓟ See Pantry essentials, p 179.

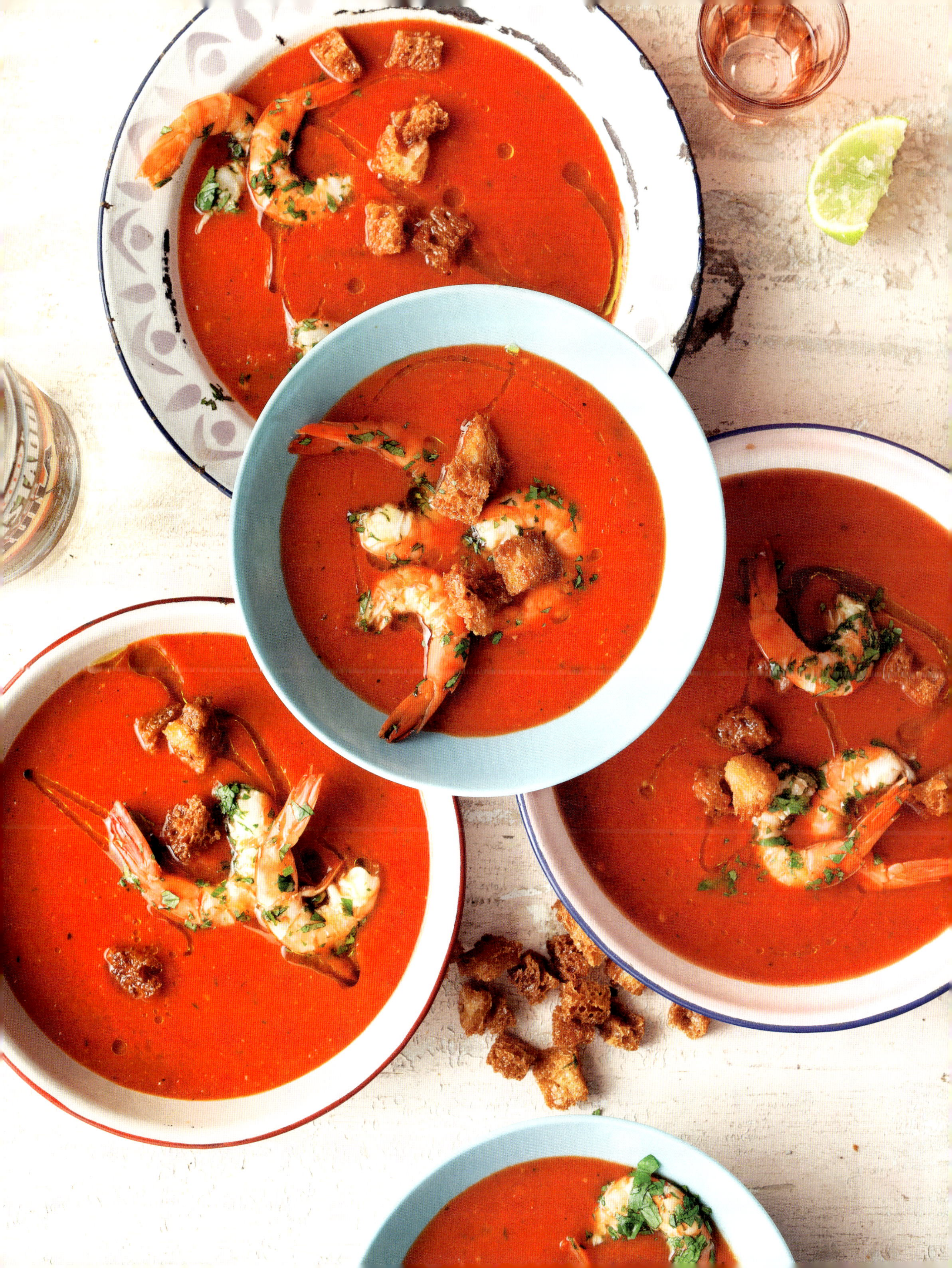

Corn cakes with Mexican green sauce

2/3 cup (100g) plain flour
1/2 tsp bicarbonate of soda
1 egg, plus 1 egg yolk
100ml milk
2 corn cobs
1 red chilli, seeds removed, chopped
3 spring onions, thinly sliced
Sunflower oil, to shallow-fry
Tomato wedges, to serve

Mexican green sauce

1 jalapeno, Ⓟ seeds removed, chopped
1 garlic clove, chopped
1 cup coriander leaves
1 cup mint leaves
1 tbs oregano leaves
4 spring onions, chopped
2 tsp brown sugar
Juice of 1 lime
50ml olive oil
1/2 tsp toasted cumin seeds

For the Mexican green sauce, place all the ingredients in a blender or food processor and whiz to a puree. Transfer to a bowl, cover and refrigerate until needed.

Sift the flour, bicarbonate of soda and 1/2 tsp salt into a bowl. Add egg, egg yolk and milk, and whisk gently to combine. Cut corn kernels from the cobs and add to the batter with the chilli and spring onion. Set aside for 10 minutes.

Heat 2cm oil in a frypan over medium-high heat. Cook heaped tablespoons of corn mixture, in batches, for 1 minute each side or until golden and crisp. Drain on paper towel.

Serve corn cakes drizzled with Mexican green sauce, with tomato wedges. **Makes 10**

Ⓟ See Pantry essentials, p 179.

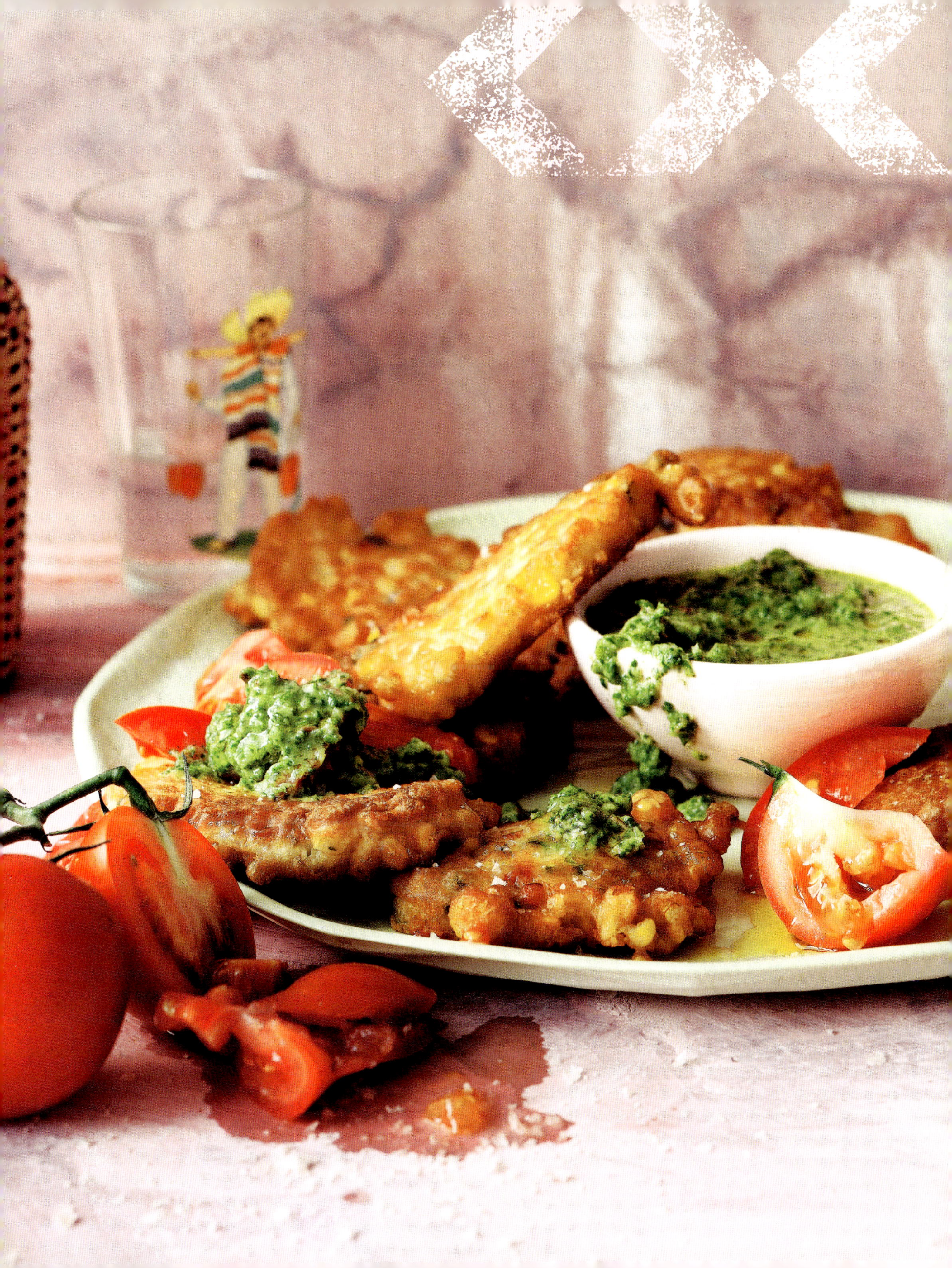

Baked kumaras with chipotle butter and pico de gallo

Tomato salsa, or pico de gallo (also sometimes known as salsa fresca), is a Mexican staple. For the freshest flavour, make it on the day of serving.

200g unsalted butter, softened
2 garlic cloves, finely chopped
¼ cup finely chopped coriander
Finely grated zest and juice of 1 lime
2 tbs chopped chipotle chillies in adobo (P)
4 medium (about 1.6kg) kumaras, unpeeled, scrubbed
Olive oil, to brush
Lime wedges, to serve

Pico de gallo
4 tomatoes, seeds removed, finely chopped
1 small red onion, finely chopped
1-2 jalapenos, (P) seeds removed, finely chopped
½ cup finely chopped coriander
Juice of 1 lime
¼ cup (60ml) extra virgin olive oil

For the chipotle butter, whiz butter, garlic, coriander, lime zest and juice, and chipotle chillies in a small food processor until combined (or mix with a fork in a bowl). Form into a log on a piece of plastic wrap, then wrap tightly, twisting the ends to secure. Refrigerate for 30 minutes or until firm.

Preheat the oven to 190°C. Brush kumaras with a little olive oil, then wrap each in two layers of foil. Place on a baking tray and bake for 30 minutes, then open up the foil and bake for a further 15-20 minutes until the skin is crisp and flesh is tender.

Meanwhile, for the pico de gallo, combine all the ingredients in a bowl and season.

Remove kumaras from the foil, split open lengthways, then serve topped with pico de gallo and slices of chipotle butter, with lime wedges. **Serves 4**

(P) See Pantry essentials, p 179.

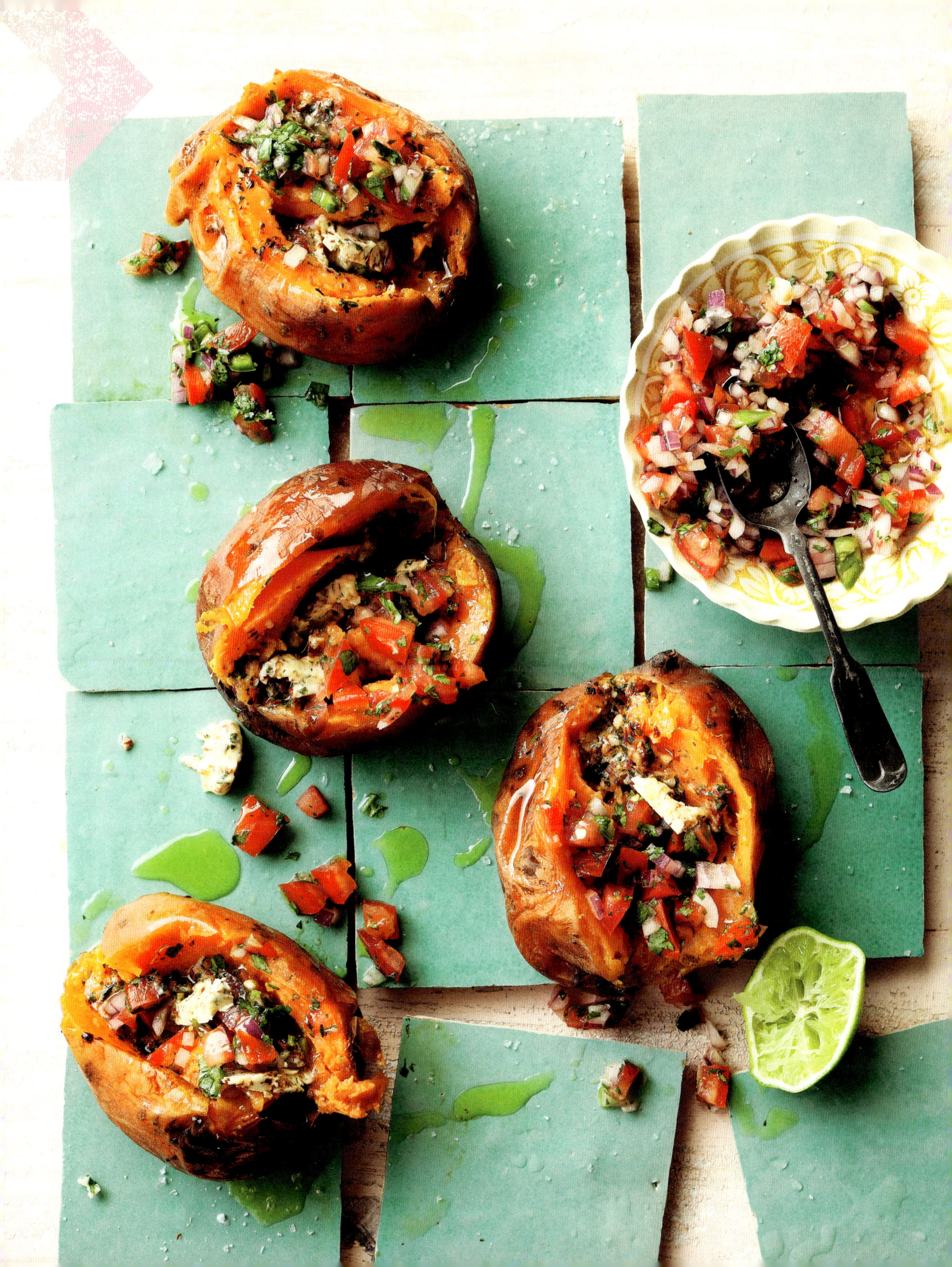

Ceviche with coconut and mango

Make sure you buy the freshest fish possible for this recipe.

300g snapper fillet, skin removed, pin-boned, thinly sliced
Juice of 2 limes, plus lime wedges, to serve
½ red onion, finely chopped
1 garlic clove, finely chopped
2 long green chillies, seeds removed, finely chopped
2 flour tortillas Ⓟ
1 tbs olive oil
1 mango, flesh cut into 1cm pieces
⅓ cup (80ml) coconut cream
Micro coriander or chopped coriander leaves, to serve

Preheat the oven to 170°C.

Place the fish in a glass or ceramic dish. Add lime juice, season with salt, then cover and refrigerate for 15 minutes or until fish turns opaque.

Meanwhile, combine the onion, garlic and chilli in a bowl and set aside.

Using scissors, cut each tortilla into 8 wedges. Place on a baking tray and brush with the oil. Bake for 8-10 minutes until pale golden and crisp. Cool.

Divide fish among plates, then scatter with the onion mixture and mango. Drizzle with coconut cream and top with coriander. Serve with tortilla chips and lime wedges. **Serves 4**

Ⓟ See Pantry essentials, p 179.

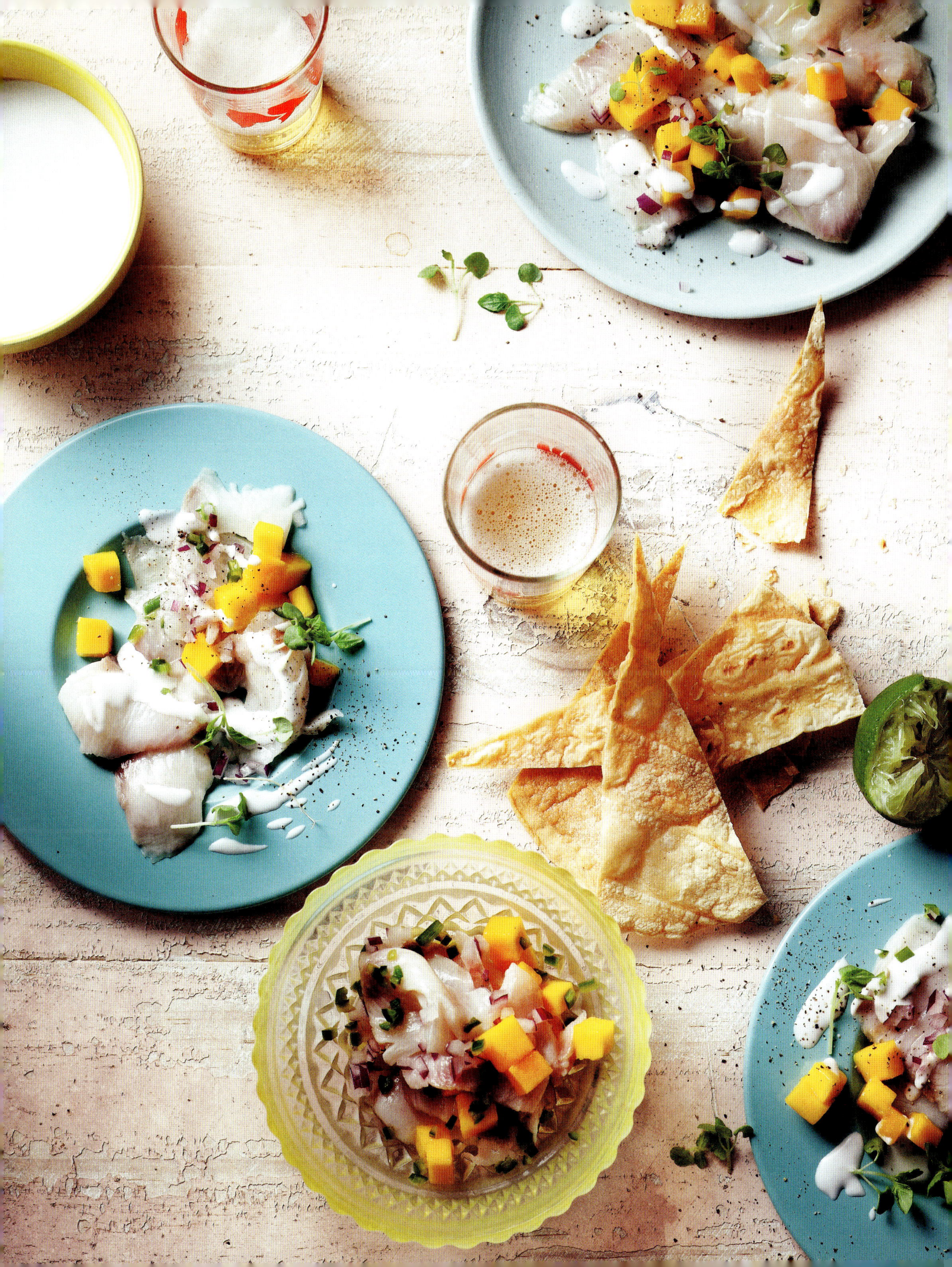

Matambre with chimichurri

Matambre translates as 'kill hunger' in Spanish, and is often served with that other Argentinian staple, chimichurri, a vibrant herb salsa.

¼ cup (60ml) olive oil, plus extra to drizzle

¼ cup (60ml) red wine vinegar

2 tsp each dried oregano and dried thyme

½ tsp dried chilli flakes

4 garlic cloves, crushed

1kg flank steak, butterflied (ask your butcher to do this for you)

1 bunch English spinach

½ cup (40g) grated parmesan

½ bunch flat-leaf parsley, finely chopped

1 bunch each oregano and marjoram, finely chopped

½ cup chopped black olives

2-3 roasted red capsicums

5 hard-boiled eggs, peeled

6 bay leaves

Chimichurri

1½ cups flat-leaf parsley, roughly chopped

¼ cup oregano leaves

1 eschalot, chopped

¼ tsp dried chilli flakes

½ cup (125ml) extra virgin olive oil

2 garlic cloves, chopped

Juice of ½ lemon

For the marinade, whisk oil, vinegar, dried oregano and thyme, chilli flakes and 2 cloves garlic in a bowl, then pour over steak in a shallow dish. Cover and refrigerate for 3-4 hours.

Preheat the oven to 180°C.

Trim spinach, discarding stems, then blanch leaves, drain and pat dry with paper towel. Combine the parmesan, parsley, oregano, marjoram and remaining 2 cloves garlic. Remove meat from marinade, discarding marinade, and place on a board. Season, then spread over the parmesan mixture. Spread spinach over, then scatter with olives. Arrange the roast capsicum over the top, then place the hard-boiled eggs, end-to-end, in a line along one end. Starting at the egg end, roll up meat, securing at 3cm intervals with kitchen string. Tuck bay leaves between the meat and string. Place the roll in a roasting pan, drizzle with a litte extra olive oil, then cook for 45 minutes. Rest, loosely covered with foil, for 20 minutes.

Meanwhile, for the chimichurri, combine all the ingredients in a food processor, season, then whiz to a coarse paste, adding more oil to loosen, if needed.

Slice matambre and serve with chimichurri. **Serves 6-8**

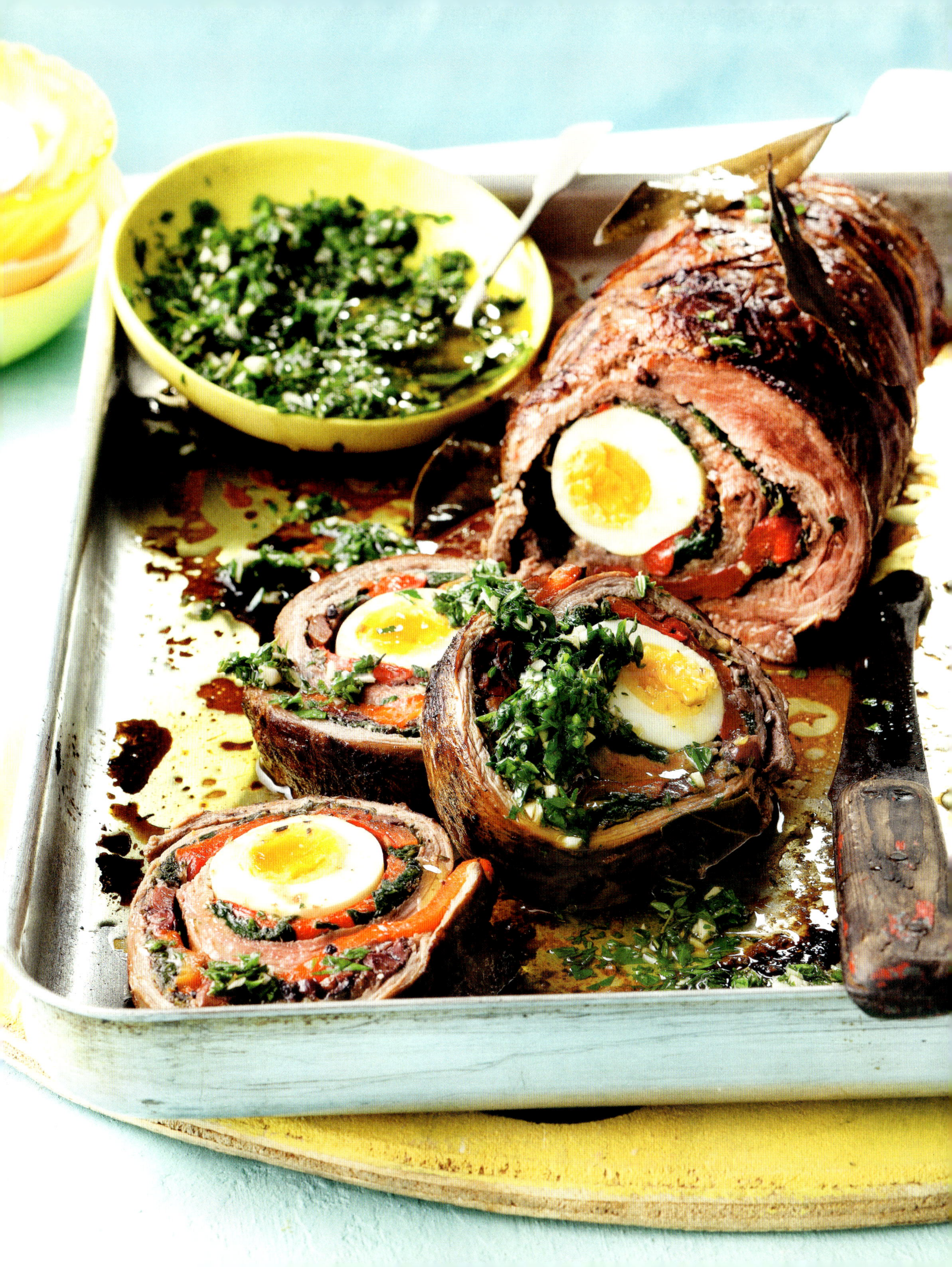

Slow-cooked Mexican beef with guacamole and lime crema

2 tbs olive oil
1.5kg beef chuck steak, cut into 5cm pieces
3 garlic cloves, chopped
1 onion, chopped
2 jalapenos, ⓟ seeds removed, chopped
600ml passata (sieved tomatoes)
1 tsp ancho chilli powder ⓟ
1 tbs ground cumin
3 bay leaves
1 tbs Worcestershire sauce
1 tbs red wine vinegar
2 cups (500ml) beef stock or beef consomme
¼ cup (60ml) tequila ⓟ
400g can red kidney beans, rinsed, drained
300ml sour cream
1 tbs finely grated lime zest
Warmed flour tortillas ⓟ and coriander leaves, to serve

Guacamole
2 avocados
¼ cup finely chopped coriander
Juice of 1 lime
1 long red chilli, seeds removed, finely chopped
1 tsp ground cumin

Preheat the oven to 160°C.

Heat the oil in a casserole or large ovenproof saucepan over medium-high heat. Cook beef, in batches, until browned all over. Transfer to a plate. Add garlic, onion and jalapenos to the casserole and cook, stirring, for 2-3 minutes until softened but not browned. Return beef to the casserole with the passata, chilli powder, cumin, bay leaves, Worcestershire, vinegar, stock and tequila. Cover with a cartouche (a round of baking paper), then a lid and transfer to the oven for 3 hours or until the beef is meltingly tender. Fifteen minutes before the beef is ready to serve, add kidney beans and return to the oven to heat through.

Meanwhile, for the guacamole, using a spoon, scoop out the flesh from the avocados into a bowl. Add the remaining ingredients and mash well with a fork. Season with sea salt, then cover with plastic wrap and refrigerate until needed.

For the lime crema, combine sour cream with the lime zest.

Serve beef with warmed tortillas, guacamole and lime crema, topped with coriander. **Serves 4**

ⓟ See Pantry essentials, p 179.

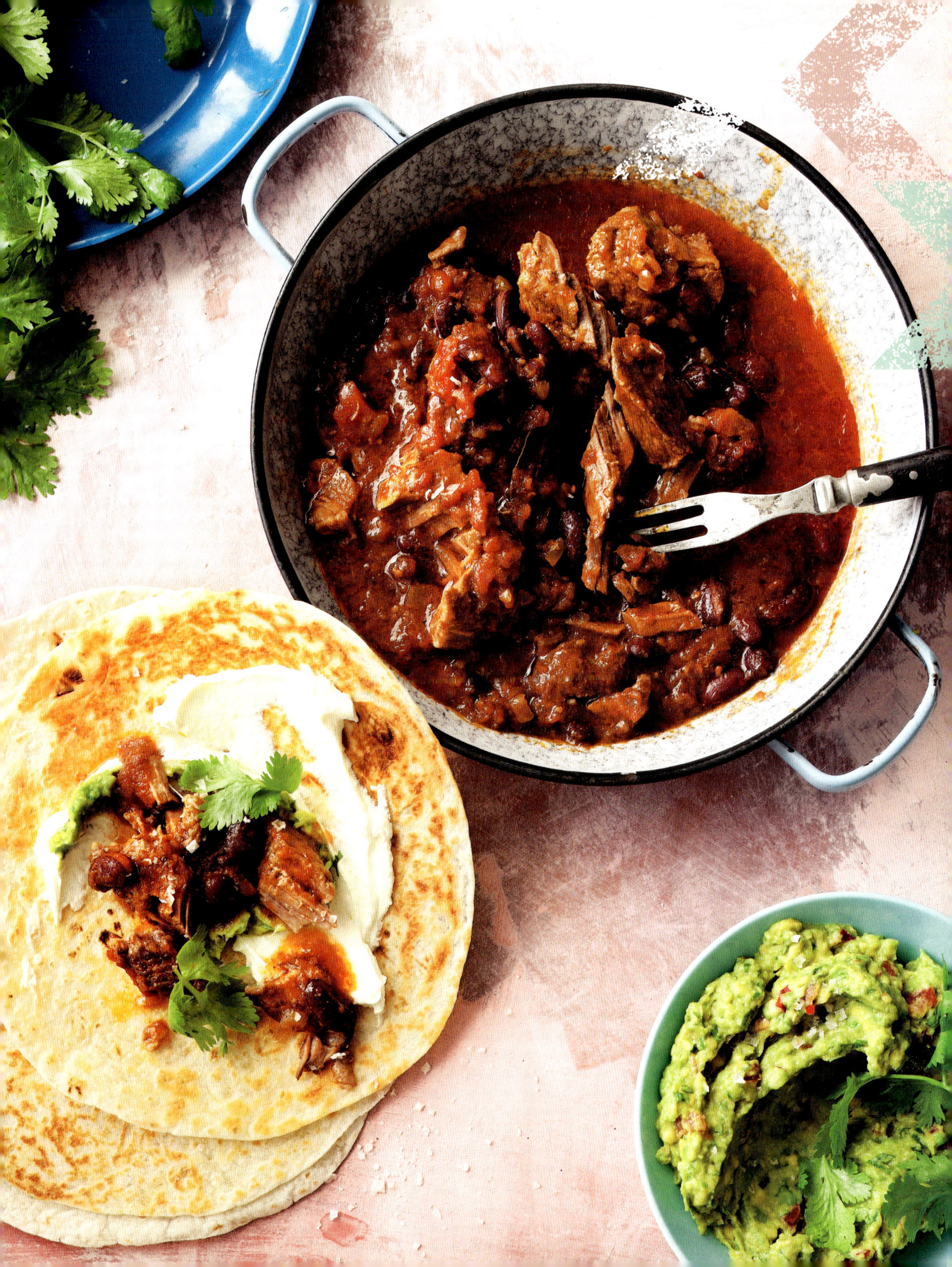

Pork ribs with chipotle barbecue sauce

2 garlic cloves, crushed
¼ cup (60g) brown sugar
1 tbs dried oregano
1 tbs mustard powder
Finely grated zest of 1 orange
2-3 racks (1.2kg) baby pork spare ribs

Chipotle barbecue sauce
2 cups (500g) tomato ketchup
1 cup (250g) good-quality barbecue sauce
1 cup (250ml) fresh orange juice
¼ cup (60g) brown sugar
¼ cup (60ml) red wine vinegar
2 tbs chopped chipotle chillies in adobo Ⓟ

Combine garlic, sugar, oregano, mustard powder, orange zest and 1 tbs sea salt in a bowl. Rub all over the ribs, then wrap in foil and refrigerate for 2 hours for flavours to develop.

Preheat the oven to 180°C. Place the foil-wrapped ribs on a large baking tray and cook for 1 hour.

Meanwhile, for the chipotle barbecue sauce, combine all the ingredients in a saucepan over medium heat and bring to a simmer. Reduce heat to low and cook, stirring occasionally, for 10 minutes or until slightly reduced.

Remove ribs from oven and open their foil wrapping, then brush both sides with the barbecue sauce. Re-wrap in the foil, then cook, basting with more sauce every 15 minutes, for a further hour or until ribs are tender and sticky.

Serve ribs with any remaining sauce. **Serves 4-6**

Ⓟ See Pantry essentials, p 179.

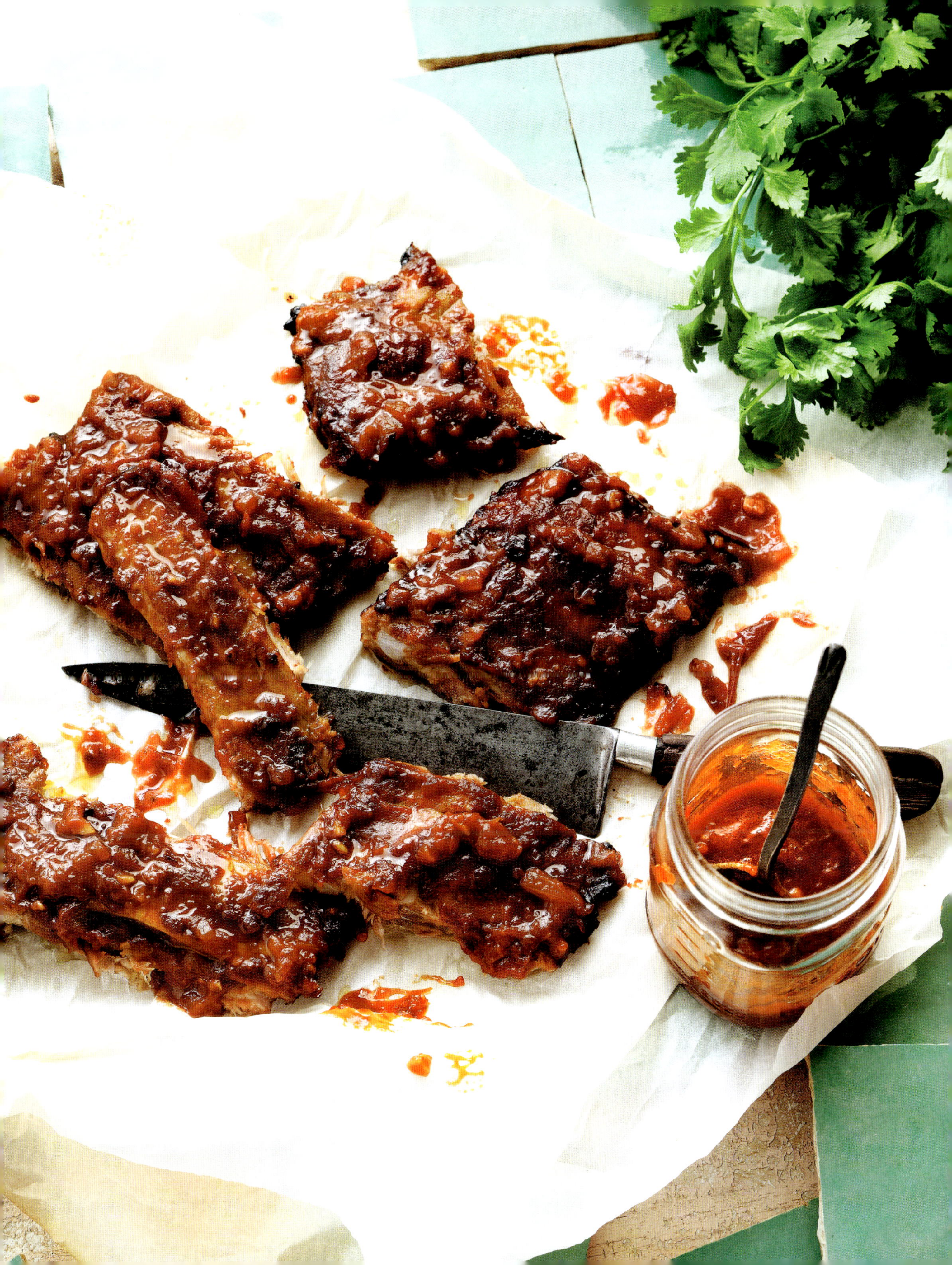

Margarita chicken with watermelon salsa

¼ cup (60ml) tequila ⓟ
¼ cup (60ml) lime juice
2 small red chillies, seeds removed, finely chopped
3 garlic cloves, crushed
¼ cup finely chopped coriander
1 tbs olive oil
4 chicken breasts, skin on, (with the wing bone attached, often referred to as supreme or Kiev)
Mint leaves and chargrilled lime halves, to serve

Watermelon salsa
¼ cup (60ml) lime juice
¼ cup (60ml) extra virgin olive oil
2 tbs tequila
1 jalapeno, ⓟ seeds removed, finely chopped
4 cups (about 700g) chopped seedless watermelon
1 red onion, halved, thinly sliced

Combine tequila, lime juice, chillies, garlic, coriander and oil in a large ziplock bag. Using a sharp knife, slash the chicken skin and flesh, then place in the bag, seal and massage to coat with marinade. Refrigerate for 2-3 hours for flavours to develop.

For the watermelon salsa, whisk lime juice, oil and tequila in a bowl. Add jalapeno, watermelon and onion, and toss gently to combine. Season and set aside.

Preheat a barbecue or chargrill to medium-high. Remove chicken from bag, draining and discarding excess marinade, and season. Cook, skin-side down first, for 3-4 minutes until lightly charred. Turn and cook for a further 3-4 minutes until cooked through. Rest in a warm spot on the barbecue or in a low oven, loosely covered with foil, for 10 minutes.

Serve chicken with watermelon salsa, scattered with mint leaves, with chargrilled lime halves. **Serves 4**

ⓟ See Pantry essentials, p 179.

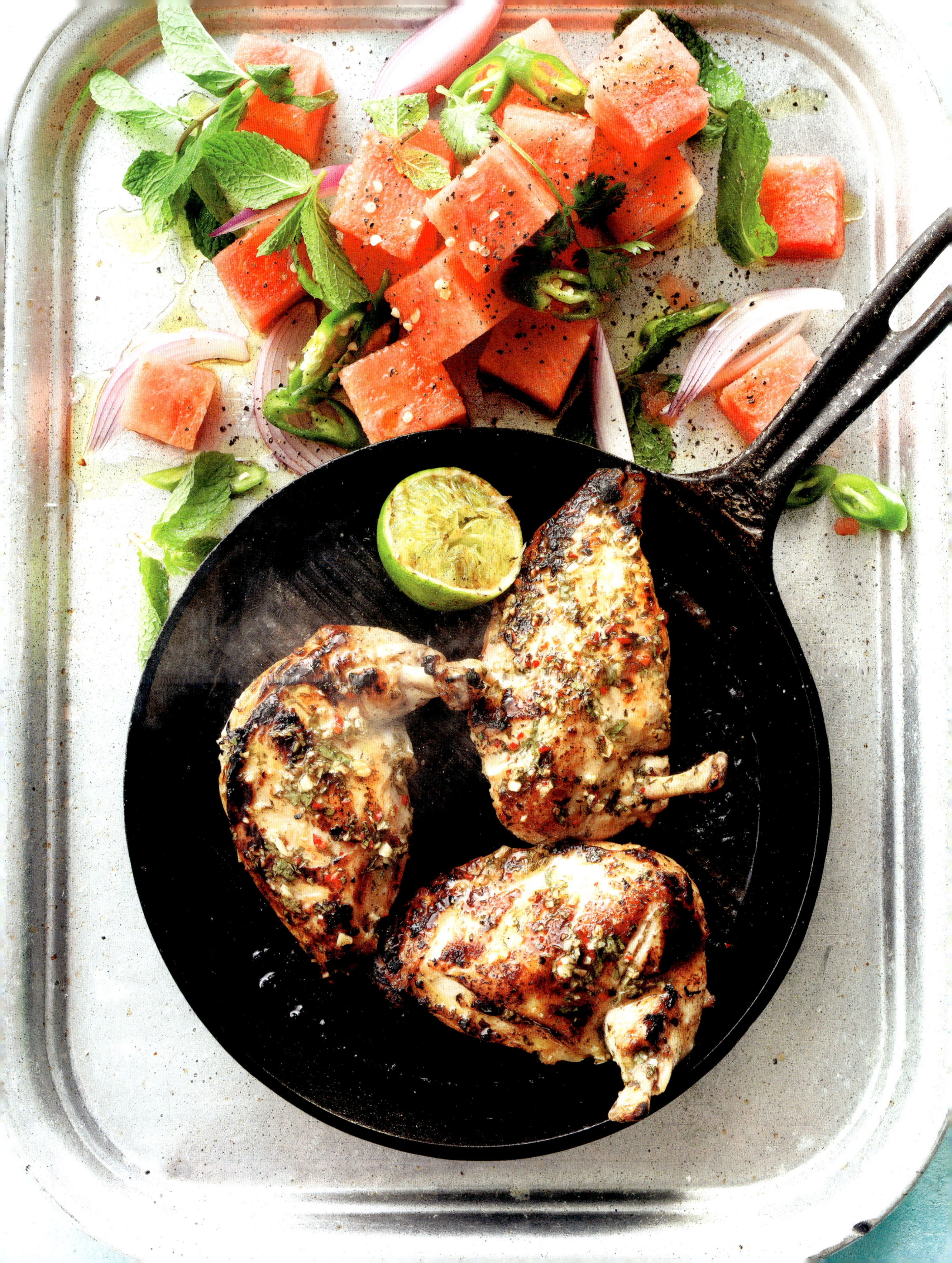

Doughnuts with dulce de leche

1 cup (250ml) milk
60g unsalted butter, chopped
7g sachet dried yeast
3⅓ cups (500g) strong (baker's) flour
250g caster sugar
2 eggs, lightly beaten
1 tsp ground cinnamon
Sunflower oil, to deep-fry
450g jar dulce de leche ⓟ (or see Basics, p 297)

Place milk and butter in a saucepan and warm over low heat until the butter melts. Set aside to cool for 5 minutes.

Line a large baking tray with baking paper. Place yeast, flour, 2 tbs sugar and 1 tsp salt in the bowl of an electric mixer. Add milk mixture and eggs, then knead with the dough hook attachment for 5 minutes (mixture will be very sticky). Turn out dough onto a lightly floured surface and knead for 5 minutes or until smooth and elastic. Divide dough into 20 portions and roll into balls. Place on prepared tray, cover with a clean tea towel and set aside in a warm place for 1 hour or until doubled in size.

Combine cinnamon and remaining sugar in a bowl.

Half-fill a deep-fryer or large saucepan with oil and heat to 190°C (a cube of bread will turn golden in 30 seconds when the oil is hot enough). Fry the dough balls, in batches, gently turning with a metal spoon or tongs to ensure even browning, for 1-2 minutes or until golden. Drain on paper towel, then dust all over with the cinnamon sugar. When all the doughnuts are cooked, cut a small slit into the side of each. Fill a piping bag fitted with a 1cm plain nozzle with the dulce de leche and pipe into the doughnuts (or spoon in using a teaspoon).

Serve doughnuts warm. **Makes 20**

ⓟ See Pantry essentials, p 179.

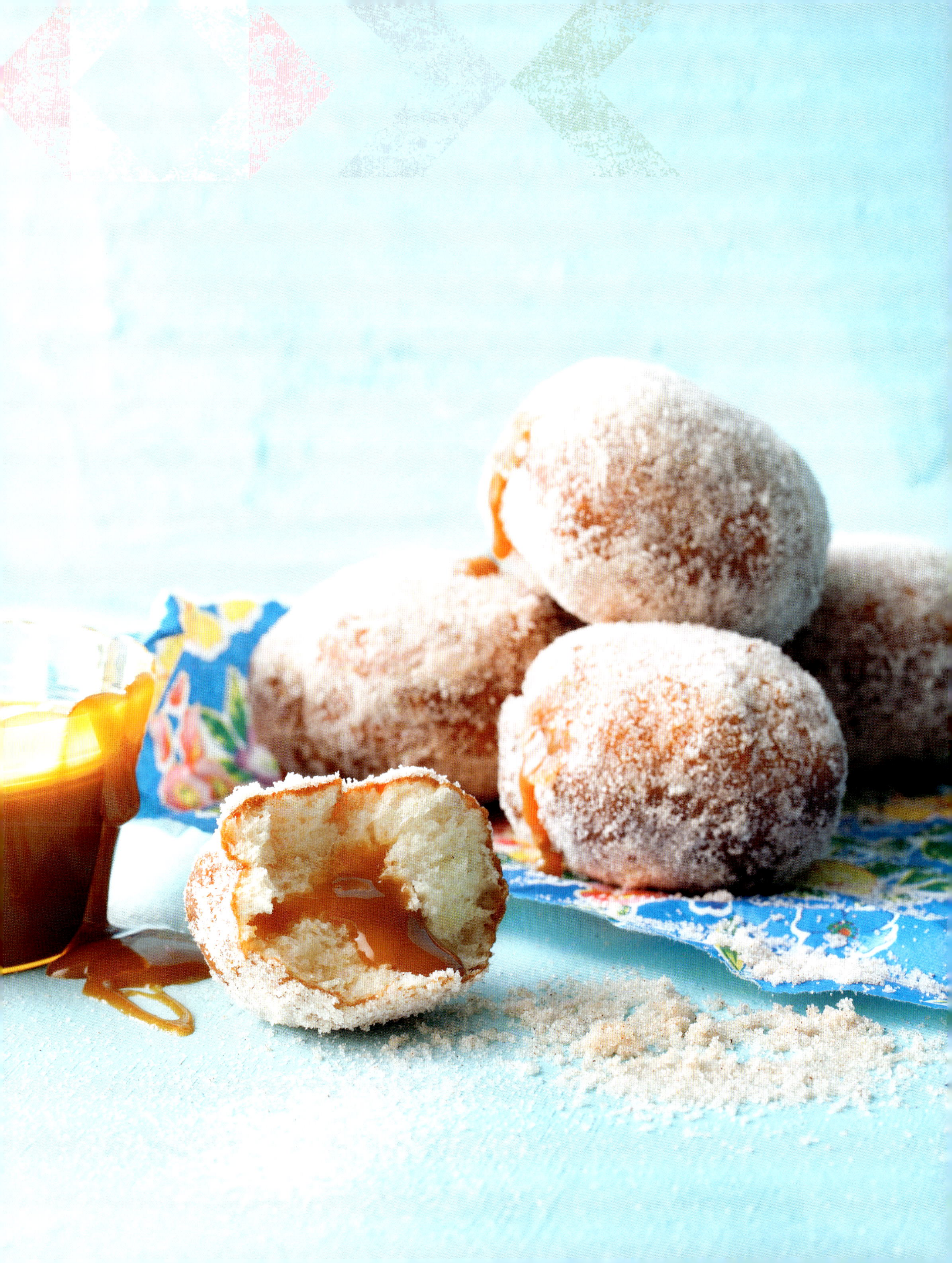

Chilli chocolate puddings

2 cups (500ml) milk
½ cup (110g) caster sugar
2 tbs cornflour
2 tsp cocoa powder
2 egg yolks
20g unsalted butter, chopped
1 tsp vanilla extract
100g dark chilli chocolate (we used Lindt), plus extra shaved (optional) to serve
Whipped cream and 1 quantity caramel sauce (see Basics, p 297), to serve

Combine 1½ cups (375ml) milk and ¼ cup (55g) sugar in a saucepan and bring to the boil over medium-high heat. Place cornflour, cocoa and remaining ½ cup (125ml) milk and ¼ cup (55g) sugar in a bowl and stir to combine. Using a balloon whisk, gradually add the hot milk mixture, whisking constantly until smooth, then whisk in egg yolks. Return mixture to the pan and stir over very low heat until smooth and thickened. Strain through a sieve into a bowl, then add the butter, vanilla extract and chocolate, stirring until the chocolate melts and mixture is smooth. Pour mixture into 4 x 200ml-capacity glass pots or jars, then refrigerate for 2-3 hours or overnight until set.

To serve, dollop whipped cream on top of the chocolate puddings, drizzle with caramel sauce and top with extra shaved dark chilli chocolate, if using. **Serves 4**

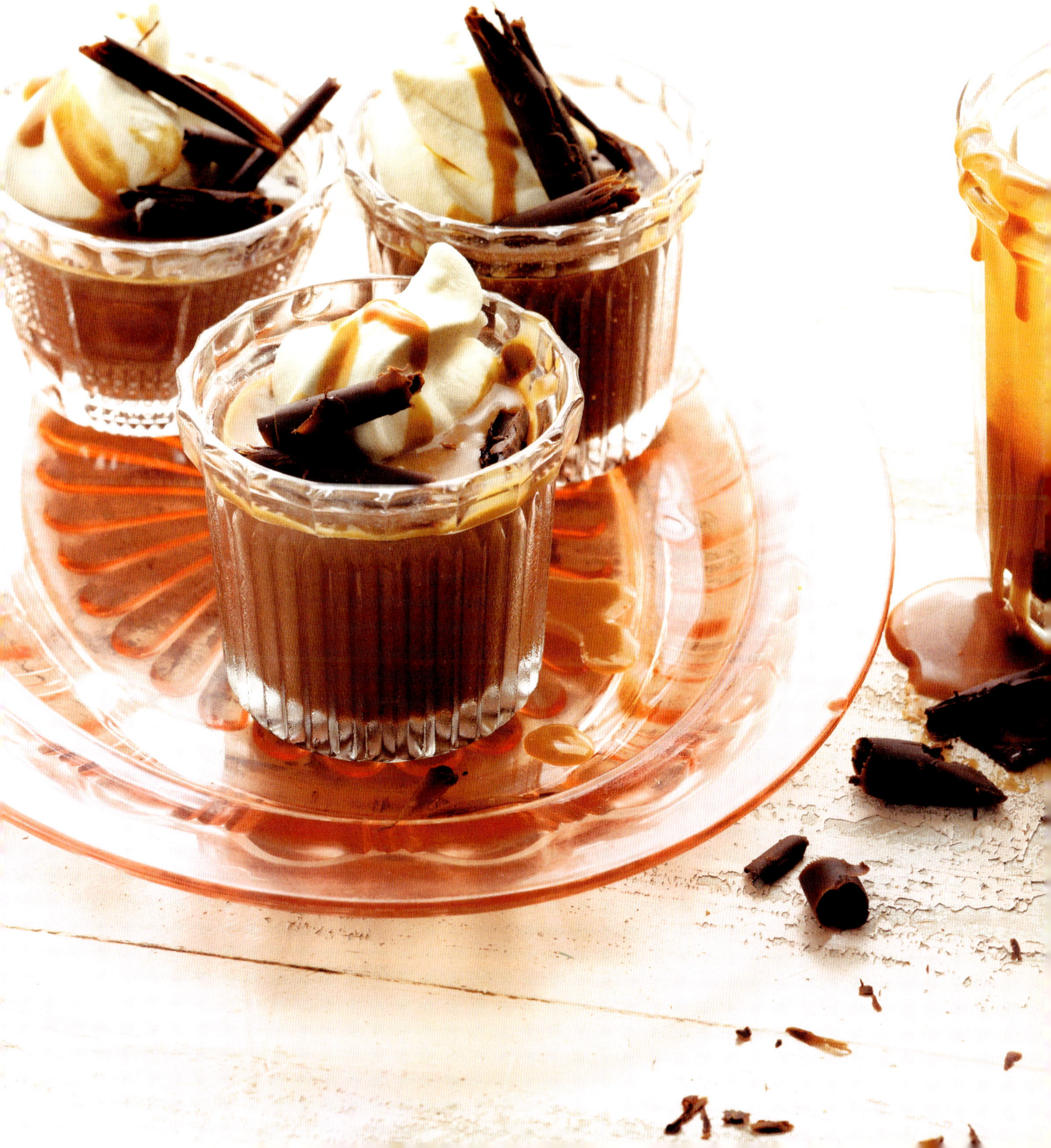

Mexican fiesta ice blocks

Try sprinkling or dipping these ice blocks in a mixture of sea salt and lime zest. For the best results, turn your freezer to the coldest setting to prevent ice crystals forming. You will need 8-10 moulds for each of these flavours.

Mango
- 1/4 cup (55g) caster sugar
- 4-5 mangoes, flesh chopped
- 2 tbs lime juice

Watermelon
- 65g caster sugar
- 4 cups (about 700g) chopped seedless watermelon
- 100ml lime juice
- 1/4 cup (60ml) tequila Ⓟ (optional)

Cucumber & avocado
- 100g caster sugar
- 1 telegraph cucumber, unpeeled, chopped
- 1 small or 1/2 large avocado, chopped
- 1/3 cup (80ml) lime juice

For the mango ice blocks, combine the sugar in a saucepan with 1 cup (250ml) water over low heat, stirring until the sugar dissolves. Set aside to cool. Using a blender or food processor, whiz mango and lime juice until smooth. Add cooled sugar syrup and whiz to combine. Strain through a sieve into a jug, discarding solids, then pour into lolly moulds, leaving a 5mm gap at the top to allow for expansion. Freeze for 1 hour before inserting the sticks, then freeze until ready to serve. To unmould the ice blocks, dip moulds in hot water for 10 seconds, then carefully pull on sticks.

For the watermelon ice blocks, combine the sugar in a saucepan with 1/3 cup (80ml) water over low heat, stirring until sugar dissolves. Set aside to cool. Using a blender or food processor, whiz watermelon until smooth. Add the cooled sugar syrup, lime juice, tequila (if using) and a good pinch of salt and whiz to combine. Strain through a sieve into a jug, discarding solids, then follow freezing method as before.

For the cucumber and avocado ice blocks, place the sugar in a saucepan with 1 cup (250ml) water over low heat, stirring until sugar dissolves. Set aside to cool. Using a blender or food processor, whiz the cucumber, avocado and lime juice until smooth. Add the cooled syrup and a pinch of salt, and whiz to combine. Strain through a sieve into a jug, discarding solids, then follow method as before. **Makes 8-10 of each flavour**
Ⓟ See Pantry essentials, p 179.

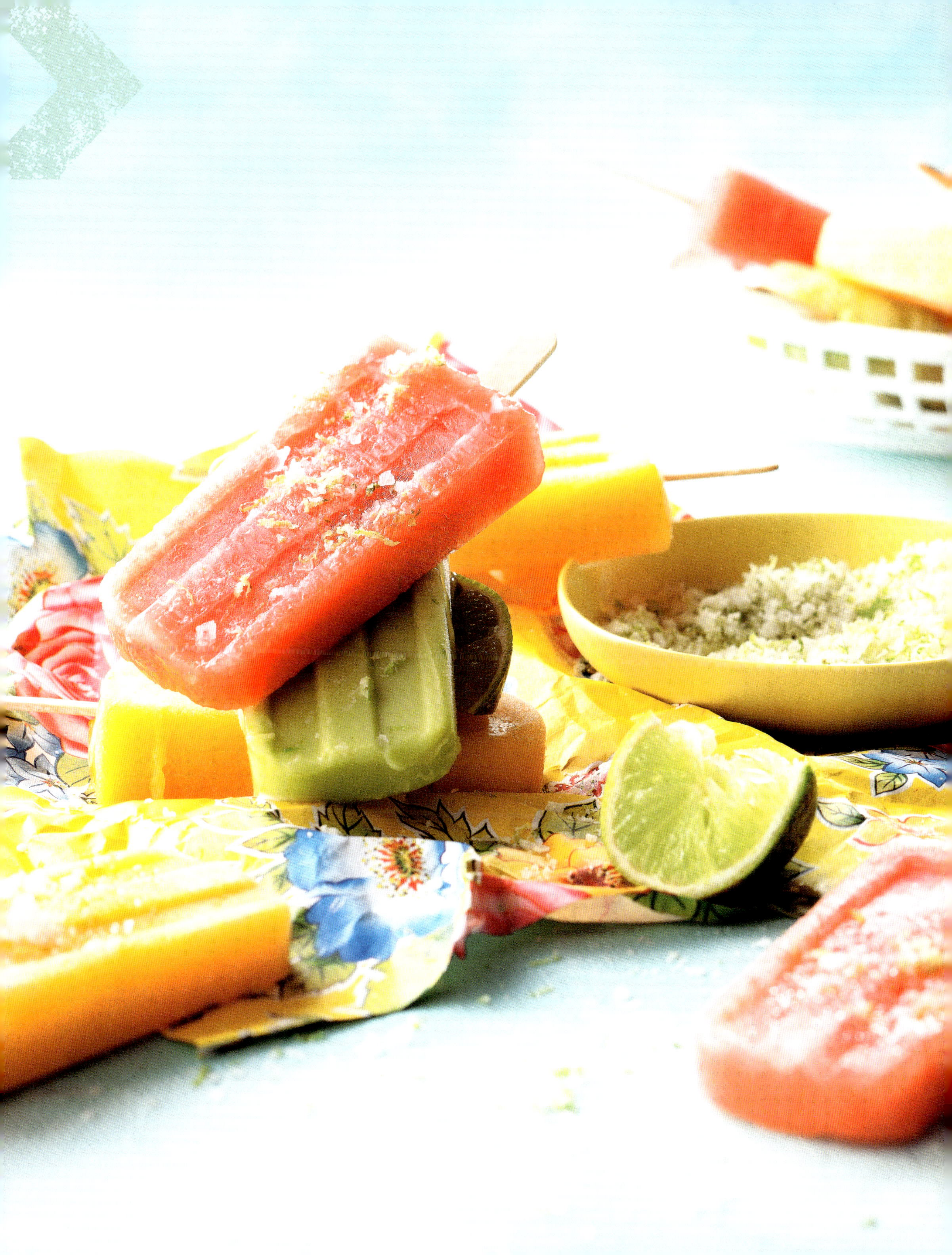

FRENCH

PANTRY ESSENTIALS

Bouquet garni
Herbs (usually parsley, thyme and bay leaves) tied with string and used to flavour soups and stews. Make your own fresh, or buy in sachets.

Capers
The unopened buds of the caper bush. Sold in jars preserved in salt or vinegar. Both styles need to be rinsed, drained and patted dry before using.

Confit duck
A method of preserving the duck that uses its rendered fat and salt to slowly cook the meat. Available from specialist food shops and selected butchers. Scrape off excess fat before cooking.

Cornichons
Tiny pickled cucumbers, traditionally served with paté. Available from delis and selected supermarkets.

Creme fraiche
A thick soured cream with a lighter flavour than regular sour cream. It's good for cooking, as it doesn't split or curdle when heated. Available from delis and selected supermarkets. Substitute sour cream.

Dijon mustard
A mild mustard whose original recipe included verjuice, ground yellow and white mustard seeds and various spices.

Fleur de sel
Hand-harvested salt from the north and western coasts of France, it has a high mineral content and is often mixed with flavourings such as seaweed.

Gelatine leaves
Available in a variety of setting strengths. Always check the packet for setting instructions. Leaf is preferable to powdered gelatine, as it gives a smoother, clearer result and has no flavour. From specialist food shops and selected delis.

Goat's cheese
Soft goat's cheese, also known as chevre (the French word for goat) is used in savoury and sweet dishes. It has a distinctive, sharp, slightly musty flavour. Available from supermarkets.

Herbes de Provence
A dried herb mix of savory, marjoram, rosemary, thyme, oregano and sometimes lavender that reflects flavours typical of France's south-west. Used in a variety of savoury dishes and sauces.

Kirsch
A clear fruit brandy originally made from distilled morello cherries. Available from bottle shops.

Tarragon
There are two types of tarragon available in Australia. French tarragon has long, serrated-edged leaves and has a distinctive anise aroma and flavour – a classic match for chicken. Russian tarragon has long, smooth-edged leaves, with little flavour or scent.

Truffles & truffle oil
Black Perigord truffles are now cultivated in Australia. Available, in season, from specialist food shops, or visit perigord.com.au. Truffle oil is a cheaper alternative, but should be used sparingly, as its earthy flavour and aroma can be overpowering.

Verjuice and wine vinegars
Verjuice is unfermented grape juice with a mildly acidic flavour. Use it in a similar way to lemon juice to deglaze pans, and for dressings and sauces. Red wine, white wine and Champagne vinegar are used variously in dressings and sauces, including classic vinaigrette and bearnaise.

Luxurious foie gras (goose liver) and truffles aside, accessible ingredients form the heart of French cooking: onions, garlic and eschalots; butter, cream, creme fraiche, cheeses; and wines and wine vinegars, often flavoured with herbs. Tarragon and chervil add their distinctive notes to savoury dishes, while eggs, flour, sugar and liqueurs are stalwarts of desserts and patisserie.

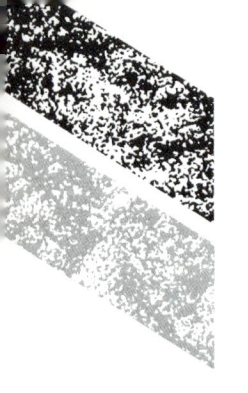

Warm goat's cheese fondue with primeurs

'Primeurs' are the first vegetables and fruits of the season and are celebrated all over France. You'll find them here at farmers' markets and selected greengrocers, especially through the spring months.

½ cup (120g) creme fraiche ⓟ
¼ cup (60ml) milk
2 sprigs thyme
1 bay leaf
1 garlic clove, crushed
160g soft goat's cheese, ⓟ crumbled
Selection of mixed baby vegetables (such as carrots, green and yellow beans, spring onions and radishes)

Place creme fraiche, milk, herbs and garlic in a saucepan over low heat, stirring until combined. Remove from the heat and set aside for 10 minutes for flavours to infuse.

Remove and discard herbs, then return saucepan to a low heat. Sprinkle over the goat's cheese, season, then stir until the cheese melts and the mixture is warmed through.

Serve with baby vegetables for dipping. **Serves 4-6**

ⓟ See Pantry essentials, p 206.

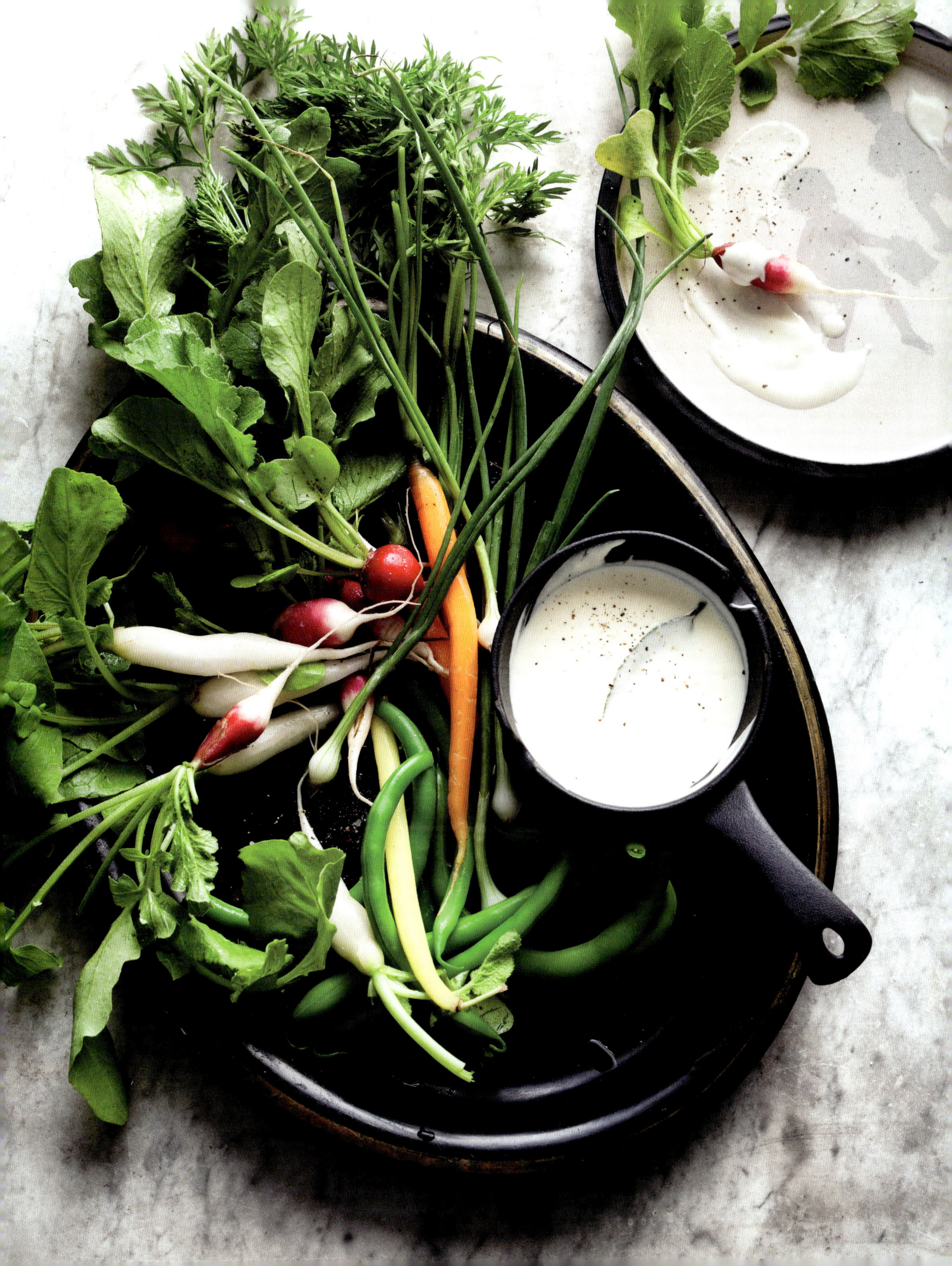

Carrot soup Vichy with herbed croutons

'Carottes Vichy' uses a classic French technique of adding a little water or stock, butter and occasionally sugar to cook and glaze the vegetables.

30g unsalted butter
1 tbs olive oil
1 leek (white part only), chopped
1 onion, chopped
Bouquet garni ⓟ
5 carrots, scrubbed, chopped
1 large potato, peeled, chopped
1.5L (6 cups) chicken stock
¼ cup (60g) creme fraiche, ⓟ plus extra to serve

Herbed croutons
½ baguette or 1 ficelle, torn into large chunks
½ cup (125ml) olive oil
2 garlic cloves, crushed
¼ cup each finely chopped flat-leaf parsley and basil

Heat the butter and oil in a large saucepan over medium-low heat. Add the leek and onion, and cook, stirring, for 2-3 minutes until softened but not browned. Add the bouquet garni, carrot, potato and stock. Season. Increase heat to medium-high and bring to the boil. Reduce heat to low, then cook, partially covered with a lid, for 20-25 minutes until vegetables are tender.

Meanwhile, for the croutons, toss bread in a large bowl with ¼ cup (60ml) olive oil. Place remaining oil in a food processor with garlic and herbs, and process to a smooth paste. Heat a frypan over medium-high heat and fry the bread, turning, for 6-8 minutes until golden and crisp. Add the herb mixture to the pan and toss to combine.

Remove bouquet garni from the soup and discard. Cool the soup slightly. Using a blender, blend until smooth. Return soup to the saucepan over medium heat and stir in creme fraiche.

Ladle soup into bowls, swirl through extra creme fraiche and serve with herbed croutons. **Serves 4-6**

ⓟ See Pantry essentials, p 206.

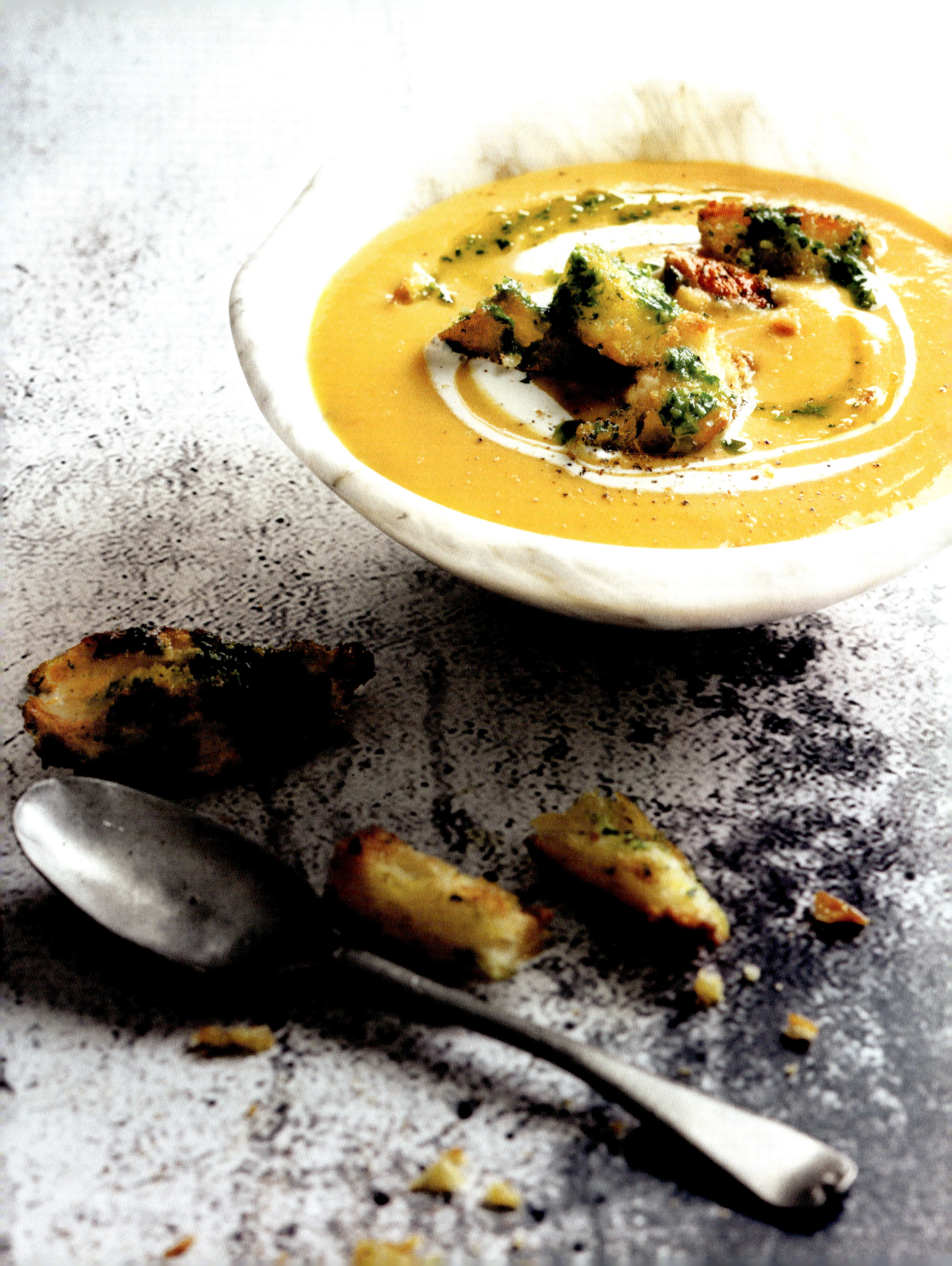

Heirloom tarte Tatin

20 mixed heirloom truss tomatoes (a mixture of small and large, enough to fit snugly into the dish)
Olive oil, to grease
2 tbs caster sugar
1 sheet frozen butter puff pastry, thawed
2 tbs Dijon mustard Ⓟ

Preheat the oven to 140°C. Place the large tomatoes upside down in an oiled 22cm Tatin dish or ovenproof frypan. Cut a small cross in the base of each, season with salt, then roast for 40 minutes until slightly softened. Remove from the oven and add the smaller tomatoes (no need to cut a cross in these), packing in well so they fit snugly in the pan. Roast for a further 10 minutes, then carefully tilt the pan to drain away any cooking juices that have accumulated.

Sprinkle the tomatoes with the sugar, season with pepper and leave to cool slightly for 10 minutes. Meanwhile, increase the oven temperature to 180°C.

Cut a circle from the pastry slightly larger than the pan, then spread with mustard. Place the pastry round, mustard-side down, over the top of the tomatoes, tucking in excess pastry around the edges. Place the Tatin dish or frypan on a baking tray, then return to the oven for 20-25 minutes until the pastry is golden and puffed. Remove from the oven and rest in the dish for 10 minutes. Carefully tip the dish again to drain off any excess liquid, then carefully invert the tart onto a plate. Season and serve immediately. **Serves 6**

Ⓟ See Pantry essentials, p 206.

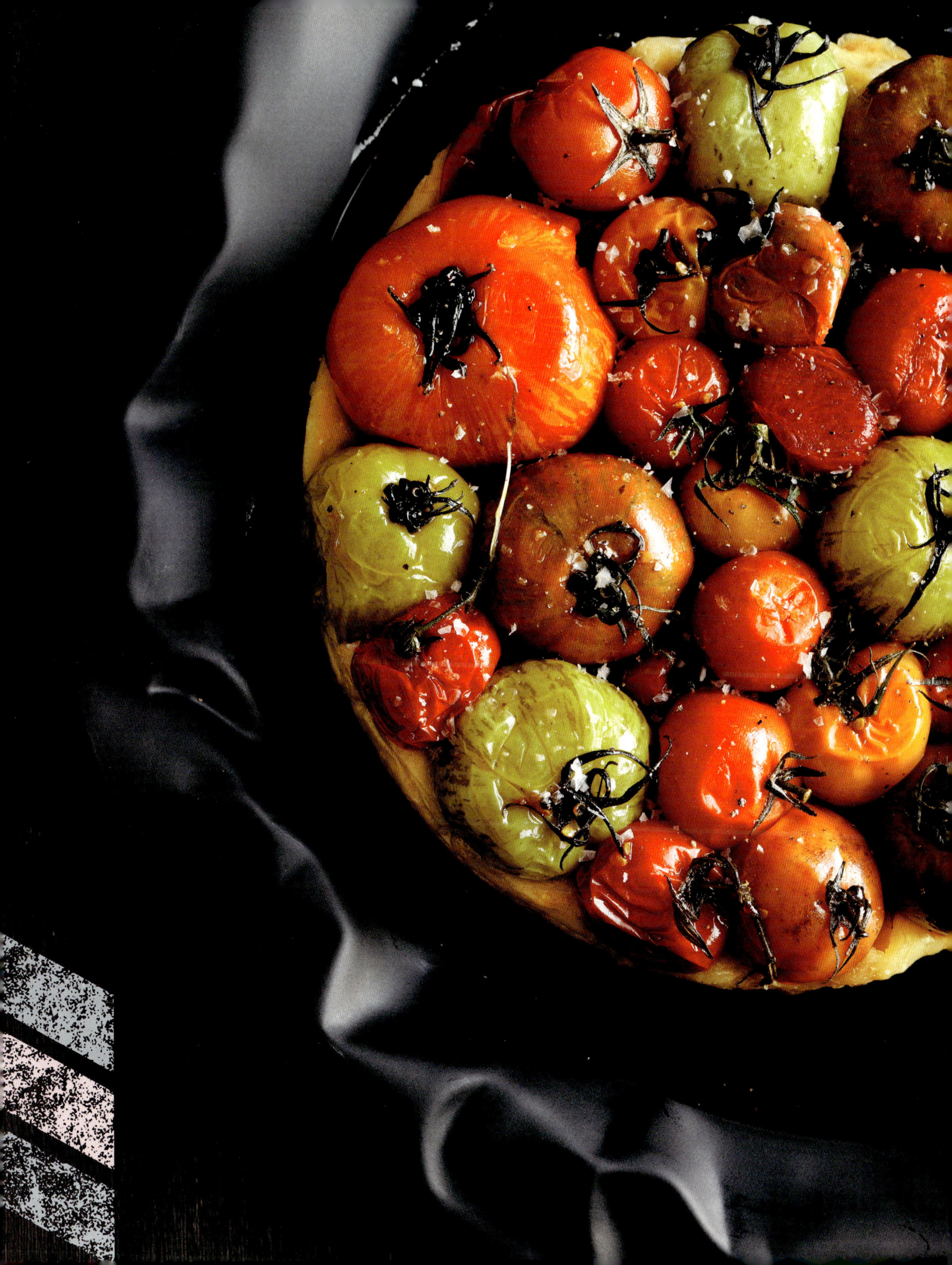

Smoked trout & celeriac tartines

1 baguette, cut diagonally into long, thin slices
2 tbs olive oil
1 (about 350g) celeriac, peeled
2 tbs lemon juice
2 tbs salted baby capers, ⓟ rinsed
2 tbs finely chopped flat-leaf parsley
2 tbs finely chopped tarragon ⓟ
1/3 cup (100g) garlic mayonnaise (see Basics, p 296) or see note, right *
250g smoked trout or salmon
Dill sprigs and lemon halves, to serve

Preheat the oven to 170°C. Line a baking tray with baking paper. Place bread on tray and brush both sides with olive oil. Bake for 8-10 minutes until golden and crisp.

Using a mandoline, finely shave the celeriac and immediately place in a bowl of iced water with the lemon juice (this will prevent it from browning).

When ready to serve, drain the celeriac and combine with the capers, parsley, tarragon and garlic mayonnaise.

Top bread with celeriac mixture, smoked trout and dill, season with black pepper and serve with lemon halves.

Serves 4 as a starter

* *Alternatively, combine 1/4 cup (65g) whole-egg mayonnaise with 2 tbs creme fraiche and 2 grated garlic cloves.*

ⓟ See Pantry essentials, p 206.

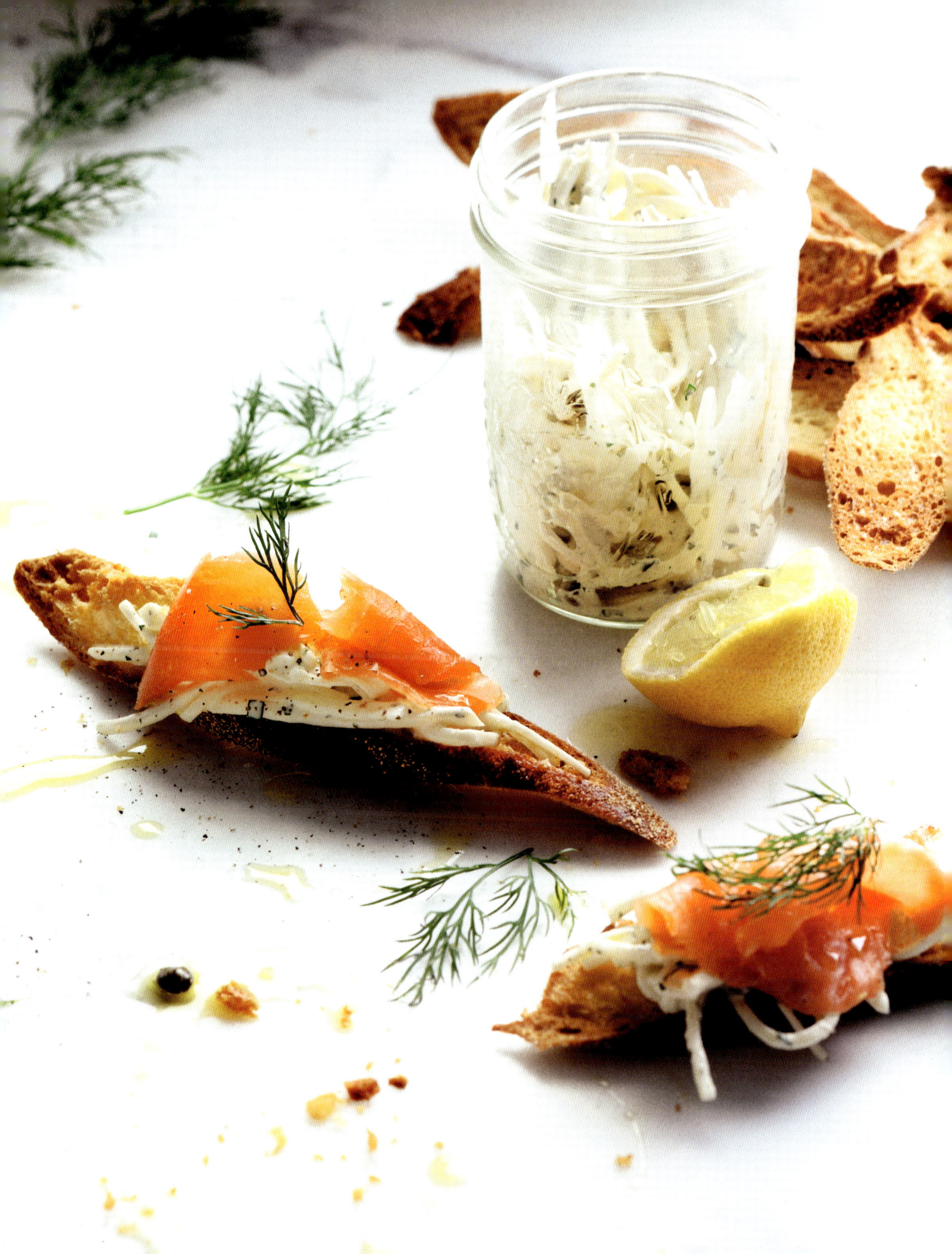

Salmon en papillote with honey mustard sauce

Cooking in paper parcels is a great way to cook fish, as it seals in all those precious juices and not-so-precious aromas!

2 tbs Dijon mustard (P)
1 tbs wholegrain mustard
⅓ cup (80g) creme fraiche (P)
1 tbs honey
1 tbs olive oil
1 tbs chopped tarragon, (P) plus extra chopped and whole leaves to serve
4 x 150g skinless salmon fillets, pin-boned
Steamed green beans and pan-fried potatoes, to serve

Preheat the oven to 200°C. Cut out 4 x 20cm squares of foil and top each with a sheet of baking paper the same size.

Combine mustards, creme fraiche, honey, oil and tarragon in a bowl and season.

Place a piece of salmon on each piece of foil, then drizzle over the mustard mixture. Seal the parcels by folding over the edges of the foil and crimping. Place on a baking tray. Bake for 12 minutes or until fish is just cooked. Carefully open the parcels and transfer fish and sauce to plates. (Alternatively, serve the fish still in their parcels and open them at the table.)

Serve with steamed green beans and pan-fried potatoes, sprinkled with extra chopped and whole tarragon leaves.

Serves 4

(P) See Pantry essentials, p 206.

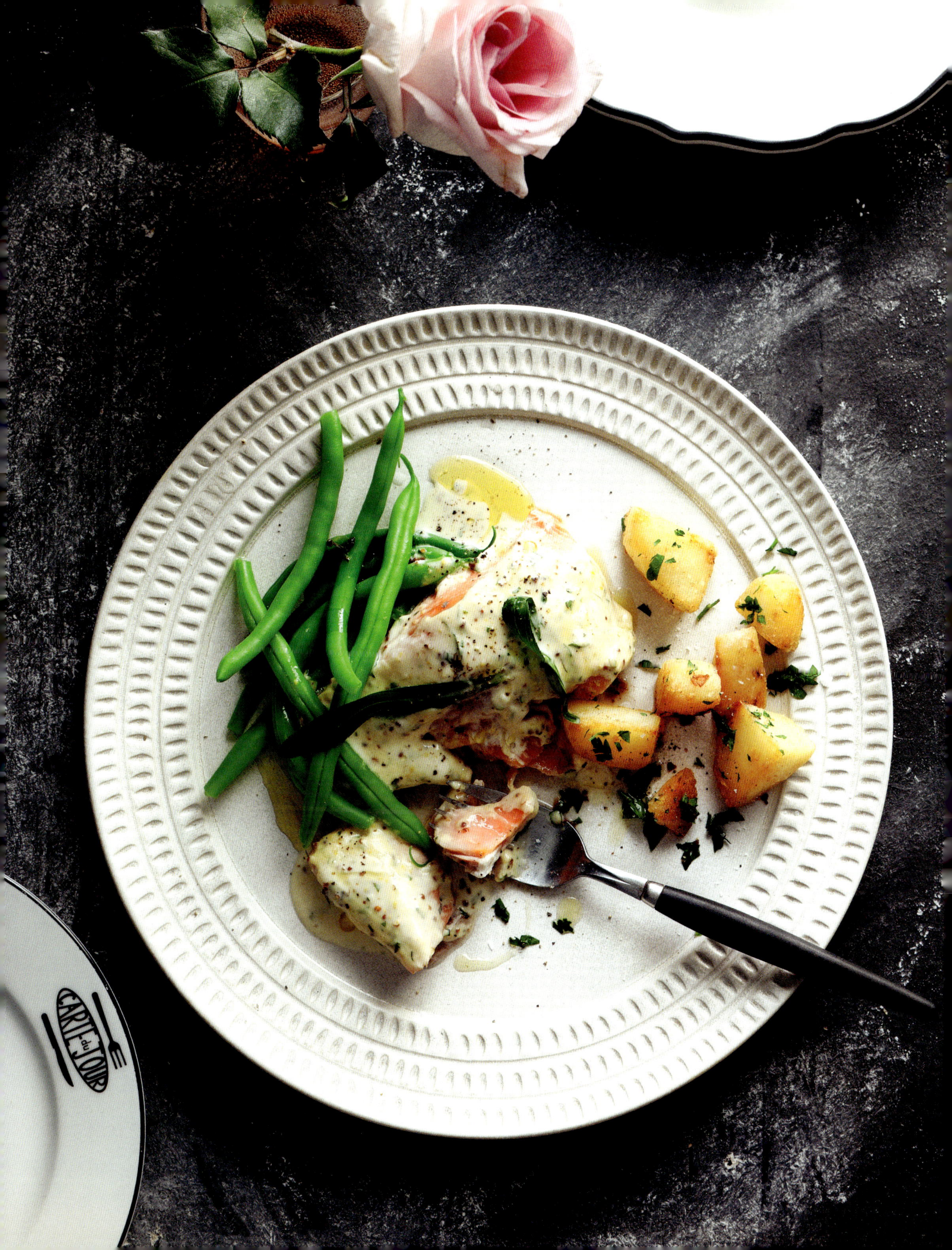
CARTE du JOUR

Beef ribs daube style

¼ cup (60ml) olive oil
3kg beef short ribs on the bone, cut into 6-7cm lengths (ask your butcher to do this for you)
3 carrots, thickly sliced
4 celery stalks, cut into 5cm lengths
12 spring onions with bulbs, white part only, trimmed
6 garlic cloves, finely chopped
¼ cup (70g) tomato paste
1L (4 cups) full-bodied red wine
½ cup (125ml) Port
1.5L (6 cups) beef or veal stock
Bouquet garni Ⓟ
Finely chopped flat-leaf parsley leaves, to serve

Dijon mash
1.5kg sebago potatoes, peeled, chopped
150ml pure cream
75g unsalted butter, chopped
1 tbs Dijon mustard Ⓟ

Preheat the oven to 160°C.

Heat the oil in a large casserole or ovenproof pan over medium-high heat and cook beef, in batches, turning, until well browned. Transfer to a large bowl. Drain excess oil, leaving 2 tbs in the pan. Add carrot, celery, whole onions and two-thirds of the garlic, and cook for 5-6 minutes until vegetables are starting to soften. Add tomato paste and cook, stirring, for 1 minute. Add wine, port, stock and bouquet garni. Season. Bring mixture to the boil, then return beef ribs to the pan, ensuring they are well covered in the liquid. Cover with a lid, then transfer to the oven and cook for 3 hours or until meat is very tender.

For the Dijon mash, place potato in a large saucepan and cover with cold salted water. Bring to the boil over medium-high heat, then reduce heat to medium and cook for 15-20 minutes or until tender. Drain, then return potatoes to the saucepan over low heat, shaking gently until excess liquid evaporates. Using a potato ricer or masher, mash until smooth. Using a wooden spoon, beat cream, butter and mustard into the potato until the mash is smooth and creamy. Season, then cover and keep warm.

Using a slotted spoon, transfer ribs and vegetables to a serving dish and cover. Place casserole over medium-high heat and simmer wine mixture for 8-10 minutes until sauce has reduced slightly. Return the beef and vegetables to the casserole to warm through.

Meanwhile, combine chopped flat-leaf parsley with the remaining finely chopped garlic. Remove bouquet garni from casserole, then serve beef ribs, vegetables and sauce sprinkled with parsley mixture, with Dijon mash. **Serves 4-6**

Ⓟ See Pantry essentials, p 206.

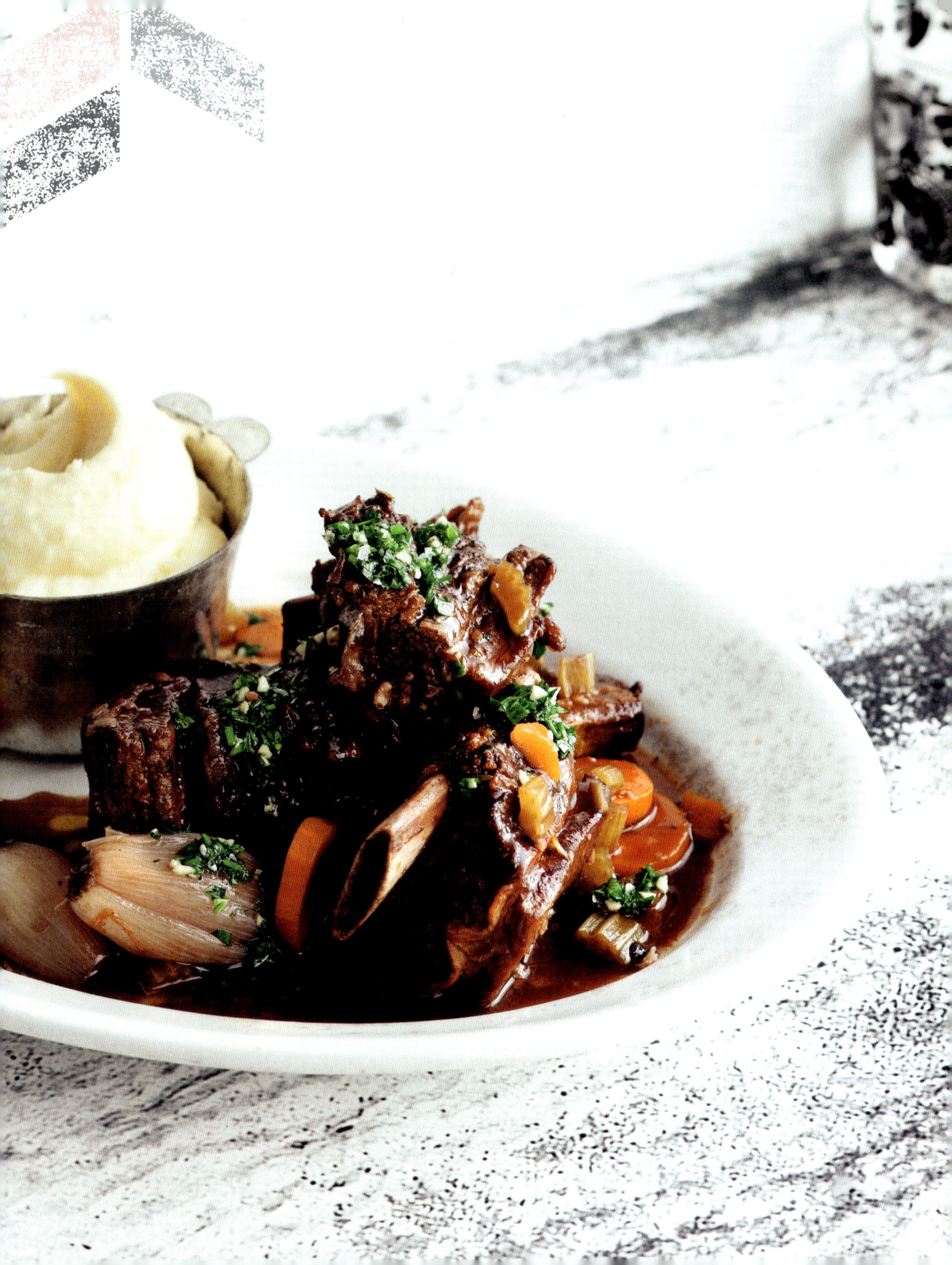

Confit duck with potatoes sarladaises

'Pommes de terre sarladaises' is a French classic – potatoes cooked in duck fat, here, conveniently reserved from the confit duck with which it's often served.

4 confit duck legs *
4 large floury potatoes
   (such as King Edward
   or sebago), peeled
2 garlic cloves, crushed
1 bunch thyme,
   leaves picked
1 bunch watercress,
   sprigs picked
2 tbs finely chopped
   flat-leaf parsley leaves

Sweet mustard dressing
2 tbs Dijon mustard ⓟ
¼ cup (55g) caster sugar
50ml white wine vinegar ⓟ
100ml grapeseed or olive oil

Preheat the oven to 180°C. Line a large baking tray with baking paper.

Scrape the excess fat from the duck legs and melt in a small saucepan over low heat. Transfer melted fat to a large bowl.

Using a mandoline, thinly slice potatoes into 2mm-thick rounds. Add to the duck fat, with the garlic and thyme leaves, then season and toss to combine. Spread the potato mixture in a single layer over the prepared baking tray. Roast for 25 minutes, turning halfway through cooking, or until crisp and golden. Place the confit duck legs among the potato slices, then return to the oven for a further 15-20 minutes until the duck is heated through and golden.

Meanwhile, for the dressing, combine ingredients in a jar and shake well. Season. Toss the watercress with sweet mustard dressing. Serve with the duck and potatoes, sprinkled with flat-leaf parsley. **Serves 4**

* *Confit duck legs are available from gourmet shops and selected butchers.*

ⓟ *See Pantry essentials, p 206.*

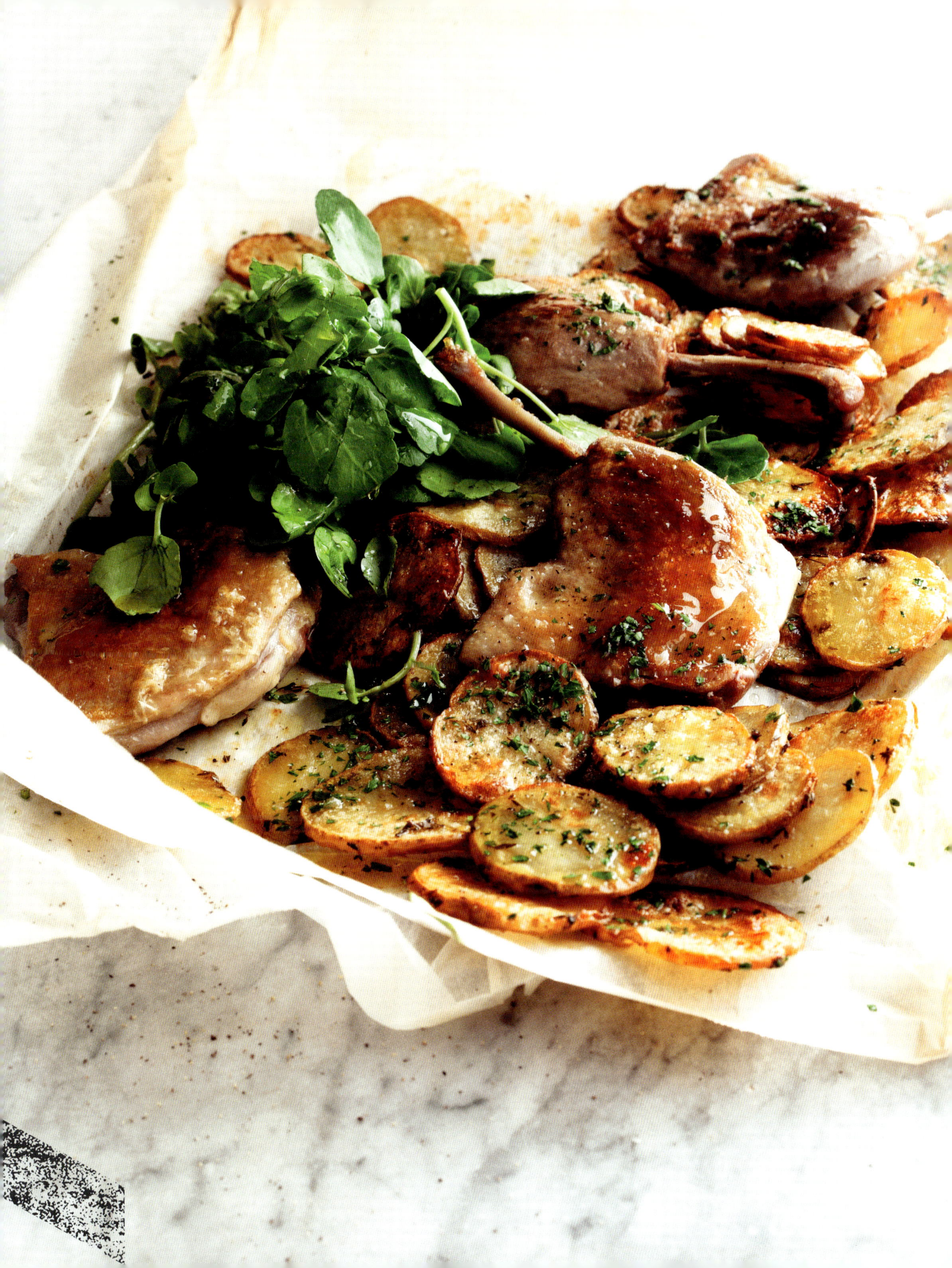

Truffled chicken with Champagne sauce

This luxurious dish is inspired by a recipe from my good friend, Jane Lawson. Truffles in season are a wonderful (but expensive!) ingredient. You can find cheaper preserved truffles in gourmet food shops, or use a drizzle of truffle oil.

- 3 leeks (white part only), each cut into 4 lengths
- 60g unsalted butter, softened
- 2 cups (500ml) chicken stock
- 4 chicken breast fillets, skin on (with the wing bone attached, often referred to as supreme or Kiev)
- 1 small black truffle ⓟ
- 1 tbs olive oil
- 1-2 tsp truffle oil ⓟ (optional)
- Steamed baby vegetables, to serve

Champagne sauce
- 20g unsalted butter
- 1 tbs plain flour
- 1 garlic clove, crushed
- 100ml Champagne or other sparkling white wine
- 2 sprigs thyme
- ½ cup (125ml) pure (thin) cream
- ½ cup (125ml) chicken stock

Preheat oven to 180°C. Grease a 2L (8-cup-capacity) baking dish.

Place leeks in prepared baking dish and dot with 30g butter. Season, then pour over the chicken stock. Place a sheet of baking paper over the top, then bake for 30 minutes or until tender. Remove from the oven.

Meanwhile, gently loosen the skin from the breasts. Thinly slice the truffle and place a few slices between the skin and flesh of each breast. Season. Heat remaining 30g butter and olive oil in a frypan over medium-high heat. Cook the chicken, skin-side down first, for 3 minutes each side or until light golden. Place the chicken on top of the leek mixture in the baking dish, then return to the oven and cook for a further 15 minutes. Remove from the oven, drain off 100ml of the cooking liquid and reserve. Set aside chicken, loosely covered with foil.

Meanwhile, for the Champagne sauce, heat the butter in a frypan over medium heat, add the flour and cook, stirring, for 1 minute. Add the garlic, Champagne, thyme, cream, stock and reserved cooking liquid, gently whisking until smooth. Simmer for 2-3 minutes until slightly reduced. Season well.

Thickly slice each chicken breast. Divide leeks among 4 plates, top each with a sliced chicken breast, then drizzle with Champagne sauce and truffle oil, if using. Serve with steamed baby vegetables. **Serves 4**

ⓟ See Pantry essentials, p 206.

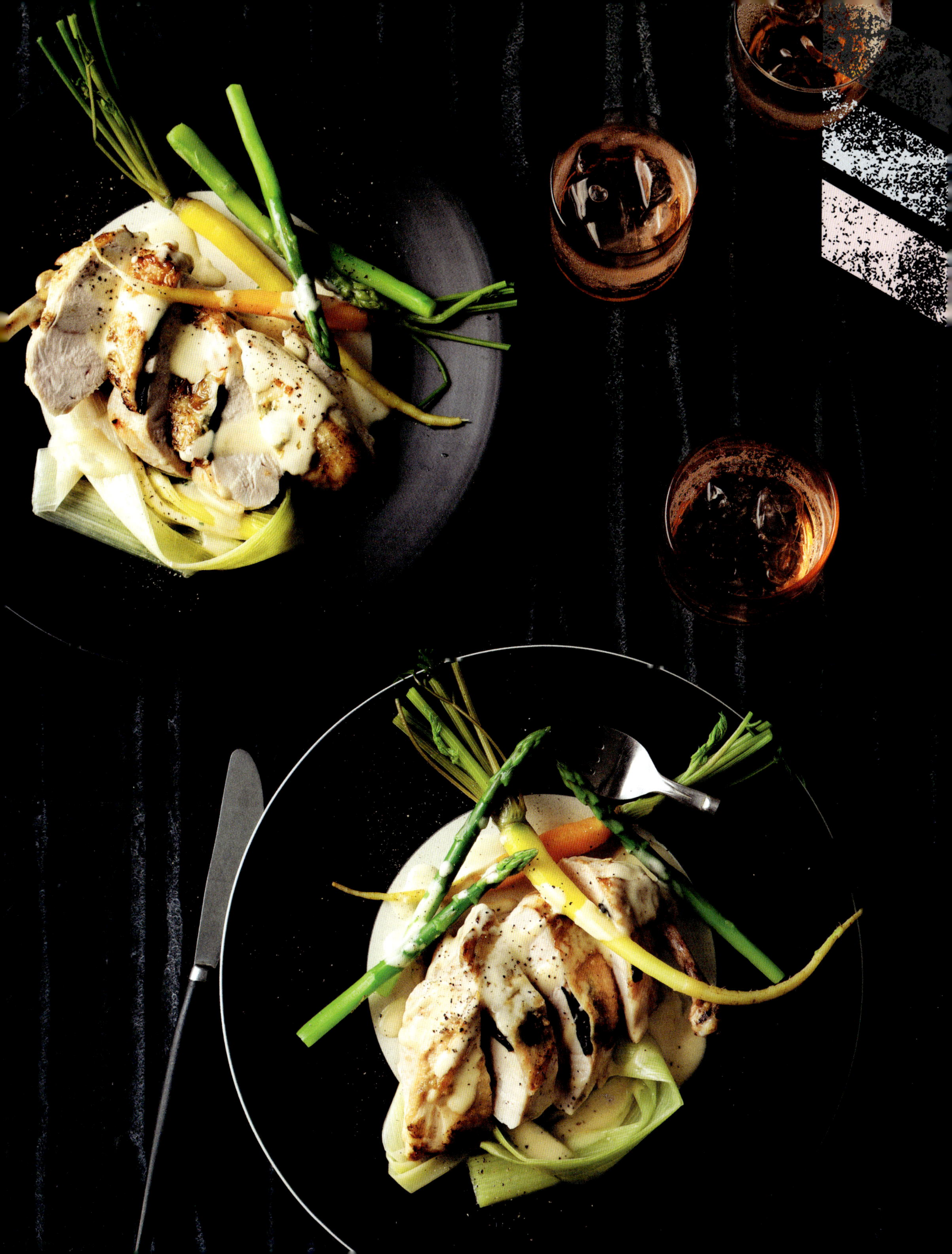

Sweet goat's cheese tarts with roasted blueberries

Roasting fruit seems to intensify its flavour. Try this method with strawberries and rhubarb, too. Serve any leftovers with yoghurt for breakfast – delicieux!

375g fresh blueberries (or frozen, defrosted)
²/₃ cup (150g) caster sugar
1 vanilla bean, split
435g frozen vanilla bean sweet shortcrust pastry,* thawed (or 1 quantity sweet shortcrust pastry, see Basics, p 294)
1 egg, separated
½ cup (120g) fresh ricotta
½ tsp ground cinnamon
125g soft goat's cheese ⓟ

Place the berries, 100g sugar and vanilla bean in a baking pan. Drizzle over 2 tbs cold water and stir to combine. Bake for 10 minutes or until the berries have released plenty of juices. Set aside to cool for 10 minutes, then refrigerate.

Grease 6 x 10cm loose-bottomed tart pans. Roll out the pastry on a lightly floured surface to 2mm thick. Using a 12cm round cutter, cut out 6 rounds. Line the pans with the pastry, then refrigerate for 30 minutes.

Preheat the oven to 180°C. Prick the pastry bases with a fork, then line with baking paper and fill with pastry weights or rice. Bake for 6-8 minutes or until pale golden. Remove the paper and weights. Lightly whisk the eggwhite with a fork, then brush over pastry cases. Return to the oven for a further 2 minutes or until golden and dry. Cool in the pans.

Combine egg yolk, ricotta, cinnamon and remaining 50g sugar in a food processor and whiz until smooth. Add goat's cheese and pulse a few times to combine. (Alternatively, using a wooden spoon, beat all the ingredients together in a bowl until smooth.)

To serve, divide cheese mixture among pastry cases and top with berry mixture. **Serves 6**

* *We used Carême brand, available from specialist food shops. For stockists, visit: caremepastry.com.*
ⓟ *See Pantry essentials, p 206.*

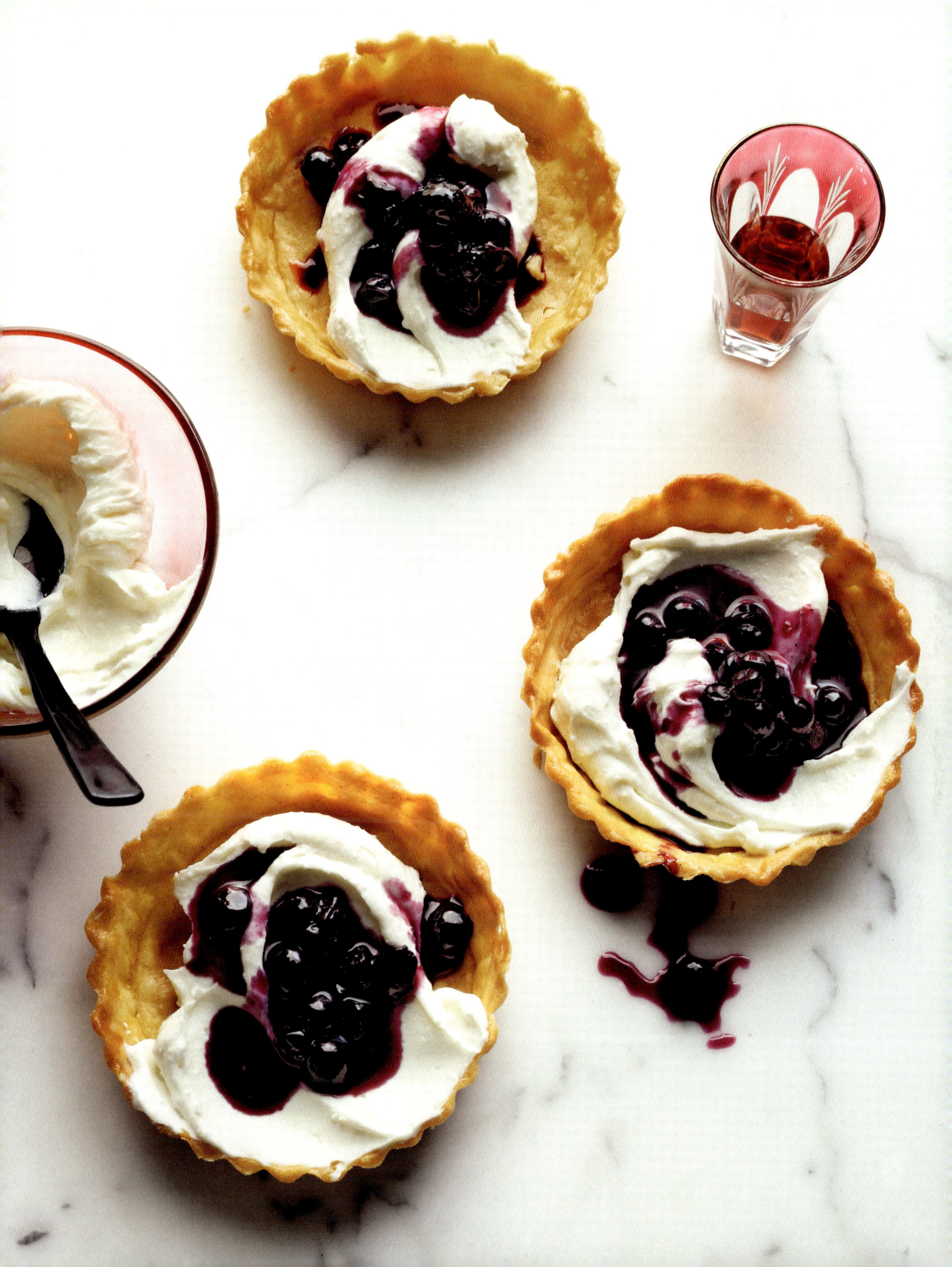

Crepes Suzette with a touch of spice

While the batter in this recipe is enough for 10 crepes, keep in mind that there are always a couple that don't work; you're aiming for two crepes per person.

¼ cup (55g) caster sugar
150ml orange juice
2 tbs lemon juice
2 oranges, finely zested, pith removed, segmented
2 cardamom pods
1 cinnamon quill
30g unsalted butter, chopped
⅓ cup (80ml) Grand Marnier
Vanilla ice cream, to serve

Crepes
¾ cup (110g) plain flour
2 eggs
200ml milk
50g unsalted butter, melted

For the crepes, sift flour into a bowl with a pinch of salt. Whisk the eggs with the milk and ⅓ cup (80ml) water. Gradually add the egg mixture to the flour, whisking well to combine. Add 2 tbs of the melted butter to the mixture, then set aside to rest for 15 minutes.

Brush a 20cm crepe pan or frypan with a little of the remaining melted butter and heat over a high heat. Reduce heat to medium-high, then add ¼ cup (60ml) batter, swirling to coat the base of the pan. Cook for 1 minute or until golden, then flip with a palette knife and cook for 30 seconds on the other side. (Don't worry if you have to discard the first crepe; it often doesn't work.) Layer crepes between sheets of baking paper and keep warm on a plate over a pan of simmering water. (Alternatively, freeze in an airtight container for up to 3 months and reheat.)

Heat the sugar and 2 tbs water in a frypan over low heat, stirring until sugar dissolves. Increase heat to medium-high and cook, without stirring, for 5-6 minutes until a golden caramel forms. Slowly add orange and lemon juice, orange zest and spices (take care, as mixture may spit), stirring gently to combine. Add butter and Grand Marnier, and stir to combine.

Fold each crepe into quarters, then add to the pan with the orange segments to warm through.

Serve crepes, orange segments and sauce with scoops of vanilla ice cream. **Serves 4**

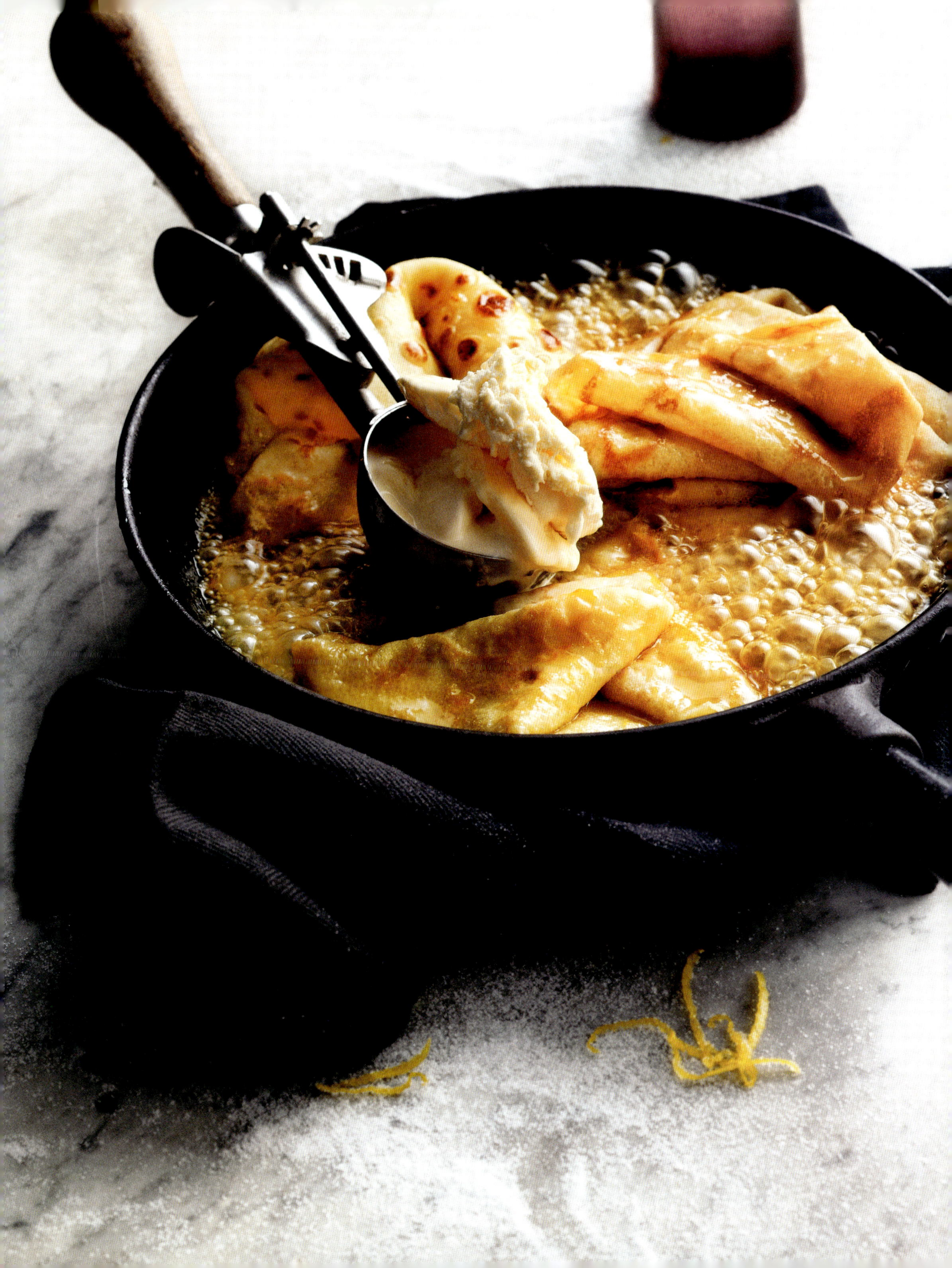

Breton apple cake

I've been making a version of this classic for years. The rich, buttery pastry melts in your mouth and it reheats beautifully the next day – if there's any left!

250g unsalted butter, softened
1½ cups (330g) caster sugar
2 tsp vanilla extract
5 egg yolks
3 cups (450g) plain flour, sifted
8 large Granny Smith apples, peeled, cored, chopped
1 cinnamon quill
Pure (thin) cream, to serve

Grease a 26cm loose-bottomed tart pan.

Beat butter and 1 cup (220g) caster sugar in the bowl of an electric mixer for 2-3 minutes until thick and pale. Add 1 tsp vanilla, then 4 egg yolks, one at a time, beating well after each addition. Add 1 tbs iced water. Using a metal spoon, fold in the flour. Using your hands, bring dough together and cut into a one-third and a two-third portion. Roll out the larger portion of dough on a lightly floured surface, then use to line the base and side of the pan. (This pastry can be a little difficult to handle, especially on a warm day, but just press and pat into the pan to line evenly.) Roll out the remaining third of the dough between 2 sheets of floured baking paper large enough to cover the pan. Refrigerate pastry case and lid.

Combine apples in a saucepan with the cinnamon, remaining ½ cup (110g) sugar and 1 tsp vanilla, and ¼ cup (60ml) water. Cook over low heat until apple starts to soften. Cover and cook, stirring occasionally, for 12-15 minutes until very soft. Drain in a colander, discarding liquid and cinnamon (it's essential that the filling be quite dry, or the pastry will be soggy). Set apple aside to cool completely.

Preheat the oven to 180°C. Fill the pastry case with apple and brush the edges of the pastry with a little water. Using the baking paper as a guide, slide the pastry lid over the filling. Trim the edges and crimp to seal. Run the tines of a fork over the pastry in a decorative pattern. Lightly whisk the remaining egg yolk and brush the top of the pastry. Bake for 45-50 minutes or until golden.

Serve warm or cold with cream. **Serves 6-8**

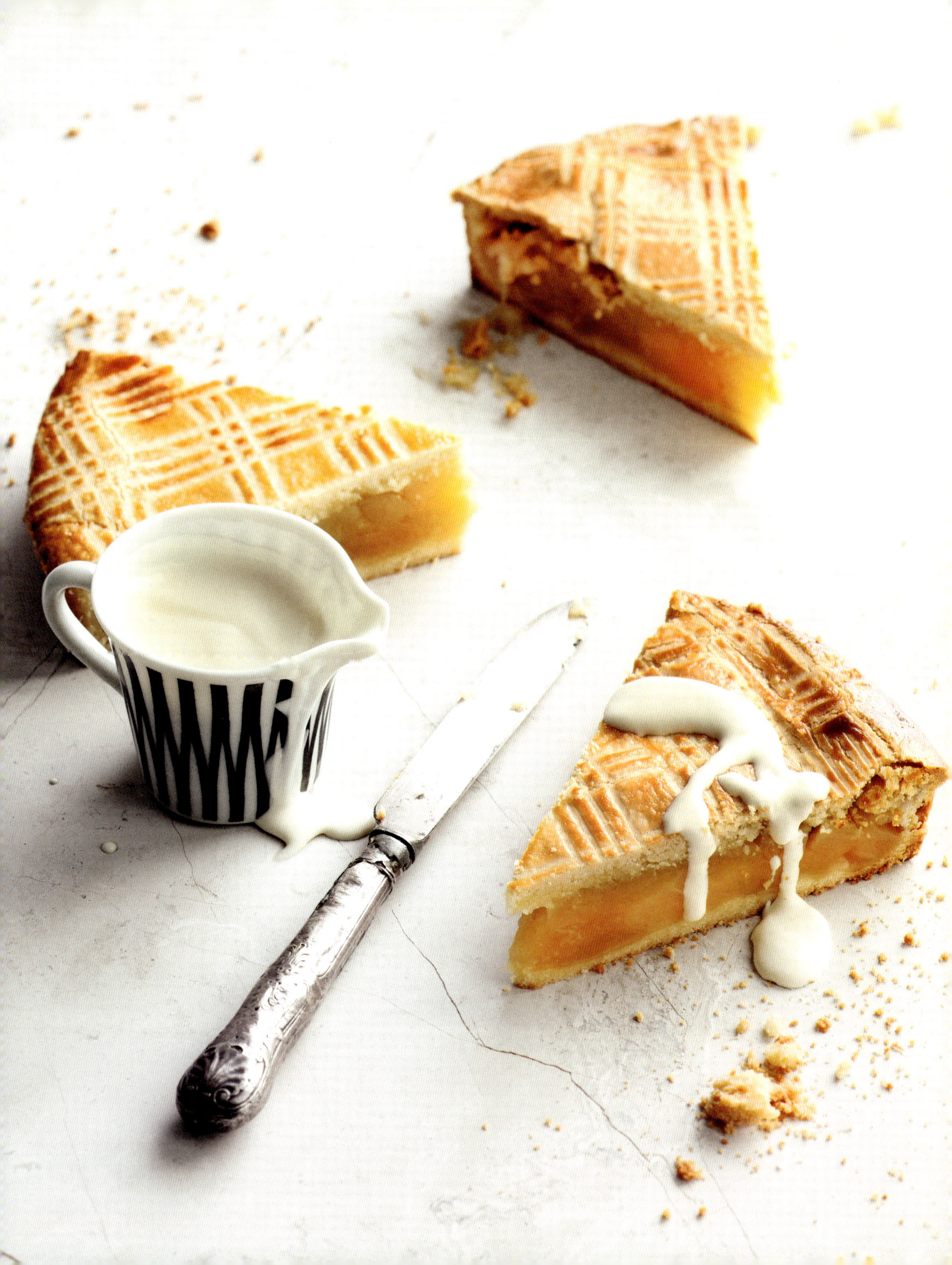

Cheat's fraisier cake

*This is a special-occasion cake, usually filled with creme patissiere.
My version is still as spectacular, but without all the hard work!*

2 good-quallity round
  sponge cake bases *
100g caster sugar
2 tbs kirsch ⓟ
5 gold-strength gelatine
  leaves ⓟ
300ml thickened cream
2 tsp vanilla extract
600ml thickened custard
400g strawberries, hulled
Icing sugar, to dust

Using a 22cm springform pan as a guide, trim both sponge cakes to fit pan snugly.

Combine 50g caster sugar and 100ml water in a saucepan. Bring to a simmer over low heat, stirring until sugar dissolves. Add kirsch and stir to combine. Cool.

For the filling, soak gelatine in cold water for 5 minutes or until softened. Bring ½ cup (125ml) cream to a simmer in a small saucepan over low heat. Squeeze gelatine to remove excess liquid and add to the cream, stirring until gelatine dissolves. Using electric beaters, whisk remaining 175ml cream and 50g caster sugar with the vanilla to soft peaks. Add gelatine mixture and custard, and gently whisk to combine.

Place 1 sponge round in the base of the 22cm springform pan. Brush with half the kirsch syrup. Halve enough strawberries to place side by side, cut-side out, around perimeter. Chop remaining strawberries and spread over sponge. Pour over custard mixture. Top with second sponge round. Brush with remaining kirsch syrup. Cover and refrigerate for 4 hours.

To serve, remove cake from pan and transfer to a plate. Thickly dust with icing sugar. Heat a long metal skewer over a flame until very hot, then scorch the cake in a criss-cross pattern, reheating skewer as necessary. **Serves 8**

* *Available in packs of three from delis.*
ⓟ *See Pantry essentials, p 206.*

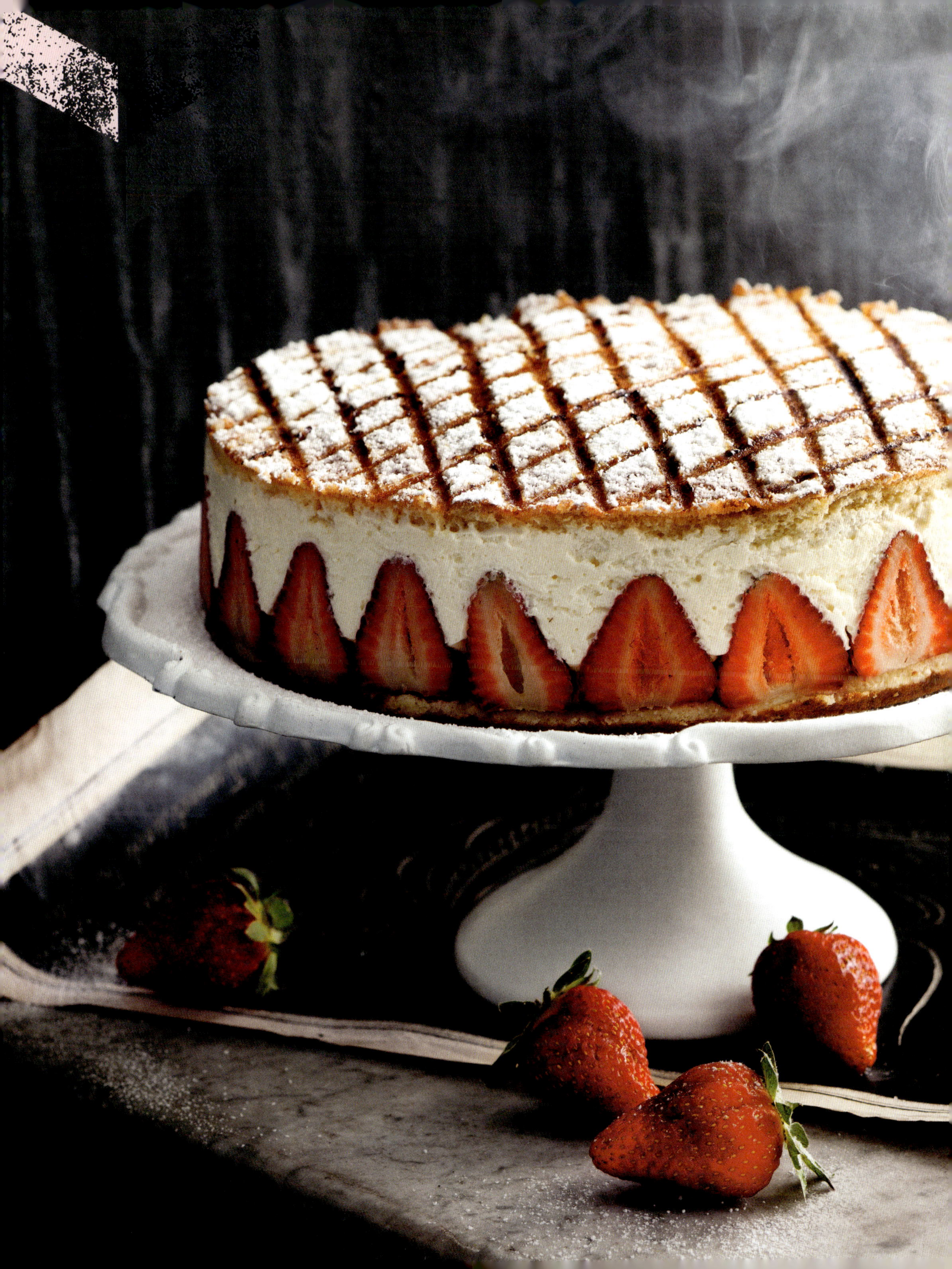

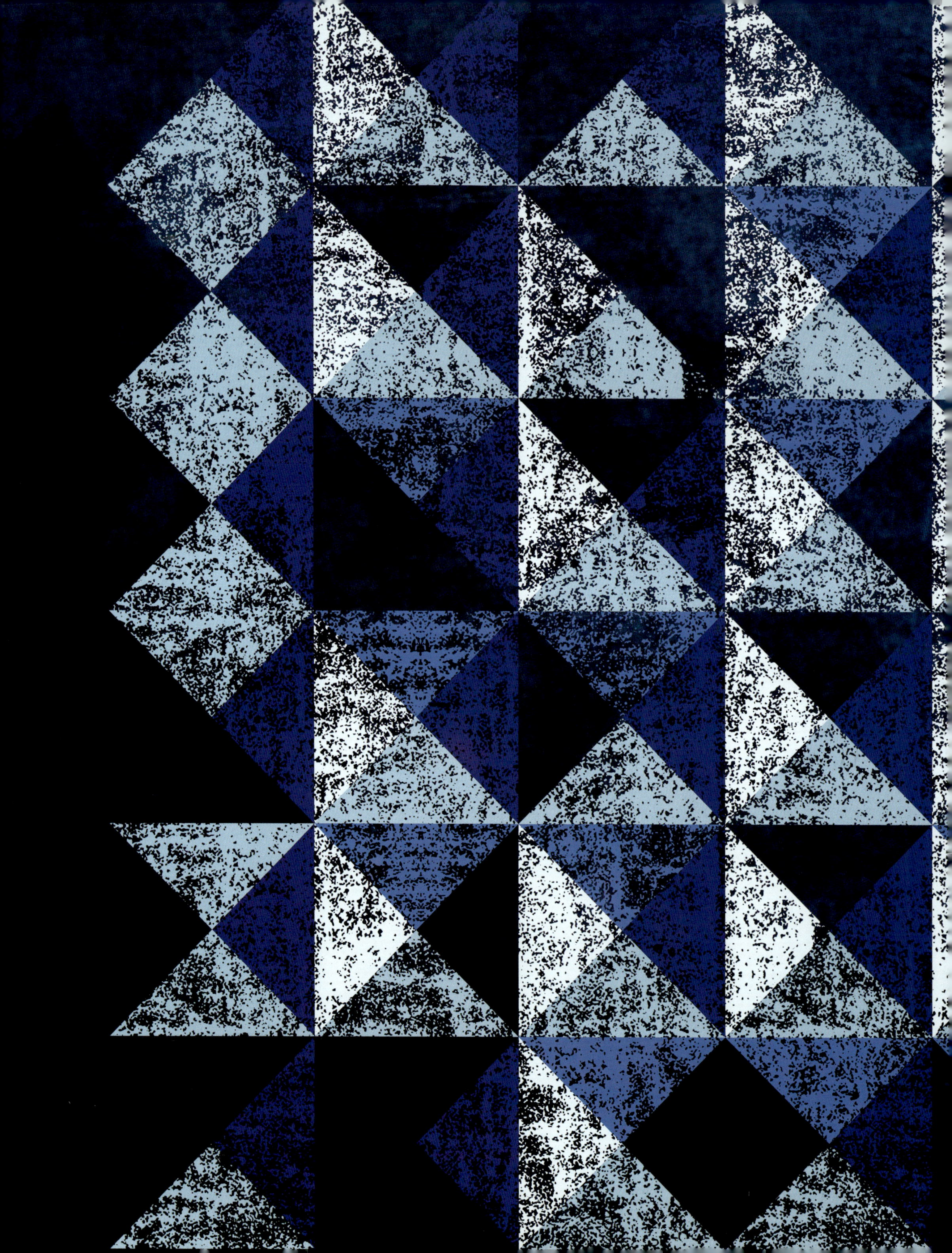

BRITISH

FINE ENGLISH
WATER CRACKERS
FINE ENGLISH
Walkers
FINE
OATCAKES
firefly
ROSE'S
RASPBERRY
CONSERVE
TAWNY ORANGE
Digestive
McVitie's
Hobnobs
Maldon
Colman's
Mustard
HP
HP
FRUITY
HAYWARDS
Piccalilli
Tracklements
ONION
MARMALADE
Mrs Darlington's
Farmer's Pickle
MADALENE

PANTRY ESSENTIALS

Beer, ale & stout
These feature variously in British recipes, from crisp batters to unctuous beef and ale stews, and even Nigella Lawson's famed chocolate Guinness cake.

Cheddar & Stilton
The two stalwarts of the British pantry: cheddar, a crumbly, richly acidic cow's milk cheese that originated in Somerset, south-west England, in the village of the same name; and Stilton, a creamy blue-vein cow's milk cheese with a strong, nutty-sweet flavour, whose official places of origin are Derbyshire, Leicestershire and Nottinghamshire in England's centre.

Cider & malt vinegars
Cider vinegar has a mild apple flavour that works well in savoury or sweet dishes. Dark brown malt vinegar (the classic accompaniment to fish and chips) is based on barley malt.

Clotted cream
Traditionally made in England's south-west (Somerset, Devon and Cornwall), it's the cream of choice for a scones and jam 'cream tea' ('Devonshire tea' everywhere else). Thick and buttery, it is made using scalded milk. Substitute thick cream.

Elderflower cordial
A syrup made using the flowers of the elderberry plant, which has a distinctively delicate floral-honey flavour. It is often served diluted with sparkling water.

English mustard
A bright yellow hot mustard, made with black and white mustard seeds, turmeric, salt and wheat flour. Buy it as a powder (mix with a little cold water to serve) or in paste form in jars.

Golden syrup & treacle
Golden syrup is a cane sugar product with a rich, caramel flavour. Black treacle is an intense, bittersweet refined molasses.

Pickles & relish
Pickled onions (usually preserved in malt vinegar and various spices) are an essential ingredient of the classic ploughman's lunch. Branston is a dark, sweet vegetable chutney, also perfect with a ploughman's. A derivation of Indian pickles, piccalilli relish gets its bright yellow colour from turmeric and has a sharp, tart flavour. Serve it with cheese and cold meats.

Walnut oil
Used in dressings, it adds a warm, earthy flavour. Not ideal for cooking, as it can become bitter when heated.

Worcestershire sauce
A tangy, peppery condiment used in everything from bloody Marys to stews and sauces. Ingredients include anchovies, chillies, molasses, white vinegar, tamarind, sugar and onions. HP Sauce, with its signature Houses of Parliament label, is favoured with a full English breakfast, steak or sausages, and has a similar flavour profile.

Food rationing and the rise of processed food after WWII gave British cuisine a bad reputation (often justified!), but the past 20 years have seen a resurgence of regional artisan produce, including some 700 cheese varieties, and traditional ingredients, such as elderflower. The influence of immigrants - from Portuguese Jews, said to have introduced fried fish, to those from the Indian subcontinent and West Indies (think chutneys, pickles and relishes) - has added to the diversity of the new British cuisine. Most of these ingredients are available in supermarkets or specialist food and cheese shops.

Buck rarebit

While most people are familiar with Welsh rarebit (or rabbit), there are plenty of variations, including this one with a fried or poached egg on top.

2 tbs olive oil
100g unsalted butter
2 leeks (white part only), thinly sliced
⅓ cup (50g) plain flour
300ml strong ale or stout ⓟ
250g mature cheddar, ⓟ grated
2 tbs creme fraiche or sour cream
2 tsp Worcestershire sauce ⓟ
1 tsp hot English mustard powder ⓟ
8 thick slices sourdough, lightly toasted
4 fried eggs
Roughly chopped flat-leaf parsley, to serve

Heat oil and 50g butter in a frypan over low heat. Add the leeks and cook, stirring occasionally, for 10 minutes or until softened but not browned. Season.

Heat remaining 50g butter in a pan over medium-low heat. Add flour and cook, stirring, for 2-3 minutes until golden. Whisking constantly, gradually add ale, whisking until smooth and thickened. Add cheese, creme fraiche, Worcestershire sauce and mustard powder, and stir to combine. Season.

Preheat grill to medium-high. Place toasted sourdough on a large grill tray, top with leek mixture, then with cheese mixture. Grill for 2-3 minutes until bubbling and golden. Serve topped with a fried egg and scattered with parsley. **Serves 4**

ⓟ See Pantry essentials, p 235.

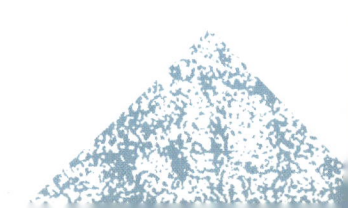

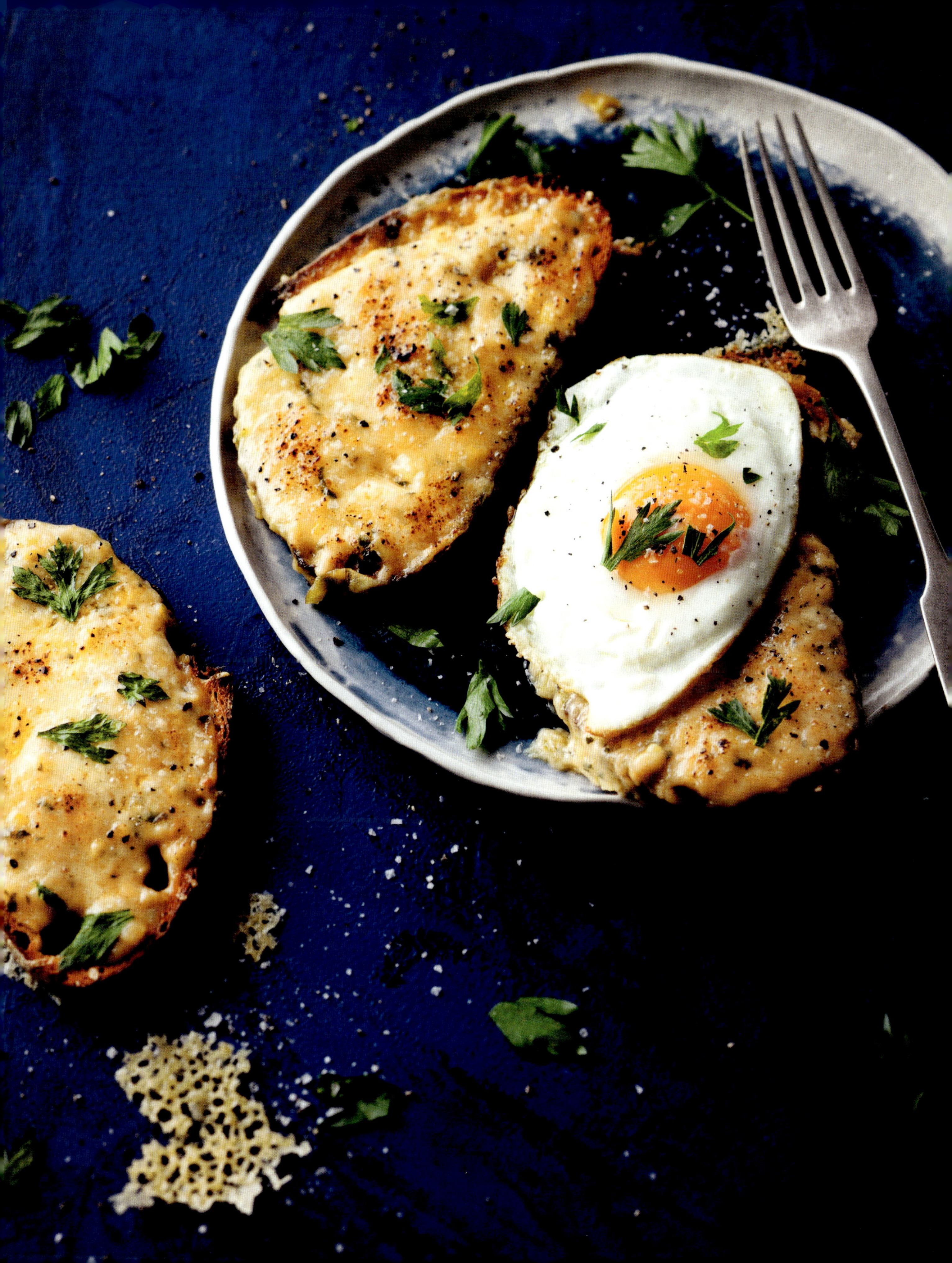

New-wave prawn cocktail

There was a time when prawn cocktail was on every dinner party menu, but then it fell out of favour. This version includes some contemporary variations to give a classic dish a new lease of life.

1½ tbs fish sauce

2 tbs sweet chilli sauce

Finely grated zest and juice of 1 lime, plus extra lime wedges to serve

⅓ cup (95g) thick Greek-style yoghurt

2 tbs whole-egg mayonnaise

1 tsp caster sugar

¼ iceberg lettuce, cut into 4 wedges

1 telegraph cucumber, halved lengthways, cut into thin wedges

600g cooked prawns, peeled (tails intact), deveined

Whisk fish and chilli sauces, lime zest and juice, yoghurt, mayonnaise and sugar in a bowl until sugar dissolves and mixture is smooth.

Divide lettuce wedges and cucumber among 4 large glasses or jam jars, add prawns, then drizzle over cocktail sauce and serve with extra lime wedges. **Serves 4**

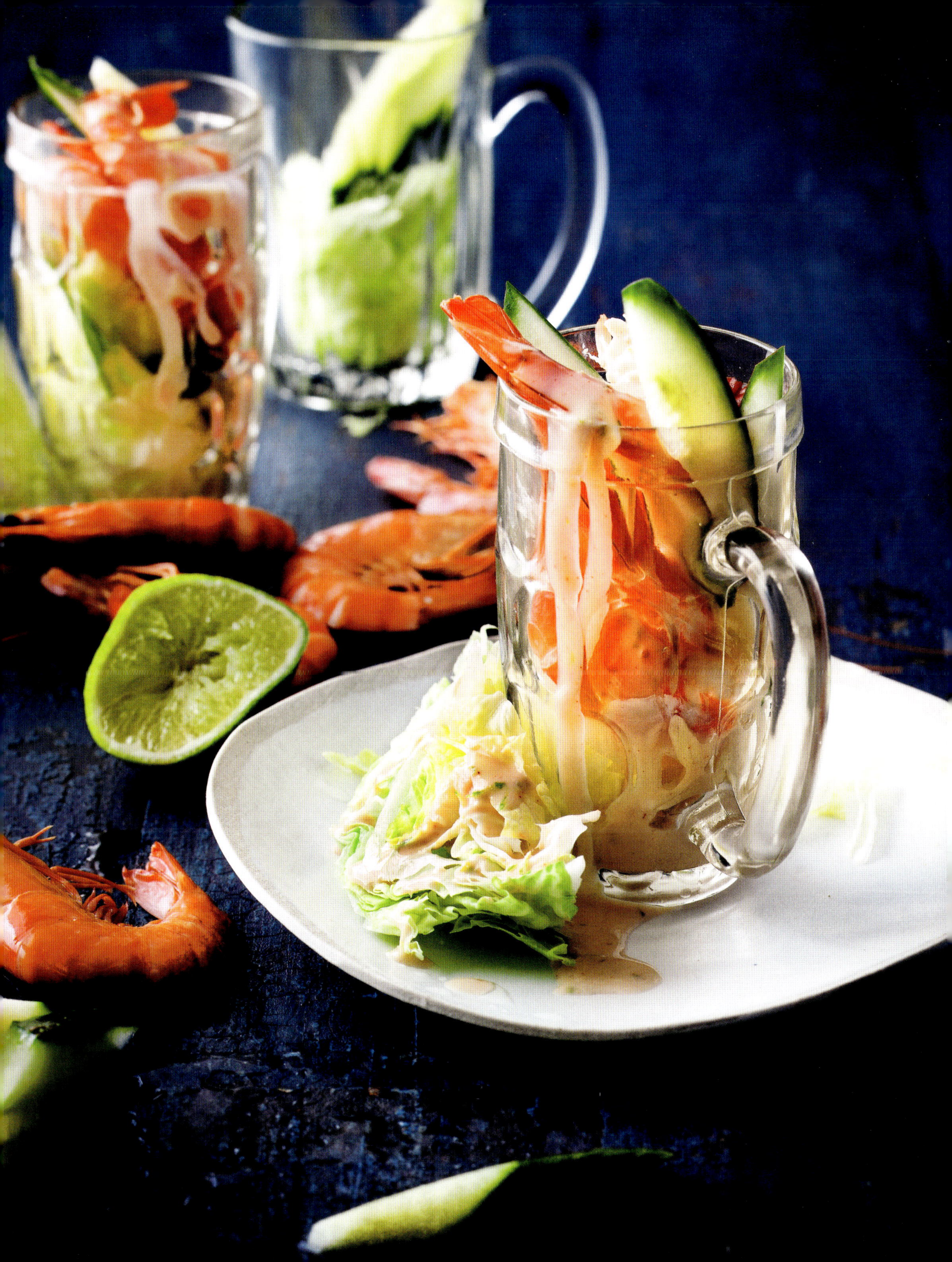

Beer-battered fish with peas and tartare sauce

5 large floury potatoes (such as pontiac or King Edward), peeled, cut into 1cm-thick chips
1/3 cup (80ml) sunflower oil, plus extra to deep-fry
2 1/2 cups (300g) frozen or (400g) fresh podded peas
30g unsalted butter
125g plain flour
200ml cold beer Ⓟ
500g thick boneless fish fillets (such as flathead), cut lengthways into 3cm-thick pieces

Tartare sauce
1/4 cup finely chopped dill pickles
1 tbs baby capers, rinsed
1 eschalot, finely chopped
1/4 cup (60g) sour cream
3/4 cup (180g) whole-egg mayonnaise
1 tbs lemon juice
1 tbs finely chopped flat-leaf parsley

Preheat the oven to 200°C. Line a large baking tray with baking paper.

Place potatoes in a saucepan of cold salted water and bring to the boil over high heat. Reduce heat to medium-low and simmer for 5 minutes. Drain well and pat dry with paper towel, then toss with the oil. Transfer to the prepared baking tray in a single layer. Season, then bake for 25-30 minutes, turning once, until golden and crisp.

Meanwhile, for the tartare sauce, combine all the ingredients, then season. Cover and refrigerate.

Cook peas in boiling salted water for 3 minutes or until tender. Drain, then return to the pan with the butter. Season, then cover and keep warm.

Whisk 1/2 cup (75g) flour and beer in a bowl until combined. Place the remaining 1/3 cup (50g) flour on a plate and season. Half-fill a deep-fryer or large saucepan with oil and heat to 190°C (a cube of bread will turn golden in 30 seconds when the oil is hot enough). Dust fish in seasoned flour, shaking off excess, then dip in the batter, allowing excess to drain. Fry fish, in batches, for 3-4 minutes until golden and crisp.

Serve fish with chips, peas and tartare sauce. **Serves 4**
Ⓟ See Pantry essentials, p 235.

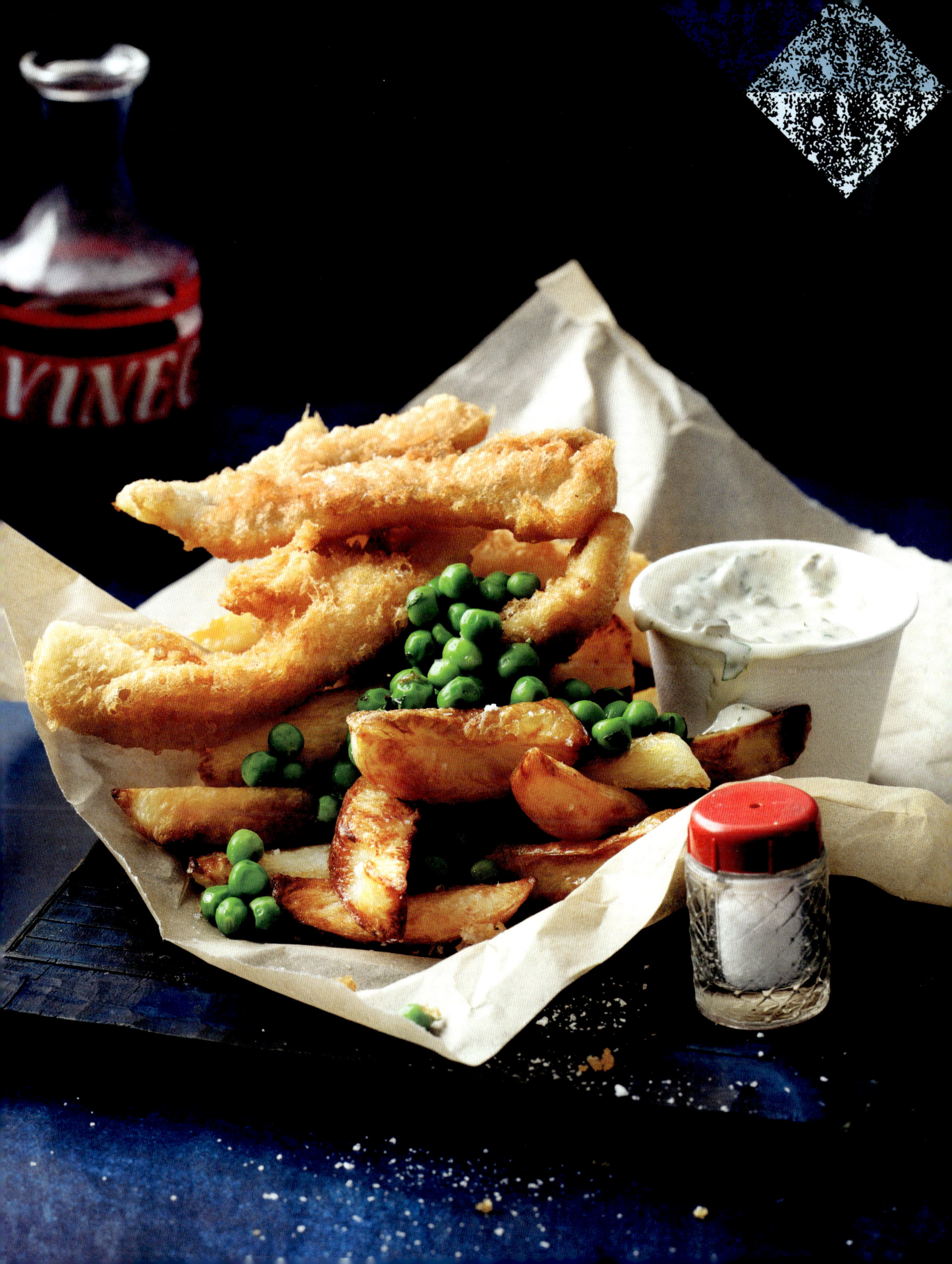
VINEG

Ploughman's salad

Whenever I go back to the UK, one of my favourite things to do is to go to a country pub for ploughman's lunch and a pint of cider. Here, I've used all those flavours in a 'dig in' salad that would make Jamie Oliver proud.

- 4 slices grain bread, crusts removed
- ½ cup (125ml) olive oil
- 2 tbs cider vinegar ⓟ
- 2 tsp brown sugar
- 2 tsp hot English mustard ⓟ
- 2 tsp Worcestershire sauce ⓟ
- 2 tbs walnut oil ⓟ
- 100g watercress, leaves picked
- 1 baby cos lettuce, leaves separated
- 1 red apple, cored, sliced
- 3 celery stalks, cut into 4cm batons
- 4 radishes, quartered
- 100g mature cheddar, ⓟ shaved
- 100g Stilton, ⓟ crumbled

Quick pickled onions
- 1 red onion, thinly sliced
- 2 tsp caster sugar
- 4 whole cloves
- 2 tbs red wine vinegar

For quick pickled onions, combine onion in a bowl with the caster sugar, cloves, red wine vinegar, ½ tsp salt and 2 tbs boiling water. Set aside for 15 minutes, then drain, discarding liquid and cloves.

Meanwhile, using a food processor, whiz bread to coarse breadcrumbs. Heat 2 tbs oil in a frypan over medium heat. Cook breadcrumbs, stirring, until golden and crisp. Drain on paper towel. Cool.

For the dressing, whisk cider vinegar, brown sugar, mustard, Worcestershire sauce and walnut oil in a bowl. Season. Place watercress, lettuce, apple, celery and radish in a bowl or on a platter and toss to combine. Drizzle over dressing. Gently toss the cheeses through the salad and scatter over crumbs and quick pickled onion to serve. **Serves 4-6**

ⓟ See Pantry essentials, p 235.

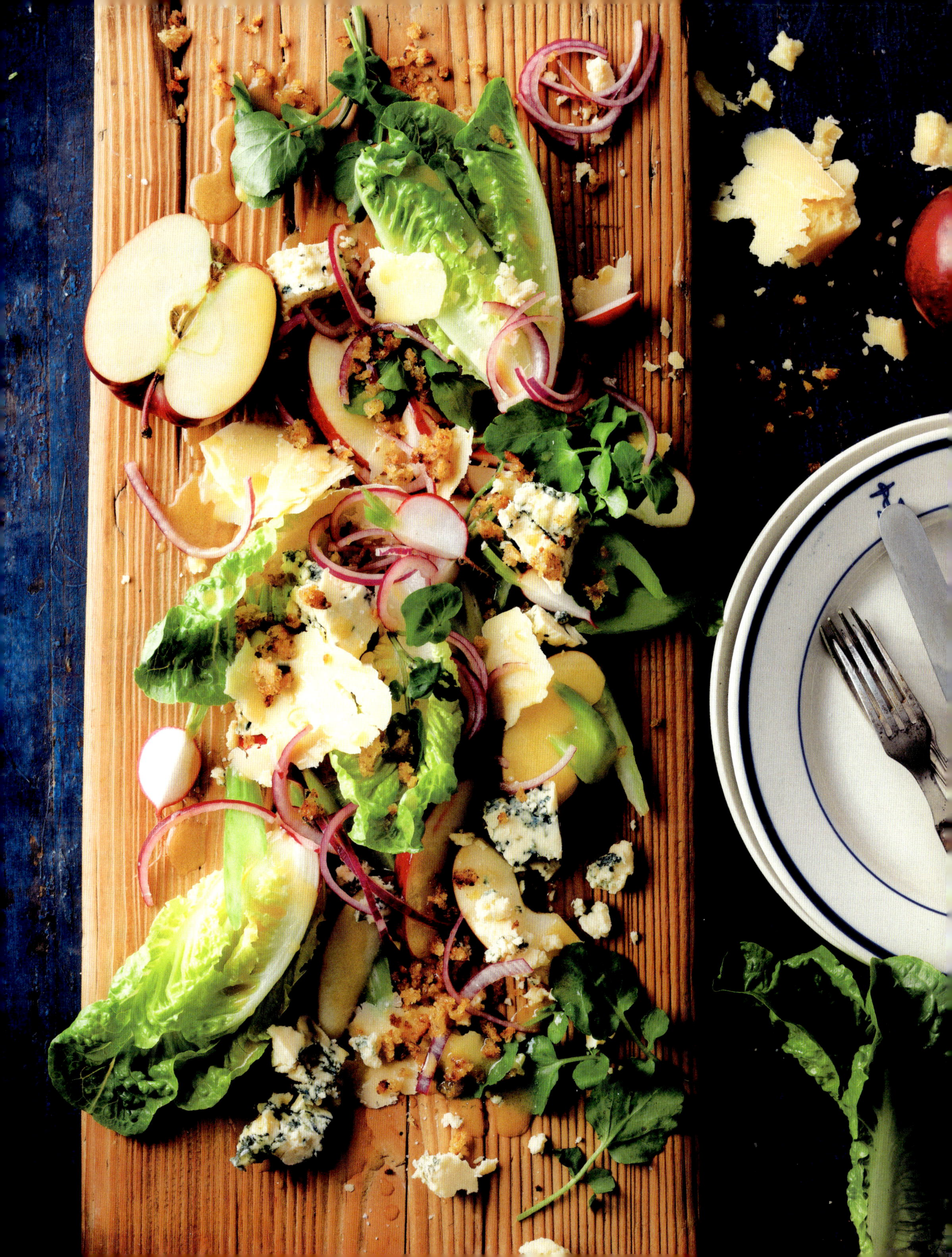

Salmon tarts with crushed pea sauce

1²/₃ cups (250g) plain flour
100g chilled unsalted butter, chopped
2 eggs, plus 2 yolks
200ml thickened cream
Finely grated zest of ½ lemon
2 tbs chopped chives
300g hot-smoked salmon, skin removed, flaked
15g grated parmesan
Pinch cayenne pepper
Pea shoots (optional), to serve

Crushed pea sauce
1 cup (120g) frozen peas
6 mint leaves, finely chopped
½ cup (120g) creme fraiche or sour cream
¼ cup (20g) grated parmesan
½ tsp finely grated lemon zest

Grease 6 x 12cm loose-bottomed tart pans.

Place flour, butter and a pinch of salt in a food processor and pulse until mixture resembles fine breadcrumbs. Add 1 egg yolk and 2 tbs iced water, then process until the mixture just comes together. Form into a disk, cover in plastic wrap and refrigerate for 30 minutes. Roll out pastry on a lightly floured surface to 5mm thick, then use to line the tart pans. Refrigerate for 15 minutes.

Preheat the oven to 190°C. Prick the pastry bases with a fork, then line the pastry with baking paper and fill with pastry weights. Bake for 10 minutes or until light golden, then remove paper and weights and bake for a further 5 minutes or until dry and crisp.

Meanwhile whisk eggs, remaining yolk, cream, lemon zest and chives in a bowl. Season. Divide flaked salmon among tart shells, pour over the egg mixture, then sprinkle with parmesan and cayenne pepper. Return tarts to the oven and bake for 20 minutes or until filling is just set.

Meanwhile, for the crushed pea sauce, pour boiling water over the peas in a bowl and stand for 5 minutes. Drain, refresh in cold water, then drain again. Add mint, roughly crush with a fork or potato masher, then stir through the creme fraiche, parmesan and zest.

To serve, dollop crushed pea sauce on the tarts and top with pea shoots, if using. **Makes 6**

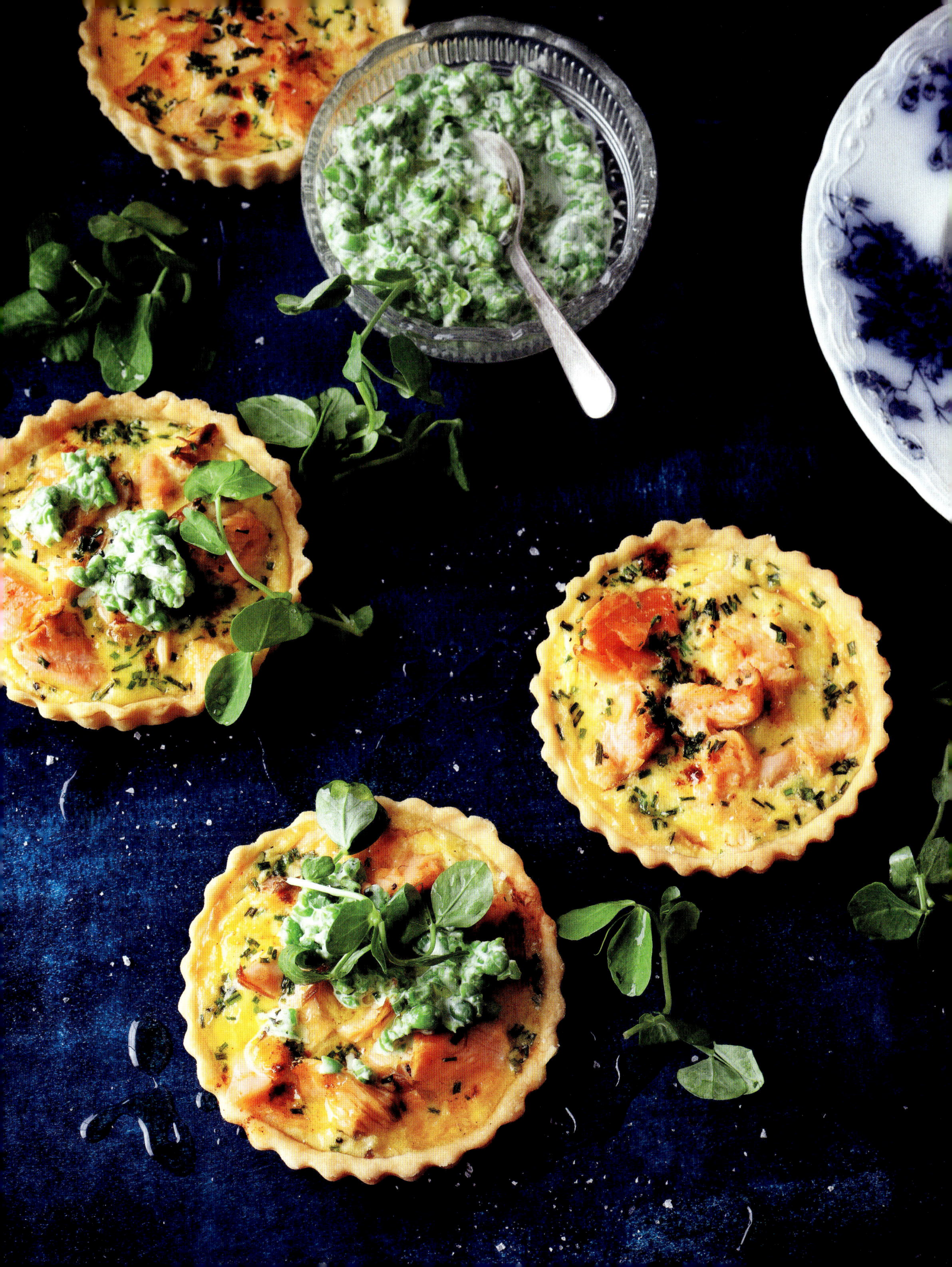

Bubble and squeak with a twist

600g potatoes,
    peeled, chopped
25g unsalted butter
300g Brussels sprouts
1 egg, lightly beaten
100g grated cheddar ⓟ
⅓ cup (50g) plain flour
300g cherry truss tomatoes
¼ cup (60ml) olive oil,
    plus extra to drizzle
6 thyme sprigs,
    leaves picked

Place potatoes in a saucepan and cover with cold salted water. Bring to the boil over medium-high heat, then reduce heat to medium and cook for 10-12 minutes until tender. Drain, then return potatoes to saucepan over low heat, shaking gently until excess liquid evaporates. Add butter, then, using a potato ricer or masher, mash potatoes until smooth. Transfer to a bowl.

Preheat the oven to 180°C. Meanwhile, cook the sprouts in a saucepan of boiling salted water for 5 minutes. Drain and refresh. Set aside 1 sprout to garnish, then finely shred the remainder. Combine shredded sprouts with the mashed potato, egg and cheese. Season. Place flour on a plate. Form mixture into 8 patties, then dust with flour, shaking off excess. Transfer to a tray and refrigerate for 15 minutes to firm up.

Place tomatoes on a baking tray and drizzle with extra olive oil, season, scatter with thyme, then roast for 5 minutes or until just starting to soften.

Meanwhile, heat oil in a frypan over medium-high heat. Fry the patties, in batches, for 1-2 minutes each side until golden. Transfer to the oven to keep warm.

To serve, separate the leaves of the reserved Brussels sprout, then scatter over the patties and roasted tomatoes. **Serves 4**
ⓟ See Pantry essentials, p 235.

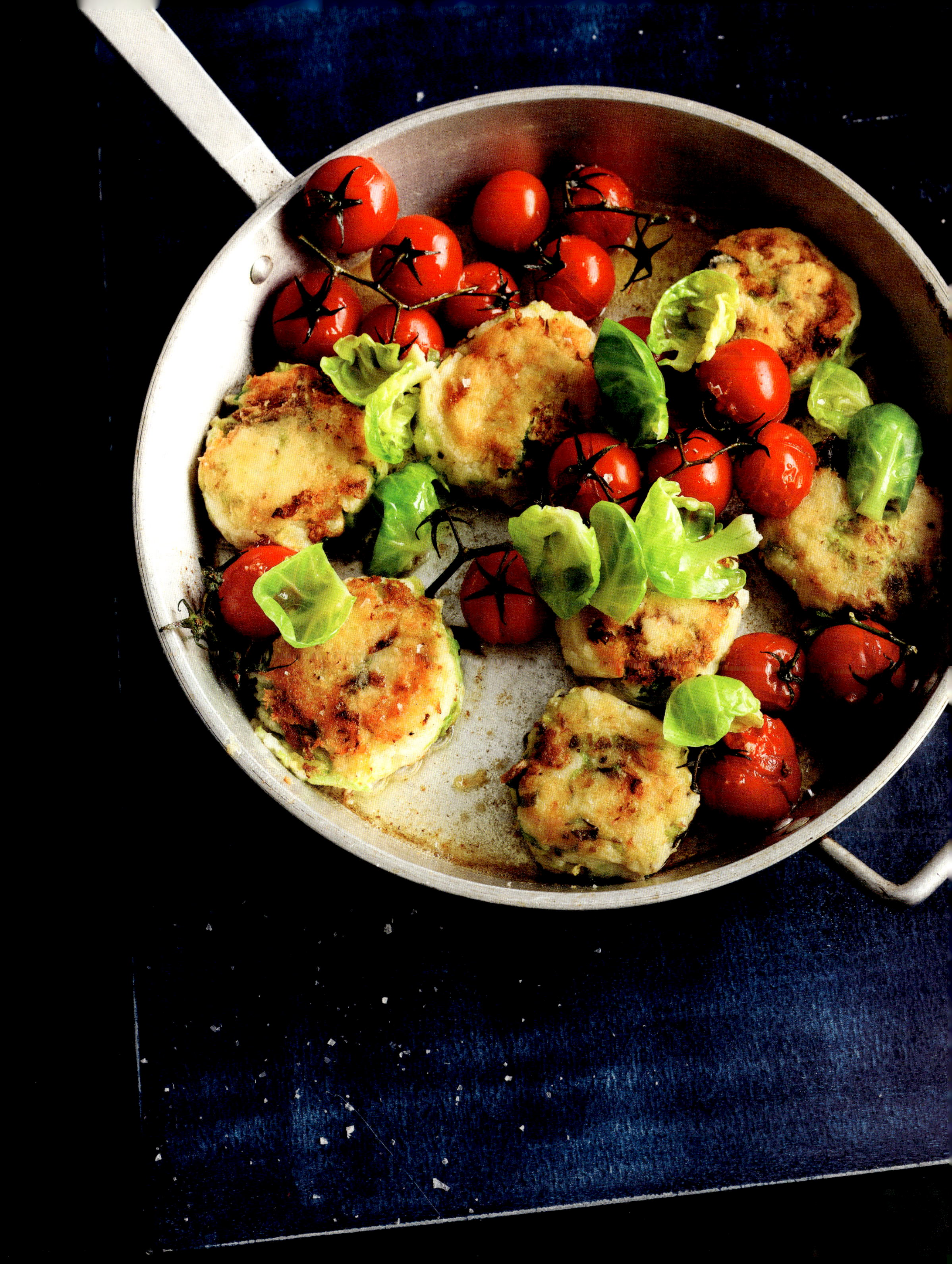

Roast beef with Yorkshire puddings and ale gravy

2.5-3kg standing 6-rib beef roast
2 tbs Dijon mustard
1 tbs chopped thyme leaves
2 tbs olive oil
2 tbs plain flour
1½ cups (375ml) mild, English-style light ale ⓟ
1½ cups (375ml) beef stock or consomme
2 tbs redcurrant jelly
Watercress sprigs, to serve
Yorkshire puddings
¾ cup (110g) plain flour
2 eggs
300ml milk
½ cup (125ml) sunflower oil or reserved beef dripping

Preheat the oven to 230°C. Brush the skin side of the beef with mustard, season, then sprinkle with thyme and drizzle with olive oil. Place in a roasting pan and roast for 15 minutes. Reduce heat to 190°C and roast for a further 15 minutes per 500g, plus an extra 15 minutes for medium-rare or until cooked to your liking. Transfer to a plate, reserving roasting pan, and rest, loosely covered with foil, for 20 minutes. Drain all but 2 tbs fat from the roasting pan, reserving the remainder to cook the Yorkshire puddings, if desired.

Meanwhile, for the Yorkshire puddings, whiz the flour, eggs and milk in a blender or food processor until smooth. Season, then transfer to a jug and stand for 30 minutes. Divide sunflower oil or reserved beef dripping among 8 holes of a 12-cup muffin pan. Place pan in the oven for 5 minutes or until oil is smoking. Carefully remove from the oven and divide the batter among the holes. Bake for 20 minutes or until puffed and golden.

Meanwhile, while the meat is resting and the 'yorkies' are cooking, place the roasting pan over medium heat. Add the flour and cook, stirring and scraping the bottom of the pan, for 1-2 minutes. Add beer, stock, redcurrant jelly and any beef resting juices, bring to the boil over high heat, then reduce heat to medium and cook for 5-6 minutes until reduced and slightly thickened. Season, then strain into a jug.

Slice the beef and serve with Yorkshire puddings, ale gravy and watercress. **Serves 4-6**

ⓟ See Pantry essentials, p 235.

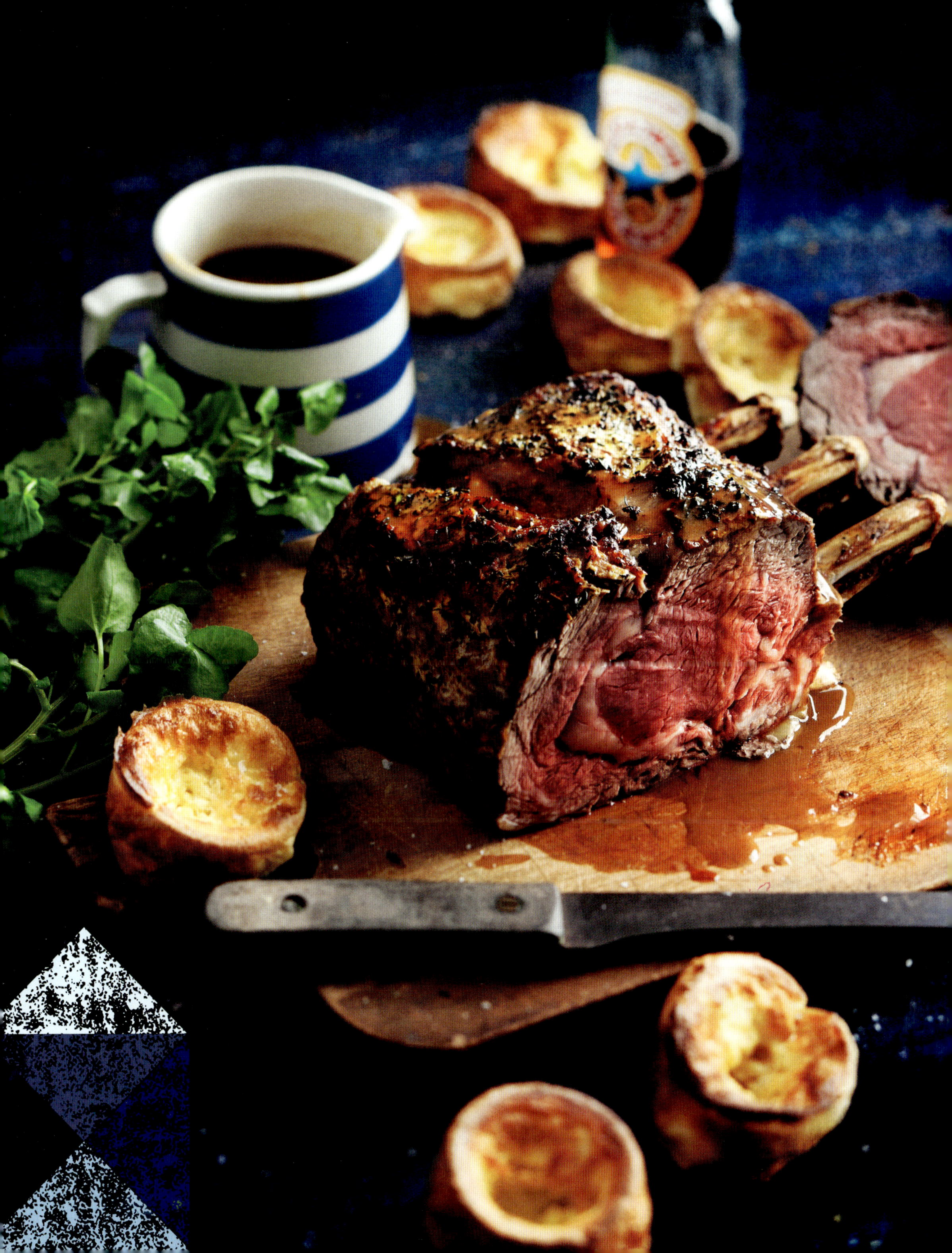

Chicken pie with stuffing balls and potato pastry

The idea for the potato pastry came from Lizzie Kamenetzky, former food editor of UK delicious. *magazine. It works so well for savoury pies.*

1.8kg whole chicken
Bouquet garni
1 onion, halved
30g unsalted butter, softened
6 pork and herb sausages
1 tbs olive oil
1 tbs plain flour
200ml white wine
1 cup (250ml) chicken stock
½ cup (125ml) thickened cream
2 tbs finely chopped flat-leaf parsley
1 egg, lightly beaten
Potato pastry
1⅓ cups (200g) plain flour
125g cold unsalted butter, chopped
160g cold mashed potato (from about 2 potatoes)
1 egg yolk

Preheat the oven to 200°C. Rinse the chicken inside and out with cold water, then pat dry with paper towel. Place in a roasting pan, then place bouquet garni and onion in cavity. Spread butter over skin. Season. Roast for 1 hour or until juices run clear when the thickest part of the thigh is pierced.

Meanwhile, for the pastry, sift flour into a bowl with ½ tsp salt. Rub in the butter until the mixture resembles breadcrumbs, then add the mashed potato and egg yolk. Using a fork, stir to form a smooth dough. Form into a disk, cover with plastic wrap and refrigerate for 30 minutes.

Meanwhile, remove casings from sausages, then roll sausage meat into 20-cent-sized balls. Refrigerate for 15 minutes to firm up. Heat oil in a frypan over medium heat and fry stuffing balls, turning, for 10 minutes or until pale golden. Drain on paper towel.

Transfer chicken to a plate, then drain all but 1 tbs oil from the roasting pan. Place pan over medium heat, add flour and cook, stirring and scraping the bottom of the pan, for 1-2 minutes. Add wine and simmer, stirring, until slightly reduced. Add stock and any chicken resting juices, then add cream and bring to the boil over high heat, stirring for 1-2 minutes until reduced and thickened. Season and stir through parsley.

When cool enough to handle, shred the chicken meat and skin (if desired), discarding bouquet garni, onion and bones. Transfer to a 2L (8-cup-capacity) pie dish with the stuffing balls. Pour over the sauce and set aside to cool.

Roll out pastry on a lightly floured surface to 5mm thick. Brush the rim of the pie dish with a little beaten egg, then place pastry over the top of the filling, trimming the edge. Use the pastry offcuts to decorate (in a Union Jack if you like!), then brush with more beaten egg. Bake for 30 minutes or until filling is bubbling and top is golden. **Serves 4-6**

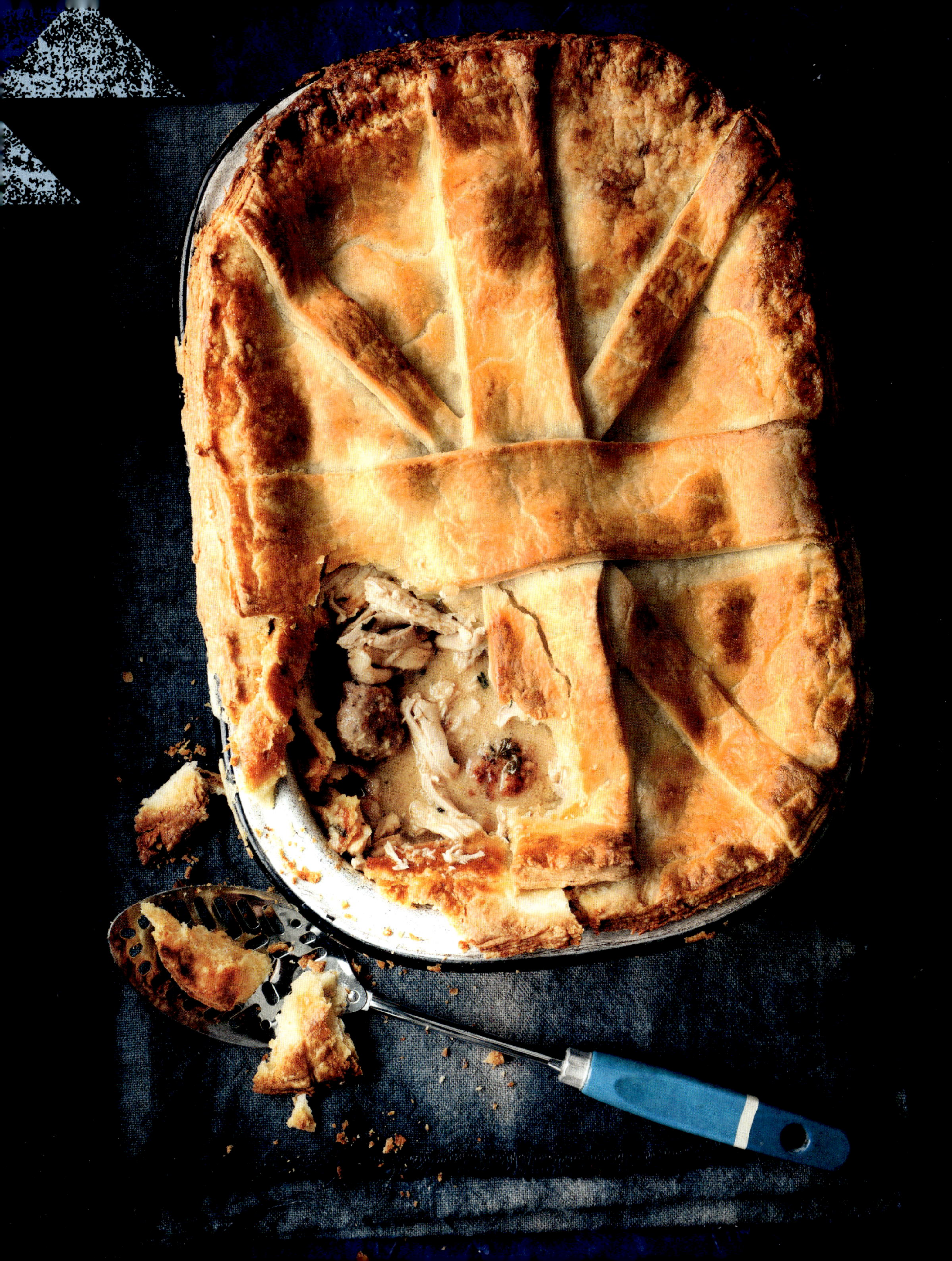

Great British trifle

This is trifle just like my mum used to make for high days and holidays. I'm the first to try out new ideas, but in this case you just can't beat the original. You will need a 2-litre (8-cup-capacity) glass bowl for this.

2 x 85g packets strawberry jelly crystals
450g jam Swiss roll
100ml sweet sherry
2 cups (500ml) milk
⅓ cup custard powder
⅓ cup caster sugar
250g raspberries
300ml thickened cream
2 tbs toasted flaked almonds

Prepare the jelly according to packet instructions, then set aside the hot liquid to cool slightly. Slice the Swiss roll into 2cm-thick rounds, then use to line a 2L (8-cup-capacity) glass bowl. Use any remaining slices to fill the centre. Drizzle with sherry, then pour over the jelly. Refrigerate for 2-3 hours until the jelly is set.

Whisk ¼ cup (60ml) milk with the custard powder in a bowl until smooth. Heat sugar and remaining milk until almost boiling, then, whisking constantly, add to the custard powder mixture. Return custard mixture to the pan and cook, stirring, over very low heat for 2-3 minutes until smooth and thickened. Cover surface of custard with baking paper to prevent a skin from forming and cool slightly. Remove bowl from fridge and scatter half the raspberries over the jelly. Pour over the custard, then return bowl to the fridge to chill completely.

Meanwhile, whisk the cream to soft peaks, then refrigerate until ready to serve.

When ready to serve, spread whipped cream over custard and scatter with almonds and remaining raspberries.

Serves 6-8

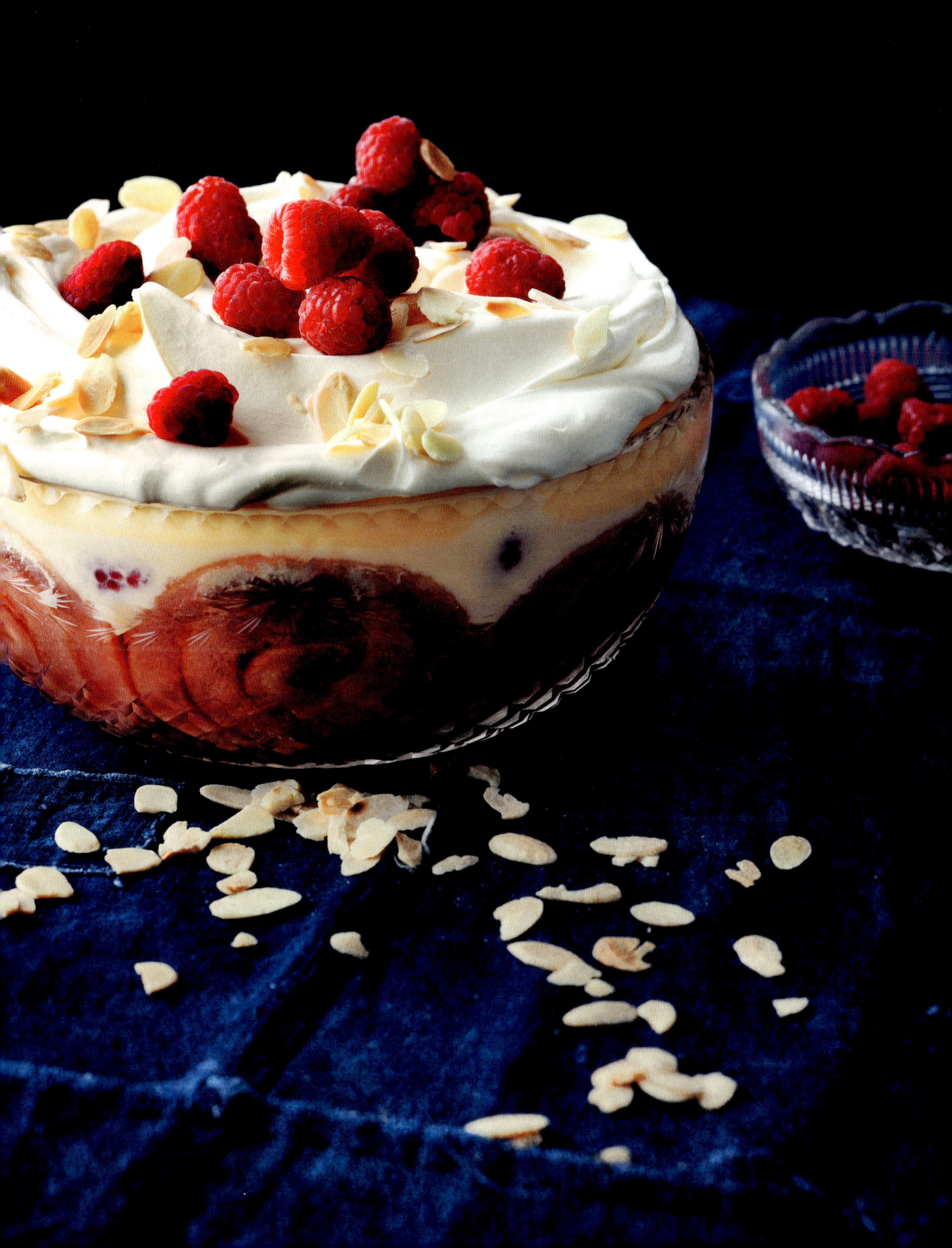

Sticky date pudding cake

1 cup (160g) pitted dates
1 tsp vanilla extract
1 tsp bicarbonate of soda
50g unsalted butter, softened
150g dark brown sugar
2 eggs
1 cup (150g) plain flour
1½ tsp baking powder
⅓ cup (35g) toasted walnuts, chopped
Vanilla ice cream, to serve
Sticky sauce
400ml thickened cream
110g dark brown sugar

Preheat the oven to 160°C. Grease and line the base of a 24cm, 4cm-deep round pie dish.

Place dates in a saucepan with vanilla and 1 cup (250ml) cold water and bring to the boil over medium-high heat. Remove from heat and add the bicarbonate of soda. Cool slightly, then transfer to a food processor and whiz to a smooth paste.

Beat butter and sugar with a wooden spoon until smooth, then add the eggs one at a time, beating well after each addition. Add date mixture, then fold in the flour with the baking powder. Transfer batter to the prepared dish, then bake for 45 minutes or until a skewer comes out clean.

Meanwhile, for the sauce, combine both ingredients in a saucepan over low heat, stirring until sugar dissolves. Continue to cook, stirring occasionally, for a further 10 minutes or until smooth and thickened.

Invert warm cake onto a shallow bowl. Drizzle with hot sticky sauce and scatter with walnuts. Serve with vanilla ice cream.

Serves 6-8

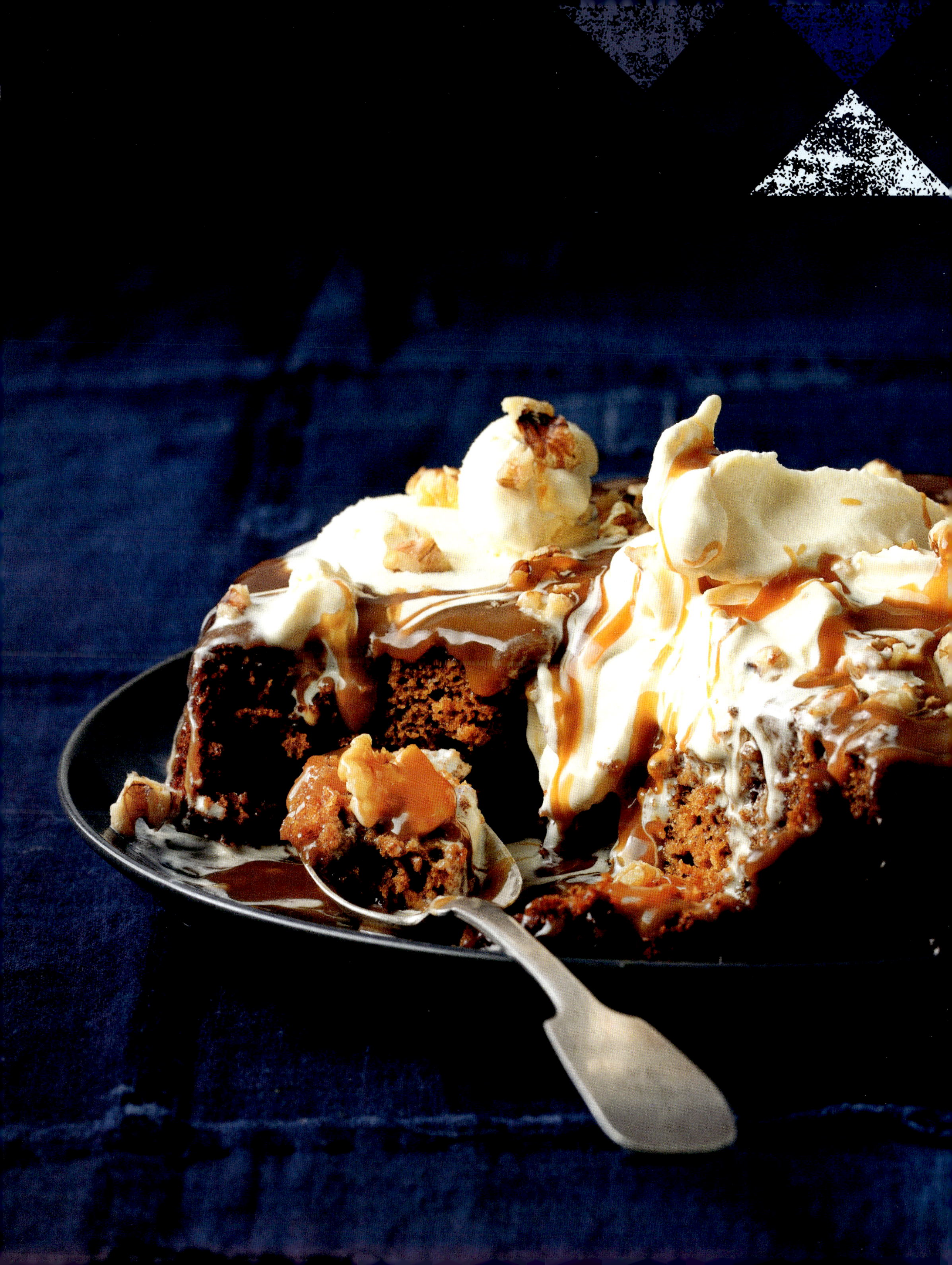

Strawberry & elderflower summer puddings

125g caster sugar
1 vanilla bean, split, seeds scraped
¼ cup (60ml) elderflower cordial ⓟ
500g strawberries
1 tbs finely chopped basil, plus extra small leaves to serve
12 slices white bread, crusts removed
1 cup (250g) clotted cream ⓟ or mascarpone

Place the sugar, vanilla pod and seeds, and ¼ cup (60ml) water in a saucepan over low heat, stirring until sugar dissolves. Increase heat to medium-high and simmer for 2 minutes or until slightly reduced. Stir in 2 tbs elderflower cordial. Cool. Makes ½ cup.

Remove vanilla pod from elderflower syrup. Finely chop 250g strawberries and combine with the chopped basil and half the syrup. Place remaining syrup and whole strawberries in a food processor or blender and whiz until smooth. Strain through a sieve into a bowl, discarding solids.

Lightly grease 4 x 1-cup-capacity (250ml) dariole moulds, then line with plastic wrap, leaving enough overhanging to completely cover the mouth of the moulds. Cut 4 small rounds from the bread to fit the base of the moulds. Dip each round into the strawberry sauce, then place in the base of the moulds. Halve 4 more slices of bread, dip in the strawberry sauce and line the sides of the moulds.

Half-fill the lined moulds with chopped strawberry mixture, gently packing it down. Place 1 tsp clotted cream in the centre, then top up with remaining chopped strawberry mixture. Cut out 4 rounds from the final 4 slices of bread to fit the top of the moulds, then dip in strawberry sauce and place on top of filling. Bring up the overhanging plastic wrap to cover completely. Refrigerate for 2-3 hours to firm up.

Stir remaining 1 tbs elderflower cordial through the remaining clotted cream. Remove moulds from fridge, invert puddings onto plates and brush with any remaining strawberry sauce. Scatter with extra basil leaves and serve with elderflower clotted cream. **Serves 4**

ⓟ See Pantry essentials, p 235.

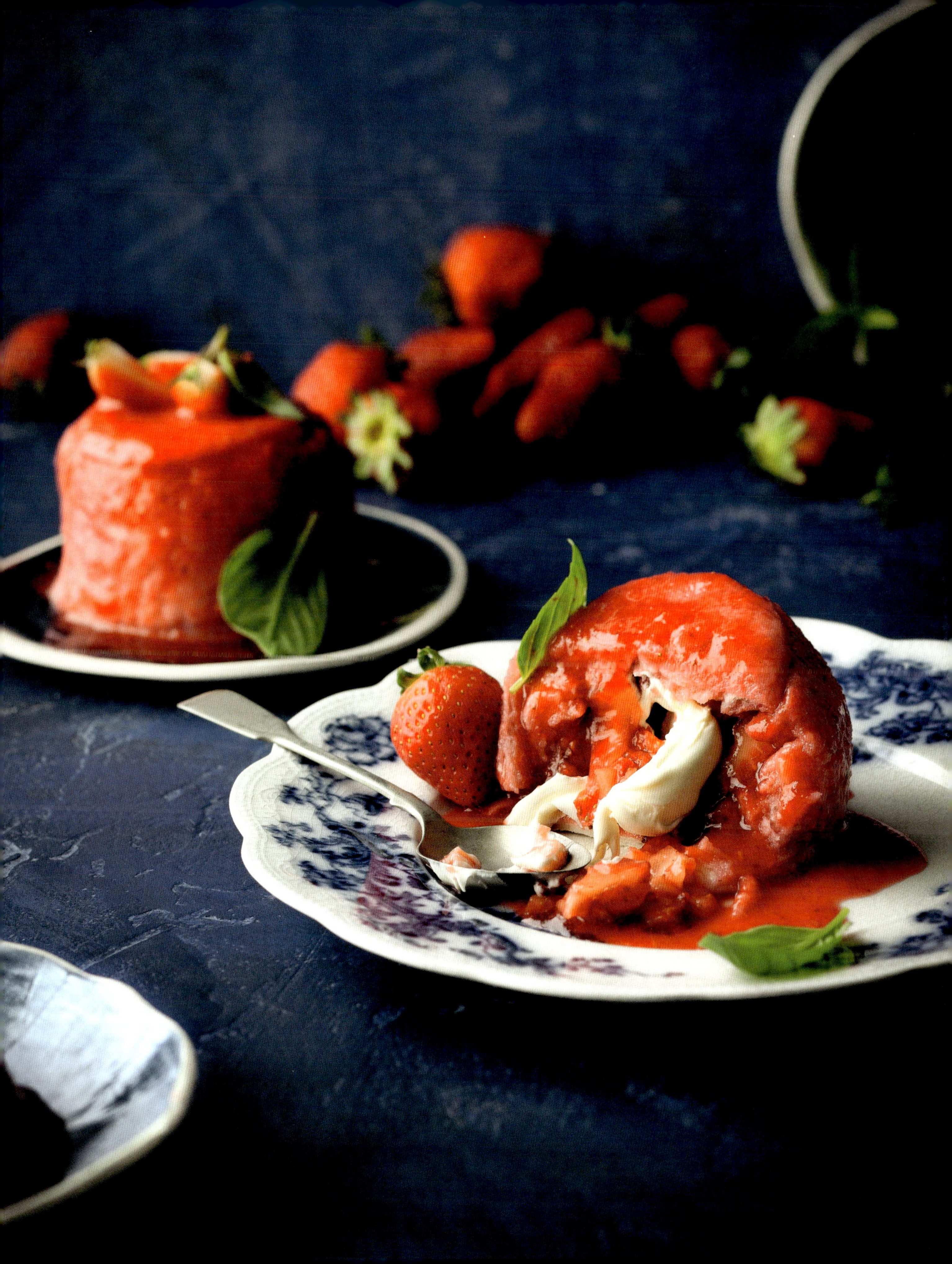

Banoffee cake

You will need a kitchen blowtorch for this recipe.

4 bananas
2/3 cup (80g) sour cream
2 tsp vanilla extract
175g unsalted butter, softened
1 2/3 cups (370g) caster sugar
4 eggs
2 1/2 cups (350g) self-raising flour, sifted
1 quantity caramel sauce (see Basics, p 297)
Roughly chopped honeycomb and shaved dark chocolate, to serve

Caramel icing
125g unsalted butter, softened
2 1/2 cups (350g) icing sugar, plus extra to dust
1/3 cup (80ml) milk

Preheat the oven to 180°C. Grease and line a 23cm springform cake pan.

Using a food processor, whiz 3 bananas with the sour cream and vanilla to a smooth puree. Using electric beaters, beat butter and sugar until thick and pale. Add eggs, one at a time, beating well after each addition. Fold in the flour and banana mixture. Transfer to the prepared pan and bake for 50 minutes or until a skewer comes out clean (loosely cover with foil if the cake is browning too quickly). Cool slightly, then turn out on a wire rack to cool completely.

For the icing, using electric beaters, beat butter and icing sugar for 2-3 minutes until thick and pale. Add the milk and 1/3 cup (80ml) caramel sauce, then beat gently until combined.

Slice remaining banana diagonally. Place on a baking tray and dust with extra icing sugar. Caramelise with a kitchen blowtorch. (Alternatively, grill the banana under a preheated medium-high grill for 1 minute or until caramelised).

To assemble, spread the icing over the top of the cake, drizzle with caramel sauce and top with caramelised banana, chopped honeycomb and shaved chocolate. Serve with the remaining caramel sauce. **Serves 8-10**

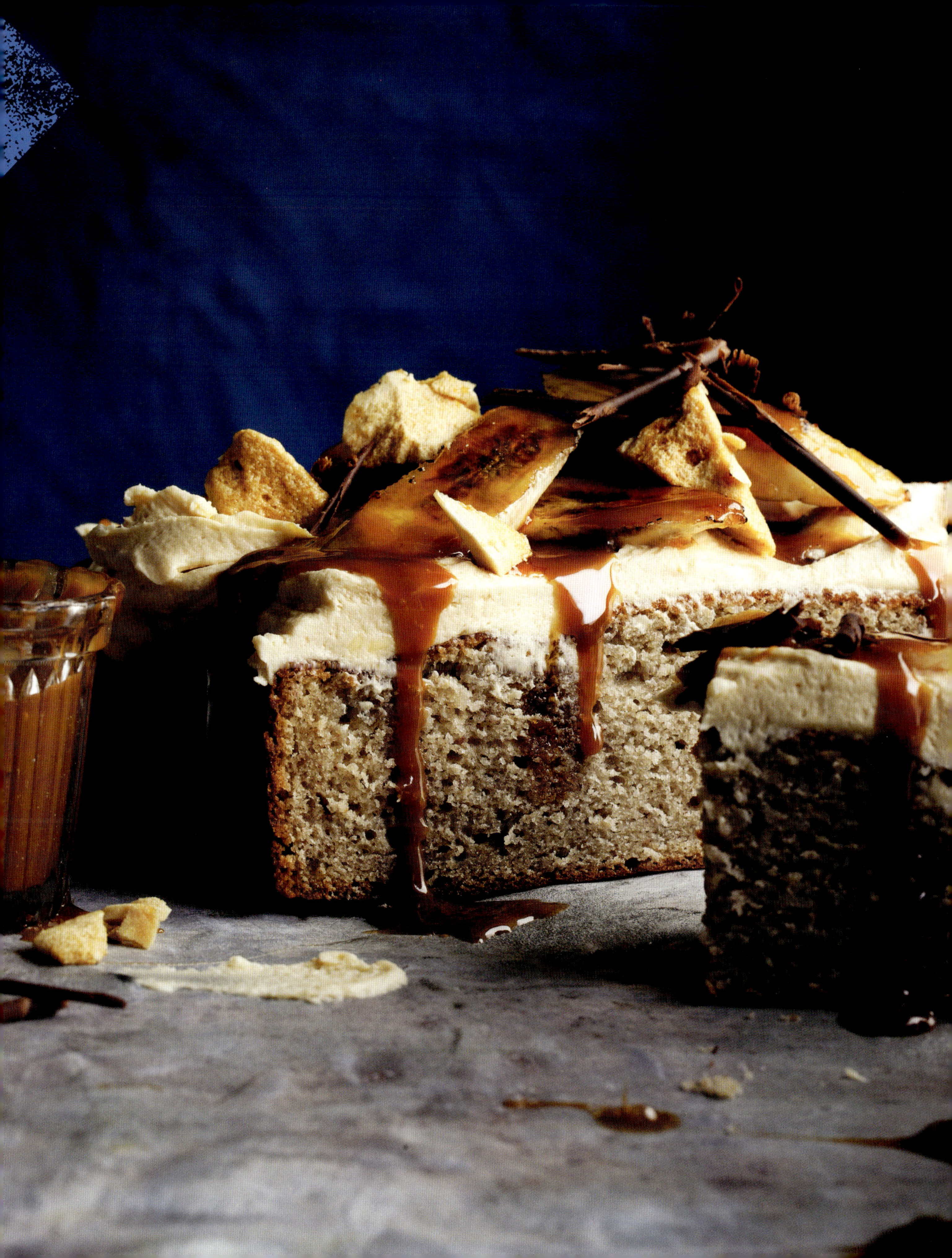

MIDDLE EASTERN

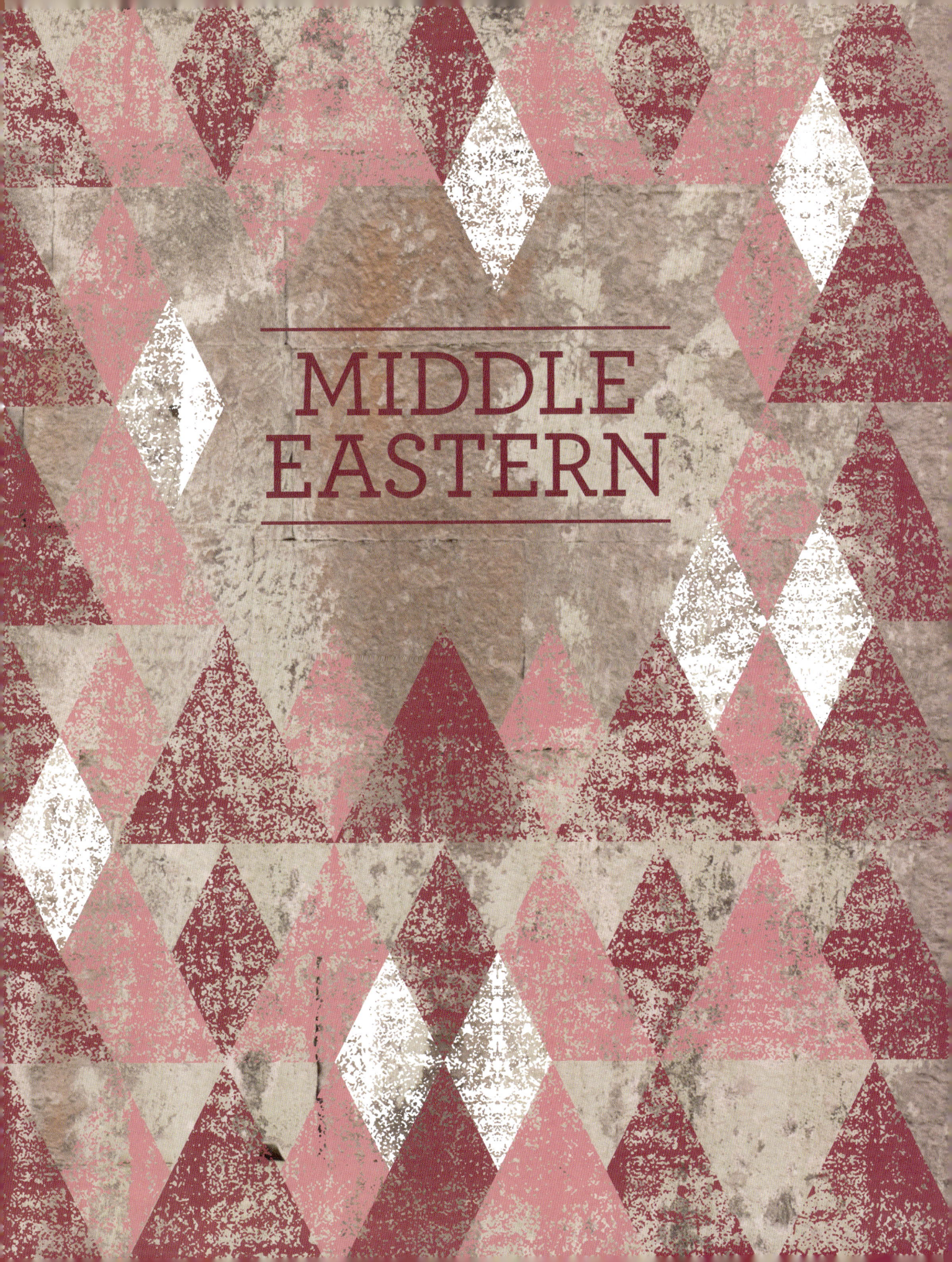

PANTRY ESSENTIALS

Barberries
A sour dried fruit usually added to chicken, rice and meat dishes.

Burghul
Also known as cracked wheat, this is whole wheat that has been partially boiled, then cracked and dried.

Couscous
All couscous is made from ground wheat or semolina. Regular and pearl couscous can be found in supermarkets.

Dried rose petals
Find edible dried rose petals and buds online at pariya.com, as well as in Middle Eastern shops.

Dukkah
This Egyptian spice, seed and nut blend is used as a seasoning, or as a dip with olive oil for flatbreads.

Filo/brik pastry
Filo is made from flour and water, and rolled paper thin. Brik pastry is the Tunisian version and is slightly tougher than filo.

Freekeh
Made from durum wheat, which is harvested while it is still green and soft, then roasted and cracked.

Harissa
A Tunisian chilli paste, made from red capsicum, dried chillies and spices.

Labne
Goat's, sheep's or cow's milk yoghurt, strained through muslin cloth.

Orange blossom water & rosewater
The first is made by soaking Seville orange blossom in distilled water; the second, using rose petals.

Pomegranate molasses
A reduction of pomegranate juice, sugar and water to a sweet-sour syrup.

Preserved lemons
Lemons preserved in salt and often extra lemon juice, sometimes with the addition of herbs such as bay leaves.

Ras el hanout
A Moroccan spice blend, made from the merchant's finest. The ingredients vary, but can include up to 30 spices.

Rose syrup
A combination of rose petals, sugar and water cooked down to a syrup.

Tahini
A paste of sesame seeds, and a vital ingredient for hummus and other dips.

Turkish delight
Made with sugar and cream of tartar, lemon juice and flavourings such as rosewater, it is then tossed in a mixture of cornflour and icing sugar. Nuts are often included in the mixture, too.

◇

The Middle Eastern pantry is an amalgam of centuries of culinary traditions, including Berber, Moorish and Arab. Characterised by warmly pungent spices, fresh herbs and contrasting textures, this is food made for the shared table – grain-based salads, dips, flatbreads, the heat of chilli, cooling yoghurt and slow-cooked meats, with desserts enhanced by orange blossom and rosewater.

◇

Lightly pickled beetroot with minted labne and dukkah

You will need to start making the minted labne a day ahead.

2 bunches baby beetroot (we used red and gold beetroot), trimmed
1 onion, cut into wedges
100ml cider vinegar
¼ cup (55g) caster sugar
4 thyme sprigs
2 bay leaves
4 cloves
200g hummus
¼ cup (40g) dukkah Ⓟ
Mint leaves, to serve

Minted labne*
500g thick Greek-style yoghurt
⅓ cup chopped mint leaves
1 tsp dried mint

For the minted labne, spoon yoghurt into a piece of muslin, bring corners together and tie to enclose. Place in a sieve over a bowl and leave in the fridge overnight to drain.

Remove labne from muslin (discarding liquid in bowl), place in a bowl, then stir through the chopped and dried mint. Season. Cover and refrigerate until needed.

Place beetroot, onion, vinegar, sugar, thyme, bay leaves and cloves in a large saucepan. Add enough water to cover. Cover with a cartouche (circle of baking paper). Bring to the boil over medium-high heat, then reduce heat to medium-low and simmer for 15-20 minutes until beetroot are tender. Cool in the liquid. Remove the beetroot from the liquid, reserving liquid, and peel (wear rubber gloves to avoid staining your hands), discarding skin. Slice into rounds, then place red and gold beetroot in separate shallow dishes (to prevent the peeled beetroot from 'bleeding' their colour). Set aside.

Return saucepan to a medium heat and bring liquid to a simmer. Simmer, uncovered, for 6-8 minutes until syrupy. Strain, then divide syrup between the two dishes of beetroot. Set aside for up to 1 hour.

Serve beetroot with hummus and torn pieces of minted labne, scattered with dukkah and mint leaves. **Serves 4**

* *If you prefer, you can buy herbed labne (yoghurt balls) from Middle Eastern shops and selected delis and supermarkets.*
Ⓟ *See Pantry essentials, p 262.*

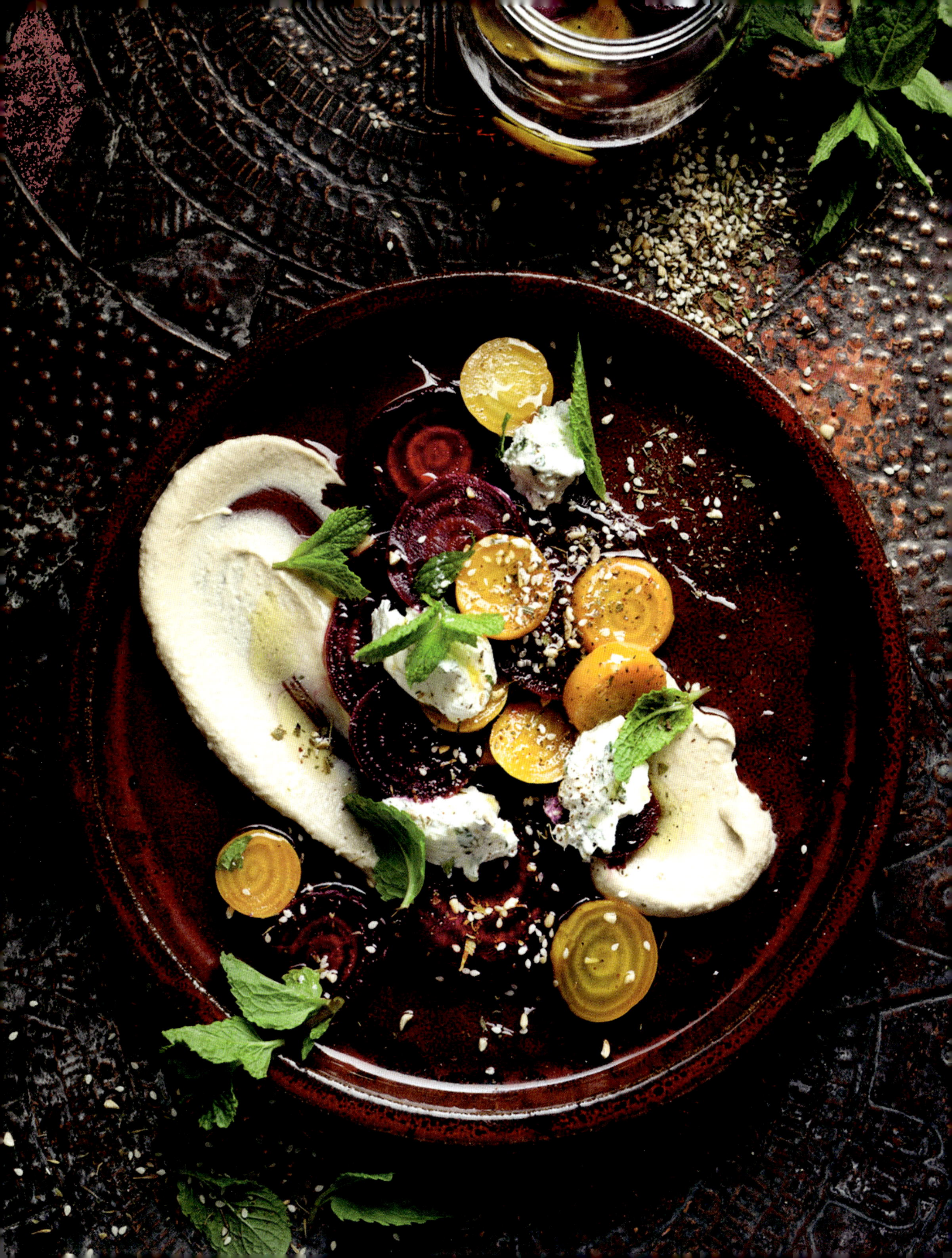

Kofta with Yotam Ottolenghi's baked couscous

For years, I've searched for the best way to cook couscous, and of course I needed to look no further than one of my favourite chefs, Israeli-born Yotam Ottolenghi. Oven-baking results in a perfectly light texture – and no lumps!

1½ cups (300g) couscous
140ml olive oil
20g unsalted butter, chopped
2 onions, thinly sliced
1 tsp honey
2 tsp ras el hanout ⓟ
⅓ cup (55g) sultanas
500g cherry tomatoes
¼ cup (40g) toasted pine nuts
½ bunch rocket, chopped
½ bunch coriander, leaves chopped
1 bunch mint, leaves chopped
1 tbs lemon juice, plus lemon halves, to serve
Thick Greek-style yoghurt (optional), to serve

Kofta
500g lamb mince
½ cup finely chopped flat-leaf parsley
2 tbs finely chopped mint
1½ tbs ras el hanout

Soak 8 wooden skewers in cold water for 30 minutes. Alternatively, use 8 woody rosemary stems.

For the kofta, combine the lamb, parsley, mint and ras el hanout in a bowl and season. Divide into 8 equal portions, then, using damp hands, form each into a log. Thread onto skewers, then refrigerate for 30 minutes to firm up.

Preheat the oven to 150°C. Line a 20cm x 30cm baking dish with baking paper.

Add couscous to baking dish, pour over 800ml boiling water and stir in 2 tbs oil. Set aside for 10 minutes, then dot with butter. Cover with foil and bake for 15 minutes.

Meanwhile, heat 2 tbs oil in a frypan over medium-low heat. Add the onion, honey and ras el hanout. Cook, stirring occasionally, for 10-15 minutes until golden and soft. Transfer to a bowl and stir in the sultanas.

Heat 2 tbs oil in a frypan over medium heat. Add the tomatoes and cook, stirring, for 3-4 minutes until starting to soften. Season and add to the onion mixture.

Fluff couscous with a fork, then stir in onion mixture, pine nuts, rocket, coriander, mint and lemon juice. Season well.

Preheat a barbecue or chargrill pan over medium-high heat. Brush kofta with remaining 1 tbs oil. Cook kofta, turning, for 6-8 minutes until lightly charred and cooked through.

Serve kofta on baked couscous with lemon halves and yoghurt, if using. **Serves 4**

ⓟ See Pantry essentials, p 262.

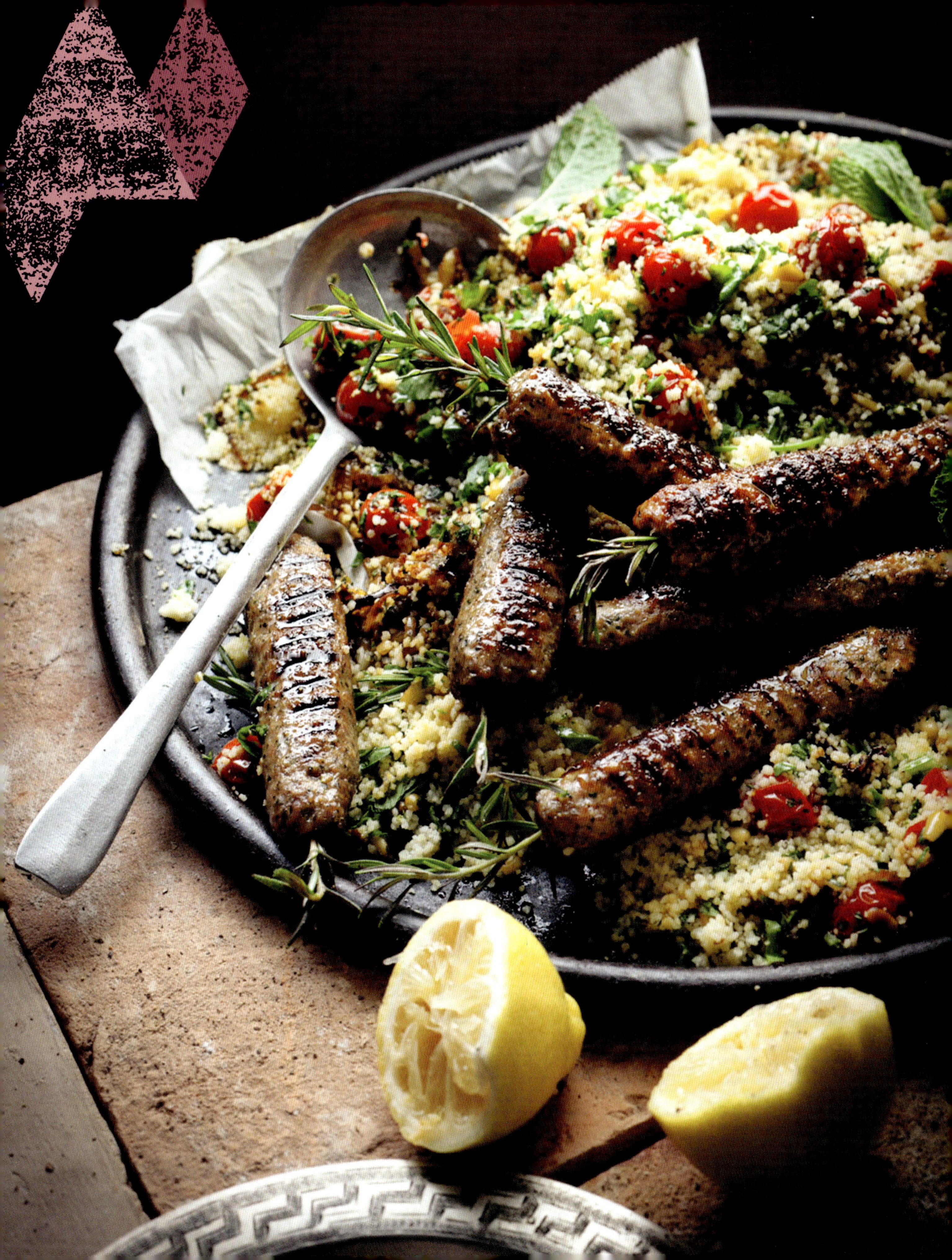

Harissa salmon with pearl couscous

Harissa is a wonderful fiery spice paste, but it does vary in heat depending on the brand. I would suggest trying a few to find the one that suits you best.

- 1 tbs coriander seeds
- 6 cardamom pods
- 1/2 tsp ground cinnamon
- 1/2 tsp ground ginger
- 1/4 cup (75g) harissa ⓟ
- Finely grated zest and juice of 1 lemon
- 1/4 cup (60ml) extra virgin olive oil
- 600g piece centre-cut skinless salmon fillet, pin-boned
- 800ml chicken or vegetable stock
- 250g pearl couscous ⓟ
- 1/4 cup chopped flat-leaf parsley
- 1/4 cup chopped mint leaves, plus extra leaves to serve
- 1/4 cup chopped coriander leaves, plus extra sprigs to serve
- 1 cup (280g) thick Greek-style yoghurt

Stir the coriander seeds and cardamom pods in a frypan over medium-low heat for 1 minute or until fragrant. When cool enough to handle, remove the seeds from the pods, discarding pods. Using a mortar and pestle, crush seeds until finely ground. Add cinnamon, ginger, 2 tbs harissa, half the lemon zest and 2 tbs olive oil.

Line a baking tray with baking paper. Place the salmon on prepared baking tray and spread the marinade over. Refrigerate for 1 hour.

Preheat oven to 170°C. Bring salmon to room temperature, then roast for 10 minutes or until just cooked.

Meanwhile, place stock in a saucepan over medium-high heat and bring to a simmer. Add couscous and cook for 8 minutes or until tender. Drain, cool slightly, then toss with herbs, lemon juice and remaining zest, and 1 tbs olive oil. Season.

Swirl the remaining 1 tbs harissa through the yoghurt, then spoon over plates. Divide couscous among plates, flake salmon over and serve topped with extra herbs. **Serves 4-6**

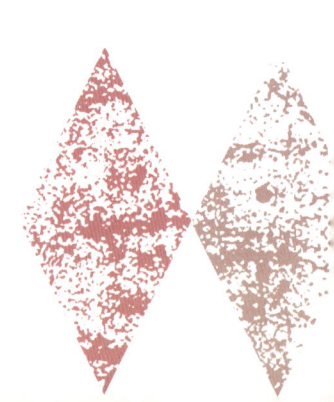

ⓟ See Pantry essentials, p 262.

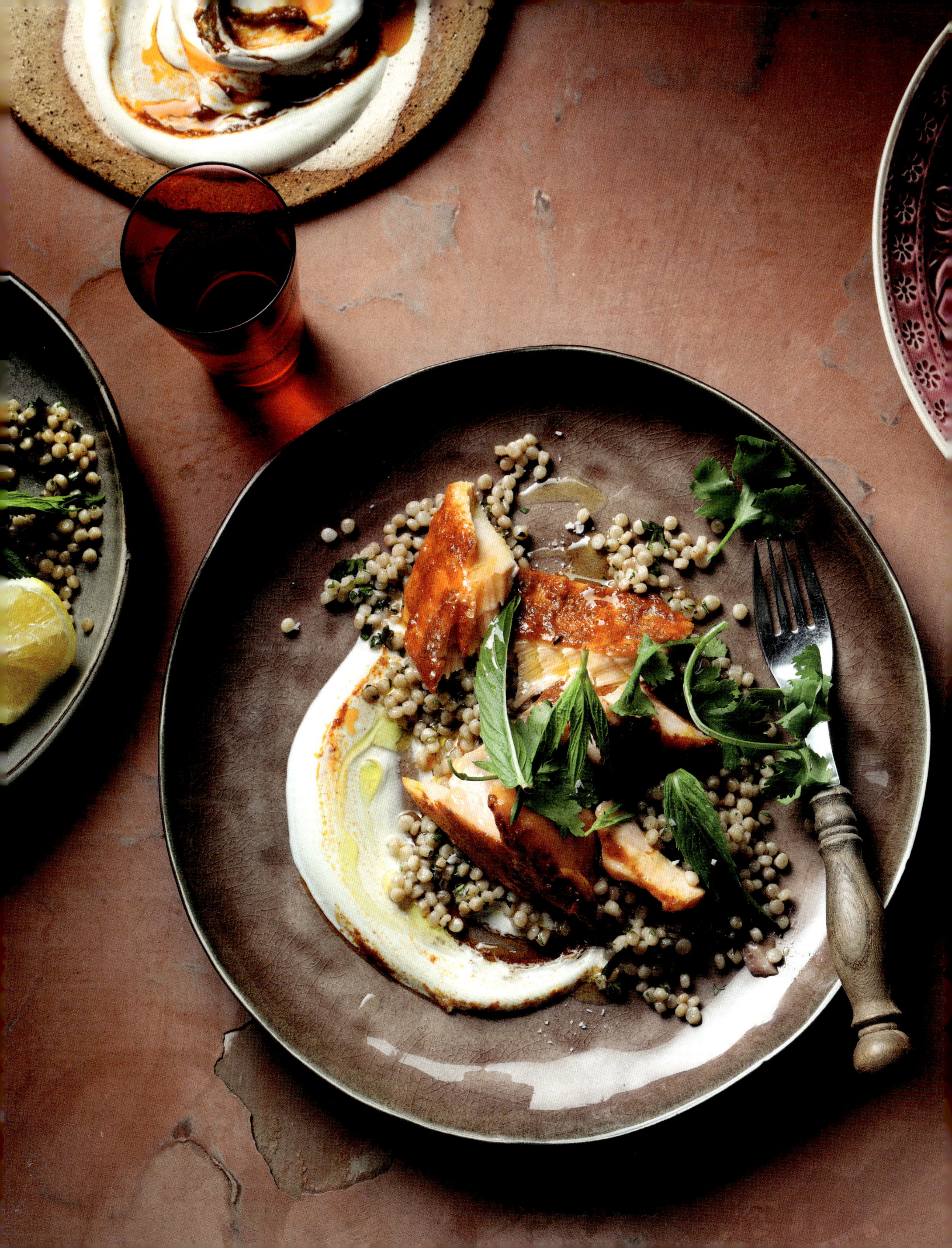

Moroccan chicken skewers with pea tabbouleh

¾ cup (200g) thick Greek-style yoghurt
1 onion, grated
½ cup (125ml) olive oil
2 tbs lemon juice
2 garlic cloves, crushed
1½ tsp sweet smoked paprika (pimenton)
1½ tsp ground coriander
1½ tsp ground cumin
600g chicken thigh fillets, cut into bite-sized pieces
2 tbs sesame seeds, lightly toasted

Pea tabbouleh
100g burghul ⓟ
2½ cups (300g) frozen peas
250g cherry tomatoes, halved
1 bunch flat-leaf parsley, roughly chopped
½ bunch mint, roughly chopped, plus extra leaves to serve
3 spring onions, thinly sliced
200g marinated feta, drained
⅓ cup (80ml) olive oil
Juice of ½ lemon
½ tsp cinnamon

Combine the yoghurt, onion, oil, lemon juice, garlic, paprika, coriander and cumin in a bowl and season. Add chicken to yoghurt mixture and toss to coat, then cover and marinate in the fridge for 2 hours.

Soak 8 bamboo skewers in cold water for 30 minutes.

Meanwhile, for the pea tabbouleh, soak burghul in 1 cup (250ml) boiling water for 30 minutes. Drain well, pressing down with the back of a spoon, to remove any excess water. Cook peas in a saucepan of boiling salted water for 3 minutes. Drain and refresh in cold water. Combine drained burghul, peas, tomatoes, parsley, mint, spring onions and feta in a bowl. Whisk oil, lemon and cinnamon together in a small bowl. Season, then toss with the burghul mixture. Set aside.

Thread chicken onto skewers. Preheat a barbecue or chargrill over medium-high heat. Cook skewers, turning, for 8-10 minutes until lightly charred and cooked through. Sprinkle skewers with sesame seeds.

Serve chicken skewers with pea tabbouleh scattered with extra mint leaves. **Serves 4**

ⓟ See Pantry essentials, p 262.

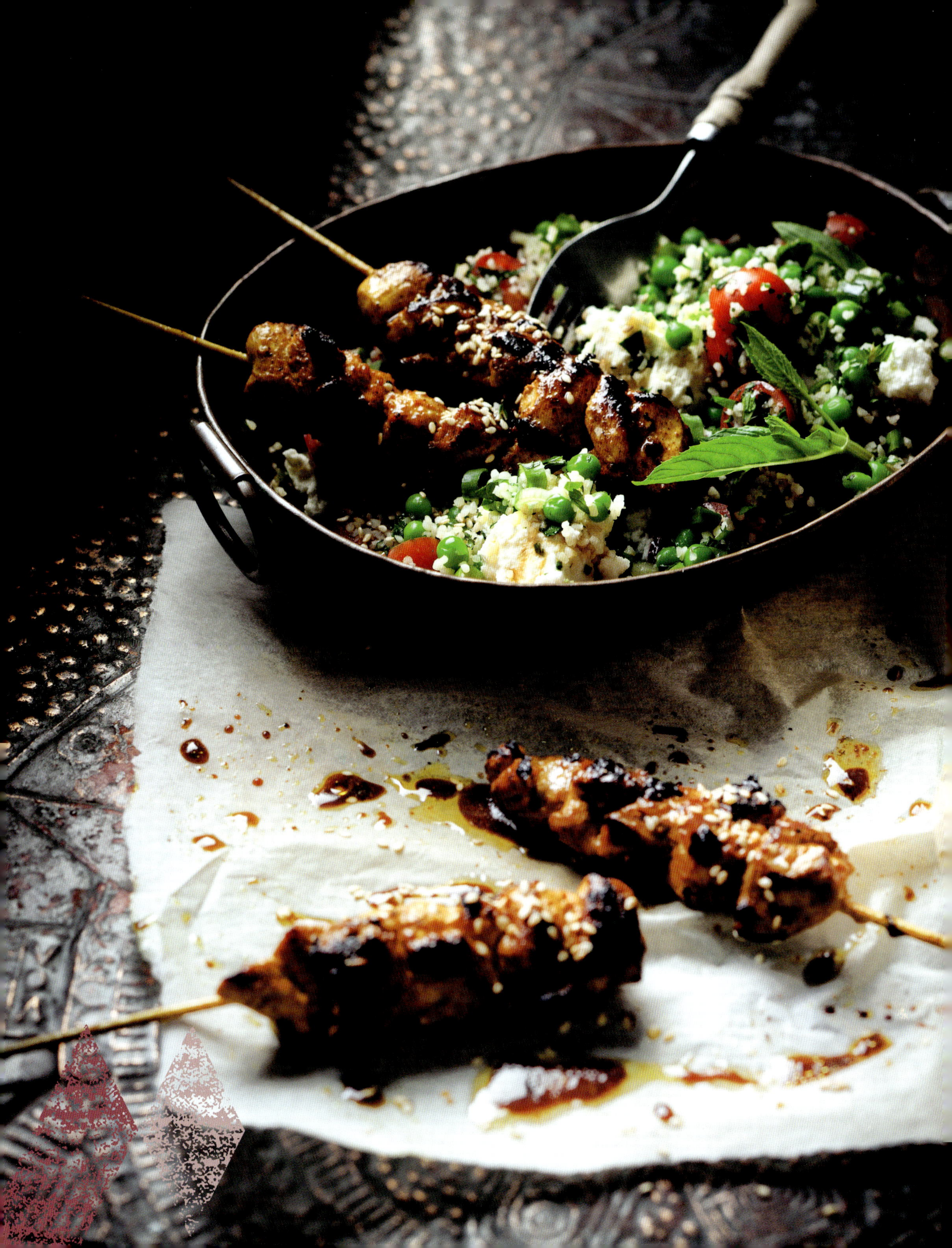

Lamb & vegetable pie with harissa yoghurt

Barberries have a tart flavour that balances the richness of the filling. If you substitute dried cranberries, bear in mind that the dish will be a touch sweeter.

2 tbs olive oil
500g lamb mince
1 garlic clove, crushed
2 tsp grated ginger
½ tsp each ground cumin, coriander, cinnamon and chilli flakes
1 tsp ras el hanout ⓟ
4 (about 300g) carrots, grated
2 raw beetroot, grated
75g dried barberries ⓟ or dried cranberries
⅓ cup (50g) toasted pine nuts
1 tbs honey
Juice of ½ lemon
25g unsalted butter, melted, cooled
375g packet filo pastry ⓟ
3 tsp harissa ⓟ
1 cup (280g) thick Greek-style yoghurt

Heat oil in a frypan over medium heat. Add the lamb and cook, breaking up with a wooden spoon, for 5-6 minutes until browned. Add the garlic, ginger and spices. Season. Cook for 1 minute, then add the carrot, beetroot, barberries, pine nuts, honey and lemon juice, then stir to combine. Cool.

Preheat the oven to 190°C.

Brush a deep 28cm loose-bottomed tart pan with a little melted butter. Place 1 sheet filo in the pan (it will overhang the edge). Brush with butter. Repeat with a second sheet of filo, so that it overlaps the first. Repeat with a further 8 sheets of filo, brushing with butter between each sheet and overlapping the previous sheet so the base is entirely covered.

Spoon the cooled mince mixture into the pastry base, then fold the overhanging pastry over the filling. Scrunch up the remaining filo sheets and arrange on top. Brush pie with remaining butter, then bake for 35 minutes or until filling is hot and the top is golden and crisp.

Swirl the harissa through the yoghurt and serve with the pie.

Serves 6-8

ⓟ See Pantry essentials, p 262.

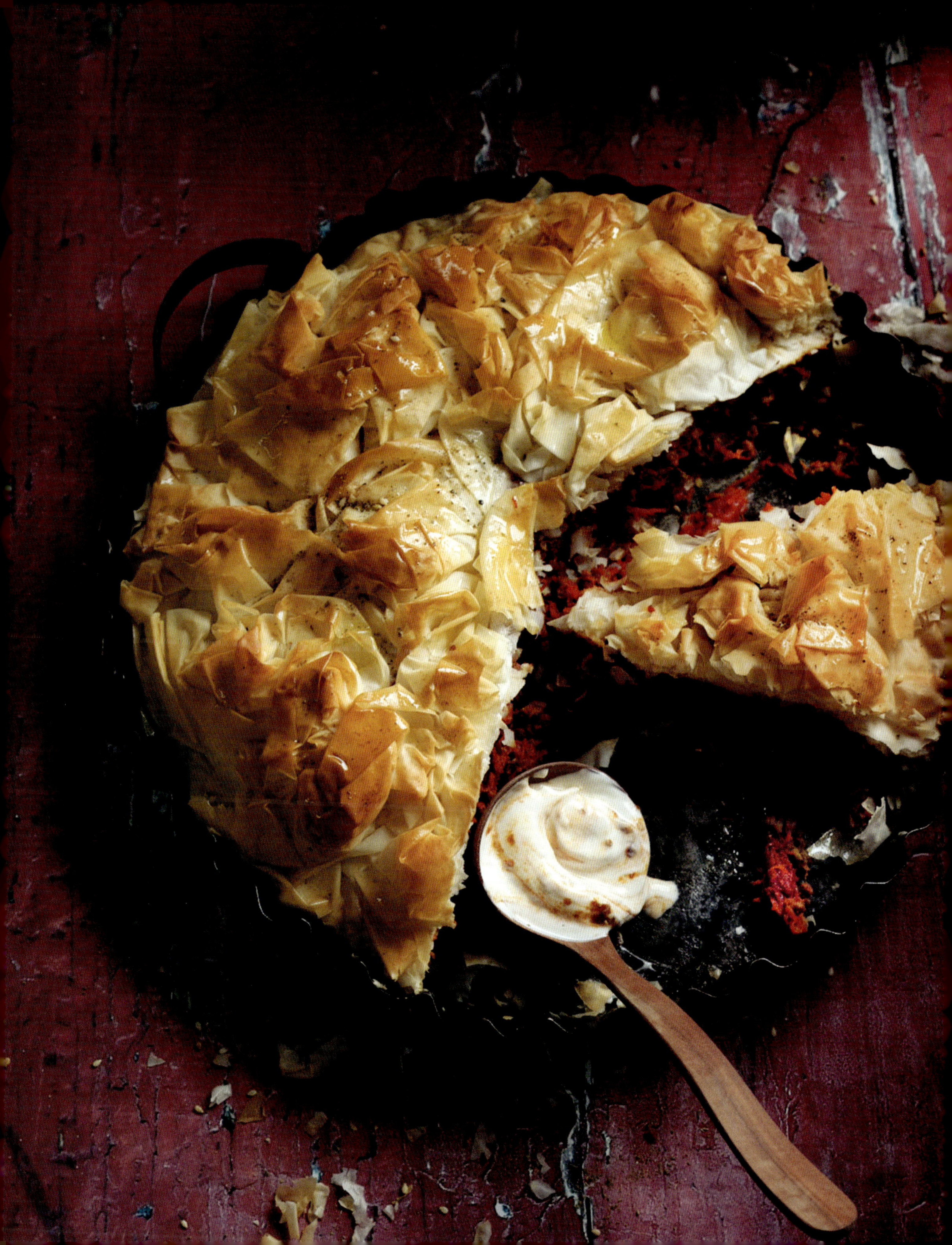

Chermoula snapper

Chermoula is a wonderful Middle Eastern spice blend that complements lamb, chicken and vegetarian dishes, too.

- 2 x 500g whole snappers, cleaned, scaled
- 2 lemons, sliced
- 1 red onion, thinly sliced
- 1 cup flat-leaf parsley leaves

Chermoula
- 1 tbs ground coriander
- 1 tbs ground cumin
- 4 garlic cloves, chopped
- 1 preserved lemon ⓟ quarter, pulp and pith discarded, rind chopped
- 2 cups flat-leaf parsley leaves
- 1 tsp chilli flakes
- 1 tsp sweet smoked paprika
- 2 tbs lemon juice
- 1/2 cup (125ml) olive oil

Preheat the oven to 180°C.

For the chermoula, combine all ingredients in a small food processor and process to a coarse paste. Season well.

Line a large baking tray with baking paper. Place fish on tray. Using a sharp knife, score skin two or three times on both sides. Spread both sides with chermoula. Place half the lemon slices in the fish cavities. Scatter the remainder around the fish.

Bake for 20-25 minutes until cooked through (test by flaking the thickest part of the fish with a fork).

Meanwhile, combine onion and 1 tsp salt in 1 cup (250ml) boiling water for 15 minutes. Drain well.

Serve chermoula snapper sprinkled with red onion and flat-leaf parsley. **Serves 2-4**

ⓟ See Pantry essentials, p 262.

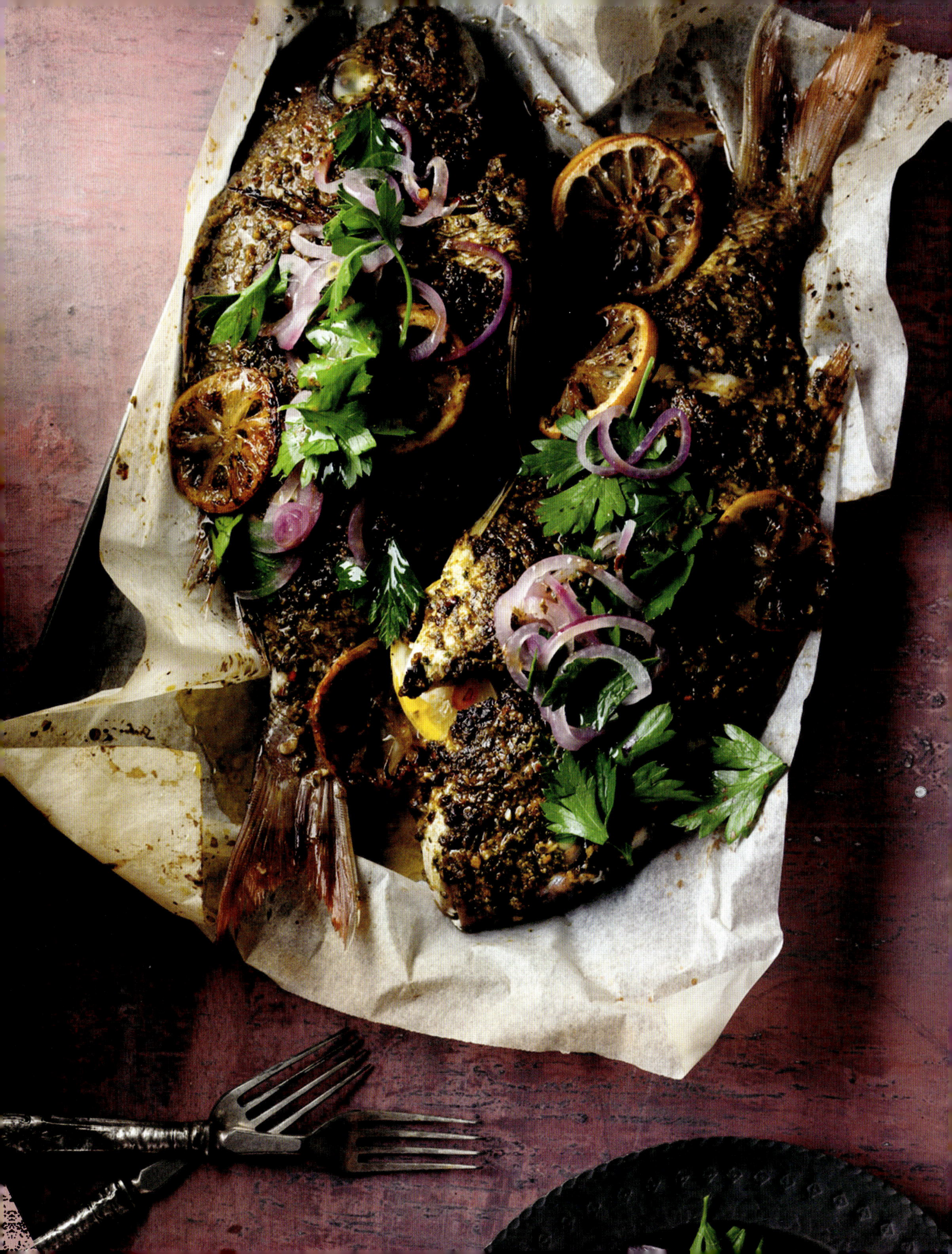

Moroccan slow-roast lamb with ancient-grain salad

- 1/3 cup (80ml) pomegranate molasses ⓟ
- 2 garlic cloves, crushed, plus 1 bulb garlic, halved
- 1 tbs ras el hanout ⓟ
- 2 tbs lemon juice
- 1 tbs olive oil
- 2 red onions, thickly sliced
- 2kg shoulder of lamb on the bone
- Rocket, to serve

Ancient-grain salad
- 1/2 cup whole green Puy-style lentils
- 1 cup (165g) freekeh ⓟ
- 1/3 cup mixed seeds and nuts (we used pepitas, sunflower seeds and pine nuts)
- 2 tbs baby capers, rinsed, drained
- 1/2 cup barberries ⓟ or dried cranberries
- Seeds of 1 pomegranate
- 1/2 cup chopped flat-leaf parsley leaves
- 1/2 cup chopped coriander leaves
- 2 tbs lemon juice
- 2 tbs olive oil

Preheat the oven to 140°C.

Combine the pomegranate molasses, crushed garlic, ras el hanout, lemon juice and olive oil in a small bowl. Season and set aside.

Place the halved garlic bulb and onion in a roasting pan. Using a sharp knife, score a cross-hatch pattern into the flesh of the lamb. Place on top of the onion in the pan. Brush lamb with half the marinade and pour 1 cup (250ml) water into the base of the pan. Cover with foil and roast for 3 1/2 hours. Remove foil, then strain the pan juices into a bowl and transfer to the fridge for 30 minutes. Brush lamb with remaining marinade and return to the oven. Cook, uncovered, for a further 30 minutes or until tender and falling off the bone.

Meanwhile, for the ancient-grain salad, cook lentils in a saucepan of boiling water for 25 minutes. Cook the freekeh in a separate saucepan of boiling salted water for 20 minutes. Drain both well, then transfer to a bowl with the mixed seeds and nuts, capers, barberries, pomegranate seeds, flat-leaf parsley and coriander. Whisk lemon juice with olive oil. Season. Add to the freekeh mixture and toss to combine.

Skim fat from strained pan juices. Heat pan juices in a small saucepan over medium heat.

Slice the lamb and serve with roasted garlic, pan juices, ancient-grain salad and rocket. **Serves 6**

ⓟ See Pantry essentials, p 262.

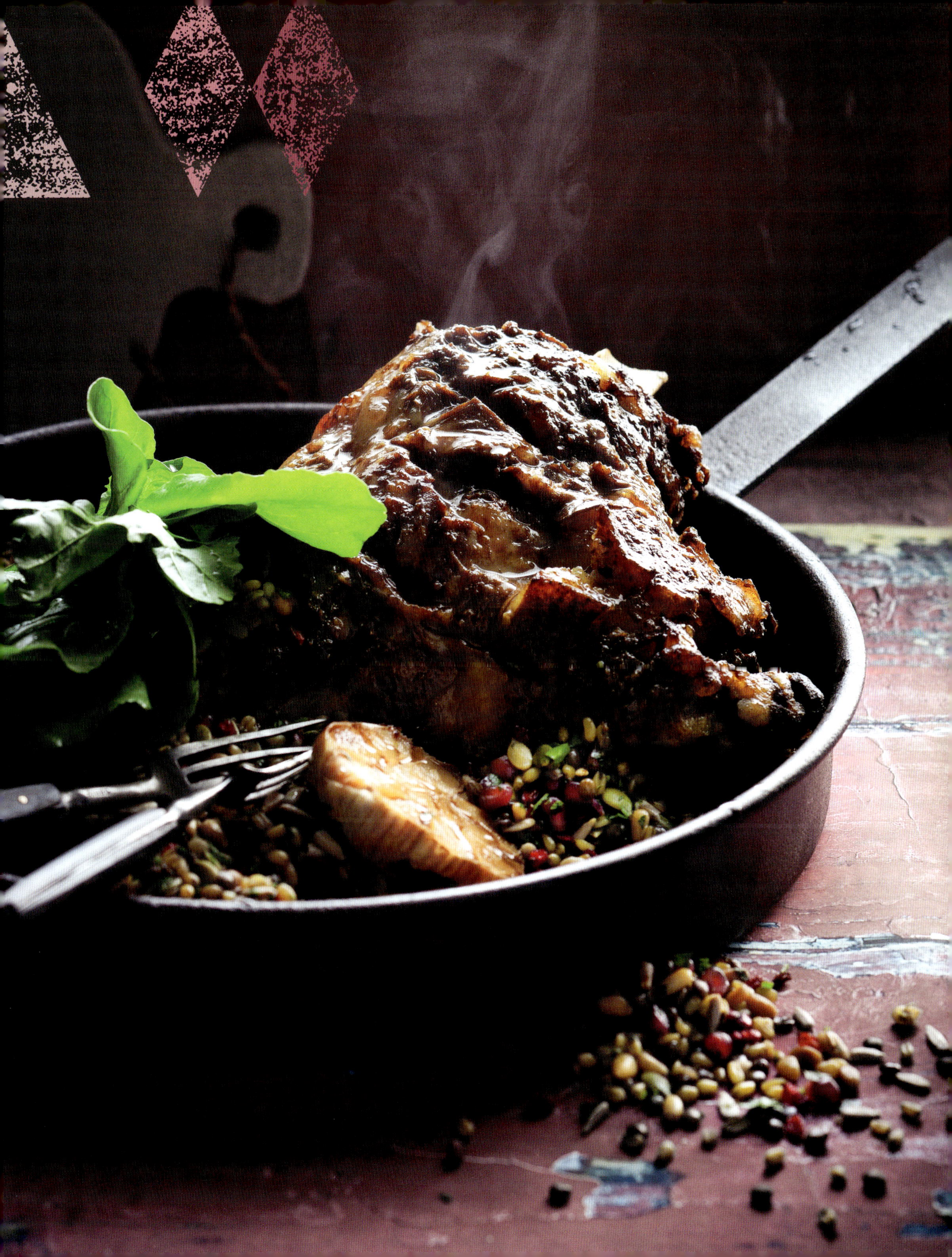

Spiced spatchcock with mujaddara

Versions of mujaddara, a Levantine staple of rice and lentils topped with crisp onion, can be found throughout the Middle East.

1¼ cups (250g) small brown lentils
1 cup (200g) long-grain rice
2 tsp cinnamon
1 tsp ground cumin
1 tsp ground paprika
4 x 500g spatchcocks
⅓ cup (80ml) olive oil
⅓ cup (80ml) pomegranate molasses ⓟ
30g unsalted butter
4 onions, thinly sliced
½ bunch flat-leaf parsley, roughly chopped
Juice of ½ lemon
Thick Greek-style yoghurt and mint leaves, to serve

Place the lentils in a saucepan of cold water. Bring to the boil over medium-high heat, then reduce heat to medium-low, cover and cook for 20 minutes or until tender. Drain. Set aside to cool.

Meanwhile, cook the rice in boiling salted water until tender. Drain. Set aside to cool.

Preheat the oven to 180°C.

Combine cinnamon, cumin and paprika in a small bowl. Place spatchcocks in a roasting pan and rub all over with 2 tbs olive oil and half the spice mixture. Season with salt. Roast for 30 minutes, then brush with 2 tbs pomegranate molasses. Return to the oven for a further 10 minutes. Remove spatchcocks from the oven and brush with remaining 2 tbs pomegranate molasses. Set aside to rest, loosely covered with foil, for 10 minutes.

Meanwhile, while the spatchcocks are roasting, heat the butter and remaining 2 tbs oil in a frypan over medium-low heat. Add the onion and 1 tsp salt, then cook, stirring occasionally, for 20 minutes or until onion is soft. Stir in the remaining spice mixture, increase heat to medium-high and cook, stirring, for a further 5 minutes until onion is crisp. Add the rice and lentils and stir gently until warmed through. Season, then add the chopped parsley and lemon juice.

Serve the spatchcocks with mujaddara, yoghurt and mint.

Serves 4

ⓟ See Pantry essentials, p 262.

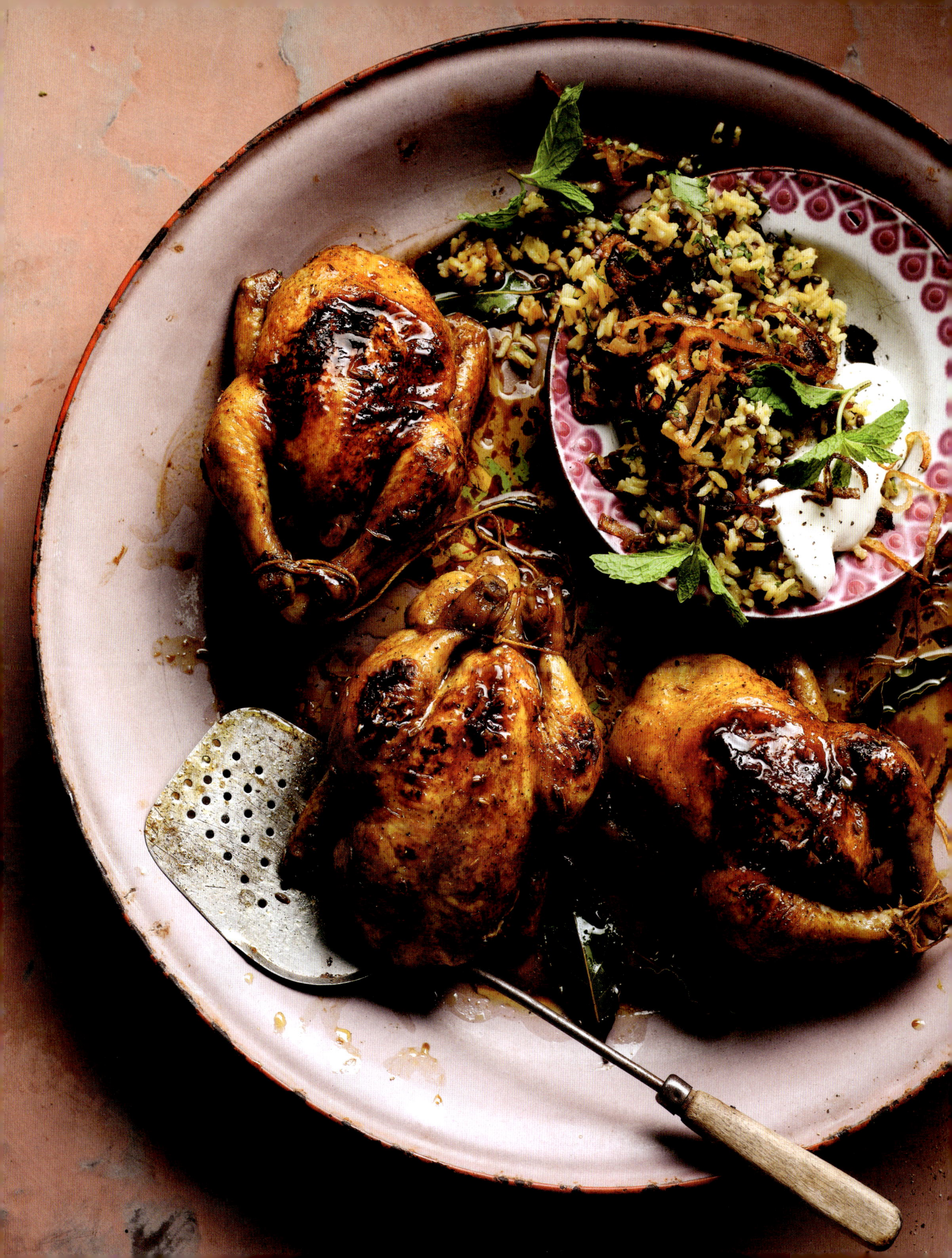

Fig & berry filo crisps

You could make this even more spectacular by layering filo crisps with the cream mixture, figs and raspberry sauce to make a mille-feuille-style dessert.

4 sheets filo pastry ⓟ
60g unsalted butter, melted, cooled
½ cup (75g) slivered or finely chopped pistachio kernels, plus extra to serve
85g icing sugar
250g raspberries
¼ cup (55g) caster sugar
1 tsp rosewater ⓟ
1 tbs redcurrant jelly
100ml thickened cream
100g mascarpone
⅓ cup (95g) thick Greek-style yoghurt
Scraped seeds of 1 vanilla bean
Finely grated zest and juice of ½ lemon
4 figs, sliced

Preheat the oven to 180°C. Line 1 large or 2 small baking trays with baking paper.

Place 1 sheet of filo on the workbench and brush with butter. Scatter with a quarter of the pistachios and dust with 1 tbs icing sugar. Place a second sheet on top, brush with melted butter, scatter with another quarter of the pistachios and dust with another 1 tbs icing sugar. Repeat this process twice more until you have a stack of 4 sheets. Cut into 12 rectangles and place on the baking tray. Bake for 15 minutes or until golden. Remove from oven and immediately dust with another 1 tbs icing sugar. Set aside to cool.

Place the raspberries, caster sugar, rosewater and ¼ cup (60ml) water in a saucepan over low heat. Stir gently until the berries release their juices. Drain berries through a sieve, then return juices to the pan with the redcurrant jelly. Simmer for 4-5 minutes until syrupy. Return the reserved raspberries to the pan. Set aside to cool.

Using electric beaters, beat cream, mascarpone, yoghurt, vanilla, lemon zest and juice, and remaining 2 tbs icing sugar until smooth and combined.

To serve, spread the filo crisps with spoonfuls of cream mixture and top with fig slices, raspberry sauce and extra pistachios. **Serves 4**

ⓟ See Pantry essentials, p 262.

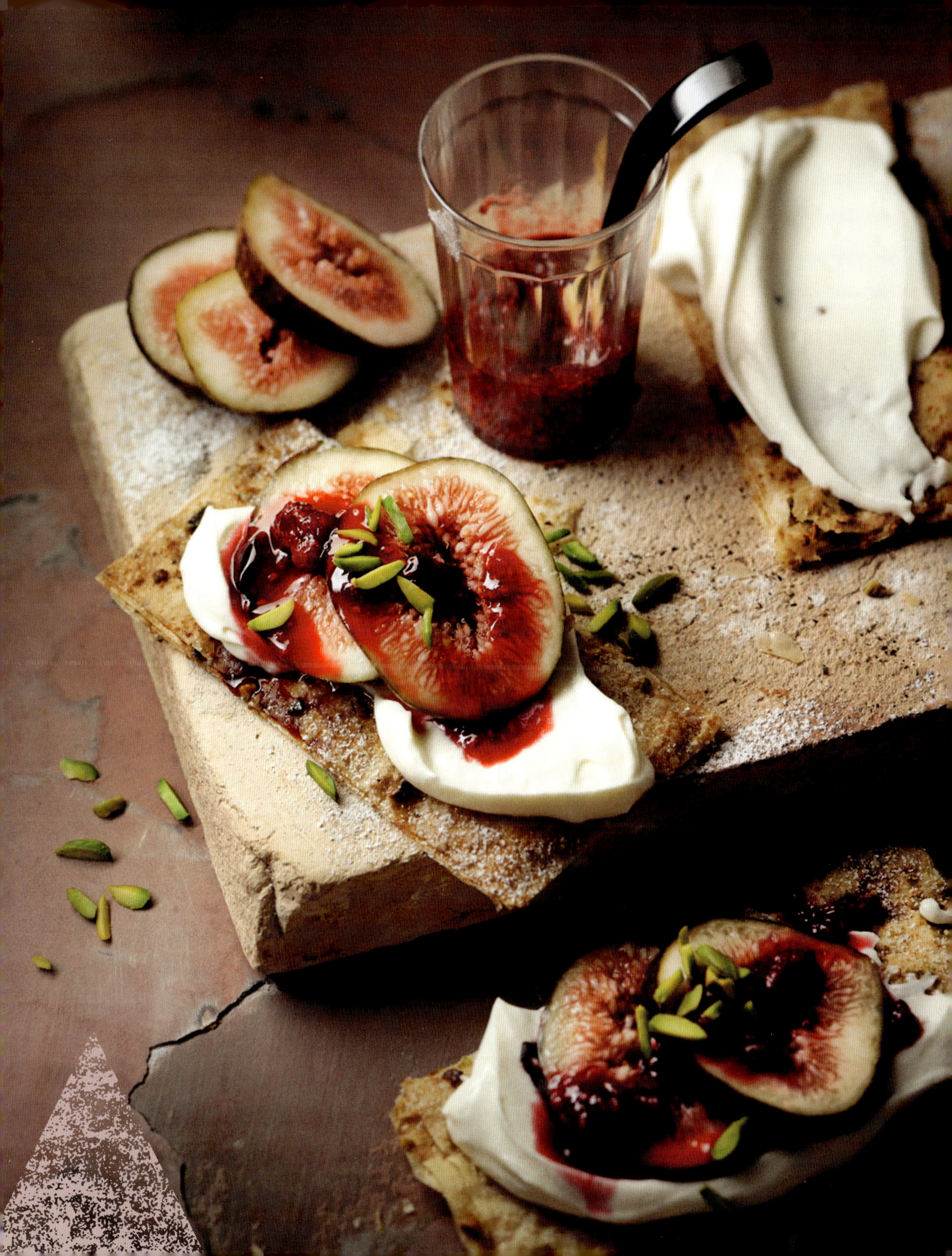

Orange blossom semifreddo cones

You will need 6 sheets of A4 paper, 6 sheets of baking paper cut to A4 size, and a sugar thermometer. Start this recipe a day ahead.

2/3 cup (150g) caster sugar
2 tbs honey
3 eggwhites
1/4 tsp cream of tartar
300ml thickened cream, whisked to soft peaks
2 tsp orange blossom water ⓟ
Finely grated zest of 1 orange
40g pistachio kernels, finely chopped, plus extra to serve
50g dark chocolate, very finely chopped

Caramel oranges
5 oranges
1 1/3 cups (295g) caster sugar
8 cardamom pods
1 cinnamon quill

To prepare cone moulds, place 1 sheet of baking paper over 1 sheet of A4 paper. Bring the top right-hand corners down to the centre, then roll to form a cone shape. Secure with a small piece of sticky tape. Repeat with remaining sheets of baking paper and A4 paper, then place cone moulds, narrow-end down, into 6 champagne flutes or narrow wine glasses (these will help support the moulds while the semifreddo is freezing).

Place sugar, honey and 200ml water in a saucepan over low heat, stirring until sugar dissolves. Increase heat to medium-high and boil, without stirring, for 6 minutes or until mixture reaches 120°C on a sugar thermometer.

Meanwhile, using electric beaters, whisk eggwhites and cream of tartar to soft peaks. Whisking constantly, slowly drizzle in hot sugar syrup, then whisk for 12-15 minutes until mixture has cooled. Fold in cream, orange blossom water, zest, pistachios and chocolate. Tap bowl on bench to remove air bubbles. Divide mixture among moulds in glasses. Freeze overnight.

For the caramel oranges, peel 4 oranges, discarding pith. Thinly slice and place in a shallow dish. Combine sugar, spices and 200ml water in a saucepan over low heat, stirring until sugar dissolves. Increase heat to medium-high and bring to the boil. Boil (do not stir), occasionally brushing down side of pan with a wet pastry brush, for 8-10 minutes until a deep caramel colour. Add juice of remaining orange (be careful as mixture may spit) and simmer for 2-3 minutes until smooth. Remove from heat, cool slightly, then pour over sliced orange. Cool completely.

When ready to serve, invert cones onto serving plates and remove tape and paper moulds. Serve cones with caramel oranges, sprinkled with extra pistachios. **Makes 6 cones**
ⓟ See Pantry essentials, p 262.

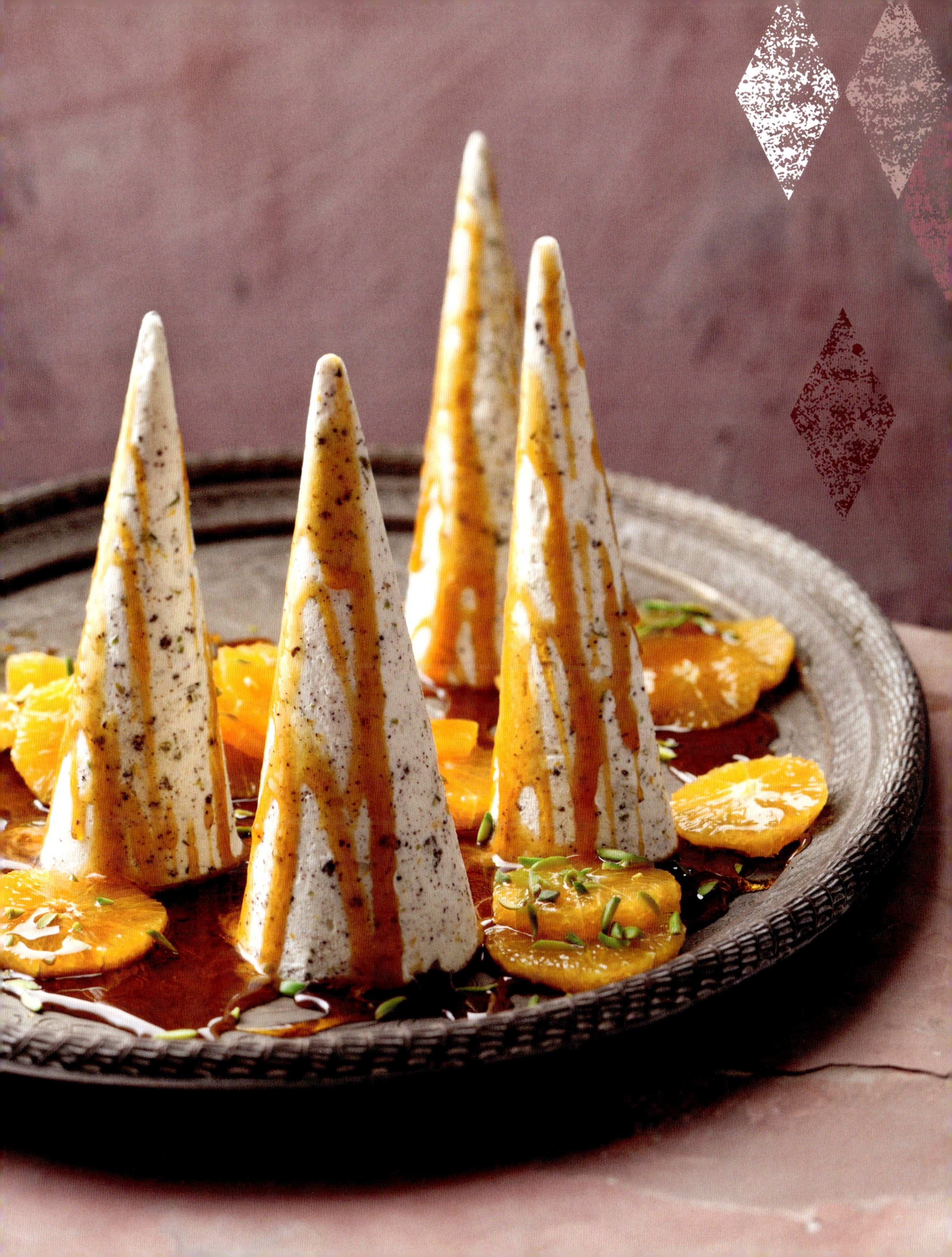

Rose-scented poached peaches with honeyed yoghurt

4 white peaches
1 1/3 cups (295g) caster sugar
2 tsp rosewater ⓟ
1/2 cup (140g) thick Greek-style yoghurt
1 1/2 tbs honey
1 1/2 tbs lemon juice
2 tbs finely chopped pistachios
Dried rose petals ⓟ (optional), to serve

Cut a small cross in the base of each peach. Set aside.

Place the sugar, 1 tsp rosewater and 3 cups (750ml) water in a saucepan over low heat, stirring until sugar dissolves. Add peaches, then bring to a simmer for 3-4 minutes until just tender (the time will depend on the ripeness of the peaches; you may need to cook them a little longer). Using a slotted spoon, transfer peaches to a shallow dish, reserving poaching liquid in pan. Cool peaches slightly, then peel away skins and add to the poaching liquid (this will give the liquid a beautiful pink hue). Increase heat to medium-high and simmer for 6-8 minutes until mixture is reduced by half and syrupy. Strain mixture through a sieve, discarding solids. Pour over peaches and set aside to cool.

Meanwhile, combine the yoghurt, honey, lemon juice and remaining 1 tsp rosewater in a small bowl. Add 1-2 tbs poaching mixture to give a pouring consistency.

Serve peaches with honeyed yoghurt, sprinkled with pistachios and rose petals, if using. **Serves 4**

ⓟ See Pantry essentials, p 262.

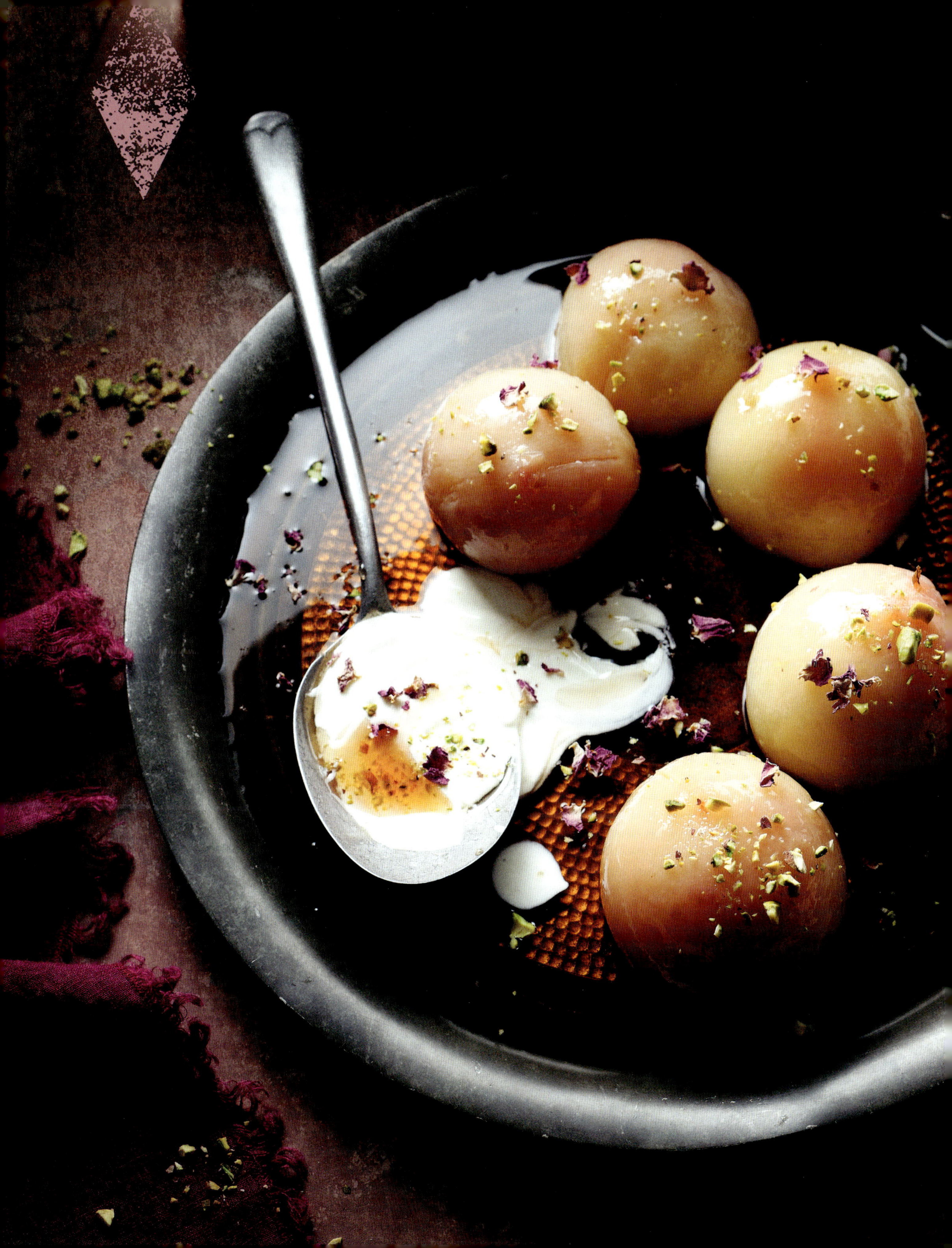

Turkish delight pavlova

Starting your eggwhites and sugar over a bowl of simmering water is a foolproof way to ensure a perfectly crisp meringue that doesn't weep.

300ml thickened cream
1 tsp rosewater ⓟ
¼ cup (35g) icing sugar, sifted
Seeds of 1 vanilla bean
1 cup roughly chopped pink Turkish delight ⓟ
125g raspberries
2 tbs slivered or finely chopped pistachios
Unsprayed fresh rose petals* and rose syrup ⓟ (both optional), to serve

Meringue
7 eggwhites
1½ cups (330g) caster sugar
2 tsp cornflour
1 tsp white wine vinegar
A few drops pink food colouring (optional)

Preheat the oven to 130°C. Cut a piece of baking paper large enough to line a baking tray. Trace a 24cm circle on the paper (you could use a large dinner plate as a guide), then place on baking tray, traced-side down.

For the meringue, place eggwhites in a bowl set over a saucepan of gently simmering water. Using a large balloon whisk, gradually whisk in the sugar. Continue whisking until mixture starts to froth and sugar dissolves. Transfer mixture to the bowl of an electric mixer, then whisk to stiff peaks. Using a metal spoon, fold in the cornflour, vinegar and food colouring (if using). Spread meringue mixture over the circle on the baking paper, making an indent in the centre for the filling. Bake for 1 hour, then turn off the oven and leave meringue in the oven with the door propped open until the oven is cold or overnight.

Whisk cream, rosewater, icing sugar and vanilla to soft peaks. Pile into the meringue and serve topped with Turkish delight, raspberries, pistachios, rose petals and rose syrup, if using.

Serves 6-8

If you're lucky, you may have unsprayed rose petals in your garden; otherwise, ask your florist, or use edible dried rose petals (see Pantry essentials, p 262).

ⓟ *See Pantry essentials, p 262.*

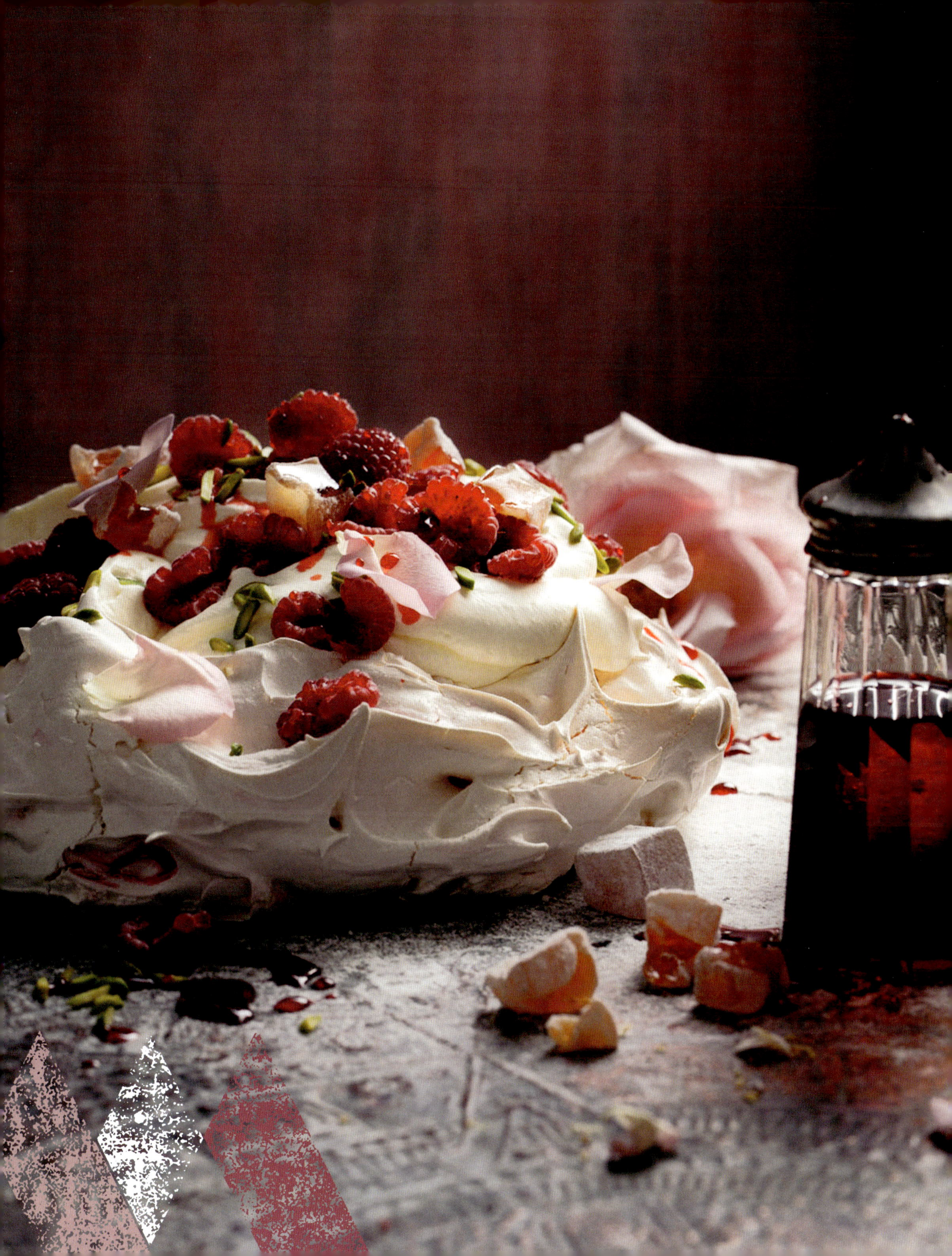

TOOL KIT

Three of the best

Vegetarian

186 Baked kumaras with chipotle butter and pico de gallo

Tarka dhal with spinach and tomato
104

208 Warm goat's cheese fondue with primeurs

Barbecue

68 Barbecued sausage rolls with beer-braised onions

98 Indian salmon kebabs

56 Steak with escalivada and manchego butter

Salads

40 Pear & manchego salad with jamon-wrapped breadsticks

70 Barbecue chicken salad with passionfruit dressing

128 Meatball caesar

>>

Show-stopping desserts

Cheat's fraisier cake
230

282
Orange blossom semifreddo cones

Chocolate-orange cake
60

Winter warmers

18
Taleggio & cauliflower risotto with hazelnut pangrattato

52
Rioja chicken

Carrot soup Vichy with herbed croutons
210

Easy weeknights

216 Salmon en papillote with honey mustard sauce

44 Chorizo burgers

168 Tom yum fried rice

Brunch

236 Buck rarebit

88 Tropical granola with lime yoghurt

198 Donuts with dulce de leche

Basics

Shortcrust pastry

Whiz 1 1/2 cups (225g) plain flour, 125g chilled, chopped unsalted butter and a pinch of salt in a food processor to fine crumbs. Add 1 egg yolk and 2 tbs chilled water, then whiz until the mixture just comes together. Shape into a ball, enclose in plastic wrap, then chill for 30 minutes before rolling out. The pastry will keep in the freezer for up to 1 month. **Makes one 23cm tart shell, one 20cm x 30cm tart shell, or six 12cm tart shells**

Sweet shortcrust pastry

Whiz 1 2/3 cups (250g) plain flour, 2 tbs icing sugar and a pinch of salt in a food processor to combine. Add 180g chilled, chopped unsalted butter and whiz to fine crumbs. Add 1 egg yolk, the scraped seeds from 1 vanilla bean and 1 tbs chilled water, then whiz until the mixture just comes together. Shape into a ball, enclose in plastic wrap, then chill for 1 hour before rolling out. The pastry will keep in the freezer for up to 1 month. **Makes one 23cm tart shell, one 12cm x 36cm tart shell or six 10cm tart shells**

Chocolate pastry

Whiz 1 cup (150g) plain flour, 2 tbs cocoa powder and 1/3 cup (50g) icing sugar in a food processor to combine. Add 80g chilled, chopped unsalted butter and whiz to fine crumbs. Add 1 egg and whiz until mixture just comes together. Shape into a ball, enclose in plastic wrap, then chill for 30 minutes before rolling out. Pastry will keep in the freezer for up to 1 month. **Makes one 23cm tart shell or six 10cm tart shells**

Sour cream pastry

Whiz 2 cups (300g) plain flour, 200g chilled, chopped unsalted butter and a pinch of salt in a food processor to fine crumbs. Add 1/2 cup (120g) full-fat sour cream, then whiz until the mixture just comes together. Shape into a ball, enclose in plastic wrap, then chill for 30 minutes before rolling out. The pastry will keep in the freezer for up to 1 month. **Makes one 23cm tart shell, one 20cm x 30cm tart shell, or six 12cm tart shells**

Pilaf
Place 2 cups (400g) basmati rice, 400ml coconut milk, 1½ cups (375ml) cold water, 1 cinnamon quill, 8 cardamom pods and 1 tsp mild curry powder in a large saucepan. Bring to the boil over medium-high heat, then reduce heat to low and simmer, covered, for 12 minutes or until rice is tender. Set aside, covered, for 5 minutes, then fluff with a fork. **Makes 6 cups**

Saffron rice
Using a mortar and pestle, crush ¼ tsp saffron threads with 1 tsp sea salt. Heat 1 tbs olive oil in a large saucepan over medium heat. Add 1 finely chopped onion and cook, stirring, for 5-6 minutes until softened but not browned. Add the saffron mixture, 1½ cups (300g) basmati rice and 700ml boiling water. Reduce heat to medium-low, then cook, covered, for 20 minutes or until the rice is tender. Set aside, covered, for 5 minutes, then fluff rice with a fork. **Makes 4 cups**

Coconut rice
Rinse 2 cups (400g) jasmine rice in cold water. Place in a large saucepan with 3 cups (750ml) cold water, 400ml coconut milk, a 3cm piece of ginger and 1 tsp salt. Bring to the boil over medium-high heat, reduce heat to low and simmer for 10 minutes or until rice is tender. Cover and set aside for 10 minutes. Discard ginger. Drain rice, if necessary, then return to the pan and fluff with a fork. **Makes 7 cups**

Flour tortillas
Combine 3 cups (450g) sifted plain flour, 1 tsp baking powder, 1/3 cup (80ml) vegetable oil, 1 tsp salt and 1 cup (250ml) hot water in a food processor fitted with a dough hook and knead for 3 minutes or until smooth. (Alternatively, combine in a large bowl, bring together with your hands, then knead on a lightly floured surface.) Cover with a clean tea towel and rest for 15 minutes. Divide dough into 16 portions, then shape into balls. Roll out on a lightly floured surface to 15cm rounds.

>>

Lightly brush a frypan with a little oil, then cook tortillas, in batches, over medium-high heat for 1 minute each side or until bubbles appear on the surface and patches of brown appear. Keep tortillas warm in a low oven. You can make these in advance and reheat in a microwave. **Makes 16**

Baked croutons

Preheat the oven to 180°C. Remove and discard the crusts from 4 thick slices sourdough, then tear into rough 3cm pieces. Place in a bowl, toss with 2 tbs olive oil and season with salt. Spread over a baking paper-lined baking tray, then bake, turning once, for 15-20 minutes until golden and crisp. Store for 3-4 days in an airtight container.

Small fried croutons

Remove and discard the crusts from 6 thin slices sourdough, then cut into 1cm cubes. Heat 30g butter and 2 tbs olive oil in a frypan over medium heat. Add 1 whole garlic clove and cook for 1 minute, turning once, to flavour the oil. Discard the garlic. Add the bread and cook, turning, for 4-6 minutes until golden and crisp. Drain on paper towel and season with sea salt. Store for 3-4 days in an airtight container.

Patatas bravas

Preheat oven to 190°C. Peel 1kg pontiac or desiree potatoes and cut into 2cm pieces. Place in a pan of cold water and bring to the boil over medium-high heat. Parboil for 3 minutes. Drain well. Transfer to a baking dish, pour over 1/3 cup (80ml) dry white wine, drizzle over 2 tbs olive oil and season. Toss to combine. Roast for 30-35 minutes until golden. Meanwhile, heat 1 tbs olive oil in a pan over medium heat. Add 2 chopped garlic cloves and 1/2 tsp chilli flakes and cook, stirring, for 1 minute. Add 400g chopped canned tomatoes, 1 tbs tomato paste, 1 tsp sweet smoked paprika (pimenton) and a pinch of caster sugar. Season. Bring to a simmer and cook, stirring occasionally, for 20-25 minutes until reduced and thickened. Cool slightly, then whiz in a food processor until smooth. Return to a saucepan. Reheat gently over low heat. Toss potatoes in tomato sauce and serve sprinkled with chopped flat-leaf parsley.

Garlic mayonnaise

Combine 200ml sunflower oil and 2 1/2 tbs olive oil in a small jug. Whiz 2 crushed garlic cloves, 2 egg yolks and 1 tbs Dijon mustard in a food processor, then, with the motor running, slowly add the oil mixture, drop by drop at first, then in a slow, steady stream until mixture is thick and emulsified. (Alternatively, using a balloon whisk, whisk ingredients in a bowl, adding the oils in the same way.) Stir in 1 tbs lemon juice and season. Store in an airtight container in the fridge for up to 2 weeks. **Makes 1 cup**

Mint jelly

Place 1kg unpeeled, chopped Granny Smith or other green-skinned apples in a large saucepan with 1.5L (6 cups) water and bring to the boil over medium-high heat. Reduce heat to low and cook for 1 hour or until the apple is pulpy. Line a sieve with muslin or a clean chux cloth and place over a large bowl. Transfer apple mixture to lined sieve and stand for 3 hours or until the liquid stops dripping (don't squeeze or press the pulp, or the jelly will be cloudy). Measure the strained juice and return to a clean pan. Add 1 cup (220g) caster sugar per 1 cup (250ml) of liquid, stirring over low heat until sugar dissolves. Bring to the boil over medium-high heat, then boil for 30 minutes or until liquid reaches setting point* (see note below). Pour into a jug, then add a few drops of green food colouring. Blanch 1 cup firmly packed mint leaves in boiling water for 30 seconds. Refresh in iced water, then drain and pat dry with paper towel. Finely chop, then add to the jelly. Pour into sterilised jars and seal. Mint jelly will keep for up to 3 months. Refrigerate after opening. **Makes 6 cups**

* To test if the jelly is set, place a teaspoonful on a saucer in the fridge for a few minutes to cool. Run a finger through the jelly: if the surface wrinkles, it's ready; if it doesn't, return the pan to the stove and boil rapidly for a further 5-10 minutes before testing again.

Crepes

Sift 3/4 cup (110g) plain flour into a bowl with a pinch of salt. Whisk 2 eggs with 200ml milk and 1/3 cup (80ml) water. Gradually add egg mixture to flour mixture, whisking well. Add 2 tbs melted unsalted butter. Set aside to rest for 15 minutes. Brush a 20cm crepe or frypan with a little extra melted butter and heat over high heat. Reduce heat to medium-high and add 1/4 cup (60ml) batter, swirling to coat base of the pan. Cook for 1 minute or until golden, then flip with a palette knife and cook for 30 seconds. (Don't worry if you have to discard the first crepe.) Layer crepes between sheets of baking paper. **Makes 16-20**

Caramel sauce

Combine 2/3 cup (150g) caster sugar and 1/4 cup (60ml) cold water in a saucepan over low heat, stirring until sugar dissolves. Increase heat to medium and cook, without stirring, for 5-6 minutes until a golden caramel forms. Remove from heat. Carefully stir in 100ml thickened cream, 1 tsp vanilla extract and 75g chopped unsalted butter (mixture may spit). Return to a low heat and stir until just combined and smooth. Cool. **Makes 1 1/4 cups**

Italian meringue

Using electric beaters, whisk 2 eggwhites until frothy. Add 2 tbs (30g) caster sugar and whisk to soft peaks. Combine 2/3 cup (150g) caster sugar with 100ml water in a saucepan over low heat, stirring until sugar dissolves. Increase heat to medium and simmer for 2 minutes or until mixture reaches 115°C on a sugar thermometer. Whisking constantly, gradually pour sugar syrup into eggwhite mixture in a thin, steady stream, whisking until mixture is thick, glossy and cold.

Dulce de leche

Remove labels from two 400g cans sweetened condensed milk. Use a can opener to make 2 small holes in top of each. Place in a saucepan, pierced-side up, then add water almost to the top of the cans. Bring to the boil, then reduce heat to low and simmer for 3 hours, topping up with boiling water as needed. Cool before opening cans. This recipe makes quite a stiff dulce de leche, which may need to be warmed to loosen in order to pipe into the doughnuts (p 198).

Index

Starters & light meals

Asian tartare with crisp wontons.......................... 160
Baked kumaras with chipotle butter and pico de gallo........... 186
Barbecue chicken salad with passionfruit dressing................. 70
Barbecued sausage rolls with beer-braised onions.................. 68
Boston baked beans..................... 132
Bubble & squeak with a twist...... 246
Buck rarebit................................ 236
Carpaccio with strawberry panzanella............................... 14
Carrot soup Vichy with herbed croutons...................... 210
Ceviche with coconut and mango.............................. 188
Chicken & banana blossom salad........................ 154
Chorizo burgers............................. 44
Chorizo-stuffed mushrooms........... 46
Corn cakes with Mexican green sauce................ 184
Crying tiger beef with dipping sauce........................... 158
Deep-pan pizza............................136
Empanadas................................. 180
Heirloom tarte Tatin.................... 212
Indian salmon kebabs................... 98
Jamon & manchego croquetas..... 42
Kashmiri prawns..........................106
Korean beef with quick kimchi......152
Lightly pickled beetroot with minted labne and dukkah.........264
Mac 'n' cheese slice.....................138
Maryland crab cakes with dill pickle mayo.........................122
The new caprese...........................12
New-wave prawn cocktail 238
Not so sloppy Joes...................... 130
Pear & manchego salad with jamon-wrapped breadsticks....... 40
Piedmont peppers.......................... 20
Ploughman's salad.......................242
Popcorn prawns with ranch dipping sauce.................126
Potato wraps................................. 96
Prawn 'nizzas'............................. 100
Salmon tarts with crushed pea sauce....................244
Scallops with peas and pancetta.............................. 16
Smoked trout & celeriac tartines.. 214
Smoky pepper soup with drunken prawns.........................182
Taleggio & cauliflower risotto with hazelnut pangrattato.................18
Tarka dhal with spinach and tomato.................. 104
Warm goat's cheese fondue with primeurs 208
Wasabi-crumbed squid with chilli dipping sauce...................156

Salads & vegetables

Baked kumaras with chipotle butter and pico de gallo.......... 186
Bubble & squeak with a twist 246
Carrot soup Vichy with herbed croutons...................... 210
Heirloom tarte Tatin..................... 212
Lightly pickled beetroot with minted labne and dukkah........ 264

The new caprese.............................12
Pear & manchego salad with
  jamon-wrapped breadsticks......40
Piedmont peppers........................20
Ploughman's salad......................242
Potato wraps................................96
Tarka dhal with
  spinach and tomato..................104
Warm goat's cheese fondue
  with primeurs............................208

Pasta, rice & noodles
Baked gnocchi with spinach,
  figs and gorgonzola....................26
Mac 'n' cheese slice.....................138
Orecchiette amatriciana................30
Paella..54
Pasta with prawns and
  macadamia pesto.......................74
Prawns with arroz negro
  and chorizo crumbs....................48
Spaghetti vongole.........................22
Taleggio & cauliflower risotto
  with hazelnut pangrattato...........18
Tom yum fried rice......................168

Seafood
Asian tartare with crisp wontons...160
Baked ocean trout with
  smashed cucumber salad..........162
Barramundi baked in paperbark
  with chilli ginger dressing..........76
Beer-battered fish with peas
  and tartare sauce......................240
Ceviche with coconut
  and mango................................188
Chermoula snapper.....................274
Cioppino (seafood stew)..............140
Harissa salmon with
  pearl couscous..........................268
Indian salmon kebabs...................98
Kashmiri prawns.........................106
Maryland crab cakes with
  dill pickle mayo.........................122
New-wave prawn cocktail............238
Paella..54
Pasta with prawns and
  macadamia pesto.......................74
Popcorn prawns with
  ranch dipping sauce..................126
Prawn nizzas..............................100
Prawns with arroz negro
  and chorizo crumbs....................48
Salmon en papillote with
  honey mustard sauce................216
Salmon tarts with
  crushed pea sauce....................244
Scallops with peas
  and pancetta...............................16
Smoked trout & celeriac tartines..214

>>

Smoky pepper soup with
    drunken prawns.........................182
Spaghetti vongole...........................22
Tandoori swordfish with pilaf
    and coconut raita.....................102
Tom yum fried rice.........................168
Wasabi-crumbed squid with
    chilli dipping sauce..................156

Poultry
Barbecue chicken salad with
    passionfruit dressing..................70
Chicken & banana blossom salad...154
Chicken pie with stuffing balls
    and potato pastry.....................250
Confit duck with
    potatoes sarladaises................220
Margarita chicken with
    watermelon salsa.....................196
Massaman duck curry
    with pineapple..........................164
Moroccan chicken skewers
    with pea tabbouleh..................270
Oven-baked chicken curry..........108
Rioja chicken..................................52
Roman chicken with
    creamy polenta..........................24
Southern fried chicken................134
Spiced spatchcock
    with mujaddara........................278

Truffled chicken with
    Champagne sauce....................222
Vegemite roast chicken with
    macadamia couscous.................80

Meat
Barbecued sausage rolls with
    beer-braised onions...................68
Beef ribs daube style....................218
Braised pork belly with black
    vinegar and pickled chillies......166
Braised pork with
    chorizo and olives.....................50
Carpaccio with
    strawberry panzanella................14
Chorizo burgers.............................44
Chorizo-stuffed mushrooms...........46
Coconut beef curry......................110
Crying tiger beef with
    dipping sauce..........................158
Jamon & manchego croquetas......42
Lamb & vegetable pie with
    harissa yoghurt........................272
Kangaroo fillet with parsnip
    gratin and cherry chutney..........78
Kofta with Yotam Ottolenghi's
    baked couscous.......................266
Korean beef with quick kimchi.....152
Matambre with chimichurri..........190
Meatball caesar............................128

Moroccan slow-roast lamb with
    ancient-grain salad...................276
Not so sloppy Joes.......................130
Pork ribs with chipotle
    barbecue sauce........................194
Rabbit pies......................................72
Roast beef with Yorkshire
    puddings and ale gravy............248
Roast leg of lamb with
    mint jelly and potato bake..........82
Slow-cooked Mexican beef
    with guacamole and
    lime crema................................192
Steak with escalivada and
    manchego butter........................56
Tandoori lamb cutlets with
    sweet and sour tomatoes.........112
Tuscan pork with roast pumpkin
    and mustard fruits.......................28

Sweet things
Almond milk cream with
    cardamom rhubarb...................116
Anzac ice cream sandwiches..........86
Banoffee cake..............................258
Breton apple cake........................228
Cheat's fraisier cake....................230
Chilli chocolate puddings............200
Chilli pears with sweet wontons
    and ginger cream....................172

Chilli pineapple mini pavs............84	Sticky date pudding cake............254
Chocolate-orange cake.................60	Strawberry & elderflower
Coconut crepe layer cake............114	summer puddings.....................256
Coconut sorbet with	Sweet goat's cheese tarts with
fruits in lemongrass syrup........174	roasted blueberries...................224
Cola cakes.......................................144	Tropical granola with
Crema Catalana................................58	lime yoghurt................................88
Crepes Suzette with	Turkish delight pavlova................286
a touch of spice........................226	

Basics & extras

Doughnuts with dulce de leche...198	Baked croutons.............................296
Fig & berry filo crisps...................280	Caramel sauce..............................297
Great British trifle........................252	Chocolate pastry...........................294
Hazelnut & Pedro Ximénez	Coconut rice..................................295
semifreddo with	Crepes...297
drunken raisins...........................62	Dulce de leche..............................297
Japanese cheesecake	Flour tortillas.................................295
with raspberries........................170	Garlic mayonnaise........................296
Lemon myrtle tapioca creams	Italian meringue............................297
with passionfruit syrup...............90	Mint jelly.......................................296
Mexican fiesta ice blocks.............202	Mustard fruits.................................28
Minimisus..34	No-churn vanilla
Mississippi mud pie......................146	ice cream....................................86
Negroni tart....................................32	Patatas bravas..............................296
Orange blossom	Pilaf..295
semifreddo cones......................282	Quick kimchi.................................152
Plum cobbler.................................142	Shortcrust pastry..........................294
Rose-scented poached peaches	Small fried croutons.....................296
with honeyed yoghurt...............284	Sour cream pastry........................294
Shrikhand with	Sweet shortcrust pastry...............294
sweet Indian biscuits................118	

Acknowledgements

Creating a cookbook is never a one-man show but the joint effort of a group of incredibly talented people. First, I want to thank HarperCollins*Publishers*, particularly Brigitta Doyle, Shona Martyn and Kate Mayes for your continued support, and the management team at NewsLifeMedia – Nicole Sheffield, Fiona Nilsson and Caspar Deman – for once again giving me the opportunity to produce this, my ninth cookbook.

I am truly blessed to be part of a fantastic team on *delicious.* Not only are they some of the best people to work with on the planet, but their hard work and dedication to the brand is extraordinary, so big hugs to Shannon Harley, Heidi, Lara, Kate and Caitlin, and a special thanks to our editor, Danielle Oppermann, for captaining the ship and keeping things on an even keel.

Shannon Keogh is the most talented art director I have ever worked with, always going the extra mile to make the end result so special – my heartfelt thanks to you.

I have also been supported every step of the way by project editor Sally Feldman, who has made the journey through the editing of this book (often the hardest part) such a breeze.

My dream food team – special thanks to Warren Mendes – has provided support throughout the whole process, as well as keeping things ticking over so efficiently on the magazine while we were busy shooting this book. It was a lucky day when you came on board, Warren, not to mention Sarah Murphy, whose assistance we couldn't have done without.

When I look at the beautiful images in this book I know how lucky I am to have the very best team to create them in stylist David Morgan and photographer Jeremy Simons. David, your talent is now legendary and it is an honour and privilege to work alongside you. Jeremy (the quiet achiever), thank you for your genius work and for being such a lovely guy (we may need to discuss your choice in music for the studio next year, though!).

Finally, love and gratitude to my friends and family, especially my husband, Phil, who's there with me every step of the way, and my gorgeous sons, Toby and Henry. Thank you for enriching my life and making all the hard work worthwhile.

delicious. uses meat supplied by Hudson Meats.
Visit: hudsonmeats.com.au

The ABC 'Wave' device is a trademark of the Australian Broadcasting Corporation and is used under licence by HarperCollins*Publishers* Australia. The *delicious.* trademark is used under licence from the Australian Broadcasting Corporation and NewsLifeMedia.

First published in Australia in 2014 by HarperCollins*Publishers* Australia Pty Limited, ABN 36 009 913 517 harpercollins.com.au

Copyright © 2014 NewsLifeMedia

The right of Valli Little to be identified as the author of this work has been asserted by her in accordance with the *Copyright Amendment (Moral Rights) Act 2000*.

This work is copyright. Apart from any use as permitted under the *Copyright Act 1968*, no part may be reproduced, copied, scanned, stored in a retrieval system, recorded, or transmitted, in any form or by any means, without the prior written permission of the publisher.

HarperCollins*Publisher*
Level 13, 201 Elizabeth St, Sydney NSW 2000, Australia; Unit D1, 63 Apollo Drive, Rosedale, Auckland 0632, New Zealand; A 53, Sector 57, Noida, UP, India; 77–85 Fulham Palace Rd, London W6 8JB, UK; 2 Bloor Street East, 20th floor, Toronto, Ontario M4W 1A8, Canada; 195 Broadway, New York, NY 10007, USA

National Library of Australia Cataloguing-in-Publication entry:
Little, Valli, author.
delicious. Love to Eat: around the world in 120 simply delicious recipes / Valli Little.
ISBN: 9780733333514 (paperback)
Cooking.
Other Authors/Contributors:
Simons, Jeremy, photographer.
Australian Broadcasting Corporation
641.5

Food Director Valli Little
Photographer Jeremy Simons
Stylist David Morgan
Art Director Shannon Keogh
Editor Danielle Oppermann
Project Editor Sally Feldman
Deputy Editor Shannon Harley
Food Editor Warren Mendes
Head of ABC Books Brigitta Doyle
Publisher ABC Magazines Liz White
Publishing Editor ABC Magazines Marija Beram
Group Publisher Food, NewsLifeMedia Fiona Nilsson
Managing Director, NewsLifeMedia Nicole Sheffield

Colour reproduction by Graphic Print Group, Adelaide, SA

Printed and bound in China by RR Donnelley

5 4 3 2 1   14 15 16 17

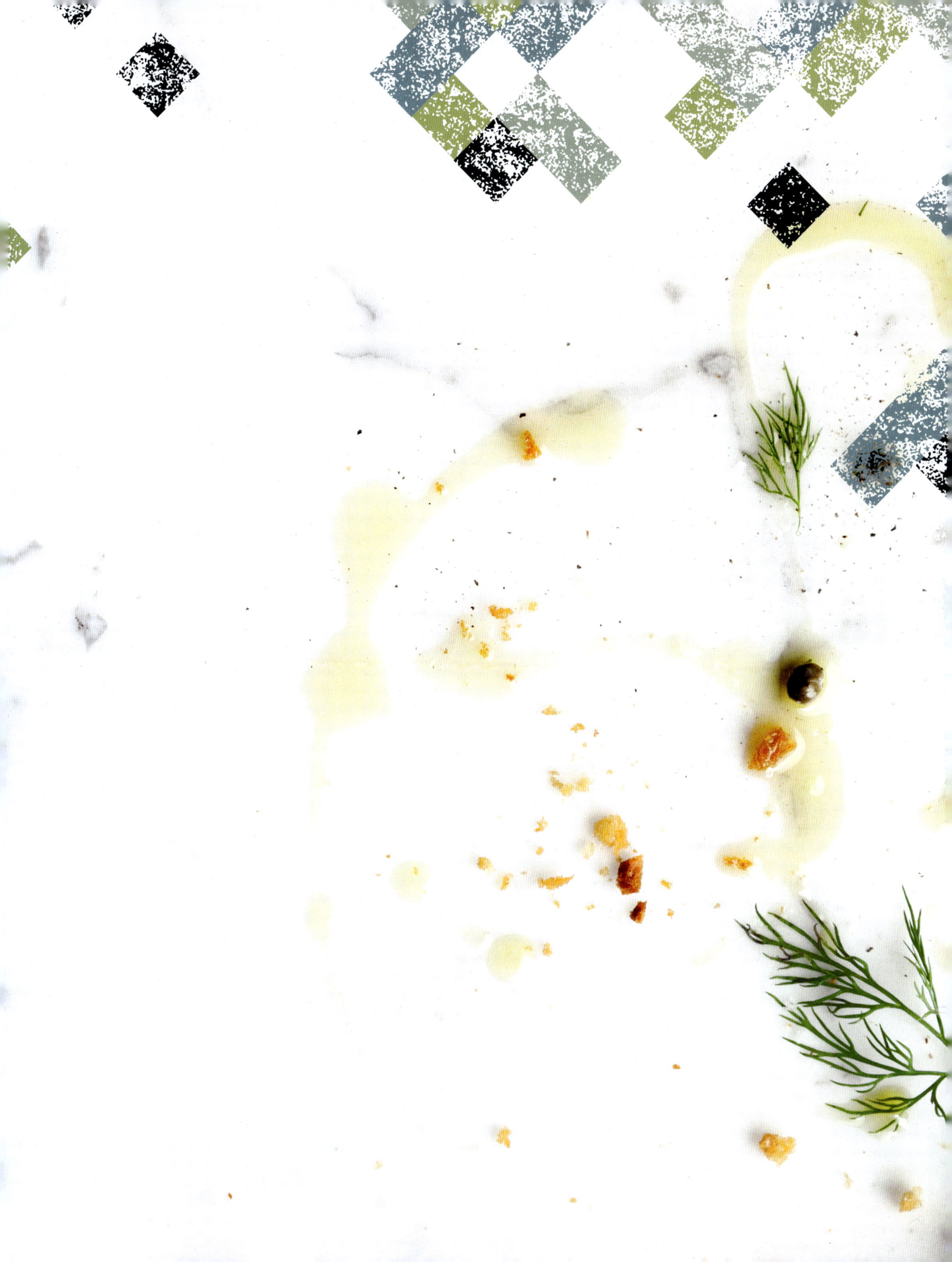